סליק

חלק היתרון והמוטבא והצלות

אמת הארץ חלק שירים ונגונים

לבנה
סרטן
☽
♋
גבריאל

כוכב
תאומים בתולה
☿
♊ ♍
מיכאל

צדק
קשת דגים
♃
♐ ♓
צדקיאל

שבתי
גדי דלי
♄
♑ ♒
קפציאל

חמה נוגה
אריה מאזני שור
☉ ♀
♌ ♎ ♉
רפאל

מאדים
טלה עקרב
♂
♈ ♏
סמאל

Palaces of Time

DATE DUE

אז מי נטה עלי קו

מי שם חוג הארץ

Palaces of Time

Jewish Calendar and Culture in Early Modern Europe

ELISHEVA CARLEBACH

The Belknap Press of Harvard University Press
Cambridge, Massachusetts
London, England
2011

Palaces of Time is being published with the generous assistance of Yeshiva University Museum, in conjunction with an exhibition on the Jewish Calendar.

Library of Congress Cataloging-in-Publication Data
Carlebach, Elisheva.
Palaces of time : Jewish calendar and culture in early modern Europe / Elisheva Carlebach.
p.   cm.
Includes bibliographical references and index.
ISBN-13: 978-0-674-05254-3 (alk. paper)
1. Jewish calendar.   2. Time—Religious aspects—Judaism.   3. Judaism—Relations—
Christianity.   4. Christianity and other religions—Judaism.   5. Judaism—
Europe—History—16th century.   6. Europe—Ethnic relations.   I. Title.
CE35.C33 2011
296.4'3—dc22
2010037583

Frontispiece: Who hath encompassed the earth. *Sefer evronot*, 1779. Cincinnati, Klau Library, Hebrew Union College-Jewish Institute of Religion, ms 902, fol. 29r.

Endpapers: The Planets and their angels. *Sefer evronot*, 1779. Cincinnati, Klau Library, Hebrew Union College-Jewish Institute of Religion, ms 902, fol. 28r.

For my grandchildren, time's sweet recompense

CONTENTS

PREFACE

My subject came trundling to me on a wooden library cart. The artifacts were so small that I nearly overlooked them; designed to be ephemeral, tossed away after a year, they had miraculously survived for several centuries. I encountered my first manuscript Jewish calendars at the New York Public Library where I spent an idyllic year at the Cullman Center for Scholars and Writers. I had outlined a rather ambitious project to Michael Terry, then Dorot Jewish Division Librarian. Within hours, Michael had wheeled out to me a garden of scholarly delights. They consisted mostly of weighty tomes printed in the sixteenth through eighteenth centuries. The pile of handwritten calendars, small enough to fit in the palm of my hand, caught my eye; I had never seen their like. Since that initial wonderment that something so personal, so fragile, and designed to last such a short time should have survived intact, I have searched for everything related to them. What I beheld was not simply another fragment from the distant past, but also a reminder and symbol of human time, its stations marked in tiny ciphers by a diligent hand. Since then, I have learned a great deal about the Jewish calendars of early modern Europe. They have never lost their power to move and surprise me.

While writing this book I have had the assistance and good counsel of many people. First and foremost, I thank "the people of the book," the librarians and curators who opened their treasure troves to me with vast expertise, endless patience, and unfailing grace. They helped and supported me in every way and shared my excitement of discovery. In addition to Michael Terry, I was assisted at New York Public Library by Annemarie Belinfante, Havva Charm, Miriam Gloger, Roberta Seltzer, and Eleanora Yadin. Jewish Theological Seminary possesses one of the great collections of material related to my subject. Professor David Kramer, its Joseph J. and Dora Abbell Librarian, has been unfailingly generous in allowing me to use the library and granting me the right to reproduce images from its collections. The Special Collections room was my home there for many wonderful hours. I thank Evelyn Cohen, Sarah Diamant, Yevgeniya Dizenko, Yisrael Dubitsky, Rabbi Jerry Schwartzbard, David Sclar, Naomi Steinberg, and David Wachtel. Sharon Liberman Mintz, Curator of Jewish Art, has been an unfailing enthusiast from the beginning of this project. Her support has been a vital source of sustenance during this project.

Palaces of Time is being published with the generous assistance of Yeshiva University Museum, in conjunction with an exhibition on the Jewish Calendar. At Yeshiva University, Dean of Libraries Pearl Berger, along with Shuli Berger, fulfilled every research request and allowed me to study their unique Sefer evronot. I thank Yeshiva University Museum Director Jacob Wisse for his assistance and interest in the calendar project. At Hebrew Union College in New York, Phillip Miller presides over a haven for scholars, and Tina Weiss assisted me ably. Phil directed me to the collection of sifre evronot in Cincinnati, where head librarian David Gilner and the library staff, including Laurel Wolfson, Gary Rettburg, and Noni Rudavsky, made my stay there most productive. I thank the library as well for its willingness to provide me with images of the manuscripts.

At Hebrew University in Jerusalem, Yael Okun and Avraham David assisted me in every way. The Institute for Microfilmed Hebrew Manuscripts proved to be an indispensible tool for my research. Within the Center for Jewish History, New York, librarians and archivists at Leo Baeck Institute, including Frank Mecklenburg, Renata Evers, and Judy Fixler, helped me find material, and those at YIVO were always ready to assist me. Arthur Kiron, Schottenstein-Jesselson Curator of Judaica Collections at University of Pennsylvania's Katz Center for Advanced Jewish Studies, as well as Michele Chesner, provided access to and images from their collection of early American Jewish calendars. At Columbia University Library, Jennifer Lee acted as point person for the Rare Book and Manuscript Collection; it was a pleasure to work with her. Yossi Galron, Jewish Studies Librarian at Ohio State University Libraries, gladly answered queries and provided images of difficult-to-access materials. Brad Sabin Hill embraced my project enthusiastically as though it were his own, and provided a stream of bibliographical leads. William Gross of Tel Aviv generously allowed me to use images from his magnificent collection of Judaica.

Colleagues, friends, and students read parts of the manuscript and made excellent suggestions that I have tried to follow. They include Eric Bressman, Yaakob Dweck, Ephraim Kanarfogel, Jordan Katz, Stanley Mirvis, Kristin Peterson, Adam Shear, Magda Teter, and Adina Yoffie. Adam Shear generously shared his early work on Jacob Marcaria and sifre evronot with me. Colleagues and friends who gladly answered my queries include Yaakov Deutsch, Rachel Elior, Sylvie Goldberg, Marion Kaplan, Ari Kinsberg, Mary Minty, Marina Rustow, Michael Silber, Sacha Stern, Tania Tulcin, and David Wachtel.

In addition to the New York Public Library Cullman Center for Scholars

and Writers, the National Endowment for the Humanities provided a grant for additional time to work on this project. At Queens College, City University of New York (CUNY), Dean Donald Scott and History Department Chair Professor Frank Warren supported me in every way. At the Graduate Center, CUNY, then History Program executive director Josh Freeman arranged for me to have a room of my own, where I could work without interruption. I remain in his debt. I thank my colleagues at Columbia University for their interest in my project, and two anonymous readers for the press who made valuable suggestions. I also thank Joyce Seltzer, senior editor at Harvard University Press, for her excellent advice; Tim Jones, art director of the Press, for his willingness to work with my vision for this book; and Julie Carlson, for her eye for fine details.

Introduction

IN 1766, Vienna was a city still shrouded in mourning for its deceased emperor, the husband of Maria Teresia. One crisp evening in very early spring, however, the muted urban bustle was disturbed by the most incongruous, festive sounds. They erupted from the direction of the Jewish quarter, where merry music played, horns blared, and sleigh bells jingled. It was Purim, a Jewish day of joy and carnivalesque celebration. Christian observers that day deplored the arrogance and insensitivity of the Jews and called for appropriate punishment. A stiff fine was imposed on all the participants.[1]

In premodern Christian Europe, similar scenes of temporal dissonance occurred routinely throughout the year, and often with far graver consequences for those involved. Jews conducted business as usual on Sundays, and feasted and fasted according to an utterly different timetable than Christians, practices that set them apart as surely as any other distinction. Those who did not celebrate the same holidays, rest on the same Sabbath, or labor alongside others on the same workdays assumed as powerful a sign of cultural difference as any badge, language, or physical marker would have conferred.

A calendar can tell us a great deal about the place of its creators and users within larger social, religious, and cultural contexts. Calendars keep members of a society working in synchrony with one another. They determine our workdays, our school days, and our holidays, not to mention the days we shop for the best buys. It is difficult to think of another product of culture that does as much work as a calendar. It merges personal time (such as birthdays), sacred communal time (holidays), and civic time (independence days) onto a grid that aligns these measures with natural rhythms and a historical framework. These temporal rhythms define who we are as surely as our names, our social identities, and our professions do.

Calendrical systems often appear to be static, neutral, and unchanging, but they are in fact dynamic systems that are continually being modified and reshaped as new considerations and calculations emerge. Calendars, then as now, were extremely sensitive to shifts in cultural habits and they changed when new

information, calculations, or commemorations were added and old ones faded into oblivion. No calendar serves as an objective instrument for marking the passage of time just as no map represents an unfiltered view of the natural landscape. Both incorporate political agendas, and often religious worldviews, into their representation.

Occasionally, the evolutionary process for configuring a society's calendar was punctuated by sharp debates and abrupt changes. Such sudden changes in any society's map of time often proved deeply divisive as some groups adopted them and others rejected them. They exposed the human and arbitrary elements embedded in calendar systems and opened them to renewed debate and evaluation. This happened to the Western calendar in the sixteenth century, when the calendar emerged as one of the most important sites of cultural conflict, sectarian identity, and political propaganda in the early modern period. The Elizabethan court manipulated the calendar to change its religious character to a nationalist one, while Reformation leaders altered the temporal order by reducing or eliminating saints' day observances and changing weekly lections. The turmoil that accompanied the Gregorian reform of the calendar in the late sixteenth century created a new source of division and confusion, while the French (and later, Russian) revolutionary calendars provided a radical embodiment of the early modern European impulse to transform, and even to obliterate, the past.

Palaces of Time focuses on this period of heightened awareness of the constructed nature of calendars and its effect on the calendar culture of European Jews. It takes into account as well the material aspects of calendar, which changed dramatically in this period. From the wooden boards or beads incised by peasants, to the painstaking handwritten calendars appended to Psalters and Books of Hours, calendars were transformed by the technology of print. Among the earliest printed broadsheets and books, they helped to create a market for printed materials, expanded the range of readers, and proved to be a most versatile and adaptable cultural medium. If culture is "an historically transmitted pattern of meanings . . . expressed in symbolic forms," even the most austere of calendars encoded and embodied in its pages a great many of those patterns.[2] When deciphered, they can unravel the questions of how a community viewed its place within the march of time and imposed cultural and religious meaning onto natural rhythms.

Calendars merit a special place in the history of the book, although they are not books in any conventional sense. In most books, the reader turns a page to

get to the next part of the text. The number on the page is unimportant to the text itself; readers often ignore it completely. Such is the function of paratexts, the apparatuses that accompany the text and help orient the reader, that readers are often unaware of their shaping presence. Simple calendars come close to being pure paratext, volumes in which the very act of turning the pages—to follow the days, months, or years—conveys the primary message. Both calendars, and works about them, emerged from the early modern crucible different from their earlier forms. They thus provide a perfect case study for the interplay between manuscript and print as vehicles of knowledge and information in the sixteenth and seventeenth centuries.

· · ·

This cultural history of the Jewish calendar in the early modern period explores the meaning of the calendar for Jews, the ideas and practices they associated with it, and how it governed their time. It asks how Jews constructed their sense of their own difference and how their calendar reflected their precarious existence as minorities within an often unsympathetic world. Chapter 1 explores the origins of medieval writings about the calendar and the reasons for its proliferation in certain periods. Literature about the calendar in medieval times provides a historical background for the body of calendrical material inherited by early modern Jews. Chapter 2 moves the narrative into the early modern period and reviews the context that set the calendar squarely into the cultural battles raging in that period, most significant among them the momentous reform of the Western calendar instituted by Pope Gregory XIII.

Chapter 3 follows the interplay among Jewish cultures over questions of calendar and computus, print and manuscript, against the backdrop of the changes in early modern Europe. Surprises await, for at the same time that printed calendars were subject to question and doubt for their sloppy execution, treatises about the calendar blossomed as a mature literary genre that invited renewed religious and aesthetic cultivation. Chapter 4 explores the manuscript tradition that arose precisely at a juncture when the calendrical text could have been purchased as a printed book. It developed a rich, allusive, and unique iconographic program whose meaning is unfolded here.

Jewish calendars and calendar literature illuminate the uneasy balance between separation and integration that marked Jewish life in that period. Chapter 5 explores the perceptions of Christian culture embedded within Jewish calendars. They contained such an intricate awareness of the calendar of the other as to mock the notion of cultural insularity.

Calendars and their literature provide apertures through which to view the circulation of many facets of a culture. Jewish calendars are rich repositories for discerning how economic activity, religious differences, and folk rituals were intertwined. Chapter 6 reflects on how calendars track the cycles of what Jacques le Goff has called "merchant's time" and "church's time." The boundary lines between Christians and Jews became sharper and stronger on Christian religious feast days, while on the days of markets and fairs special dispensations were created to allow strangers to converge in a normally restricted space. The temporal and the spatial contours of Jewish life thus affected one another directly.

Chapter 7 turns to a more immanent aspect of Jewish calendrical culture. It explores how a folk ritual of unknown origin that arose to mark the turning seasons became deeply embedded within the calendar culture of medieval and early modern Jews. The final chapter in the book, Chapter 8, reflects on the chronological dimension of the Jewish calendar. It explores the emergence of a unified chronological system among Jews—a cultural feat—along with the elastic temporal grid and the consolations of history embedded in Jewish calendars. I have not attempted to provide a comprehensive bibliography of Jewish calendars, nor a manual for their calculation, nor even to include all the potential subjects that could have been clustered around a cultural history of my subject. Instead, I hope to introduce calendar literature as an overlooked source for cultural history, particularly Jewish cultural history.

· · ·

Jewish calendar literature reveals one of the central paradoxes of Jewish existence: the need to know, to encompass, and to instruct in the culture of the other. It demonstrates how a minority culture creatively and simultaneously embraced and distanced itself from the majority culture. Fiercely proud of their own distinctive calendar, early modern Jews were nevertheless acutely aware of the European calendar, its meaning, debates over its reform, and their implications. Calendars served as agents as well as mirrors of the Jewish experience. Their pages contained a graphic representation of the fundamental duality of their lives in time, with the neatly arrayed rows of Hebrew months alongside the Christian or Muslim, Jewish holidays along with non-Jewish, portraying a double consciousness that has symbolized Jewish life for much of its history.

{ 1 }

Calendar and the Cultural Meaning of Time

It was not until I came across the heavily annotated Hindu calendar she kept hung in her room all her life that I realized how inviolably whole that world had been to her. It had been a realm of existence over and above her sorrows and disappointments on the material plane, a world with its own rhythms and seasons, virtues and habits.

Pankaj Mishra, *The Romantics: A Novel*, 2000

ONE of the most crucial cultural monuments a human society can create is a system of accounting for time. Although calendars may appear to be simply a convenient way to coordinate human movements with natural time, every culture has developed its own mechanisms for doing so. The history of calendar computation through the ages and cultures is a story of the need to balance the cycles built into nature—circadian (day and night), lunar, and seasonal (winter and summer)—with those that have purely human meaning but no natural corollary, such as feast and fast days, weeks, or the division of the day into hours.[1]

Creating this manifold system has never been a uniform or self-evident proposition. The year of the sun and the revolutions of the moon do not calculate to whole days, but are completed with fractions of days.[2] Every society has thus had to confront the question of whether, when, and how to align the dissonant circuits of the heavenly bodies by adding days, months, hours, and even seconds. Their cyclical motions have no fixed beginning point; this too is arbitrary and differs by culture and tradition. The "reckoning of time" thus has always employed a combination of astronomical and mathematical science, along with cultural and religious interpretations. Each generation of calendar writers reshaped the system they inherited in ways that reflected both historical meanings as well as advances in available technologies.

Regardless of their cultural background, writers about time presented their work as an accurate and exact representation of the rhythms of nature. They

fostered the impression that calendars simply measured and reflected organic processes, that they were utterly apolitical and independent of human influence, and therefore authoritative, divinely sanctioned, and immutable. Yet in any society, setting a system to account for time has never been, could never be, a strictly objective matter. As Sacha Stern has defined it, "Calendars represent a process of human cognition, in which the experience of time . . . is conceptualized, structured and comprehended. Calendars make sense of the dimension of time by imposing a rational, human structure upon it."[3] The calendar consists of rules designed to "harmonize incommensurable movements as closely as possible."[4] Calendars, then, amalgamate scientific data and mathematical calculation on the one hand, with religious, cultural, political, and social influences on the other. The very complex and multidisciplinary knowledge needed to master the calendar meant that each society was faced with a tremendous challenge: to train the special few who would integrate the branches of knowledge and formulate the calendar, while simultaneously disseminating its results to the rest of society.

To keep its members marching in synchrony, many societies adopted a two-tiered system to disseminate knowledge concerning their calendars. At the apex, a small circle of initiates formulated, absorbed, and taught the mathematical, astronomical, and cultural knowledge needed to construct a calendar. The second tier comprised the broadest possible circles, the entire population. Two Hebrew terms signal these tiers. The Hebrew word *ibbur*, as we will see, refers to the higher-level formulation, designed for the scholarly elite, whereas *luah* is the word for the table or calendar that presents this knowledge in a clear and accessible manner for the general public. Luah comprised the most concise and memorable formulation of calendrical knowledge, circulated in a manner designed to keep it accessible to all.

The Beginnings of Calendar Literature

The literature of the ibbur is centered on the intercalation system that Jewish society adopted to keep its calendrical cycles in close synchrony with the dissonant rhythms of two celestial bodies, the sun and the moon. The term derives from the root *ayin bet resh*, meaning pregnancy, embolism, intercalation—in this case the insertion of an additional month every few years to expand, or "swell," the number of days in that year. By the High Middle Ages, the Latin term *computus* (or *compotus*) designated the European literature at the intersec-

tion of the art and science of constructing a calendar.[5] "A medieval computus," explains Gerhard Dohrn-van Rossum, "is a handbook containing above all methods for the astronomical and calendric calculation."[6] The equivalent term for a Jewish computus manual would be *Sefer ibbur* or *Sefer evronot* (plural). The literature of the ibbur, then, represents the upper tier of knowledge about the Jewish calendar, the one studied and promoted within those circles that had access to the highest level of education and authority. Thus, ibbur and luah, computus and calendar, represent the two levels of a system to disseminate knowledge of the calendar to Jewish society in a clear and comprehensive way.

When new societies formed or new religions emerged, they adopted new values and rejected older ones, often forcing a change in the calendar system. Such conflict and change gave rise to the literature of computus, which frequently promoted a particular, contested calendar system. The literature of computus was by nature polemical: it argued that one system solved the religious, social, and technical problems of the calendar better than the alternatives. Calendar literature sometimes became the site of conflicts between folk custom and learned culture. If serious contention over a calendrical issue arose, computists tended to review carefully the religious and cultural justifications, as well as the series of interlinked calculations that undergirded their calendars. Computus literature, then, tended to flourish at a time when a society faced crisis, such as when a sectarian group claimed a superior system of calendar reckoning, or when new scientific advances rendered old tables, calculations, and assumptions outmoded. It aimed to smooth over differences, to foster social cohesion by promoting one calendar system as uniquely true, and to unify a group of people around it.

Sifre ibbur emerged first in the Middle Ages, and served as the foundation of a continuous manuscript and oral tradition for centuries. They later found new currency in the early modern period. A brief comparison with the development of Christian computus literature allows us to construct a context, a vocabulary, and a sense of the parameters of the genre. This is not an argument concerning direct lines of influence. The more fully documented unfolding of Christian computus literature simply provides basic tools for constructing a model of the Jewish genre as it evolved through the medieval and toward the early modern period. Its trajectory can help us understand the emergence of the form in medieval Jewish culture.

The central problem of the Christian calendar as it emerged and evolved

was the need to maintain some degree of balance between the solar Julian calendar it had inherited from the Roman Empire and the lunisolar calendar inherited from the Jews. The date of Jesus' death was tied through Passover to the Jewish calendar, but the early church was afraid that such direct reliance would encourage Judaizing among early Christians and grant the Jewish calendar special status within the Christian religion. In the second century, Christian society was riven over the question of whether to celebrate Easter on the fourteenth day of the Jewish lunar month Nisan, regardless of the day of the week on which it might fall, or on a Sunday only. Those who observed Easter at the same time as the Jews were called Quartodecimans, from the Latin word for fourteen, and their numbers diminished as a result of strong opposition from the popes.

In the fourth century, the bishops who had gathered at the Council of Nicea (ca. 325) decided to make the final break from the Jewish calendar. Christians were to celebrate Easter on a Sunday every year. But which Sunday? The Christian church of Antioch offered one possibility: it celebrated Easter on the Sunday after the first day of Passover. But in Alexandria, this method for calculating the date of Easter came under strong attack. The Alexandrian scholars alleged that the Jews had become sloppy in their own calculations, sometimes calculating the fourteenth of Nisan before the vernal (spring) equinox (thus sometimes observing two Passovers within one solar year). Consequently, their formula for liberating the celebration of the most sacred day in the Christian calendar from the Jewish calendar entailed celebrating Easter the Sunday after the vernal equinox.[7] How to find the correct lunar month remained a subject of dispute between Roman and Alexandrine computists, but the principle and the motivation behind it were clearly formulated at Nicea: Easter must be completely independent of the calculations of the Jews. As Emperor Constantine summarized it: "First of all, it appeared an unworthy thing that in the celebration of this most holy feast we should follow the practice of the Jews, who have impiously defiled their hands with enormous sin. . . . Let us then have nothing in common with the detestable Jewish crowd; for we have received from our Saviour a different way."[8]

The search for the perfect Easter formula remained a serious problem for Christian computists and a source of great denominational conflict. Christian astronomers treated the search for a usable Easter calendar as though it were an acceptable scientific question, but as Johannes Kepler is said to have sighed centuries later, "Ostern ist ein Fest vnd khein Stern" (Easter is a feast, not a planet).[9] Or, as another scholar summarized it: "The Church throughout held that the

determination of Easter was primarily a matter of ecclesiastical discipline and not of astronomical science. . . . The moon according to which Easter is calculated is not the moon in the heavens nor even the mean moon, i.e., a moon traveling with the average motion of the real moon, but simply the moon of the calendar. This calendar moon is admittedly a fiction."[10]

The question of the Christian calendar was stirred up once more in the West at the end of the sixth century, when Roman missionaries came to England during the pontificate of Gregory the Great (ca. 540–604) and discovered that the English church was using a method of calendar calculation that had been discarded by the Roman church centuries earlier. The struggle to persuade the English and the Irish to adopt the Roman Christian calendar continued until the mid-seventh century, inspiring further examination of the calendar's foundations and methods of calculation.

This controversy and conciliation provided rich material for the English monk Bede (673/674–735) to write his magisterial *De temporum ratione* (*On the Reckoning of Time*), the first fully realized work of Christian computus literature that has come to us in its entirety and is attributed to a known individual. By the time of Bede, it had become common for scholars to consolidate various materials related to the calendar into one manuscript anthology. These materials included computistical tables as well as introductions to the subject, brief treatises about various aspects of the calendar, mnemonic devices (especially brief rhymes), and even important correspondence relating to it.[11] Bede's accomplishment was to take these varied materials, some of which had circulated anonymously for centuries, and forge them into a coherent book.

Perhaps the most important contribution of Bede's computus is that it links the calculation of the Christian calendar with the larger question of the creation, existence, and meaning of historical time. The celestial bodies, created by God along with time, are for Bede markers of time rather than determinants of it. Bede conjoins computus in one seamless work with cosmology, chronology, history, and Christian eschatology. His predecessors were the first to suggest that cosmology and computus should be joined to form a systematic treatise, and Bede built on their legacy.[12]

The origins of the calendar and the origins of the world are often imagined to be rooted in the same point in time, prompting writers to conflate the origins of the world with their sense of time and its role in their lives. Bede incorporated a full world chronology into his computus treatise. In his work, time became universal rather than Christian—*annus mundi* rather than *annus Do-*

mini—perpetuating the patristic notion that Abraham was the father of astronomy, a notion later embraced in computus treatises.[13]

As mentioned earlier, until Bede's work, medieval computus manuscripts were anonymous. Copied or adapted, and circulated without attribution, such compositions were a staple in scholarly circles and took on particular attributes in different cultural milieus.[14] Each anthology contained some common basic tables, including perpetual Julian calendars, which showed the days and future lunar phases, and a Paschal table. Around these basic elements, a great deal of additional related information was included from subject areas like medicine, astronomy, cosmology, and so on.

Bede did not intend to write an encyclopedia of calendrical knowledge. Instead his work remained focused on its main objective—to solve a practical problem by using scientific tools available at the time. Before Bede shaped the material, there was no dearth of charts, tables, volvelles (circular charts), and other premodern calculation devices to illustrate the formulae and help those who could not follow the calendar unassisted. These mechanisms also provided a system of checks and balances for those who were constructing their own calendars based on the written instructions. Mnemonic rhymes and ditties helped students remember the numerous and arcane rules of the calendar. But they lacked uniformity, coherence, authority. Bede's book filled this gap. Consequently, it rapidly became the standard text on the subject.

During this period, computus was a central part of religious academic study, especially within the Carolingian revival of learning. In Bede's time, there was no syllabus as such for monks; instead mimesis of their seniors provided monks' basic training in all practical and doctrinal matters in their communal lives. Charlemagne instituted a curriculum for both monasteries and cathedrals that put computus on the map of European continental scholarship. The curriculum included *grammaticum* (reading), *notas* (writing), *cantus* (music), *psalmos* (liturgy), and *compotum* (computus).

The art of telling time and date was highly complicated in the empire administered by Charlemagne.[15] While it was not unusual for several calendar systems to circulate simultaneously, at least eighteen different New Years' dates were in use before the Carolingian curriculum was promulgated.[16] One of the goals of the new curriculum was to spread uniformity in calendrical matters throughout the empire. As the Carolingian schools grew more numerous and enrolled a more diverse student body, more teachers became specialists in computus, and their favorite text was Bede's *De temporum ratione*. Bede's work,

which remained in active use for half a millennium, stood at the very center of the university curriculum, because the mastery of computus included many different essential subjects such as astronomy, mathematics, geography, theology, and law; its applications, too, included medicine and agriculture.[17]

The eclipse of Bede's computus came about as a result of both inner design and external developments. Bede's computus was calculated for one complete cycle of 532 years (the product of multiplying the nineteen-year lunar cycle by the twenty-eight-year solar cycle, yielding all the possible variations). As Bede's cycle drew toward its end, new questions arose regarding his chronology. By the mid-twelfth century, the rediscovered Greek classics of mathematics and astronomy, along with the Arabic contributions and glosses, had marginalized the existing computus and emphasized its shortcomings. And so in the thirteenth century another English scholar, Oxford professor Robert Grosseteste (d. 1253) took on the challenge of reviewing the Christian computus in light of the latest astronomical and mathematical knowledge. His astronomical work *De spera* and his *Compotus correctorius* incorporated new methods and updated the literature for the next generations of students and scholars.[18] While dissatisfaction with the Christian calendar grew in the Late Middle Ages as its imperfections became more evident, these works were still copied, studied, and ultimately printed.[19]

The challenges to the traditional Christian computus in the face of the recovery of Greek science opens a path to understanding why the twelfth century turned out to be an incubation period of Jewish computus writing. Unlike other Jewish books, the ibbur never appeared in any canonical form. Its component elements—that is, its calculations, instructions, and midrashic formulations—appeared over time in widely varying forms. Unlike the calendars that resulted from the computus, the computus itself was treated as an esoteric body of knowledge, transmitted in brief and cryptic formulae, only later to emerge as a bona fide *sefer*, a book to be circulated and studied.

Development of the Jewish Computus

The Bible contains only the broadest designations concerning the calendar, linking the months to the moon and the festivals to the seasons of the solar year. This sketchy treatment of time resulted in a great deal of controversy, both among the ancients as well as modern scholars, over the calendars used by Israelites in antiquity. Enoch, some books of Apocryphal and Pseudepigraphic

FIG. 1.1. Finger of God (*top left*) showing Moses the new moon. *Sefer evronot*, 1779. Cincinnati, Klau Library, Hebrew Union College-Jewish Institute of Religion ms 902, fol. 1r.

writing, particularly *Jubilees*, along with the texts discovered at Qumran, contain a great deal of material about different calendars advocated, or in use, in the postbiblical period in Judea.[20] Later rabbinic literature addresses some aspects of the Jewish calendar but offers for other elements only desultory references or discussions of particular rituals.[21] Although time and ritual are central to Judaism, even today the "history and historiography of the Jewish calendar lag far

behind the study of any other fundamental pillar of Jewish religious thought and observance."[22]

It seems from Jewish sources that the Jewish calendar developed from one based on direct observation of the moon and the seasons and pronounced monthly by the Sanhedrin (High Court) in Jerusalem to a fixed mathematical calendar that could be calculated for all time. Hillel II, a virtually unknown fourth-century C.E. Patriarch (political leader), was widely believed to have set this calendar that served Jews throughout the world. The prerogative of pronouncing this Jewish calendar remained nominally in the hands of the patriarchate in Judea. Although Babylonian sages like Nahshon Gaon (d. 889) contributed greatly to the pedagogy of the calendar calculations, there were apparently few important disagreements between Judea and Babylonia, and the Judean patriarchate retained its formal authority.[23]

The Muslim conquest stimulated further interest in astronomy and calendar calculation. Jews quickly adopted Arabic and began to pursue scientific knowledge alongside Muslims. Astronomical knowledge was important to Islam, and the cultivation of relevant mathematical tools and accurate observational methods contributed to crucial advances.[24] Jews living in the Muslim world learned a complex calendar system that differed in many ways from their own and from that of their Christian neighbors. Still, few people at the time had the intellectual and educational background to comprehend the mechanics of calendation. The Muslim scholar al-Khwarizmi (ca. 780–850) noted about the Jews: "The generations passed one after the other, and this [counting] was hidden among the special individuals of the children of Israel, and they were not many in number, and it was hidden from the vast majority who neglected to study it and to pay attention to it, for they relied on the people who knew the tradition."[25]

In the eighth century a Jewish sect called Qaraites arose among Jews in the Muslim world. Qaraites dissented from many rabbinic traditions, among them the rabbinic calendar.[26] The challenge of Qaraism stimulated further interest in astronomical knowledge among Jews.[27] During this period a number of late *midrashim*, or parable-like teachings, that touched on calendar-making, astronomy, astrology, cosmology, and chronology were compiled and began to circulate. These include works such as *Pirqe de Rabbi Eliezer*, the *Baraita de Shmuel*, and later, *Sefer yetzira*.[28] Each of these late midrashim conveyed a worldview that included aspects of the calendar, chronology, and cosmology. None of these texts could have been used in any practical sense for computing the calendar,

because they diverged so far from any astronomical reality.[29] Further, through the tenth century, the authorities in Palestine who set the calendar each year would certainly have shunned the notion of a fixed, accessible text for making such calculations.

With the exception of the Qaraites, the authority of the patriarchate in Eretz Israel to set the Jewish calendar went largely unchallenged until a dramatic conflict known as the Sa'adiah–Ben Meir controversy erupted between the Babylonian and Palestinian authorities in 921 C.E. The following Passover, in the spring of 922, the two Jewish communities celebrated Passover on different days. Half a year later, the Babylonian computation prevailed due largely to the efforts of the towering figure of Sa'adiah Gaon (882–942).[30]

As a result of the controversy, Sa'adiah is said to have written a full-length work on the calendar called *Qittab al-ibbur*.[31] This work on the computus, which would have been the first of its kind if it was truly a full treatise, did not survive except in some fragments, and is known primarily through citations in other works, including that of his opponent, the Qaraite scholar Jacob al-Qirqisani.[32] Until the time of the controversy, several different considerations and calculations had been used by different communities to determine the calendar, although as a matter of practical observance, all deferred to the gaon in Palestine.[33] To the best of our current knowledge, their method of calculation was never published.

Sa'adiah may have intended to break the hegemony of the patriarchate in Eretz Israel not merely by besting them in the calculation of a particular year, but by publishing a set of rules by which anyone could set the Jewish calendar for any year. Such a text, if uniformly adopted, would not just eliminate future controversy, it would also undermine this source of Palestinian rabbinic authority and rebut some of the Qaraite criticism of the irregularities of the rabbinic calendar. Indeed, the passage of the ibbur to a textual and public form would have irrevocably altered the political and religious dynamics of the Jewish world. Yet for reasons unknown, Sa'adiah's book was all but lost to the following centuries. Some scholars believe that it may have circulated privately among the cognoscenti, and may have even inspired works on the ibbur that appeared almost two centuries later, half a world away, in Iberia.

For, after centuries of relative silence, Jewish computus literature came to life as a mature, fully realized genre in twelfth-century Spain.[34] Three scholarly figures stand out for their contributions: Abraham bar Hiyya Savasorda (1065–1136), who wrote *Sefer ha-ibbur* around 1123; Abraham ibn Ezra (1092–1167),

who completed his treatise by the same title in 1146 (along with the enigmatic treatise, *Iggeret ha-shabbat*); and Moses Maimonides (1135–1204).[35] Since no genre emerges suddenly in Jewish literature without the stimulus of some compelling need, we must investigate the context of these important works, along with the strategies that enabled them to survive.

The significance of Abraham bar Hiyya for the literature of the Jewish calendar can hardly be overestimated, for he wrote the first complete surviving Jewish computus treatise, which became the essential source for similar works that followed.[36] One nineteenth-century scholar wrote that "all those who followed him, such as R. Isaac Israeli in his book *Yesod olam*, copied from him."[37] Although bar Hiyya clearly drew on older material, he was a pioneer in numerous respects. He was, for example, one of the first Jews to write mathematical and astronomical-astrological treatises in Hebrew, introducing a new vocabulary of scientific terms.[38] He also conflated astronomical and astrological elements, considering them one subject, the "science of the stars, *hokhmat ha-kohavim*."[39]

Although bar Hiyya spent most of his life in northern (Christian) Spain, and was deeply familiar with its culture, he knew and read scientific works in Arabic. His scholarship paved the way for justifying the study of science on religious grounds, as an aid in understanding the divine works. One manuscript introduced bar Hiyya's *ibbur* with a claim for Jewish antecedence in the astronomical sciences: "In it the author has shown the strength of this science and has proven the precedence of the Jews in it with faithful signs. Concerning the gentile claim that all the astronomical measurements and the computus have come to the Hebrews through their [gentile] sages, the gentiles boasted in vain. . . . It also contains many useful tables that will be valid for all times."[40]

Of the three prominent Iberian figures, Abraham ibn Ezra had the most extensive scientific training, wrote the greatest number of scientific works, and was by far the most accomplished in scientific literature. His *Sefer ta'ame ha-luhot* (*Treatise Explaining the Astronomical Tables*) referred often to Greek sources and made comparisons to Arabic and Hindu systems. A purely scientific work that described the astronomical and astrological characteristics of each planet, it contained no religious material and was translated into Latin for Christian readers.[41] That translation first applied the term *computus iudaeorum* (Jewish computus) to ibbur literature.[42]

So too was Maimonides engaged in the subject. At the age of twenty-three, Maimonides had already written a treatise in Arabic on the Jewish calendar that

presented the computus along with the calendar, with the combined work intended to be an introduction to the ibbur.[43] Ultimately, Maimonides incorporated his mature formulation of the ibbur into his monumental code of Jewish law, the *Mishneh Torah*. The section of the code dealing with the computus, "Hilkhot qiddush ha-hodesh" ("Laws of the Sanctification of the New Moon"), particularly the middle third (chapters six through ten), is a more elaborate version of his earlier work. Both treatises owe a large debt to the ibbur of bar Hiyya (unless both men relied on an earlier common source that has not survived).[44]

"Laws of the Sanctification of the New Moon" constitutes a bona fide computus treatise, and might have been titled a sefer ibbur had it been presented as a self-standing treatise without the framework of the larger code. It contains the final classical form of the perpetual calendar that Jewish savants in the Islamic world had worked so hard to perfect. By incorporating it into his monumental and authoritative *Mishneh Torah*, Maimonides secured for it preeminent status among all those who study Jewish law.

Although each of these scholars mastered the Arabic scientific corpus that had been translated, and in some cases transformed, from the Greek, they wrote their treatises in Hebrew to ensure that Jews everywhere could read their works.[45] While the works of all three contained mathematical and scientific components, they were written to serve Jewish ritual, religious, polemical, and social needs.

The arrival of the works of the Greek scientists and Arab mathematicians in Spain forced a dramatic rethinking of these subjects among Jews. Greek astronomy and Arab mathematics enabled both Jewish and non-Jewish scientists to measure and predict movements of the celestial bodies with a precision that had been unimaginable earlier. This development not only called earlier calculations into question, but also, for Jews, undermined some cherished suppositions concerning the Jewish calendar in traditional sources. Rabbinic literature presented the calendar as having been divinely ordained. The particulars of its calculation were transmitted orally as part of the exclusive covenantal patrimony of the Jews. Initiates were forbidden to reveal this lore to the ignorant public and to non-Jews.[46]

The astronomical works of the Greeks, along with those of other ancient nations, would have suggested to knowledgeable Jews that many of the components of the Jewish computus were not unique. In addition to the month names, which the Talmud acknowledges "were brought up from Babylonia" (JT Rosh

Hashanah 1:2), many other aspects of the calendar, such as the division of the hour into 1,080 parts, were derived from ancient Chaldean astronomy. Faced with evidence of accumulated astronomical traditions of the ancients, the Jewish claims of exclusivity and originality, and, thus, that their computus was part of a sacred covenant, needed profound rethinking.

The exposure to Greek and Arabic works also would have revealed that Jews now lagged behind others in the exact sciences. This discovery forced them to refine their calculations to keep their calendar in line with developing knowledge and new technologies.[47] Far from keeping their computus a secret from the gentiles, it now appeared that Jews needed to assimilate the learning of the gentiles into their own calculations.

What, if anything, would remain of the tradition of secrecy surrounding the calendar? The mantle of oral transmission and esotericism surrounding the process of intercalation had always accompanied it. By maintaining the vocabulary of secrecy while violating its spirit, the three Spanish Jewish authors redefined the meaning of secrecy, or the meaning of the calendar.

Muslims, who were the first to encounter the classical scientific works, and later also Christians, were faced with similar challenges. In this period of scientific expansion Jews were confronted not only with scientific advances but with the calendars of their chief religious and cultural rivals as well.

The writers of the sifre ibbur of the twelfth century confronted these challenges in several ways. Some responses were unique to their individual treatises; others were common to all three. All three authors referred to the tradition of esotericism. Bar Hiyya's rhyming prologue alluded to the notion of the Jewish computus as a body of secret knowledge. Ibn Ezra referred to his entire treatise as one to be transmitted with caution, and to one portion in particular as "sod ha-ibbur" (the secret of intercalation, the system of insertion of leap days, weeks, or years to keep a calendar synchronized with the moon's phases).[48] Maimonides also used the term "sod ha-ibbur" in the sense of an esoteric knowledge that the sages revealed only to a few initiates.[49] Yet by writing comprehensive treatises detailing how to calculate the Jewish calendar, these authors slipped off the veil of secrecy. Ibn Ezra justified committing the ibbur to writing as a pedagogical aid in the transmission of the lore from master to disciple.[50] He wrote of the *derekh ha-me'abrim* (ways of the calendators), as well as *hakhme ha-ibbur* (wise men of the calendar), and in this way acknowledged, and often took to task, a long chain of predecessors.[51]

Esotericism has proven to be a useful tool for integrating new knowledge in

FIG. 1.2. Rabbi (Simon ben) Gamliel receives Jewish calendar formulae. *Sefer evronot*, 1552. Courtesy of the Library of the Jewish Theological Seminary ms 9487, fol. 3r.

a time of crisis, and this situation was no different.[52] When scholars claim that the knowledge has been known all along, just concealed, it is accepted more readily. Both Maimonides and ibn Ezra, however, dismissed the traditional concern with esotericism of calendar-making, seeing it only as scientific knowledge to be shared with those who had sufficient scientific training. If esotericism created a social elite of insiders who were privy to the secret knowledge, then that circle of savants would now be composed of men whose mastery of science provided a way to access the secrets of the Torah.

Abraham ibn Ezra noted that some of his contemporaries could not accept the rationale for the *dehiyyot*, the rabbinically mandated deferments that formed an integral part of the calculation formula:

> Don't allow your heart to ask in confusion, Just because it is burdensome to the public, how can I abandon the true dating of the holidays in their proper time? . . . And to the one who argues that our sages have commanded us to celebrate the holidays for two days on account of doubt [as to which day the month would begin], why have you not set the Day of Atonement for two days? There are a number of world class fools among our contemporaries who fast for two days, and I will demonstrate to them that their fast is futile, that it is vain and false.[53]

His refutation, he promised, would come in the course of his interpretation of the secret.

Ibn Ezra devoted approximately a third of his treatise on the ibbur to the section he titled "The Secret of the Intercalation."[54] He began with a plea that God open the hearts of the reader to see the truth, for those who would "deny the ibbur" have written innumerable books. All of these works are based on illusions, ibn Ezra argued, for neither the Torah nor any scripture has detailed the process by which Jews have reckoned their festivals, their months, and their years. As for the controversies, some reckon months according to their *qeviot* (predetermined formulae), others according to a sighting of the new moon or according to the mean lunation, and still others depend on the relative position of a constellation.[55] Ibn Ezra likewise discussed how different cultures come to different conclusions regarding the starting point of the solar year. "In sum: there is no clear cut evidence in scriptures as to how Israel reckoned their times in antiquity."[56] As evidence he noted that when King Hezekiah celebrated the Passover at the "wrong" time, God acceded to his reckoning.[57]

Ibn Ezra presented the sod ha-ibbur as a necessary rabbinic intervention

where the biblical text simply does not provide sufficient guidance. The very obliqueness of the text, in his view, was eloquent proof that it could never have been intended to stand unaided. Only an obvious error in calculation could override the rabbinic mandate with regard to determining any aspect of the calendar. But if a formula or tradition led to a conclusion that had been contradicted by scientific observation, it could not be the truth. Such errors, regardless of their authors, should be rejected, for "they are untrue, and simple observation refutes them."[58]

Ibn Ezra reserved the sharpest scorn and most comprehensive refutation for the calculations attributed to the talmudic sage Samuel, who had boasted, "The pathways of the heavens are as clear to me as the pathways of Nehardea."[59]

> Do not pay attention to the *tequfot* [calculated according to] Samuel, who reckoned to the quarter day and not more precisely, for his is not a true interval at all. Perhaps Samuel knew this, and set the formula for the people of his generation, for it is difficult for people to understand primary fractions, let alone secondary. I know that any wise man who reads these things that I have said about the tequfah of Samuel will wonder at my words, or mock: and I respond: it is I who wonder at you. For the Torah demands that a matter can be verified if there are two or three witnesses, and I have seven honest witnesses to refute Samuel's calculation.[60]

Take for example, ibn Ezra argued, the equinoxes. They are measurable and immediately verifiable as the days in the year when the number of hours in the night and day are virtually the same. Yet in the year of his writing, Samuel's calculation of the day when the seasons would change indicated a very late date for the equinox. "This would cause us great embarrassment before the world, and we would become, because of our reckoning, the scorn and mockery of those around us. . . . Even the most unlearned person can see when the day and the night are equal, some eleven days earlier. Heaven forbid. Our reckoning is correct and there is no need for the tequfah of Samuel."[61] He rejected the notion that the tequfah of Samuel could be promulgated to the public because it was simpler, than that of R. Ada, which was more accurate. There can only be one true tequfah. Two different calculations cannot fall eight days apart yet both be true.[62] Ibn Ezra concluded his reproof of those who clung to Samuel's reckoning with the strongest rebuke: "If the tequfah of Samuel is true, then our entire

calendation is false, and our festivals and fasts all lies, Heaven forbid. Better that our calendation is true, and what of Samuel's reckoning? It is irrelevant."[63]

In this context, ibn Ezra opposed practices that associated the equinoctial and solstitial points with danger. "Those who think that any person who eats or drinks at the time of the tequfah will be harmed and will swell up, it is a fable (*derash*)."[64] For ibn Ezra, this belief was all the more ludicrous because most Jews did not even know how to calculate the true tequfah.

The twelfth-century computus literature of the Spanish sages justified incorporating into Jewish culture, through the calendar, new wisdom, new structures, and new arguments from the science of non-Jews. Bar Hiyya accorded equal weight to rabbinic midrashic sources and to scientific works in the explanatory portion of his computus. He included the famous midrash about God minimizing the moon to punish it for complaining about the creation of two equal heavenly bodies, and he used midrashic sources in his computations.[65] Bar Hiyya also included a great deal of astrological material in all his works, even as he expressed ambivalence about reliance on astrology.[66] These traditional sources stood alongside newer scientific knowledge of his day.

Maimonides appended to his treatise on computus, *Hilkhot qiddush ha-hodesh*, an entire section on calculating the exact time that the new moon would appear, a section based primarily on the work of Arab astronomers.[67] Maimonides offered the most explicit apology for incorporating non-Jewish science into his computus. He noted that the Bible alluded to works of "sons of Issachar" on the science of time that had not been preserved. This lack of extant books on math and astronomy among the Jews meant that they had to learn these matters from the Greeks. But since these subjects were based on proofs rather than on opinion, it did not matter who wrote them.[68]

The authors of the three seminal ibbur treatises did not intend them to be contributions to an interfaith discussion of the relative merits of various systems of computus. They each wrote in Hebrew for Jewish readers, and despite their derisive references to the other faiths, they did not engage in direct polemics against these faiths. Rather, aspects of their work dealing with the Christian and Muslim calendars should be seen as apologetic literature, designed to bolster the Jewish faith from within.

Of the three sifre ibbur, bar Hiyya's employed the sharpest tone, championing the Jewish computus over all others. His comparative analysis, which exposed the deficits of those calendars that were based entirely on either solar or lunar cycles, established the Jewish computus literature as another form of po-

lemic. This is consistent with its development as an instrument of sectarian and religious differentiation. Bar Hiyya warned:

> Be aware that most of the nations who are near to us, whose ways we know and whose customs we hear of, count according to the sun, and some of them, although they count according to the sun also take the moon into account. We don't know of any nation that counts according to the moon without taking the sun into account except for the kingdom of Ishmael [Islam] alone, and those among other nations who enter into their error. We will explicate their computus, *derekh heshbonam*, first, because their months are lunar, similar to the computus of Israel in that one respect.[69]

Bar Hiyya continued with a savage characterization of Islam that may reflect his revulsion at the recent religious wars raging in Spain: "We say that in the kingdom of the Ishmaelites they began this computus from the beginning of the sin of the mad evildoer who misled them, and the onset of his error came in the month of Av, in the 12th year of the 231st cycle, which is 4382 to the creation, according to the accounting which we currently use."[70] Bar Hiyya followed this with a brief account of the Muslim computus. He emphasized that the Egyptian computists relied on eyewitnesses for the new moon, keeping their new moons close to those of the Jews.

Bar Hiyya was no more generous in his chapter to pagan nations that followed a purely solar calendar. Under the rubric of "pagan nations," he launched into a derogatory and polemical description of the Christian calendar:

> The entire evil kingdom of Edom [the nation of Esau, referring to Christianity], who count according to the hanged one (*ha-talui*), compute most of their civil matters according to the solar calendar like the Greeks, however they are forced to compute according to the moon along with the sun to set their fasts and some of their calamities [*eydeyhem*, rabbinic dysphemism for feast days], because they liken themselves to Israel in this counting.[71]

He also derided the Christian chronology as both portending evil and filled with error.

> They count these calamities [feasts] from the year in which they are certain their misleader was born. According to them, he was born in

the year 3761 after the creation, on the twenty-fifth day of the month of December, which is the Sabbath day (Saturday), the ninth day in Tevet, eighteenth year in the 198th cycle, to our counting. If their words were true, it is fitting that this evil man should be born on that day. However, no one believes their words when they say of the birth of the hanged one that they know the date of his birth and that he was born on the 25th of December, as this is not written in their evangelion [written polemically in Hebrew, *aven gilyon*, scroll of sin] nor in the writings of the disciples of the makh'is (one who angers).[72]

Bar Hiyya alleged that when the apostles went forth to proselytize among the pagans, they allowed the pagans to retain their holiday of the winter solstice, "turning it from impurity to impurity and from sin to sin." Their own priests, he charged, have no idea when he was really born and they err famously by an entire year in their reckoning of the number of years since his birth. The Christian reckoning within the nineteen-year metonic (lunar) cycle was similarly erroneous. Christians, mocked bar Hiyya, were divided over the age of Jesus at his death and some had even resorted to asking the Jews to help them figure it out. Indeed, bar Hiyya explained the entire Christian moveable cycle in pungent polemical terms.[73] He then demonstrated the interdependence of the systems, for Jews could figure their own calendar knowing certain facts about the Christian calendar, and vice versa.[74]

In an atmosphere of scientific competition in which each religious community claimed superiority for its computus, bar Hiyya proudly staked a claim for the Jewish sages of old whose calendrical structure had withstood the test of time and comprehended both major cycles, solar and lunar. The polemical imprint was to remain an enduring feature of computus literature through the early modern period.

Writing several decades later, Abraham ibn Ezra broke the tedium of the genre by adopting a more literary tone and by presenting the dry and difficult algorithms in the form of riddles and poems. He introduced methods to remember the *molad* (conjunction of the moon) and the qeviot "*be-shirim shequlim* (in metered rhymes)."[75] This playfulness endured in calendar literature, not only in mnemonic ditties, but also with iconographic traditions that sprang up in the margins (and in some cases the center) of the text in a later period.

Nevertheless, ibn Ezra did not refrain from using his calendar treatise for polemical ends. He sharply criticized parts of the Christian computus as having

been based on erroneous computations, citing astronomers of many nations in support of his views. He pointed out that the Christian calendar was dependent on the Jewish one, and noted the old controversy between the Quartodecimans and those who argued that Easter should fall only on Sundays.[76] But ibn Ezra reserved his fiercest attacks for his fellow Jews, among them bar Hiyya. He also sharply refuted the Qaraites and rejected the basis for their calendar, and repudiated the 247-year calendar cycle attributed to Nahshon Gaon of the mid-ninth century. By attacking other scholars in this way, his treatise cemented the twelfth-century Sephardic ibbur literature as a genre that was at once pedagogic and polemic.

Of the three major Spanish Jewish treatises on the computus written in the twelfth century, Maimonides' had by far the largest circulation. Embedded in his monumental code of Jewish law *Mishneh Torah*, his "Laws of the Sanctification of the New Moon" remains a classical exposition of the traditions pertaining to calculation of the Jewish calendar. While acknowledging the emphasis in biblical tradition on the court's sanctification of the moon based on lunar observation, Maimonides argued that it was equally important to know the astronomical calculations in the event that the court could not fulfill this function or ceased to exist.[77] Maimonides used mean values for basic calendrical calculations and for computing the molad and tequfah. The authoritative status of his code ensured that his accounting for the calendar would become a new standard.[78]

It appears that in Spain and Provence, the ibburim of bar Hiyya and ibn Ezra circulated at approximately equal rates.[79] Bar Hiyya's ibbur traversed the borders of Spain and became popular in Italy and Byzantium. Not until the late fifteenth century did sifre ibbur appear as separate, self-standing treatises in Ashkenaz.[80]

The Italian and Ashkenazic Ibbur

One of the earliest medieval manuscripts to contain a treatise titled *Sod ha-ibbur* is an anonymous eleventh-century Byzantine and Italian Jewish anthology. Among the collections of laws, midrashim, geonic responsa, and a list of all the tractates in the Mishnah is a section of seven folios beginning with the tantalizing phrase, "He who wishes to plumb the secret of the intercalation."[81] The manuscript is undated and bears no colophon; it is difficult to know whether its contents were gathered to suit one particular reader or more than one.[82]

The manuscript is also notable because it includes a section called "Laws of Torah Reading and Public Prayers for All the Days of the Year," which hints at the development of what was to become the favored vehicle of computus literature within medieval Ashkenazic circles, the *mahzor*. The word *mahzor* literally means cycle; in Jewish literature it refers to a liturgical compendium containing prayers for the holidays and the seven special Sabbaths of the Jewish year. In the Italian rite, the term included both daily and festival prayers. Mahzor could refer to a holiday prayer book; in German lands a large-format manuscript would be made for the cantor's use.[83] Mahzor was also used to designate a compendium that included customs, rites, and prayers for the ritual year, as well as commentaries on the prayers, laws related to the annual festival cycle, laws of the permitted and prohibited, as well as *shtarot* (model contracts).[84]

As in the case of Spain, tracing the path of transmission of Jewish calendar literature in medieval Ashkenaz leads scholars to the twelfth century, in this case to disciples of the renowned teacher and scholar Rashi (1040–1105). Although mahzorim were compiled even before this period, Rashi's circle of disciples in France was intensively involved in mahzor cultivation (which was not the case at the time in Germany).[85] Four of Rashi's disciples compiled mahzorim, which served as guideposts for the religious life of the Jewish community both in and out of the synagogue.[86] The most famous of the mahzorim is *Mahzor Vitry* of R. Simha of Vitry; it was preceded by, and drew material from, the mahzor of Rashi's closest disciple, R. Shemaya. Perhaps the clarifications of many liturgical texts and customs that emerged from the teachings of Rashi spurred his disciples to codify the new material.

After R. Shemaya left the group, R. Jacob bar Samson (ca. 1070–1140), who lived in northern France, became the most influential of Rashi's disciples, and the first in that circle to become deeply interested in astrology and astronomy. During the year 1123–1124, Jacob bar Samson composed his enigmatically titled *Sefer elqoshi*, which survives only in a fragmented state.[87] It was comprised of three segments, one astronomical, one cosmological, and one related to the sod ha-ibbur, the intricate discussion of the computus. Jacob bar Samson based his work on the Talmud, on the lost treatise of Sa'adiah Gaon, and on the ibbur of bar Hiyya. While bar Samson referred explicitly only to Sa'adiah, he apparently also knew of and used bar Hiyya's ibbur, a fact that highlights the relationship between the Jewish culture of northern France and that of Spain.[88] Bar Hiyya composed his ibbur in 1123, and within months, in France, Jacob bar Samson included portions of it in his work.[89] The works are similar in several ways.[90]

Despite these influences, R. Jacob forged a unique path when he composed his ibbur. He acknowledged his debt to the Babylonian geonim, and to Sa'adiah in particular, yet he followed the tradition of Eretz Israel for some calculations. There is no way to ascertain the exact path of its transmission to France, but the *dehiyyat Nissan* (deferment of the month Nissan) that he used in his computus formula had been used in Eretz Israel and was rare in medieval European manuscripts.[91]

R. Jacob's work is important for Ashkenazic cultural history because it shows that in late eleventh-century northern France, both Babylonian and Eretz Israel traditions (as well as those of Muslim Spain) exerted influence over Ashkenazic culture and practice.[92] The history of ibbur literature confirms that the long-regnant notion of an exclusive line from Palestinian to medieval Ashkenazic culture cannot be sustained; the Babylonian tradition is just as likely as the Palestinian tradition to have influenced medieval Ashkenazic Jews.

The first medieval ibburim served as foundations for development of the genre in several ways. Some situated the ibbur within the context of scientific learning. Although Jews were not primarily attracted to scientific study for religious reasons, once such interests had developed, religious pretexts helped justify Jews' pursuit of the sciences, particularly astronomy (not then separate from astrology), which was so closely linked to the construction of the calendar.[93]

The tendency to integrate mathematical and astronomical science into one work related to the calendar reached its fullest realization in the *Yesod olam* of Isaac ben Israel (or Israeli, fl. Toledo, 1310).[94] *Yesod olam* differed considerably from the earlier Jewish computus works.[95] In twelfth-century sifre ibbur, scientific knowledge was included only if it served the primary religious purpose of the computus, whereas Israeli presented nonreligious subjects as inherently valuable. The ibbur informed his work but did not justify it. *Yesod olam* became the epitome of the Spanish Jewish achievement: science, language, and Jewish learning bound together in one coherent volume.[96]

Another Spanish figure took the ibbur in a different direction. The fourteenth-century scholar David Abudarham, from Seville, authored an influential compendium of Jewish liturgy and custom that included a *seder ibbur* with readings from the Bible and Prophets for the entire year as well as astronomical and calendrical tables. His work used Spanish and Provençal as well as French, German, and Italian Jewish sources.[97] Unlike *Yesod olam*, it situated the ibbur in a purely religious context.

In medieval Ashkenazic literature, the *Sefer elqoshi* of Jacob bar Samson ap-

parently stands as the only independent treatise on the calendar.[98] All the extant medieval ibbur treatises in Ashkenazic script are embedded within larger texts. For centuries, the twelfth-century Sephardic ibburim did not find much purchase in Ashkenaz. Not one free-standing treatise on the calendar has been preserved from the thirteenth century in Ashkenazic script.

From the thirteenth through the sixteenth centuries, several trends can be seen in the Ashkenazic ibbur material. Some ibburim contained midrashic elaborations on the calendar, or judaized aspects of it. For example, one manuscript contained a small midrashic section titled "Names of the Months." Its opening verses explained the meaning of all twelve month names: "Why is [the first month] called Nissan? Because in it *nissim* (miracles) were performed for Israel. Iyar, because the entire world is hanging in the *avir* (air) in it," and so on.[99] Almost all Ashkenazic ibbur material was included in larger collections of custom and liturgy and usually drew from a mix of sources: geonic, Spanish, Eretz Israel, and Ashkenazic.

By the early fifteenth century, ibburim circulating in Ashkenaz began to expand. Some contained a much more extensive section on the calendar called "The Order of the Secret of the Intercalation."[100] A manuscript completed in the second decade of the fifteenth century (1414 C.E.) is one of the earliest recognizable sifre evronot, as they were later called in Ashkenaz.[101] It contained a complete Christian calendar including the month names and saints' day names in a combination of German and Hebrew, a chart with the best and worst days for bloodletting, and a perpetual chart for each year of a twenty-eight-year solar cycle that indicated the exact hour of the equinoctial points.[102] These features, signs of Jewish engagement with the larger culture, had been rare in earlier surviving ibbur manuscripts, but were becoming more commonplace.

Ibbur literature was the product of a centuries-long process of amalgamation and sifting. The twelfth-century Sephardic ibburim reflected their authors' confrontation with the calendar knowledge of other cultures, and they remained stable as texts through the medieval period—that is, they were "closed" books. In Ashkenaz, by contrast, the formulation and the transmission of ibbur remained in flux through the medieval period. Ibbur formulae appeared within various types of collections: liturgical, religious, custom-based, historical, medical, and literary.[103] The text varied from one exemplar to the next, so that the Ashkenazic tradition was very much "open book."[104] It was not to receive a stand-alone, full-bodied treatment until the sixteenth century in Western Europe.

The Politics of Time in Early Modern Europe

The Calendars of these computers, and the accounts of these dayes are very different; the Greeks differing from the Latins, and the Latins from each other; the one observing the Julian or ancient account, as great Britaine and part of Germany; the other adhering to the Gregorian or new account, as Italy, France, Spaine, and the united Provinces of the Netherlands.

Sir Thomas Browne, *Pseudodoxia epidemica*, 1658

No single vehicle of culture reflected the dynamic changes in early modern European society as clearly as the calendar, which functioned both as a system for accounting for time and as an artifact for displaying it. Beginning in the sixteenth century, the calendar emerged as a locus of religious, cultural, and political conflict. Great European thinkers as well as petty pamphleteers channeled their scientific, religious, and political passions into the development of humble and quotidian printed calendars that soon became indispensable to ordinary Europeans. Far from remaining compendia of dry computational tables, calendars reflected some of the most important cultural currents of their time, evolving into a literary genre, political tool, and marker of religious denomination.

The calendar played a central role in the Catholic-Protestant conflicts of the sixteenth and seventeenth centuries. Each denomination sought to strengthen its control over adherents, a struggle that changed the religious face of European society and shattered the hegemony of the Catholic Church—along with its calendar. Even before the changeover to the Gregorian calendar deepened the divide, observances and Bible readings differed greatly among denominations. Not only *what* people believed and observed divided the various groups, but also *when* they observed it. The sight of a festive religious procession by one group when another was still immersed in somber devotion enraged Christians of every denomination. Neighbors often set upon one another if they deemed

each other disrespectful of their calendars. Whereas in previous times Europeans had directed such resentment of discordant calendars primarily onto the Jews in their midst, with the Reformation, and later the reformation of the calendar, they expressed their anger against members of Christian groups as well.

Calendars in the early modern period also played a pivotal role in fostering the national consciousness in Elizabethan England, and later, revolutionary France. Civic holidays were intended to replace religious ones, and calendars became useful tools in the hands of anyone hoping to shape new dynastic and political loyalties. This development coincided with the debate in scientific and theological circles over the changes necessary to bring the Western Christian (Julian) calendar in closer alignment with natural cycles. The Gregorian reform of the calendar in 1582 reflected and stimulated new thinking about science, religion, and the political order, and in particular, facilitated the transfer of knowledge and power regarding time-keeping from clerical and religious circles to the secular realm.

Production of Calendars

Helping to propel calendars to the forefront of cultural and political change in the early modern period was the expansion of print. Booksellers and printers marketed calendars and almanacs to ever-expanding segments of the population. Calendars soon became profitable items on many printers' lists as people came to depend on them. Some of the earliest printed works were calendars, and the ability to produce them in large numbers affected not only their circulation, but also the type of information they could carry. Consequently, printing did not just change the technology of disseminating calendrical information; it altered as well the very nature of what Europeans meant by "the calendar."

Before the invention of printing, medieval Europeans determined their days in a variety of ways. Farmers and peasants would learn about Sundays and feast days from their parish priest, then incise these instructions on a stick, with larger notches indicating holy days. For instance, Natalie Davis describes a peasant device that consisted of marks made "in figures on little tablets of wood." In the late seventeenth century, "on a morsel of wood no bigger than a playing card," peasants marked "all the months and days of the year, with the feast days and other notable things."[1] Some simply tied knots on a string, making larger knots for Sundays. In medieval England, people used "clog almanacs," carved sticks or

rods made of wood, brass, or horn on which notches or symbols indicated lunar cycles and Christian feasts. Small ones were made to fit into a pocket, whereas larger ones would be hung in a central place near the hearth in the home.[2]

Homemade devices like these glyphic calendars were supplemented by oral ditties, traditional proverbs, and memorable poems of various kinds that helped people who could not read or did not own a manuscript calendar.[3] Students had to learn the calendar by heart in school, and it is possibly for them that mnemonic devices emerged to help count the days on their fingers and to learn the feasts.[4] Among the most widely used of these devices were the *cisiojanus* poems, rhyming mnemonic couplets originating in the late twelfth century that were named for the first two syllables of the Latin words for "circumcision" and "January."[5] Designed to help people remember the order of the feast days throughout the year, they contained 365 syllables, one for each day of the year, and were grouped into twelve couplets, one for each month. Each syllable corresponded to a saints' day or feast day, so these poems varied by locale. They were later appended to calendars and Books of Hours, and began to appear in the vernacular from the late fourteenth century.[6] When annual printed calendars replaced perpetual calendars, mnemonics like these gradually fell into disuse.[7]

Through the medieval period, a great deal of attention in the calendar-calculating—or computus—literature was devoted to "reckoning of time and holy days by means of the hand and fingers."[8] The great eighth-century Northumbrian monk Bede recalled the method of counting by using the fingers and joints of the hand:

> Some people, in order to simplify calculation, have transferred both cycles, the lunar and the solar, onto the joints of their fingers. Because the human hand has 19 joints if we include the tips of the fingers, by applying each year to one of these joints they begin the lunar cycle on the inside of the left hand. . . . Again, because the two hands together, if you do not count in the fingertips, have 28 joints, they assign the years [of the solar cycle] to these, beginning at the little finger of the left hand.[9]

These instructions themselves were too complicated to follow without some accompanying illustration, and many calendar calculation manuals, including Hebrew *ibbur* manuscripts, contained these and other ingenious mnemonic charts to help the user keep track of the many factors and variables nec-

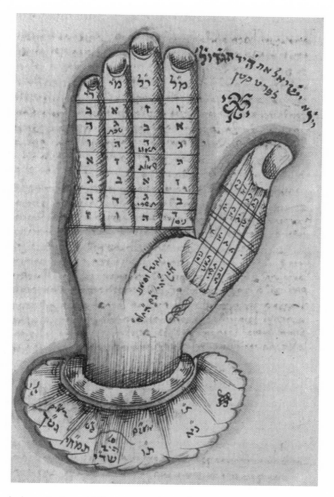

FIG. 2.1. Hand-shaped chart. *Sefer evronot*, 1779. Cincinnati, Klau Library, Hebrew Union College-Jewish Institute of Religion ms 902, fol. 20r.

essary to come up with the correct result.[10] Bede himself did not place too much faith in written charts, because the chance of copyist or calculation error was too great. As he recognized: "Many aspects of this discipline, just as of the other arts, are better conveyed by the utterance of a living voice than by the labor of an inscribing pen."[11]

Official calculations remained the domain of the learned elite, mainly university professors and clergymen who had studied mathematics, astronomy, and theology. Priests and monks would write the calendar in the back pages of their

missals and breviaries, or near the end of their Psalters, while members of the legal profession would put calendars behind the local statute collections or their law books.[12] Books of Hours, those keys to medieval Christian piety, served as a common venue for calendars. Although their primary purpose was to accompany their owners through the liturgical hours of the day, they also provided the divisions of the year, so that European calendars appeared in them early on.[13]

Calendars were, of course, prepared painstakingly by hand, often by the very person who had calculated them. In fact, most calendars were not calculated to one specific year. Rather, they consisted of tables containing the information necessary for computing any year's calendar. Some perpetual calendars contained volvelles, paper spheres carefully superimposed on top of one another so that they could be rotated to calculate for any year: these permanent mandalas were executed with precision and beauty. Others were simple charts showing the day of the week that corresponded to March 1; from them one could calculate any other date in the year.[14] Most manuscript calendars provided information to determine dates for many years ahead, with hundred-year calendars the favorites. They illustrated the "perpetual" calendar principle: after a certain number of years, every cycle would repeat itself, so once the pattern was established the calculations could extend far into the future.

As soon as printing was invented, printers could technically have produced annual calendars much like the ones we use today. Yet the earliest printers, wary of investing resources into such an ephemeral product, did not print single-year calendars. Instead they continued to model their product on medieval perpetual calendars, providing users with the golden number, the holy days, and the lunar phases, so they could construct their own calendars.[15] Until printed calendars began to display the days, weeks, months, and years in a graphic and accessible manner, they did not become a truly popular form. In order to entice new buyers each year, enterprising printers began to add various extraneous materials to their calendars, sometimes vastly expanding their cultural scope.

In the late fifteenth and early sixteenth centuries, makers of calendars, almanacs, and household reference books began to include a variety of popular materials in their calendar compendia.[16] These early compendia were modeled first on peasant almanacs, anthologies ostensibly designed to guide peasants through the multilayered and overlapping rhythms of their lives: agricultural time, church time, and astrological time. In English, these were called "shepherds' calendars," in German, *Volkskalender*, and in French, *Calendrier des bergers*.

The earliest surviving exemplar of a German Volkskalender dates to the early fifteenth century, and was probably based on a Latin model. Its core section, the *Kalendarium*, contained methods for calculating the seasons and leap years, a cisiojanus, the twelve signs of the zodiac, the seven planets, as well as chronological calculations and astronomical treatises. A medical-themed Volkskalender appeared in southern Germany around the mid-fifteenth century, and was first printed in 1481.[17] Such folk calendars included dietary, medical, and hygienic information according to month and season, as well as advice about propitious times for bloodletting, bathing, sexual relations, pruning trees, buying clothes, or moving to another place. The early sixteenth-century *Kalender of Shepherdes* came with beautiful illustrations, rhymes that connected seasonal attributes to religious events of the month, charts of lunar appearances and eclipses, explanations of the connection between a person's birth month and character, the planets and parts of the body they influenced, the human figure, and a bloodletting chart.[18] Most calendars contained predictions about the weather, the outcomes of duels or wars, and other important matters. These prognostications were intended by the compilers and taken by the consumers to be a vital reason to buy the calendars.

Despite their name, shepherds' calendars were probably not accessible to most shepherds and peasants. These faux naïve works were not intended directly for the field laborers but for those who read to them, instructed them, or employed them—those who could now "correct" their superstitious ways.[19] Those who were closest to nature's rhythms did not need written manuals. Yet regardless of the class of their readers, so-called shepherds' calendars circulated in huge numbers. In seventeenth- and eighteenth-century France alone, some 150,000–200,000 copies were printed annually.[20]

German pioneers of the printing industry were quick to grasp the steady profit from utilitarian calendars that would need to be replaced every year. In the fifteenth century, fifty-six printers in twenty-five cities printed calendar books and broadsides. By the sixteenth century more than five hundred *Praktiken* and *Prognostiken* had been printed, and German printers overtook the Italian calendar printers to dominate the European printing industry.[21]

By the 1660s, the books that sold the most copies every year were almanacs and calendars. An estimated 400,000 copies were sold annually, bought by one of every three families in Europe.[22] By the eighteenth century, calendars and almanacs comprised the single most frequently printed item in all Europe. They far surpassed Bibles as the best selling printed works, for the simple reason that

people could use and read their Bibles for many years but they needed to purchase new calendars annually.[23] Thus while more families owned Bibles than kept almanacs, far more almanacs entered the marketplace. Calendars fell into a category between sacred literature, such as Bibles and hagiographies, and the ephemera that constituted the lion's share of the printers' and booksellers' economy. While broadsides, ballads, and sensational pamphlets were printed to convey fresh news and to be read for amusement, calendars and almanacs fell somewhere in the middle of the spectrum. Printers expected people to turn to calendars for daily consultation to obtain medical, astronomical, religious, and economic information. Calendars had to be simple enough to be accessible to a wide readership, yet both comprehensive enough to be useful in many ways and accurate enough to be credible.

Calendars presented a special challenge to printers. Because the public viewed them as ephemera, printers were loathe to squander on them precious resources such as expensive paper or specially commissioned illustrations.[24] Title pages were often taken from older prototypes. Yet the poorer the paper quality, the harder it was for printers to print them correctly. This was particularly true for calendars printed with two colors of ink, black for weekdays and red for holy days. These calendars were modeled after Bibles that printed the words of Jesus in red, so that the two colors, red and black, represented blood and ink, spirit and letter. In such cases, the paper would need to be pulled though the press twice, and all the tiny marks next to various days would need to be aligned correctly.[25]

One eighteenth-century description of an ideal calendar details sets of columns with the left used for the day of the week, followed immediately by the number of the week in the year. The second column would contain the number of the day in the month and the name of the day. Next to that column, in bright red ink, would be the names of the feast and fast days. Additionally, brief notices of evangelica and epistles, the portion to be read that Sunday, and the type of Sunday, would be noted there. Next would be information concerning the sun and the moon, when each rose and set, and the zodiac symbols. The last column would contain information on the appearance and disappearance of the moon. An intricate system of glyphs was to follow this column. By the eighteenth century, encyclopedist Johann Georg Krünitz was complaining that no one understood the glyphs anymore, so he provided a key: † symbolized a good day, and ‡ stood for a very propitious day for bloodletting (printers of Jewish calendars used the neutral symbol ° for a good bloodletting day, to circumvent

the use of crosses); ♣ marked a favorable time for planting; while a double fish strongly recommended the time for fishing. The next column was reserved for weather forecasts, a vestige from the time, not too far back, when that realm still stood under the influence of astrologers.[26]

As the printing industry matured, calendars expanded and ultimately blossomed into an extremely diversified print category comprising a profusion of specialized volumes to serve every conceivable interest and constituency. The staples included astronomical, geographical, military, historical, economic, household, and gardeners' calendars. Decorated in wood and copper cuts, early calendars were designed with charts, astrological signs, figures, and images so they would be comprehensible even to people who were barely literate. Calendars were printed in various formats, some small enough to fit in pockets, others intended for display on walls, and still others, the *Contoir-* or *Stifts-kalender*, made for the desks of businessmen. *Schreibkalender* contained blank pages interspersed with the calendar material to encourage note taking. They became a staple of the printers' industry and the booksellers' inventory, and were produced in staggering quantities and varieties, tailored to every segment of the population that could afford them.

Porous cultural boundaries meant that calendar printers used designs from a broad range of sources throughout the early modern period. Even the early shepherds' calendars included design elements from across national boundaries; German and French woodcuts, for example, could end up adorning the same volume.[27] One eighteenth-century German printer modeled his wares on the French revolutionary calendars, which were designed to win German farmers to radical Jacobin thinking.[28] An eighteenth-century German scholar lamented that the French produced more interesting calendars than the Germans; he noted enviously that the French even marketed an *Almanach des Centenaires*, a calendar that listed the names of centenarians since antiquity, and so provided a comforting antidote to the relentless passage of time reflected on the pages of the calendar.[29] The scholar's comment demonstrates the high level of competition that existed in the marketplace for calendars.

As calendars evolved from oral and handwritten works to a printed medium, and from perpetual and permanent books to annual and ephemeral leaflets or broadsheets, their function changed. They became accessible reference works rather than instructions for reckoning with a complicated set of overlapping rules. Lunar and solar cycles, golden numbers, and epacts (which give the moon's age in days on January 1 of a particular year) ceased to exist as real con-

cepts even for people who had formerly mastered them.[30] Printing transformed a specialty item into a mass medium, and facilitated the transfer of knowledge regarding the marking of time from clerical and religious circles to the secular realm, out of the Psalter and Book of Hours and into the kitchen and laborer's pockets. Printers in Europe aimed to appeal to the broadest possible customer base. Narrow ideological and didactic goals were eclipsed by the economic interests of printers who aimed to suit the largest number of buyers with each edition.

Had events not conspired to propel calendars to the center of the European denominational wars, they would have remained useful trackers of time much as they are in our own day, with their users feeling no deep engagement with the history of calendars or with what they represent. But such was the fate of these particular books that they came to stand at the center of the era's great strife.

In early modern Western Europe, technological and social change proceeded at an intense pace. Governments, religious bodies, even trade and mercantile guilds, began to use calendars strategically as a means of molding and shaping social thought. Calendars thus emerged as one of the important didactic and polemical instruments of the age.[31] They were used to disseminate not only information, but also values. Just like other printed books, calendars could be manipulated, edited, censored, and controlled.

The Gregorian Calendar Reform

It is one of the ironies of early modern history, and a warning against superficial characterizations, that the Catholic Church advocated and instituted the reform of the calendar in order to align it with current scientific understanding. Astronomers and scientists had long been aware that the calendar Christians had inherited from the Roman Empire, the Julian calendar, contained inaccuracies.[32] The minutes per year that the Julian calendar deviated from the solar cycle seemed trivial in themselves; accumulated over many centuries, however, they added up to many days. The discrepancy set the stage for urgent and widespread debate among scientists and theologians over the flaws in the Julian calendar and their remedies, a discussion that had begun centuries earlier. The accumulated deviation had become so significant that it would prevent the church from being able to observe Easter at its required time, or as Dante wrote in the early fourteenth century, January would eventually be "unwintered by the hundredth part which is neglected."[33] The convergence of Easter and the spring

equinox was a perfect example of how the Christian calendar had once naturalized religious rituals. The gradual drift that had separated Easter from true spring made it ever more obvious that the manmade calendar was out of step with celestial movements.

Intense deliberations over the introduction of a revised calendar lasted for decades and raged among all groups of Europeans. The Catholic Church had delayed the calendar reform due to fear of provoking further divisions. The reform ought to have come as part of the sweeping overhaul called for by the Council of Trent, which met for more than two decades. But the council remained so preoccupied with doctrinal issues raised by the Protestants that the bishops never got to the calendar. In 1577, Pope Gregory XIII, haunted by a sense of responsibility to complete that council's mandate, sent around to Catholic princes a "Compendium of New Ways to Restore the Calendar."[34] Then, on February 24, 1582, he prepared the Catholic world for a momentous change: in October of that year, ten days would be dropped from the calendar.[35]

Pope Gregory instituted another less heralded, but perhaps more significant, shift in the calendar: a new method of calculating the date of Easter. His calendar's calculation of Easter by counting back to the fourth-century Council of Nicea (by now identified as Catholic), rather than to an earlier apostolic date that had no denominational overtones, rankled Protestant astronomers such as John Dee in England.[36] Protestants, who had not been consulted prior to the change, interpreted Pope Gregory's decision to excise the famous ten days as a show of vigor by a proactive counter-Reformation church—and indeed the pope considered it to be a continuation of the work of the Council of Trent, convened to counteract the rise of Protestantism. Eastern churches also rejected the new method for calculating Easter, concerned that the wide-ranging possibilities for fixing the date of Easter would lead to "one person celebrating the Passion at the same time as another will be celebrating the Resurrection."[37] It seemed as though Gregory had found the perfect way to harden lines already deeply incised into the religious and political landscape.

Once the Catholic Church had unilaterally instituted the new calendar, calendar observance became one of the chief signs of denomination in Europe. While the reform was accepted and implemented most easily in Italy, Spain, Portugal, and Poland, Protestant states resisted the change until the eighteenth century. They feared that accepting it in the time and manner prescribed by the Catholic Church would be giving in to papal authority at a critical time in their growth. As one Englishman said, "We should seem to some . . . that we doe it

for fear of the Pope's curse and excommunication, because he doth command it under payne of execution to be observed by all men."[38] Although some Protestants publicly advocated adopting the new calendar for the sake of social unity, their voices were ignored.

Protestants in Germany—where people of one denomination were clustered in a small area next to people of another, in a kind of checkerboard pattern of denominational distribution—were among the fiercest resisters to the calendar change. Polemical anti-Catholic literature portrayed the pope as the anti-Christ and his proposed reforms as demonic. Even when the German princes decided to adopt the Gregorian calendar in 1700, they adhered to the old rules for calculating Easter until 1775.[39]

In Eastern Europe, the reaction was similarly contentious, with those who used the Orthodox calendar remaining resistant—although not everywhere. When the Catholic Church in Poland adopted the new calendar, the Polish-Lithuanian state followed suit without objection. An anonymous nobleman in the court of Sigismund August wrote in his calendar for the year 1582: "*Hoc anno calendarium reformatum* (This year, calendar reformed)," noting the reform and making the necessary changes in the calendar. He did not register any complaint about the change.[40]

Outside the cities, however, the agricultural nature of society, which was centered on the land and featured dispersed populations, meant that an old sense of time prevailed through the eighteenth century. And the Eastern Orthodox churches of Wallachia, Moldavia, Poland, and Rus linked the Gregorian reform of the calendar with the Roman Catholic desire to unify all the Christian denominations under one roof: its own. They were thus reluctant to enter into any arrangement that might end the millennium-long rupture in a manner that favored the Catholic Church. The Eastern Orthodox Church had a third set of rules for calculating the date of Easter, and it refused to bow to Roman innovations in this matter.[41]

Other groups also resisted the change. When the commonwealth that united Poland and Lithuania dissolved in the eighteenth century, Lithuania restored its old calendar.[42] Even among East European Jews, Qaraites continued to follow their own calendars, rather than the rabbinic calendar, for most internal matters. And Lithuanian Tatars adopted a hybrid system in which they noted the months according to the Muslim calendar and the year according to Christian chronology.[43]

Meanwhile, the state tried to prohibit the conducting of business on days

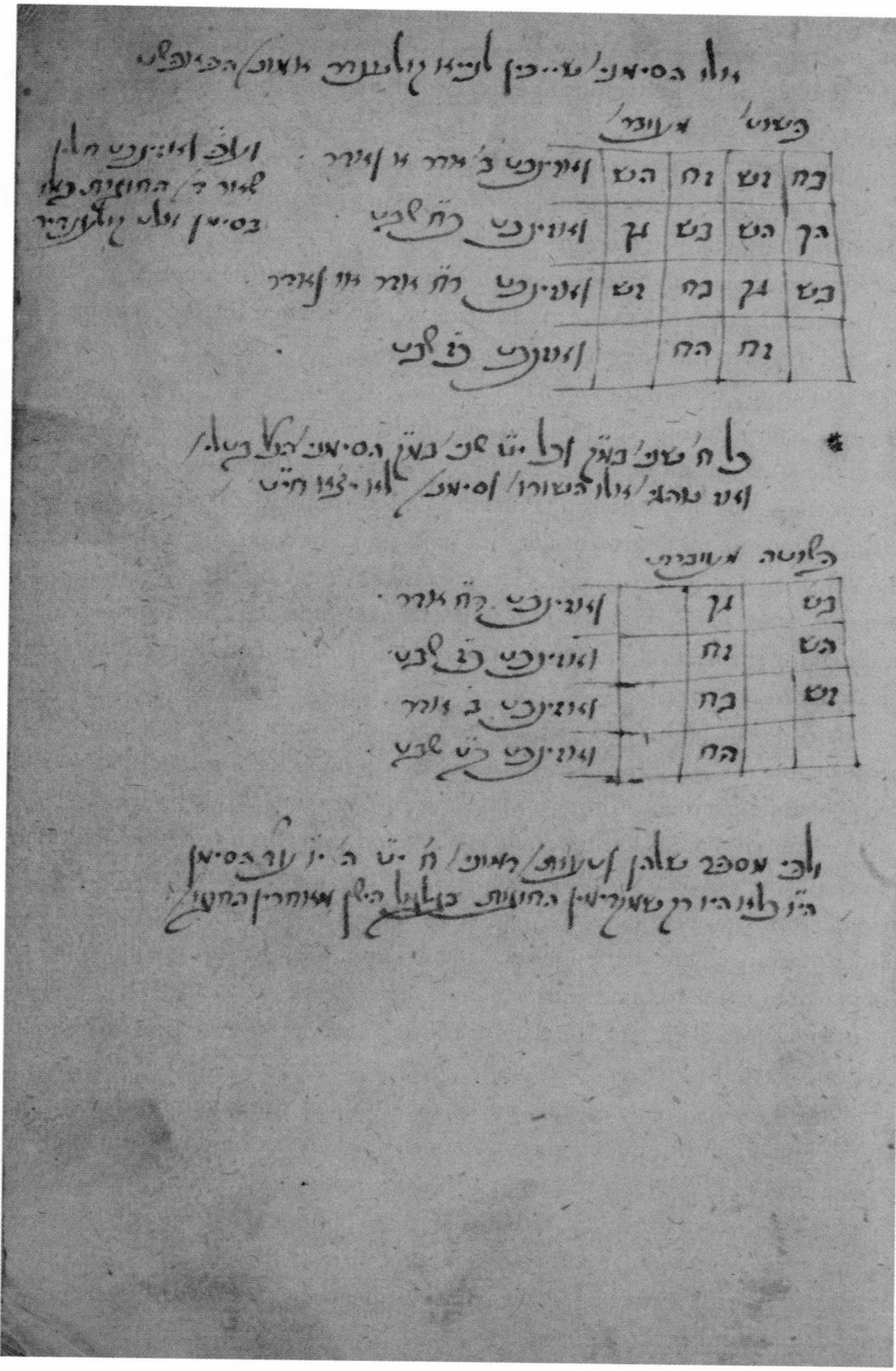

FIG 2.2. Hebrew calendar manual referring to "new calendar instituted by the Pope." *Sefer evronot*, 1583. Courtesy of the Library of the Jewish Theological Seminary ms 2547, fol. 7r.

when the "new" calendar proclaimed a holy day or feast, while the minority tried to protect its right to refuse to appear before the courts or to be compelled in any way to violate their own holidays. Jewish calendars printed in central Europe listed all three Christian European calendar dates for every Christian holiday alongside the Jewish calendar date. Despite the multiplicity of calendars, Jews could still not extricate themselves from the temporal rhythms of the Christian majority.

Almost a century after the Gregorian calendar reforms, mathematician Johann Henrich Voigt made a strong argument to Protestants that the time had come to adopt the Gregorian calendar as well. His argument was based on technical grounds: the equinox and solstice were now thirteen days off their true occurrence on the old calendar; the Christian holidays of the moveable cycle were slipping ever further from their true seasonal time. He argued on historical grounds as well, revisiting the centuries-long debate among mathematicians, astronomers, kings, and popes about how to best correct the calendar. Finally, he argued for social reasons. The strife over the calendar was ripping apart the fabric of European society. Already, he lamented, "spouses observe one another's festivals with derision, craft guilds, wandering societies, markets and fairs, everything is in disarray as one segment of society works while the other feasts."[44] Neighbors looked into each others' pots to deride those who cooked meat on fast days, and guilds learned to march with only a fraction of their members on their patron saints' days.

In fits and starts, over the course of two centuries, Europe struggled to move toward a unified calendar. From 1582 through 1700 in central Europe, and until 1752 in England; then from 1789 for the next twelve years into the nineteenth century in France, the calendar never ceased to be a central focus of political and religious conflict and debate. Farther east, the Russian revolutionaries of 1917 introduced radical changes in the Soviet calendar along with other momentous cultural shifts.[45]

The long-term effect of this debate, including the institution of a new calendar accepted only by some Europeans, is difficult to measure. Certainly it shattered the illusion of one eternal and stable method for marking the passage of time. The very idea of tampering with any aspect of such a fundamental instrument of the social order as a calendar, which people had tended to take for granted as fixed and uncontested, led them to question other long-held assumptions. Almost any serious change in the calendrical order introduced the notion that the framework that people had conflated with a natural and immutable or-

der of time was, after all, an artificial construct. By repudiating the old calendar, reformers implicitly conceded that the new calendar was a contrived and possibly temporary innovation, leaving the door open for further changes. When these destabilizing factors combined with the emerging nationalism of early modern states, the question of who determined the public character of time became sharper still.

On Calendar and Nation

The parameters of the debate over calendar reform in England demonstrate how emerging conceptions of national identity converged with those informing the calendar question. After a period of initial wavering, the English resisted the change to the Gregorian calendar. As one observer noted, England had long gone its separate way by beginning the New Year on March 25, three months later than the rest of the continent. A nation that reckoned a different year three months out of every year would have no difficulty being ten days out of step. [46] Seventeenth-century printers had become accustomed to using the legal year in dating official and scholarly literature, while using the calendar year (beginning January 1) for popular works such as almanacs.[47] "In all dates between the first of January and the 24th of March inclusive they mark the double year in this manner: 169⁶/₇."[48] When the English government finally instituted the change in 1752, the British public is reputed (erroneously, it turns out) to have cried, "Give us back our eleven lost days!"

The eighteenth-century change marked the culmination of England's long struggle to replace loyalty to church with loyalty to nation. After England had broken from the Roman Church in the sixteenth century, the number of old festivals was reduced by about four-fifths, from 125 to 27 days throughout the year, and their influence diminished.[49] During the reign of Elizabeth, too, new patriotic days of observance came to populate the calendar.[50] Accession days, royal birthdays, and victories such as that over the Spanish Armada helped forge a separate and distinctive identity for Britons. Days devoted to honoring the virgin queen paralleled those devoted to the virgin mother of God. Celebrations of national events and iconic monuments took their place beside religious observances, thereby helping to shape a new civic identity within the nation-state. England used "calendar consciousness" to bind the nation to its ruling dynasty and to secure a providential interpretation of English history.

The newly invented vocabulary of patriotism spread not only via printed

calendars and almanacs, but also through royal proclamations, sermons, and watchful wardens. The "bells and bonfires" were transformed from symbols of a vigorous church to sounds of the new civic identity in a strong nation-state.[51] As David Cressy has written, "No other nation employed the calendar as the English did to express and represent their identity."[52]

Through the seventeenth century, the calendar was at the center of the struggle for the soul of England. When the Puritans came to power in 1640, "they set out to level time itself."[53] Not only did they abolish saints' days as completely idolatrous, they intended to efface all Christian holidays that marked the highs and lows of the ritual year, including Christmas and Easter. Only Sundays and monthly fasts were to remain, for to a true Christian, every day in his life was Lent. Changes were proposed even for the names of the months and days; these never took effect. As Robert Poole remarked of the pitched battles that followed such extreme refashionings of the calendar, the contests were as much about the ownership and quality of public time as they were about the identity of the true church. During the Puritan period, which lasted some fifteen years, the Anglican calendar circulated clandestinely (much as the Catholic calendar had a subterranean life when the Anglican one had been adopted). With the Restoration came the revival of the Anglican calendar, "a new almanack after the good old fashion," as one calendar heralded it. Still the date of Easter continued to be problematic for decades. The Gregorian reform led to variations of as much as five weeks from the Anglican calendar.

The lively scientific and religious deliberations in England over whether to adopt the Gregorian calendar (or one that would correct even *its* deficiencies by dropping even more days, thus leaving England on a different calendar, as before) continued through the seventeenth century. They reached a crescendo in 1699 when Denmark, the Protestant German states, and the Netherlands adopted the Gregorian calendar, leaving England isolated from the rest of the continent. The turn of the new century would have added another day's difference, creating a full eleven-day gap between the Gregorian calendar and the old-style Julian version, which was lagging behind the true times of the equinox ever more significantly. This prospect had provided sufficient impetus for many Protestant states to swallow their distaste and adopt the now nearly universal Gregorian calendar. Yet the English resisted—even though English merchants would be more inconvenienced than ever, for every document and commercial calculation would need to take the two calendars into consideration—because they felt the adoption of the Gregorian calendar was "out of line with the devel-

oping nationalist Protestant vision of England's place in the world."[54] Thus as the rest of the Protestant world capitulated in 1700 and entered the Western European synchrony, England remained defiant, and alone. But the matter could not, and did not, rest there. External commercial and diplomatic pressure on England to bring its calendar into conformity with the rest, along with the embarrassment of repeated anomalies in the calculation of Easter, meant that England continued to be pressed to adopt the calendar of the majority.

In 1752 those pushing for change finally triumphed and the English calendar was reformed to comport with the Gregorian. The government introduced the change cautiously so as to keep interruptions to a minimum. Markets and fairs were left to their natural times so that the sale of wool would not occur before the sheep were ready to be sheared, "nor the sale of fruits before they are ready to be gathered; or for cheese, or cattle, before they are come to their perfection, fit for sale."[55] After the long delay, the reform of the calendar in England went smoothly. Newspapers carried detailed descriptions of the changes, reassuring their readers that other than changes in the nominal dates of the days, nothing had been moved. Money and property, rental and other contracts would not be affected. Printed calendars for 1752 repeated the message (in the space created by the eleven missing days). Almanac printers attended carefully to the changes and to the commercial opportunity this reform presented in sales. They continued to print the important "old dates" for almost half a century longer for those markets and fairs and commercial contracts that might refer to them.

The mythical reluctance of the lower orders to relinquish their saints' days probably played little role in the reluctance of the English to relinquish the old calendar. Not only religious festivals, but also university terms, legal calendars, quarter days, and markets and fairs were intertwined with saints' days. Indeed, the calendar reformers of 1752 cleverly managed to persuade those who remained resistant to the Gregorian calendar that their reluctance was itself a sign of popishness, of relying on old peasant superstitions.[56] The mutable and adaptable character of the European calendars is nowhere better illustrated than by this turn of argument and change of mind.

No professing Jews lived in sixteenth-century England and very few did through most of the following century. But the absence of professing Jews did not mean that the image of Jews was lacking from the calendar discourse.[57] Antipapist rhetoric often linked the image of Jews and Judaism to that of the pope and Catholicism. One seventeenth-century minister thought saints' days "smell hugely of Judaism, paganism, and papism."[58] By contrast, some philo-semitic

circles of scholars and millenarians in seventeenth-century England maintained the lunisolar Jewish calendar as the gold standard against which all reforms were to be measured. Henry Jessey published a "Scripture-kalendar" in which the Jewish-style use of scriptural terms replaced the "heathen" terms of the old calendar.[59] The notion that "the Jews" would mock the ever-erroneous Julian calendar (that the English adhered to) provided ammunition for the forces of change.[60]

A Revolutionary Calendar: "Bouleversement des habitudes"

That French (and much later, Russian) revolutionaries attempted to impose completely new patterns of time on their society indicates how thoroughly aware they were of the power of the calendar to regulate society.[61] The revolutionaries cast the existing Christian calendar as the ultimate symbol of oppression and of all that was evil about the old regime. The prolegomenon to a French revolutionary calendar, for instance, stated that the French nation had been "oppressed many centuries by the most insolent despotism."[62] It described the old calendar as witness to eighteen centuries of growing fanaticism, vice, stupidity, and persecutions, as well as to a scandalous triumph of arrogance. Erasing that calendar would be as close as they could come to effacing the past itself. Memories of all the inequities of traditional society would be lost as the old book of time was closed and the new revolutionary calendar was launched, signaling the new world order they hoped to implement.[63]

While some designers of the new French calendar hoped that it would be so universal in character that it would appeal to all forward-thinking Europeans, others saw it as an instrument to instill republican values.[64] The Committee of Public Instruction's initial mandate was to harmonize the new republican order (for example, counting years from the Fall of the Bastille) with the "old" Gregorian calendar. The committee soon exceeded this mandate, however, by structuring an utterly new calendar that not only renamed units of time such as months and days, but also decimalized them all the way to the smallest elements: hours, minutes, and seconds.[65] The autumnal equinox would provide the beginning date of the new year. This identification of the calendar with the most radical aspects of the revolution, and its roughshod flattening of habits so deeply ingrained in European culture, contributed greatly to the new calendar's ultimate failure.

In early republican France, observance of the new calendar instantly turned

into a measure of political "reliability" rather than a marker of temporality. The Jacobin government, through its Committee on Public Instruction, used every avenue to realize the new calendrical order. All government offices would run according to the new calendar, and all official documents and legal instruments would be dated according to it. The new calendar was adopted by judicial offices, record offices, and schools. Children and their parents, along with anyone registering a birth, marriage, contract, will, or death, would immediately need to know the new calendar days, months, and years. Printers saw a vast opportunity and hastened to produce calendars and conversion charts for their multifarious customer base.[66] Journalists, writers, playwrights, choreographers, and lyricists tried to incorporate the new calendar and instill awareness of it.[67] And markets and fairs, which had often been held near certain saints' days or festivals, were now to be held according to new schedules. Further, the governments of the Terror were not content with laws and propaganda alone. Police departments vigorously enforced the new order, arresting those who did not observe the new republican rest days, or those who observed the old ones in a traditional fashion. Under this new regime, taking a leisurely walk on a Sunday implied perfidy to the republic, not just reverence for past traditions.

These vigorous efforts to usher in the new timescape ultimately failed for both ideological and practical reasons. First, the overt identification of the calendar with republican virtue tainted it as a political instrument. As Matthew Shaw explains, "Reactions to the calendar . . . continued to provide an important focus for debates about the Revolution and the State of France."[68] And second, it clashed with ingrained cultural and personal habits that died hard. Many villagers could not bring themselves to observe the republican-ordained rest days, *décadies*, just as they could not help observing Sundays in the traditional manner.

Economic habits proved most difficult to uproot. Farmers' markets had followed the same traditional rhythms for centuries, staggered so that local competition was never too great, and always tied to the arrival of crops at market according to specific harvest times. The new calendar tables ignored some of these considerations, causing hardships for individual households unable to purchase basics, and throwing farmers and merchants into a panic as commodities accumulated without the prospect of immediate sale.[69] Disruption of the old system led to many disagreements between individuals and towns, caused incalculable damage to trade beyond the borders of France, and disrupted diplomatic relations.[70] After ascending to power, Napoleon gradually abandoned

the harsh position of the Jacobins. Ultimately, after a dozen years, on January 1, 1806, he abolished the republican calendar and reinstated the Gregorian.[71]

The French experiment provides remarkable evidence of how the calendar has been used for purposes far beyond its central one as an instrument for marking time. In the two centuries since the Gregorian reform, the power of the calendar as a tool to disseminate and consolidate political and religious lessons had become apparent. The calendar had become a platform on which early modern societies played out the great political, religious, and national dramas of their time.

{ 3 }

The Jewish Calendar in the Age of Print

Those who rely on the error that these printers [of calendars] have perpetrated eat leavened food on Passover and consume their hearts' delight on Yom Kippur.

Issachar ibn Susan, *Sefer ibbur shanim*, 1578–1579

THE intense level of public interest in the calendar spurred a "rethinking of temporality that seems to have preoccupied the age."[1] This growing focus on calendrical matters in early modern Europe paralleled, and in some measure directly influenced, a renewed interest among Jews in their own calendar. Signal events in early modern Jewish history, combined with the advent of print technologies and new channels for dissemination of printed material, helped propel this reexamination of the place of the calendar in Jewish culture.

Starting in the late fifteenth century, the Jewish populations of Europe shifted and reconfigured in dramatic ways as a result of expulsion, migration, and resettlement. The expulsions of Jews from the territories of the Spanish and Portuguese crowns as well as from many central European cities, and the immigration of Jews to new settlements in the Ottoman Empire, Poland, and Lithuania, brought together exiles who followed very different Jewish traditions. Pieces of a cultural mosaic that had been placed precisely and not moved for centuries were suddenly shaken up and scattered about in entirely new combinations. Exiles from all over the map gathered in new places, dissolving a long-standing pattern in which each Jewish community was congruent with its city. This imposed mobility resulted in an extraordinary level of contention, particularly when customs long cherished by members of one locale clashed with those of another. Which tradition would dominate in the new communities? The newly resettled Jewish emigrants came to grief often as they argued over Jewish rituals, quarreled over ancestral customs, and sparred over their calendars.

The revival of Jewish life in Ottoman Palestine in the early sixteenth century led to a bitter controversy over *semikha* (rabbinic apostolic ordination) in

which the calendar played a prominent role. The reinstitution of that ordination could have led to the establishment of a Sanhedrin, a high religious court, one of whose prerogatives would have been to set the calendar based on sightings of the moon. Opponents of the revival of a Jewish high court argued that such a change would render obsolete the fixed calendar that had served Jews so well through the medieval period. If each month could only be proclaimed once the moon had made its appearance, Jews would not know the exact dates of their holidays in advance; the entire Jewish world would have to contend with the ensuing chaos and confusion.[2] The plan did not succeed.

During this period, critics of the rabbinic Jewish calendar arose from various quarters. Christian Hebraist scholars questioned rabbinic calendar innovations that had no apparent biblical basis, an attack echoed by former Iberian conversos such as Uriel d'Acosta (d. 1640).[3] In Italy, the author of *Kol Sakhal* (*Voice of a Fool*), presumably Venetian rabbi Leone Modena, produced the most original and thoroughgoing critique of the Jewish calendar since the medieval Qaraite schism of the eighth century. He subjected many aspects of rabbinic tradition to withering scrutiny, and he did not spare the calendar. He attacked rabbinic additions to the calendar such as observing the second day of holidays only in the diaspora.[4] He also singled out for derision the *dehiyyot*, deferments of the New Moon, which, he argued, caused Jews to observe the biblically mandated holidays on the wrong date.[5] Addressing Modena's critique would have required returning the calendar to its scriptural foundations—an unworkable solution since so many of the elements of the Jewish calendar derived from rabbinic readings of and elaborations on biblical texts.

Such attacks on the Jewish calendar stimulated defenses of the traditional methods of calculation. David Nieto (1654–1728), noted Sephardic rabbi, physician, and Jewish apologist, devoted a significant portion of his defense of Judaism to an argument in support of its traditional rabbinic calendar.[6] While the early modern Jewish calendar never underwent a reform on the model of the Christian calendar, it had become a locus of cultural anxieties for early modern Jews.

Both calendar and ibbur emerged from the early modern crucible different entities from what they had been. In the sixteenth century, conflicts over the nature of the Jewish calendar, after some four centuries of stasis, coincided with other related developments. The process of shaping the ibbur gathered momentum during the fifteenth century as compilers added narrative material to the computations and standardized the text. By the sixteenth century, writers,

scribes, and copyists of Hebrew ibburim had largely standardized their characteristics and contents. The ibbur in Western Europe evolved from a concise component of the ritual and liturgical compilations, such as mahzorim, into a separate book, a self-standing cultural and religious artifact called *sefer evronot*. This text continued to be cultivated in manuscript while simultaneously emerging in print.

The trajectories of these print and manuscript versions of sifre evronot, much like those of print and manuscript calendars, diverged in many cases and intersected in others. The calendar and its literature present a perfect case study for the interplay between manuscript and print as vehicles of knowledge and information. For even as the printed calendar materials were subject to question and doubt during this era, the ibbur was blossoming as a mature literary genre that invited renewed religious and aesthetic cultivation.

Printing the Ibbur

The now discarded notion that print culture displaced manuscript culture has given way to the idea that the two coexisted far longer than had previously been believed.[7] In fact, scholars now argue against the "ingrained contrast between script and print" because the two media interacted very productively for centuries.[8] Unlike today, readers during the sixteenth and seventeenth centuries did not categorize texts primarily on the basis of whether they were handwritten or printed.[9] Consequently, the trajectories of print and manuscript evronot cannot be easily separated from one another. Even if at times their development seems independent, they influenced one another throughout the early modern age.

The distinction of printing the first ibbur treatise belongs to the great cosmographer, cartographer, philologist, and Hebraist Sebastian Münster (1488/1489–1552). Münster's book belonged with a group of auxiliary works, such as grammars, dictionaries, and introductions to various genres, that were printed to help the first generations of Christian Hebraists study Hebrew and Judaism without the direct tutelage of Jews.[10] Famous for printing beautiful maps and lavish scholarly tomes, Münster had studied Hebrew and then taught it, first at the University of Heidelberg, and later at the University of Basel. At the time of Münster's arrival, Hebrew publishing at Basel had been established for over a decade, and the city was reaping the first fruits of the confluence of its printers' exacting techniques and its reputation as a scholarly entrepôt. Münster was instrumental in bringing many basic works of Hebrew language, etymol-

ogy, and grammar to the press of Johann Froben of Basel (one of the printers who published the works of Erasmus).[11]

In 1527, Münster published a small book, *Kalendarium Hebraicum*, at Froben's press. On the title page of *Kalendarium Hebraicum*, Münster announced that he had translated the material himself into Latin. He intended the book to be a small compendium of useful information about the Jewish calendar and Jewish chronology, with primary sources in Hebrew, and Latin translations on facing pages that would be useful for Christian humanist students and for theologians. It contained a brief introduction to Jewish calendation, along with a pitch for its value to Christians: Jesus, after all, had celebrated Passover as the Jews still did. He explained the system of Jewish chronology and how to decipher the numerical value of the Hebrew letters to extract the anno mundi. He also decoded for his readers the Jewish tendency to take those letters and rearrange them to form meaningful and positive words.[12] Münster included several works of Jewish chronology such as an abbreviated *Seder olam*, and parts of Abraham ibn Daud's *Sefer ha-qabbalah*.

A section of Münster's book titled "Treatise on finding moladot and tequfot" contained computus texts found in many medieval Ashkenazic compendia attributed to Nahshon Gaon under rubrics such as *seder sod ha-ibbur* (treatise on the secret of intercalation). The word ibbur (or its plural form) does not appear in Münster's title. Münster does not say where he acquired the texts, although given his close connections with Elijah Levita and other contemporary Hebrew scholars, obtaining them would have been simple.[13] Many Christian savants corresponded with early modern Jewish scholars; among the topics on which they sought clarification was the Jewish calendar.[14]

Pioneering as it may have been, Münster did not print his Jewish computus for Jews but for Christians, and there is no evidence that many Jews sought it out. Buried in a volume that contained other material, and intended for Latin-literate Christian Hebraist students or scholars, it did not call attention to itself. No other ibbur appears to have been printed for another generation.

It took a publishing entrepreneur to realize the value of the ibbur as a self-standing genre in its early modern context. Jacob Marcaria, a physician turned printing impresario, was responsible for bringing to press an impressive number of works, many for the first time. Marcaria was the first to present the text of the ibbur as a stand-alone book and he appears to be the first to have used the plural form of ibbur in the title: *Sefer evronot*.[15] The text itself, as Marcaria advertised, is a highly abbreviated form, and, like ibbur treatises of this period,

still idiosyncratic in its order and contents.[16] Marcaria's book, printed in the small town of Riva di Trento, Italy, does not have a typeface nearly as clear and elegant as the one that Münster had used in Basel.[17] In addition, Münster's text is considerably fuller than Marcaria's. Both contain similar elements, however, including sections that preserve the sense of a teacher leading a student step by step: for instance, they use phrases like "Now take the thousands that you have," or "Now I will return to the first item I mentioned."

Within five years after Marcaria published the first sefer evronot for a Jewish market in Riva di Trento, two new ibburim were published in Salonika, in the Ottoman Empire. Issachar ibn Susan (ca. 1510–ca. 1580) published his own composition, *Tiqqun Yissachar*, in 1564.[18] And the printing house of Yosef Ya'avetz brought to press in 1568 *She'erit Yosef*, compiled by Daniel ben Perahia Kohen.[19] The appearance of three new works within the span of five years, in a genre that no Jew had printed before, marks a significant "moment" in the printing history of sifre ibbur: the transition of the ibbur from esoteric to public and from manuscript to print. That this moment coincided with a very similar development in another realm of Jewish esoteric literature, qabbalah, places the printing of the ibbur within the framework of a larger cultural trend.[20] Just when it became impossible for Italian presses to print the Talmud, works of a more circumscribed nature were being printed and disseminated.

Both entrepreneurs wrote at some length about their motives and circumstances. In his introduction to the second edition of his ibbur, ibn Susan was unusually expansive about his travails. His comments explained the renewed interest in the calendar by Jews: exile, migrations, and settlement in the Holy Land. Ibn Susan was a native of Fez, in today's Morocco, although his family name seems to indicate earlier ties to Susa in the area that is today Tunisia. Thus his family was of North African, or *maghrebi*, origins.[21] Upon immigrating to Safed as a young man, ibn Susan retained his maghrebi identity and headed the North African *qehillah* (congregation) in Safed. There he encountered a bewildering array of customs. He was particularly concerned to differentiate those of the Spanish exiles from those of the maghrebis of North Africa, as well as those of the Musta'arabs, the Arab Jews who had lived in the Holy Land prior to the latest waves of immigration. He was especially interested in Musta'arab customs because he believed that they preserved authentic practices from the geonim of Babylonia as well as those of the early inhabitants of Eretz Israel. For example, he noted that the Musta'arab cantor announced on the eve of the fast of the Ninth of Av: "Today marks ____ years from the destruction of

the Holy Temple," a chrono-custom not preserved in either of the other two communities, the Sephardic or the maghrebi.[22]

In addition to visiting the Jewish communities he found in Safed, ibn Susan traveled to a number of cities throughout the region. As a young man, he had studied in Jerusalem with Levi ibn Habib, whose imprint can be seen on ibn Susan's work. Ibn Habib had been one of the central figures in the celebrated controversy over the revival of rabbinic ordination. He accused his chief opponent, Jacob Berav, of downplaying the havoc that would ensue among the dispersed Jewish populations if the fixed calendar were abandoned.[23] Ibn Habib devoted great effort to the study of the ibbur and wrote a notable commentary to Maimonides' "Laws of the Sanctification of the New Moon." His interests appear to have encouraged his disciple, ibn Susan, to devote himself to the same subject. Significantly, while ibn Susan was completing the first draft of his ibbur in 1539 he was almost certainly unaware of Münster's edition, and it was years before Marcaria's sefer evronot would come to market. That is, ibn Susan wrote his ibbur uninfluenced by these other, nearly contemporary works.

Ibn Susan subsequently traveled through the eastern Mediterranean, first as a refugee from Safed for reasons unknown, and later in attempts to support his family. He attributed his interest in the mathematical problems of the ibbur to his nomadic lifestyle: "As a result of my wandering, it was difficult to concentrate on texts, so I occupied myself by reviewing the mathematical formulae related to the ibbur to take my mind off my travails." Ibn Susan then justified his interest further. The subject was significant, nay vital, in its own right. "This *mitzvah* [good deed, in this case referring to the precept to calculate the calendar] includes within it many others, so that Israel will know how to observe the holidays, and the times, and the beginnings of months, and the order of the lections for the Sabbaths."[24]

Ibn Susan's introduction provides an unusually frank look at the state of confusion over Jewish calendation in the sixteenth century. His original impetus for preparing an edition of the calendar rules, he wrote, came from the confusing or erroneous calendars he encountered on synagogue walls.[25] He attributed the widespread distortions in chronology and calculations to the careless work of people who edited and printed calendars.

Contradictory traditions concerning the sabbatical year also contributed to the public's confusion. Ibn Susan wrote that he was moved to compose *Tiqqun Issachar* when in 1539 (5299 A.M.) a chronological controversy erupted over

whether that year was a *shemittah* (sabbatical) year—a biblically mandated seventh year when no planting or harvesting occurred and other unique observances were kept. Ibn Susan studied the work of Maimonides and of Eshtori ha-parhi (ca. 1280–ca. 1355) and resolved that that very year, 1539, was in fact a sabbatical year.[26]

Ibn Susan wrote that he had entrusted his ibbur manuscript to an editor-proofreader responsible for preparing it for the printer and shepherding it through publication. This does not appear to have expedited the process. The book did not appear in print until 1564, almost a quarter century later. When at long last he saw his book in print, ibn Susan was deeply chagrined. Solomon ben Benjamin Rey, the man to whom he had entrusted the job, had positioned his own name prominently on the title page and buried the author's name in small print on the bottom of that page. (Rey's precise role is difficult to ascertain.)[27] But this was only the beginning of Rey's misdeeds. Far from eradicating errors, ibn Susan charged that Rey had taken many liberties with his original manuscript; in particular, "The manuscript had been recopied two or three times without my knowledge from my original." The printed book appeared to have been based on an inferior manuscript copy, and in the course of the unauthorized copying, ibn Susan complained, many errors had crept into the first printing:

> He omitted diverse items from various parts of the book, he ignored some of my insertions and deletions, and throughout the entire book . . , he omitted the prepared tables, as well as the circles for the tequfot. He included only the hundred-year charts, and del Rey wrote his own name on them, although he did not compose them. He printed that edition in a money saving mode, and while I cannot blame him for what he omitted . . . I blame him for what he added of his own or of others, conjunctions, months, . . . and the turn of the seasons. These are the years for which he erred. . . . Therefore, I have seen fit to add here [in the second edition] an appendix on the tequfot with true precision.[28]

Ibn Susan brought the second edition to print by correcting and editing the work himself in order to fulfill his original mission. After seeing the many errors that had been introduced into his precise charts with their careful calculations, he could understand how errors had become so rampant in the ibburim and in the calendars posted in public spaces. Ibn Susan blamed the printers

for extreme and multiple errors of carelessness. As a result of the printers' sloppiness, he railed, "All those who rely on the error that these printers have perpetrated are eating leavened food on Passover and consume their hearts' delight on Yom Kippur [a solemn fast day]."[29] Ibn Susan set about checking the calendar manuals in print, and found, for example, two discrepant versions of the chart of R. Nahshon Gaon in circulation. "Later I set myself to checking the other qeviot that were printed by a press, and it is easy for errors to enter their work."[30]

Ibn Susan wanted to see for himself why so many errors plagued the printed texts. His testimony provides a glimpse into a typical printshop of the day. After a page of print was no longer needed, each of the Hebrew letters was hurriedly sorted into its own box.

> The printers themselves testify regarding their own work that letters can easily be exchanged with others as they quickly separate them, each letter in its own box, and they do this with all the letters. Later, they take the letters from the boxes to set up the next page, and this is how error enters printed books, in the [inadvertent] switching of letters— sometimes, very many [errors]. The printers have printed thousands and hundreds of this work, and it has spread widely to many places of Israel, in the villages and towns, and it was dispersed among travelers.[31]

Thus even the most careful calculations could easily become distorted by the substitution of one wrong letter during the printing process. Far from bringing stability and uniformity to the calendar, printing increased the level of inaccuracy and error. Consequently, paying for a scribal copy may have been the better alternative long into the age when print versions had become available.

In the introduction to *She'erit Yoseph*, another ibbur printed at the same time as ibn Susan's, Daniel Kohen claimed to be writing at the request of "people who demand and beseech me for an easy and quick way to master the science of the ibbur."[32] Like ibn Susan, Kohen decried the large number of errors that had been introduced into other ibburim. His work would "correct the many distortions of the printing press in matters both obvious and obscure, so numerous that they could have been written by a child. . . . As for the printed perpetual tables, every one of them is riddled with errors of scribes and printers, in many places." The title page promised a clear account of the Muslim and Christian months, and of how the two calendars align with one another. The book is

also filled with rhymed couplets, mnemonic aids for every segment of the ibbur. Kohen wrote the ibbur as a consolation for the tribulations of Israel, and he cited the rabbinic sources that interpreted the ibbur as a sign of God's love for His people. "As God loved His people above all others, he wanted to benefit them so He transmitted to them the keys to the sun and the moon." Unlike the texts of Ashkenazic ibburim, *She'erit Yosef* cited liberally from the sifre ibbur of Abraham bar Hiyya and Abraham ibn Ezra, and from the calendric tables of Abraham Zacuto.[33]

History and contemporary bibliography have performed a sleight of memory trick, condemning the first author-printers of the ibbur in the early modern period to oblivion and crediting a latecomer with all the accomplishments of his predecessors. Elements of the ibbur had been circulating in manuscript hundreds of years before the invention of printing. Attributing the text to one author would be similar to attributing a Jewish prayerbook or the *haggadah* (traditional Jewish book read on Passover) to one author. Each comprised many layers of material that have been reshaped and presented in various configurations over time. While setting the ibbur to print may have greatly promoted uniformity in the text, no single individual can be credited with its creation. Yet since the seventeenth century, the name Eliezer ben Jacob Belin Ashkenazi has appeared on title pages as the "author" of sifre evronot. Although his name does not even appear on the title page of the edition he brought to press, the elusive Belin came to be credited with the Jewish computus to the virtual exclusion of all the enterprising individuals who preceded him. Some contemporary bibliographers and catalogers have followed suit, attributing all sifre evronot to this "author."[34]

Unlike the loquacious Marcaria and the meandering ibn Susan, virtually nothing is known about Belin's life or how he came to be a pivotal figure in printing the ibbur. The text of the ibbur that Belin brought to press in Lublin, in 1615, is very similar to the text of manuscript evronot in circulation in German lands. It is tempting to speculate that Belin may have been related to the Worms family of that name, for his edition appeared shortly after the Jews of Worms were (temporarily) expelled.[35] But thus far there is insufficient evidence to make any assertions.

Belin's introduction emphasized the religious importance of each person mastering the calculations of the ibbur rather than relying on ready-made tables.

FIG. 3.1. Title page of first Sefer evronot edited by Eliezer Belin. Lublin, 1615. Courtesy Gross Family Collection, Tel Aviv.

We have seen only a few men, two from a city, . . . forming a small elite of masters of calculation who know how to reckon the seasons and the constellations. [Most people] rely on the calendars that they find ready each year . . . They cannot fulfill the mitzvah. Thus, in order to benefit the public . . . we have searched in new books and old in order to find the calculations, we labored and we succeeded . . . we have extracted the best portions, we have organized it in a correct and true manner, and we have added commentary where necessary. . . . It is filigreed with more than gold, like a set table open to all, in order to fulfill the obligation of the mitzvah . . . [that the calendar be calculated] by reckoning and not by seeing it within a prepared calendar, and that each person prepare his own . . . with all the festivals."[36]

A quarter century elapsed before David bar Jacob of Lomza reprinted the book that Belin brought to press. In an approbation granted in 1640, the rabbis at a Council of the Four Lands gave Lomza exclusive rights to peddle a new, corrected, edition that he had brought to print.

As a result of the errors, the times of the gentile holidays and the markets were confused and he toiled in order to remove that obstacle, a matter that no person had paid attention to. This body of knowledge [the computus] which is our "wisdom and our sapience" among the nations, . . . is virtually forgotten. Therefore, we have agreed that he has permission to print the "value" that he has added so that he should not have toiled in vain and expended a great deal to print the book.
The words above are those of the leaders of our Four Lands, who are staying here in Lublin, Tuesday, 4 Nissan, at the Gromnitz fair [1640].[37]

In 1690, the Belin edition was brought to press again. The text is similar but not identical to the original, and the introduction is still signed by "the small and the young Eliezer . . . son of Jacob Belin Ashkenazi."[38]

The printing histories of the earliest modern sifre evronot provide vivid and compelling testimony of the difficult passage of ibbur literature into print. The repeated acknowledgment in the texts that errors in the ibbur charts were likely to lead to divergences in days of holidays and fasts explains the reluctance in some circles to rely on printed calendars and printed sifre ibbur. Moreover, it becomes apparent from studying these early ibbur treatises that they would

have been less profitable for publishers than calendars were. The number of buyers was relatively small, and the initial investment in setting up the book, particularly one with charts and line drawings, would have been considerable. Not surprisingly then, printed editions of the ibbur were relatively rare through the sixteenth and seventeenth centuries, despite the central role of the Jewish calendar for maintaining Jewish religious life.[39] Moreover, through the end of the sixteenth century, no ibbur was printed by Jews in Ashkenazic lands, western or eastern. The Italian and Ottoman printed ibburim seem to have curtailed the development of similar works in German lands, where instead sifre evronot were revived in manuscript form.

The relationship between the arcane computus and the accessible calendar can be seen in the recollections of ibn Susan. Once people realized that he had developed an expertise in the ibbur, his knowledge was in great demand.

> In some of the places I passed through [in my travels] people beseeched me to provide for them a *tiqqun* (fixed calendar chart) that would last for many years. For they said that they did not know how to search the sifre ibbur that are found among us to find a particular year unless they are told the *qeviut* (set formulaic number) according to the chronology of creation or according to some other chronology such as the *minyan shtarot* (Era of Contracts), for they have no luhot (tables) that arrange this for them. They have asked me to prepare a book on this subject and to inscribe tables in it. . . . Therefore, my book contains tables from 5299 [A.M., or 1539 C.E.] through the year 6000 A.M., the end of the world, a total of 702 years. I have provided tables and rules for the tequfot as well, to track them until the end of time.[40]

Many computus treatises contained tables designed to facilitate computation of the various formulae. These tables arranged complex information in a visually accessible manner; they were not calendars. With their aid a practical and useful daily calendar could be constructed, and computists eventually began to insert full calendars into the works they wrote or copied. Authors or copyists of sifre evronot often included calendars for one or more years at the end of their text. Before the advent of printing, sifre evronot, calculation manuals, were the essential genre; luhot (prepared calendars) were the incidental form. Printing, however, which promoted ready-made, precalculated calendars containing all the information most people needed to know, reversed this.

Printing Jewish Calendars

The rise of print technology along with new paper manufacturing techniques stimulated the production and consumption of calendars on an unprecedented scale. Schisms over the reform of the European calendar also helped to keep the printers of calendars busy, since each change required a new printing. Booksellers and printers made vigorous efforts to promote and distribute the calendars.

Given the central importance of their religious, astronomical, astrological, and medical uses, it is no surprise that calendars and their related tables were essential to the genesis of Jewish printing as well. Mordechai Finzi's *Luhot* was the first Hebrew book to be published in its author's lifetime, in 1475.[41] And in 1496, the press of Abraham de Ortas published Abraham Zacuto's perpetual almanac in Portugal. (Columbus used a Latin translation of this work to intimidate the Native Americans by correctly predicting an eclipse.)[42]

The first calendars to be printed were rife with errors. One of the earliest surviving printed Hebrew calendars, a broadsheet printed for the year 1496–1497 in Barco, Italy, by the famed Jewish printer Soncino, features a glaring error: the year printed in large letters at the top is 1493, three years off. (The correct Hebrew רנ"ו differs by only one similar-looking letter from the incorrect רנ"ג that was used.)[43] Computists and printers who collaborated on the task of presenting calendrical tables in visually accessible printed form wondered aloud whether print really represented an advance over manuscript, or if it merely multiplied and compounded the rate of error and divergence in a field in which exactitude and uniformity were the greatest of virtues.[44] Three centuries after the invention of print, when Raphael Hanover prepared his *Luhot ha-ibbur* (Leiden, 1755–1756), he insisted on signing every copy of the book after he had personally inspected it: in this way, he indicated that each copy of the printed tables had met his high standards.[45] The question of whether and how to print calendars was debated in the literature of ibbur and luah for more than three centuries.

Despite these problems, calendars quickly became staple items on printers' lists. Their ephemeral nature created an annual demand, and they had to meet only the lowest of customers' expectations regarding aesthetics and other production qualities. Moreover, in larger markets, calendars could be easily customized to reflect local needs and sensibilities, such as market and saints' days.

Hebrew printers in the Ottoman Empire and in Italian cities began print-

ing calendars from the sixteenth century, and calendars from some places have survived for each year over the course of centuries. The mere existence of a Hebrew printing press did not necessarily mean that calendars were produced there. Calendar printing required the initiative of an individual printer, one who had access to the requisite knowledge or a good working calendar model from earlier years and locations, as well as the appropriate plates and fonts.

In printed calendars, as with other early printed works, the roles of the various players are not always easy to distinguish. Publishers or other intermediaries were often far more important than authors to the process of bringing a work to press. They served as impresarios who hired authors (or calendators), secured the supplies and the printing house, hired proofreaders, and took care of the distribution. Proofreading and checking were particularly important when Jews printed in Christian printing shops, because the Christian workers often made many mistakes. Some printers went to great lengths to have their calendars proofread and approved, because one serious mistake, just one wrong letter, could ruin an entire year's investment.

To focus on one example, several terms were used to describe the roles of those who worked on Venetian Hebrew wall calendars over the course of one decade. The owner of the printing house was Juan (Giovanni) da Gara, a Christian printer who served the Hebrew printing market in Venice. Israel Zafroni, the Hebrew printer who took overall responsibility for the calendar, used the term *magihah* (editor, proofreader) to describe his own role. Zafroni hired a venerable calendator to make sure it was correct; subsequently he hired others to "research and prepare" the calendar, and to make sure that the print was set up correctly (*higiha be-defus*). Later, the Venice calendar was modeled after that of Mantua, with some slight additions (*ve-hosif al hagahat Mantova*). The term *mehaber* (composer or author) was used then, possibly to describe Zafroni. The Hebrew words *nidpas* (printed) and *na'ase* (created) sometimes distinguished between different roles as well.[46] The title that Zafroni accorded to himself, *magihah* (proofreader), is a modest characterization of his actual role. His entrepreneurial spirit meant that he played a far more essential part than a typical proofreader would today; later he would have been called the "one who brings [the manuscript] to the printshop" (*mevi le-bet ha-defus*).

Zafroni was an experienced printer who worked for decades at various centers of Hebrew printing, most notably at the Froben press in Basel, before returning to Venice.[47] A close examination of the calendars he ushered into print in Venice during a concentrated period demonstrates the small variations that

were possible even within a limited format such as the broadsheet wall calendar. They also illustrate Zafroni's desire to balance tradition with innovation, to connect with his customers, and to keep them aware of his role in the product they purchased.

On the (apparently) first Venice wall calendar printed by Zafroni, for 1598–1599, he wrote a lengthy statement of purpose to introduce himself to his customers. "My soul thirsts to print one calendar and to innovate at least one feature in it. When I searched my satchel I found what you see before you, and this is sufficient for now. In the coming years, with the help of the Creator, I will introduce many additional new and important features. I will vary the features each year, and write things on the new calendars that were not seen on the old. 'And you shall not throw out the old in the face of the new,' for the 'tablets and the shards of the tablets both rested in the Ark' as a reminder for the generations."[48] While Zafroni implied that his first calendar was modeled on one already in circulation, he expressed a desire to innovate (while respecting the basic outlines of the traditional form). Among the features on his calendar were four different reckonings of the tequfah, and the times that eclipses were to be expected.

In the calendar for the following year, 1599–1600, Zafroni delivered on his promise for new and improved features. His colophon boasted: "Who can measure with his palm the waters of this great sea, this calendar? The venerable and aged master, R. Isaac Sullam, expert in the laws of *ibbur shanim* (calendation), knowledgeable in the secrets of astronomy, the conjunctions, the seasons, the eclipses of the celestial bodies, and the festivals of God. I, the young, have added innovations as I promised, and so I shall do as I said year after year, and I have written on these calendars things that were not written on the previous one, while I have not discarded the old."[49] In the next year, Zafroni's statement reappeared in abbreviated form, and his innovation for 1600–1601 appears to be more extensive weather predictions for the year.[50] In 1601–1602, Zafroni's name does not appear. Minuscule print announces that the calendar was "prepared and researched by the sage R. Yedidiah of Rimini, and the proofreading was done by R. Isaac Sullam, in the printing house of Juan da Gara in Venice."[51] Perhaps Zafroni had left Venice for a time.

Four years later, the Venice wall calendar printed in the house of da Gara still does not contain Zafroni's name, but it bears his imprint. "This calendar was prepared and researched by the learned R. Abraham of Rimini, as well as R. Yedidiah, of blessed memory, and printed in the house of Juan da Gara in

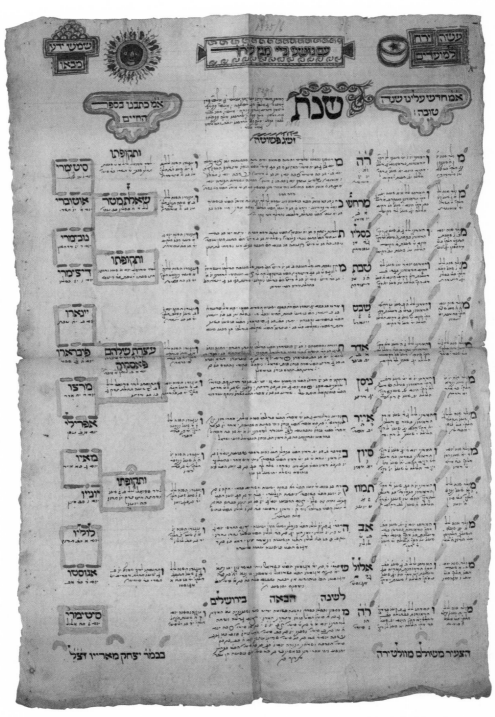

FIG. 3.2. Manuscript wall calendar, 1535–1536. Bayerische Staatsbibliothek München ms Cod. Hebr. 154.

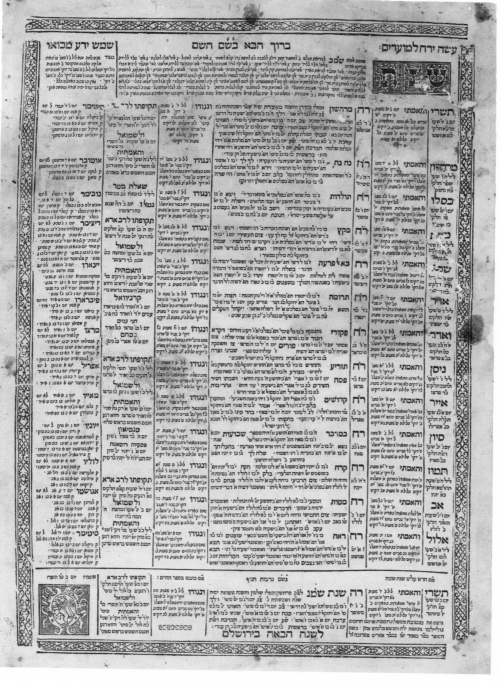

FIG. 3.3. Printed wall calendar chart, Mantua, 1581–1582. Courtesy Gross Family Collection, Tel Aviv.

FIG 3.4. Printed wall calendar, Wandsbeck, 1729–1730. For each month, Jewish dates appear on the right; Christian dates and fairs are shown on the left. Courtesy Gross Family Collection, Tel Aviv.

Venice. He saw it in the city of Mantua and praised it; it was proofread by one of the disciples of the great man R. Isaac Sullam, of blessed memory: the young scholar Matzliah b. Samuel of Arles, may his merit protect us. The composer saw it and added some things to the readings of Mantua."[52] It is unclear whether Zafroni referred to himself as the author or composer (*mehaber*) of the calen-

dar. It contains additional "innovations" from the previous years' versions: the constellations for each month, and a full column displaying the *omer* calendar, not often seen on wall calendars. Like its predecessors, it made a promise for more new features in the coming year: "In the calendar for 1606, which is to come, I will instruct you regarding the nature of the stars and the planets; you will see it and your hearts will rejoice."[53] By the calendar of 1609–1610, Zafroni's name was once again printed on it, along with the continually promised innovations. "This calendar was prepared and researched by a wise man, the sage R. Moses Trazzino, resident of the holy community of Ferrara. I, the young Israel Zafroni, prepared it for print as God pleased to show me. Printed by Juan da Gara in his house, here in Venice." In the upper left corner of the broadsheet, Zafroni's signature innovation was "an 'order of thunder' for each month. If they appear to be rules without sense, this is what we have found in the books of the ancients, and they were greater experts in every science than we are, and no harm can come from heeding them."[54] In the following year's calendar, the "innovation," which appears without the explicit signature of Zafroni, is a discussion of how to calculate the changing seasons based on the true tequfot.

A momentous event for Hebrew printing in Venice compelled Zafroni to insert a personal note once again in 1610. The message reads, "Zafroni says: The Lord who has guided me from the first until this day, has graced me after the death of the craftsman da Gara and the shuttering of the doors of his printing plant. Those who stumbled gathered strength and set up a new printing establishment, and this is its fruit. It is copied from the model of the sage R. Moses of Trazzino, may his merit protect us, and printed in the house of the partners Zanito Zanitti and Baldassare Bonnevilli in Venice."[55] Zafroni had been able to steer his calendar series for over a decade. Due to his efforts it survived even this most difficult period of de Gara's death and the closing of his print shop.

Another example of the power of a single determined entrepreneur to influence the printing of Hebrew calendars (and by extension, of other Jewish works) can be seen in Fürth. Hebrew printing began there in 1691, yet the first Jewish calendars from that press date to the arrival of a specific printer, Hayim, son of Zevi Hirsch, a printer in Wilhermsdorf. Upon his arrival in Fürth, one of the first items that Hayim printed was a pocket calendar for 1737–1738 [5498 A.M.]. After his father arrived some two years later, the calendars began bearing Zevi Hirsch's printer's mark.[56] The Fürth calendars are modeled on those of Wilhermsdorf, providing a clear example of how the expertise of a single printer would travel with him, influencing the printing trade wherever he went.

Fortunately, there are only a few years in the early modern period for which no Jewish printed calendars survive. Due to the diligence of some early collectors, many calendars printed from the sixteenth through the early nineteenth centuries in Altona, Amsterdam, Berlin, Frankfurt an der Oder, Fürth, Hamburg, Jessnitz, Mantua, Venice, and Sulzbach are available for study.[57]

Far more difficult than tracing the appearance of Jewish calendars in print, however, is understanding their dissemination, circulation, and usage. Did early modern users regard them much as we do personal calendars today? Recent discoveries of what have been called German *genizot,* treasure troves of the discarded remnants of sacred texts and artifacts stored in synagogues, have turned up large numbers of (mostly eighteenth-century) printed calendars and have stimulated new studies of them.[58] It seems from initial research that the printing of Jewish calendars continued to expand in early modern times, both in terms of numbers of editions, places of publication, and the scope of cultural information they included. By the end of the eighteenth century, they had been transformed from a tiny and bare utilitarian code into a cultural omnibus. The calendars' pages are a marvel of concision, conveying much useful information in a deceptively modest visual arrangement.

When Jewish readers picked up an early modern printed calendar, what information would they have gained? Certain characteristics marked it immediately as different from non-Jewish calendars. Early modern Jewish calendars were constituted according to the Jewish year, starting with the month of Tishre and its first day, the Jewish New Year, *Rosh ha-shanah.* They were entirely in Hebrew. Printers produced early modern calendars in two basic formats: pocket calendars, which were usually printed in small codex form, and wall calendars, large broadsheets on which the entire year could be viewed.[59] Fewer wall calendars were printed and distributed, because they were designed mainly to be hung in synagogues. From their continued printing in Italy, however, it seems that there was a sufficient demand for them to make them worth printing. Some were printed on both sides to serve for two years, resulting in a great deal of wear and tear. The earliest surviving printed wall calendar in German lands, one from Hanau for the year 1625–1626, survived only because it was used inside the binding of a book. The next surviving printed wall calendar from German lands dates from a century later, and differs little in basic structure.[60] This similarity suggests that they were in circulation throughout the period and that the form of these calendars was consistent over time.[61]

From the earliest surviving printed exemplars, we can see that there were

FIG 3.5. Man holding a pocket calendar, *Luah*, Fürth, 1789. Courtesy Gross Family Collection, Tel Aviv.

certain conventions in arranging the material. The core section of printed Jewish calendars generally consisted of five columns. On wall calendars, each month's information was lined up in five vertical rows, with the tequfot and the conjunctions noted beneath each month's section. Pocket calendars, by contrast, could devote a leaf or two to each month. The first column contained the name of the new Jewish month and notations relevant to Jewish observances that month, including the name of each week's Torah portion, and any Jewish holidays or fast days. Some calendars included reminders in this column for special holiday rituals such as *eruv tavshilin* or the date marking the new tequfah. The second column noted the day of the week, signified by a Hebrew letter (*aleph* through *zayin*), while the third column marked the day of the Jewish month, through 29 or 30, designated by Hebrew letters. The fourth and fifth columns were reserved for material of non-Jewish import. The fourth column marked the Christian day of the month, through 30 or 31, and the fifth column noted the Christian day or month name, Christian holidays, saints' days, along with

the locations of important markets, and sometimes the seasons or weather prognoses.[62]

Most early modern Jewish wall calendars were decorated simply. Paper quality varied. As a wall calendar for 1798–1800 advertised, "These stamped luhot cost 5 kreu[zer] each and on good paper, six kreu[zer]." (The stamp probably refers to a calendar tax.) Pocket calendars had fewer space restrictions. As users came increasingly to value them, printers loaded them with more features and expanded the type of information they contained. Alongside their timeless values and ancient holidays, the cramped pages of Jewish calendars served increasingly to orient their users to quotidian temporal rhythms.

Additions to the Calendars

As mentioned earlier in the case of Zafroni, Jewish calendars accrued a variety of additional features for their users. This extraneous material often overwhelmed the core in quantity if not in importance, changing the character of the compilation from that of a calendar into that of an almanac. These additions speak to people's use of calendars to organize the rhythms of daily life in ways that integrated seamlessly their ritual, economic, and social activities. Calendars came to include natural events, such as times of sunrise and sunset and weather reports; scientific and medical knowledge, as in the *oder loss tafel* (table with the best days for bloodletting); folk remedies for treating various ailments; the mundane aspects of commercial activity, such as schedules of mail delivery and pickup, coach or ship departure and arrival; and the best days for travel or moving ("Whoever wishes to move from one house to another, or to travel across the land, the following days are propitious for that").[63]

In virtually every location, the Jewish calendars shared these elements with their non-Jewish counterparts.[64] In fact, in many cases Jewish printers included information borrowed directly from non-Jewish vernacular calendars. Still, the Jewish calendar publishers appropriated material discriminatingly, rarely including features such as predictions of events for the coming year. Other culturally neutral items, such as tables describing when the sun would rise and set, were often transformed into religious signposts for prayer times and Sabbath candle lighting. Some Jewish calendars placed religious texts related to the calendar and to time, such as blessings for a new moon, or the *tashlikh* service, among the mundane addenda. Others moved toward becoming compendia of Jewish laws or customs, by including for example, instructions for koshering

meat. No single calendar included all of the same elements, and each style of calendar changed with time, reader sensibilities, and the needs of a particular locale. As late as 1817–1818, for instance, the calendar from Frankfurt am Main included among routine items like times for morning and afternoon services and for the beginning of the Sabbath a list of "Thorschlusszeiten," times when the city (or ghetto?) gates would be closed each evening.

Perhaps because Jewish calendars were unreliable or sometimes hard to find, Jews continued to write (or copy) them by hand long after they were generally available in print. A series of five small manuscript pocket calendars dating from the middle third of the eighteenth century (1730, 1734, 1739, 1742, and 1746) symbolize the close daily connection between these cultural artifacts and their users.[65] Their diminutive size indicates that these pocket calendars were intended to be carried by an individual, perhaps to serve as a model for printed calendars, or possibly copied from one and customized to suit the owner.[66] A nineteenth-century Hebrew manuscript calendar by one individual spans forty-four years without a break, one sheet per year, offering a painstakingly complete record of the passage of time in one human life. One might wonder: Why would a busy man write out a new calendar annually when printed ones were readily available? Did the scribe-owner know how to calculate the calendar on his own and hope to retain that ability? Regardless of his motivations, this individual created his own unique "book of life," a compelling record of his time on earth.[67]

The need for calendars during this era was more urgent where Hebrew printing had not yet been firmly established. Because the first printed Jewish calendar in America did not appear until 1806, German Jewish immigrants to the United States composed, or at least owned, manuscript calendars during the colonial and revolutionary periods. These calendars were apparently intended to supplement Christian calendars, for unlike all contemporaneous examples from Europe, several of them contain no references whatsoever to the Christian calendar. One of these was a luah written by Abraham Eliezer Cohen in Philadelphia for the year 1778–1779.[68] A merchant from Lancaster, Pennsylvania, Joseph Simons, who was also a member of the prominent Ettings family, commissioned and owned several manuscript calendars that are still extant, including one for a year during the Revolutionary War.[69] One exemplar in that collection stands out for the inventiveness and care that the creator took in fashioning a bicultural calendar.[70] He began with a small printed "Pocket Almanack" for the year 1780. The English title page (left opening) contains four tiny

FIG. 3.6. American pocket calendar for 1780, creatively adapted to include a Jewish calendar, in Lancaster, Pennsylvania. Courtesy of the Library at the Herbert D. Katz Center for Advanced Judaic Studies, University of Pennsylvania ms 60, fols. 1v–2r.

individual printed Arabic numerals, painstakingly cut out of another source and pasted on to spell out 5–5–4–1 (the Jewish year for 1780–1781). Handwritten beneath that is the place of production abbreviated in Hebrew as *be-k"k lenke* (*be-kehilla kedosha Lanca,* or "in the holy community of Lancaster"). The Hebrew calendar, meanwhile, is handwritten from right to left starting from the other side of the calendar booklet. Each Jewish month is allotted one page and adorned by a tiny, simple drawing to illustrate the sign of the month. The book-

let also contains an engraving of a "zodiac man," with letters pointing to the graphic symbols of the zodiac. On the inside cover, from the right opening, the compiler pasted "A Table shewing the value of any number of dollars from 1 to 10,000 at seven shillings and sixpence each."

On the back flyleaf, the owner etched his signature "Etting"—a well-known early American Jewish family name of German (Frankfurt) origins.[71] Thus the owner fashioned a homemade collage calendar, a distant echo of the calendar that he could not obtain from across the ocean, down to an imitation of the printed title page.

While most users discarded their handwritten calendars after they became obsolete, some preserved them for a useful afterlife, customizing them for other purposes. These modified calendars testify to their owner's reluctance to part from them, and to their sense that they represented something intimate and valuable (if only for the extra paper within the binding). For example, the over-leaf of the binding of a calendar published in Amsterdam for 1764–1765 was fashioned by a later owner into a purse, to hold papers or money. From December 17, 1790, until sometime during 1804, the owner also used the extra paper in the calendar to record expenses incurred in a business venture.[72]

Most calendars were (and are) created to be ephemeral. The precious survivors that remain yield frustratingly few clues about the lives of their author and owners. Those that have escaped the depredations of neglect and destruction, however, unmistakably attest to the value of these humble maps of time in the eyes of their owners and makers, to the centrality of Jewish time within the world they inhabited, and to the temporal axes around which their daily activities revolved. They demonstrate the intensely personal connection that the owners felt with their books of days.

{ 4 }

A New Jewish Book in Christian Europe

Some I have found in old books, written hundreds of years ago, some
on single pages, torn and crumbling parchments, strewn on the ground,
trampled underfoot by all who see them but do not appreciate them,
who consider them worthless. I retrieved them from the refuse heap,
and by uplifting and embracing them, established them as my own.

David b. Isaac of Fulda, ca. 1540–1607

TWO men study at a table, each one from their own copy of a Hebrew
manuscript book. The room they occupy is a scene of cozy domesticity.
One wall is lined with kitchen implements; a separate area to the right, a library
or study, contains the books, stacked vertically and bound with double clasps in
medieval fashion. One of the men sits at a side of the table; the other, perhaps
his tutor, stands opposite him. The text is clearly identified, because the books
contain the opening words of a sefer evronot: "The Holy One, blessed be He,
has commanded [us to study] the reckoning of seasons, constellations, and conjunctions." The image of the men appears in a unique drawing in a manuscript
sefer evronot from 1649, and reflects the cultivation of calendar literature in
manuscript among scholars in early modern German lands.[1] These books were
created as ritual objects, as study manuals for young scholars, as valued possessions worthy of careful preservation, and as objects of artistic embellishment.

The picture of a private tutorial in a tranquil setting seems a world away
from the religious and political rivalries that beset Europe and its Jews in the
sixteenth and seventeenth centuries. Yet the invention of the tradition rendered
in the illustration, of writing and studying evronot, and the central role of these
practices in the German Jewish culture of the period, came about as the result
of multiple layers of cultural and religious dislocation.

As mentioned earlier, the cultivation of sifre evronot as a stand-alone book
in manuscript began in the mid-sixteenth century, some decades after print
technology had come into use, and it continued well into the eighteenth century.

FIG. 4.1. Two men studying sifre evronot. *Sefer evronot*, ca. 1648–1651. Staatsbibliothek zu Berlin—Stiftung Preussischer Kulturbesitz, Berlin, Germany ms or. oct. 3150, fol. 78r. (Photo: Ruth Schacht. © Art Resource, NY.)

That manuscript evronot flourished concurrently with their appearance in print is hardly an anomaly. Scribal efforts continued long after books became available in print. Correspondence, bureaucratic records, and business contracts were written by hand long after printing had become commonplace. Nevertheless, a culture in which an entire handwritten genre emerged in the face of print technology demands a closer look. For as we will see, the little books carried a double cultural burden. They were a response to the sense of internal crisis within German Jewish culture, and they simultaneously reflected a Jewish response to the Christian religious and cultural wars of sixteenth- and seventeenth-century Europe.

Cultural Anxiety in Early Modern Jewry

From the mid-sixteenth century, students, scholars, and scribes—especially from southern and central German Jewish communities—produced a remarkable outpouring of manuscript sifre evronot. A large number of sifre evronot were written in the same region, home to a Jewish culture under siege. Indeed, its leaders, rabbis such as Hayim b. Bezalel of Friedberg (1515–1588) (brother of the famed R. Judah Loewe of Prague) fought valiantly to defend German Jewish customs and teachings against encroachments on their authority and autonomy.[2] They felt particularly threatened by Eastern European Jewish culture and the growing influence of Sephardic tradition on Jewish codes of law and of mysticism.

The rabbis' insistence on the validity and value of the local traditions should not be interpreted as parochialism. Rather, it reflected an acute historical and sociological awareness. Far from being culturally isolated, Jewish scholars from German lands were mobile, well connected, and deeply aware of their growing marginalization. As young yeshiva students, and then as communal rabbis, German Jewish scholars were well traveled within the Jewish world. They knew that there had been a time when their scholarship and authority had dominated Ashkenazic Jewish culture, and that new centers had emerged that openly and explicitly challenged that primacy.[3] The cultivation of manuscript sifre evronot emerged as an invented tradition in a culture caught between nostalgia for its past and concern for its future.

To advance German Jewish standing within the early modern Jewish world, these scholars embarked on a concerted endeavor to resurrect both real and assumed texts and practices from "ancient times," by which they meant the medi-

eval heyday of Franco-German Jewry, or some even more proximate era. The German Jewish scholars recognized that many of the sacred texts still in their possession were no longer sought after, and that those represented just a surviving fragment. Moreover, they sensed that the knowledge that had passed along with the texts through oral transmission had almost disappeared. "The art of writing represents only the slightest portion [of the knowledge being transmitted] which has been forgotten from memory, like the dead. [Instead they rely on printing.] The ... secrets ... will no longer be retrievable in memory."[4] They lamented the reliance on printed texts, which in their view only accelerated the process of forgetting the traditional wisdom.

A number of sixteenth-century scholars attempted to reverse this trajectory. R. David b. Isaac of Fulda (ca. 1540–1607) wrote about qabbalistic texts that he had copied into a digest: "Some I have found in old books, written hundreds of years ago, some on single pages, torn and crumbling parchments, strewn on the ground, trampled underfoot by all who see them but do not appreciate them, who consider them worthless. I retrieved them from the refuse heap, and by uplifting and embracing them, established them as my own."[5] R. David lamented his earlier ignorance of an old Ashkenazic custom that he had just discovered. "Only in recent days I received and found it in a *sefer yashan noshan* (very old book)."[6] Similarly, R. David wrote about a *seliha* (prayer for times of distress) that he had discovered: "I found it bound . . . in a *sefer yashan noshan*, torn, trampled, blurred, its traces barely visible."[7]

The phrase *yashan noshan* implies great antiquity; it recurs as a motif throughout the narratives of recovery from oblivion. The notion that scholars like R. David were recovering texts from a distant past, finding manuscripts of hoary provenance, also appears in discussions of the sources for German manuscript sifre evronot.[8] The sefer evronot written by Pinhas ben Isaac in 1566 concludes a paragraph with "Thus I have found in a very ancient book."[9] Moreover, the sense of loss and anxiety over the distance from their medieval culture appears to have intensified over time. In the seventeenth and even early eighteenth centuries, German Jewish writers searched the old literature to bring its comforts and secrets into their work. In the margin of an early seventeenth-century sefer evronot, the copyist noted: "I have found written in a *sefer yashan noshan* that each time a 532 year cycle ends, the cycles of the sun and the moon are even. They say that every 532 years, the gates of mercy open. Some say, the gates of paradise, some say the gates of heaven."[10]

Judah Reutlingen Mehler of Bingen, who wrote his sefer evronot in the

mid-seventeenth century, cited a long passage from a thirteen-year cycle that he had copied from an "ancient" sefer evronot, from 1552.[11] In the second half of the seventeenth century, Moses ben Benjamin Neimark noted with great specificity in his sefer evronot: "All this was copied from *sefer yashan noshan* that was found in Nuremberg; it was copied from the *quntres* (treatise, notebook) of R. Samuel Schlettstadt, of blessed memory."[12] Later in the seventeenth century, Tzvi Hirsch Koidonover (then living in Frankfurt) explained in the sefer evronot that he wrote in 1672 that he had copied the Christian calendar section from a sefer evronot he found in Frankfurt: "This I have found in a sefer evronot *yashan noshan* which had been written in 1472."[13] The recovery and preservation of authentic, nearly forgotten traditions allowed the copyists to express their pride in the past that was slipping away even as these acts revealed their anxiety over their place in the future.

Yeshiva students studying how to construct the computus and copy it properly used sifre evronot as texts to supplement oral teachings in the subject.[14] Students gained instruction individually, under the personal direction of a teacher, or collectively in a study hall. They used instructional models for copying, laying out, and spacing the texts and charts, as well as for illustrating each portion of the text. Ibbur texts thus were textual reinforcements to a body of knowledge that was still generally transmitted orally. One seventeenth-century manuscript sefer evronot described in detail the process by which it had been commissioned and copied for use as a textbook. Zusslen Meshulam bar Meir HaKohen, a scribe from Frankfurt am Main, completed "here in the Holy Community of Fulda, in 1661" a sefer evronot that he wrote for the young student Judah Leib b. Shlomo. Judah Leib inscribed the date and price of his purchase of the commissioned manuscript: "I Judah, son of my father and master Shlomo, may he live, bought this evronot and *shtarot* [book of model contracts] . . . in 1661, in Fulda." He further noted that he undertook a formal course of study in the subject for which he had commissioned the text: "I, Juda Leib, . . . studied *evrona* [sic] with our teacher and master R. Eliezer ben R. Joseph z"l, here in the holy community of Fulda in the winter of 1661."[15]

The transition of the ibbur from a cryptic formula transmitted within an oral tradition into an elaborate written book may be seen as part of a trend toward textualization in many areas of sixteenth-century Jewish culture.[16] But in the early modern period, an aura of esotericism still clung to ibbur literature, and Ashkenazic manuscripts contained many references to secrecy. Throughout the period of transition from an oral to a more textual tradition, no two

manuscripts (even those copied by the same scribe in the same year) contained exactly the same elements.[17] Many scribes boasted that they had collected the material from various sources: written, oral, or a combination of these. Moses b. Jacob of Moravia, for instance, wrote on the title page of his manuscript evronot that his text had been gathered from "many sifre evronot."[18]

The texts themselves bore the marks of orality long after they appeared in writing. Mnemonic devices only went so far, and mathematical or astronomical charts could be complicated, lengthy, and easy to misunderstand, especially for neophytes. Even the borders between handwritten and printed sifre evronot were blurred. Some printed sifre evronot bear copious handwritten notes, while scribes of some manuscript sifre evronot testified that they produced exact replicas of published texts.[19] That is, manuscript sifre evronot often served more as mirrors of the needs of the scribes or owners than as sacred transcriptions of a canonized text. Thus fluidity rather than rigidity is one of the outstanding characteristics of sifre evronot literature.

From the sixteenth century, the manuscripts acquired the paratextual elements that announced the formation of a book. Some of the manuscripts bore clearly marked introductions.[20] Others presented the contents on a title page. Some scribes placed the evronot text in the center, with additional scholia in the margins or remarks clearly marked as commentary.[21]

Some sifre evronot bore standard colophons: Itzik Kreilsheim proclaimed the completion of his sefer evronot with a festive flourish.[22] Other scribes and copyists of sifre evronot did not sign their works in this way, but instead adhered to a convention used by Christian scribes of computus at least as far back as the ninth century, if not much earlier.[23] The practice, which called for the insertion of the "present year" in all calculations, makes it possible to date an evronot manuscript to the year of its writing even in the absence of a colophon, or at the least to trace its date of origin to some extent. Of course, not all copyists bothered to update their calculations to the present year. One example comes from Elijah Loanz, a qabbalist and miracle worker well known in Southern Germany. After producing an illustrated sefer evronot, Loanz wrote that he had copied it from the manuscript of Judah Loewe Oppenheim of Worms.[24] In his colophon, Loanz admitted that he had not yet mastered the calculations and had merely copied: "You, reader, when you see that I write sometimes 'For instance, now in the year [5]312 [1552 c.e.],' but it is in fact now [5]346 [1586 c.e.] know that I have copied from the evronot written by R. Loewe Oppenheim of the holy community of Worms. I wrote and copied it word for word, as I am

not yet that expert in this book and would have erred. Therefore I have written exactly what I found before me."[25]

Two centers of southern German Jewish culture, Frankfurt and Worms, figured prominently in the early cultivation of manuscript sifre evronot—although rabbinic figures from other places are noted by scribes of sifre evronot as sources of information or as transmitters of calendar lore. These include Wolf of Moravia, Yehiel of Guenzberg, Jonathan b. Naftali Treves, Zeqlein of Metz, and Samuel of Schweinfurt.[26] In addition to R. Aqiva bar Jacob (d. 1597) of Frankfurt, who was a native of Prague, several other mid-sixteenth-century scribes of sifre evronot from southern Germany have a Prague connection. The professional scribe Elijah bar Moshe Troitlein of Worms, for instance, was a disciple of R. Nathan Shapira as well as of Abraham of Prague.[27]

As suggested earlier, within this geographic range, two centers of Jewish culture stood out, Frankfurt and Worms. Judah Loewe Oppenheim led a circle of eminent scholars in Worms, including R. Hayim of Friedberg and Abraham Wallich, both of whom were determined to recover lost wisdom from the Jewish tradition, including the ibbur and Hebrew grammar. In particular, R. Aqiva of Frankfurt played a central role in the creation and transmission of evronot: his name figures in dozens of sifre evronot over the centuries.[28] Aqiva was a native of Prague who served as preacher and member of a scholar's circle in Frankfurt during the last quarter of the sixteenth century.[29] (He was also the son-in-law of Simon of Guenzberg, one of the wealthiest Jewish men in Swabia, Germany, and a renowned collector of rare and beautiful Jewish manuscripts.[30]) Within his scholar's circle, Aqiva probably taught the computus in part by having his students make copies of formulae, charts, and other elements from early ibbur manuscripts.[31]

Equally significant, Aqiva helped transform the evronot into a midrashic compendium in which narrative material from diverse rabbinic sources was gathered. One of the elements of the evronot that has been consistently associated with Aqiva, as well as with Loewe Oppenheim, is the section of the evronot that teaches Jews how to calculate the Christian calendar, in particular by using the rules for the moveable cycle.[32] Upon fleeing Eastern Europe for Frankfurt almost a century later, Zvi Hirsch Koidonover copied a sefer evronot he had found there:

I heard about R. Loewe Oppenheim z"l, that he heard from a learned priest why *Fasnacht* [Shrove Tuesday, the last day before the somber

Lent season] sometimes occurs eight days into the month, not as it is written in the books. The priest said the reason is as follows: If the conjunction [of the moon] occurs before noon then *Fasnacht* falls on the first of the month, so that they can eat meat on one day each month. But if the conjunction falls after noon, then *Fasnacht* is deferred to the eighth day of the month, so that they can eat meat one day in the month, as what they eat on Tuesday is counted.[33]

These two elements of sifre evronot—their claim to be transmitting texts from rabbinic antiquity, and their incorporation of and response to elements of Christian culture—would define these documents' character over the next two centuries.

Illustrations in Manuscript Sifre Evronot

Early printed sifre evronot remained largely unillustrated except for the basic diagrams or charts intended to arrange information in accessible form. Handwritten sifre evronot, in contrast, were often profusely embellished. Their iconographic vocabulary expressed common cultural assumptions. Indeed, the emergence of the manuscript sifre evronot as a mature book was marked by the introduction of illustrations.

In many of these illustrations, scribes depicted the body of knowledge represented by the ibbur as a codex, a book. Some of the books within the illustration clearly opened to the talmudic passage in which Rabbi (Simon b.) Gamliel claimed to possess a tradition transmitted from his ancestors concerning the renewal of the moon. The illustration depicts him holding a book whose script, clearly visible in the illustration, is the sefer evronot text itself.[34] In another type of illustration, angels deliver the book titled sefer evronot to man, illustrating how the art of calendation is an encounter between divine gift and human cognition.[35]

When treatises on the Jewish calendar emerged as stand-alone works, they developed an expanded text and a distinctive iconography. Except for one element, the zodiac and its astrological signs, the illustration of these works has remained largely unexamined. Yet the rich iconographic conventions found in the illustrated manuscripts of early modern sifre evronot flourished for over three centuries and certainly merit a place in the pantheon of decorated texts. The illustrations complement and expand on the ideas in the text and form an

integral part of the genre. Like Bibles, *megillot*, and *mahzorim*, the calendar treatises had now come of age as a Jewish book. The text provided a new venue for scribes and illustrators of Hebrew manuscripts, with the same hand often performing both tasks.

Wealthy patrons commissioned illustrated manuscripts as luxury items, as gifts or for their own libraries as personalized works of art. Thus *megillot*, *haggadot*, *ketubbot*, *siddurim*, *sidre brakhot*, and other religious works continued to be written and illustrated by hand.[36] In many cases, scribes modeled their manuscripts and their illustrations on printed works, completing a circle of influence between print and script.

Many German Jews saw the creation of a sefer evronot as the fulfillment of a religious precept, and its adornment as a way of further enhancing their act of devotion.[37] One artist-scribe, Pinhas ben Abraham Sega"l of Halberstadt, explained why he lavishly illustrated his sefer evronot: "I illustrated it in pleasing color, as it says, 'This is my God and I will beautify Him' [Exodus 15:2], teaching a person to beautify a mitzvah, to take a flawless *lulav* [palm], to build a beautiful *sukkah* [temporary tabernacle].... My intentions were purely for the sake of Heaven. In this merit ... may God diminish our exile and send our messiah and build our Temple speedily in our days."[38]

The earliest medieval computus literature is suffused with figurative language. Both the human tendency to discern familiar shapes in the constellations as well as the centuries-old astronomical tradition of diagramming the heavens and celestial orbs contributed to the store of images available to artists or scribes. The classical notion of the universe as a set of nested spheres, along with the conceptualization of the heavens as mansions with portals, provided additional images for illuminating astronomical and calendrical material.

It seems pertinent to note that some of the sharpest formulations of the rabbinic prohibition against figural art pertained to the depiction of the heavenly bodies, which were singled out because they had been objects of pagan worship in ancient times. Talmudic sources discuss the permissibility of witnesses to the new moon making a likeness of what they saw, and questioned whether such likenesses were akin to pagan objects of worship.[39] Rabbinic reservations, however, did not prevent Jews in late antiquity from using the zodiac signs and the Helios image.[40] The discussion over celestial images continued in halakhic literature into the early modern period, and scholarly deliberations over the effect of this debate on the production of visual imagery are well known.[41]

Whatever the prohibitions or inhibitions, by the sixteenth century they had been overcome, at least for two-dimensional renderings of celestial figures.

The iconography of the sifre evronot is an integral part of the manuscript, with messages that both complement and expand on those of the text. In virtually all cases, the illustrations depict stories or personalities that were well known by most readers. Although sifre evronot featured a distinctive set of illustrations, many of the individual images had antecedents in earlier Ashkenazic illustrated works.

Ashkenazic ibbur literature originally appeared within Bibles, *siddurim*, and mahzorim, and sifre evronot borrowed some of their iconographic motifs. One example is the image of a balance, which was used to illustrate *parshat sheqalim* in mahzorim, and is used to represent the balancing of calculations in sifre evronot. The Binding of Isaac, a motif in Bibles, *haggadot*, and mahzorim for Rosh Hashanah, appears in sifre evronot as part of the illustration of the tequfot. The sun and moon, too, appear in various illustrated evronot; they had been used in mahzorim to depict *parshat ha-hodesh*.[42]

Other examples similarly show the lineage of illustrations used in sifre evronot. Each of the verses in *tefillat tal* (prayer for dew) and *tefillat geshem* (prayer for rain), which appeared in German mahzorim, were illustrated with signs of the zodiac. Artists often coupled these images of the zodiac signs with Labors of the Month illustrations, a cultural loan from Books of Hours and from medieval mahzorim.[43] For Shavuot, mahzorim depict Moses with the Tablets of Law; subsequently depictions of Moses, or of Moses with Aaron, appeared within the sifre evronot. The elaborate portals that decorated the opening of many sifre evronot and served as one of their central motifs could have taken inspiration from any of several sources, from the "Gates of Mercy" that often decorated Yom Kippur service texts, to the opening of printed Hebrew books.[44] The majority of figural depictions illustrate narratives or events in the text. Nevertheless, not every illustration in sifre evronot had a direct antecedent in some other genre, and the use of particular images in certain parts of the text ultimately developed into an autonomous and distinctive iconographic vocabulary.

Illustrations in sifre evronot fall into several categories, based on both style and substance. The overall artistic quality of the illustrations varies tremendously. Some manuscript sifre evronot were copied and prepared by professional scribes, while others were clearly the work of amateurs. Some of the ama-

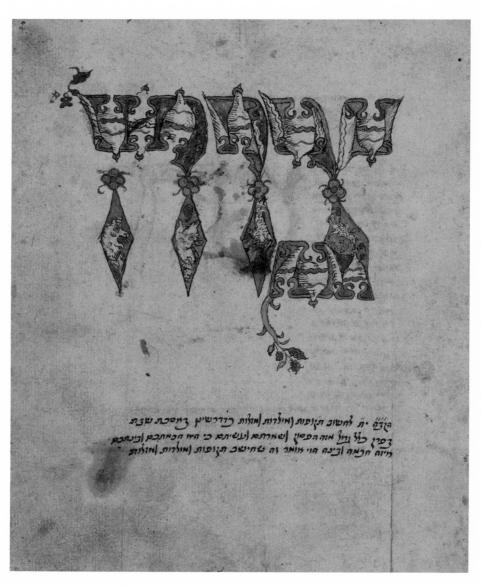

FIG. 4.2. Ornamented initial word *Tziva, Sefer evronot*, 1552. Courtesy of the Library of the Jewish Theological Seminary ms 9487, fol. 2r.

FIG. 4.3. Ornamented initial word *Tziva, Sefer evronot*, 1665–1666. Cincinnati, Klau Library, Hebrew Union College–Jewish Institute of Religion ms 901, fol. 1r.

teurs and students sketched in the most formulaic and perfunctory way, while others were clearly quite skilled at, and passionate about, illustrating their volumes. Some scribes included no figures at all, but nevertheless demonstrated great professionalism and care in writing the text, laying out the design, and the configuring and embellishing its many charts and volvelles.[45] Some of the mo-

FIG. 4.4. *Sha'ar*, Portal, *Sefer evronot*, 1557. Courtesy of the Library of the Jewish Theological Seminary ms 2548, fol. 34v.

tifs included by scribes do not appear to have any direct connection with the subject matter of the book; they are merely ornaments or doodles.[46]

The most commonly decorated elements in sifre evronot were the words within the text itself, such as opening word panels or other significant phrases. The most commonly ornamented opening word is *"tziva"* (He commanded),

which refers to a directive from God. The word emphasized the sense among the scribes that copying, calculating, and preserving this knowledge fulfilled a mitzvah, a religious precept. It also illustrated the notion that the only way to fulfill the mitzvah of *qiddush ha-hodesh* (sanctifying a new month), after the Jewish calendar had been set and publicized for all future time, was by learning how to construct the Jewish calendar and writing one's own sefer evronot.[47] For some owners or scribes, the cultivation of the text represented just such a fulfillment of the mitzvah of qiddush ha-hodesh.[48] One sixteenth-century scribe explained that he had labored so prodigiously over the calendar chart so that it would be "clarified for all those to whom God has granted understanding and wisdom. . . . I have done all this in order to allow other men of truth and uprightness [to fulfill this precept] and to serve as a safeguard forever unto all the generations. This table will not be obsolete until the coming of Shiloh [the end of time]."[49] Lavishing time and effort on the script, layout, calculations, and illustrations constituted for these scribes an act of *hiddur mitzvah*, the decoration and beautification of a religious observance in a manner pleasing to God and to man.

Evronot Illustrations

The study of iconography, "to probe meaning in a work of art by setting it in its historical context, to analyze the ideas implicated in its imagery," is in its infancy for sifre evronot.[50] Even so, we can begin our interpretation of sifre evronot iconography by examining the use of the image of a mansion or palace, the dominant classical metaphor for the heavenly spheres. An elastic and flexible image, it connotes majesty, beauty, and symmetry at the same time that it conveys a sense of boundaries and finite lines. God was infinite and unknowable, but readers of computus literature could behold the house of His design if they used the correct instruments and formulae.

Illustrators of sifre evronot often opened the manuscript with a gateway or portal and placed the title within it, thus announcing the theme of their work. This is a common enough trope inviting the reader to enter into the contents of a book; in fact, the title pages of Hebrew books are still called the *sha'ar*, or portal page.[51] In some cases the portal enclosed a table of contents or the identifying inscription of the scribe.[52] Other portals contained both the title "Sefer evronot" as well as an embellished initial word, *tziva* (He commanded).[53] In addition to the opening, portals appeared throughout sifre evronot as motifs evok-

FIG. 4.5 *Sha'ar*, Portal, decorated word. *Sefer evronot*, 1717. Cincinnati, Klau Library, Hebrew Union College–Jewish Institute of Religion ms 903, fol. 34r.

ing current as well as ancient images associated with the heavens. The opening folios of sifre evronot manuscripts alluded to, or sometimes explicitly referred to, ibbur knowledge as coming from a divine realm, and the opening of the manuscript as similar to entering the gateway to heaven. In the ancient Near East, where the sun was a divinity, portals often stood for the sun god, and later simply as a means for referring to the sun's appearance in the sky. This suggests possible echoes of the ancient gatelike structures used to chart the passage of the sun along the horizon.

Portals bear an ancient pedigree as synecdoches for the palace of the deity. Some of the sifre evronot portals were decorated with images of celestial bodies.[54] As Ellen Robbins observes, "The 'gates' in the Apocryphal Book of Enoch (Enoch 72–82) represent divisions (arcs) of the eastern and western horizon, roughly corresponding to the rising and setting amplitudes of the sun (and moon, as both travel across the same band of the sky, the ecliptic). . . . The gate of the setting sun is mentioned incidentally in the Sabbath legislation of the Qumran community."[55]

Psalms 24:7–9 refers to gates that serve as entryways for the divine king. In Jewish iconography, portals signified the entrance to the Temple, with its concentration of divine presence, or to the opening of the Ark that contained Torah scrolls, a source of divine knowledge.[56] At least one manuscript explicitly linked its illustrations of gates to those of the Temple.[57] And a number of sifre evronot manuscripts elaborate further on the Temple theme. Some contained a

shulkhan, a table that evoked the one used in the Temple, or calendrical charts in the shape of Temple implements, such as a cruse (*qanqan*) for oil, or a laver for washing hands.[58] These implements also bore symbolic significance: a table in one manuscript was captioned: "When the table is fully set [*arukh*] we will merit the longest [*arokh*] day."[59]

Some title illustrations preserved the sense that the entry portals into the manuscript were the Gates of Mercy, retaining even the captions that would have been used in a mahzor: "These are the gates of the Lord, the righteous shall enter them," followed by the verse: "Open the gates of righteousness so that I may enter them and thank God."[60] Since some of the principal components of sifre ibbur were calculation tables—referred to as the "Chart of the Four Portals" (or later "Seven Portals")—dating at least as far back as the tenth century C.E., these ancient and medieval motifs continued to be relevant and natural elements of sifre evronot illustrations.[61]

A distinctive and recurrent motif in illustrated sifre evronot was the depiction of a man on or near a ladder reaching toward heaven to obtain the secrets of the calendar. The figure on the ladder often carried an hourglass, a symbol of measurement of time.[62] In some illustrations, the human figure also mediates between the lunar and solar spheres, symbolizing the Jewish calendar's alignment of the lunisolar cycles, as well as the planetary influences.[63] Ladders have long been employed in religious imagery to symbolize bridges between domains.[64] Here the ladder mediates between the earthbound limitations of the human mind and divine knowledge of the celestial world.

Ladder imagery in Jewish and Christian religious texts is rooted in one ur-image, that of the *sullam* in Jacob's dream described in Genesis 28:12–17. The term *sullam* is found nowhere else in the Hebrew Bible, so its meaning is unclear. Given that it was used in the story of the dream for angels traveling in both directions, however, its original meaning was likely a stairway to heaven. The Greek Septuagint and Latin Vulgate translations of this passage of the Bible used terms that meant both staircase and ladder, and subsequently ladder is the definition that has prevailed.[65] Jacob's reaction to his dream vision, "How awesome is this place! This is none other than the house of God and that is the gateway to heaven" (Genesis 28:17), provides an additional link between the stairway/ladder and portal imagery that opened many early modern sifre evronot.

The ladder in Jacob's dream is a means not only of ascent to the heavens, but also of the descent back to earth. Although it was difficult for some medi-

FIG. 4.6. Angel giving calendar secrets to Issachar. *Sefer evronot*, 1716. Reproduced with the permission of the National Library of Israel ms Heb 8° 2380, fol. 10r.

eval artists to depict descent (some showed their figures descending head first to make this clear), the figure in the sifre evronot has usually ascended the ladder and acquired his precious cargo of knowledge. He is depicted on his return to earth.[66] Unlike ascents to heaven that are depicted as instantaneous (such as by chariot), ladders imply a laborious effort to attain ever higher levels of knowledge.[67]

Although the iconography of the ladder to heaven can be traced to the biblical scene of Jacob's ladder, the figure in the sifre evronot is not Jacob but one of

his sons, Issachar.[68] Based on a verse that attributed knowledge of the reckoning of time to members of this tribe, the figure of Issachar bears the credit and responsibility for relaying the heavenly secrets to the people of Israel. "And the children of Issachar know the wisdom of the times" (I Chron. 12:32–33). The text in the sefer evronot is rooted in a late-eighth-century midrash titled *Baraita de Shmuel*, which has been attributed pseudepigraphically to the talmudic sage Samuel, who was reputed by the Talmud to have been an expert in astronomy. "The Beraitha of Samuel teaches: when Issachar ascended to heaven he established one thousand and eighty parts to the hour. And [the sages] have further taught, 'And the sons of Issachar know the wisdom of the times,' the Hebrew term *ittim*, times, contains the acronym for the words *ibbur* (intercalation), *tequfah* (season), *yitron* (remainder) and *molad* (new lunar birth)."[69] The image of Issachar descending a ladder not only illustrated a particular passage of the text but also underscored the larger message of the literature of ibbur: the divine origins of the rabbinic reckoning of time, the priority and superiority of the Jewish calendar, and its place in the chain of transmission of Jewish knowledge.[70]

The message that the Jewish calendar and its chronology were divinely ordained and that time itself began at the precise moment of the creation of the world was symbolized by the iconography of Adam, Eve, and the serpent.[71] This was a simple arrangement in which the figure of Adam stands to the right of the Tree, Eve to the left, and the serpent, often extending a fruit to Eve, at the center, wrapped around the Tree of Knowledge. It is an arrangement that appears in countless Christian Bible manuscripts and was ubiquitous in early printed Bibles as well.[72] In the context of the sifre evronot, however, it also conveyed larger lessons about the Jewish calendar. The moment of creation, calculated retroactively to an imaginary set date and moment—known in Hebrew as *bahara"d* (an acronym for second day, fifth hour, 204th part)—played a prominent role in the Jewish computus as the fixed point from which all further chronological and horological calculations would proceed. The justification for this particular point of time was based on the story of creation, and particularly the creation of man, the first creature to appreciate the concept of time. The serpent symbolized the expulsion from Eden, an event that marked the end of primordial time and the beginning of historical time.

Here too, extra-biblical, apocryphal, and late midrashic sources about the calendar play a role. A late Samaritan work in the style of a catechism contains the following exchange:

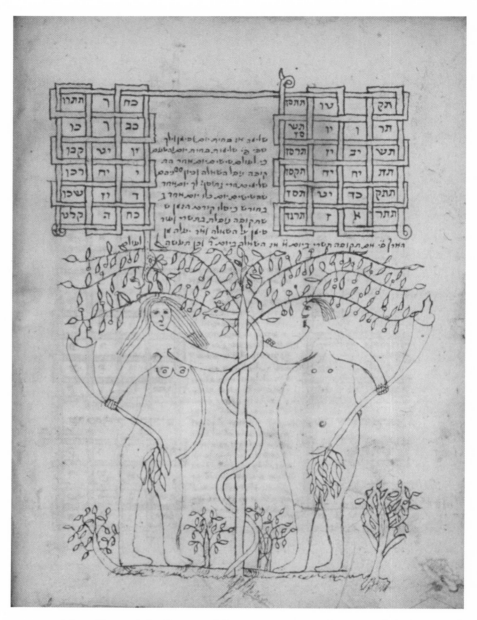

FIG. 4.7. Adam, Eve, and the Serpent. *Sefer evronot*, ca. 1625. Courtesy of the Rare Book and Manuscript Library, Columbia University ms X893 Se36, fol. 19v.

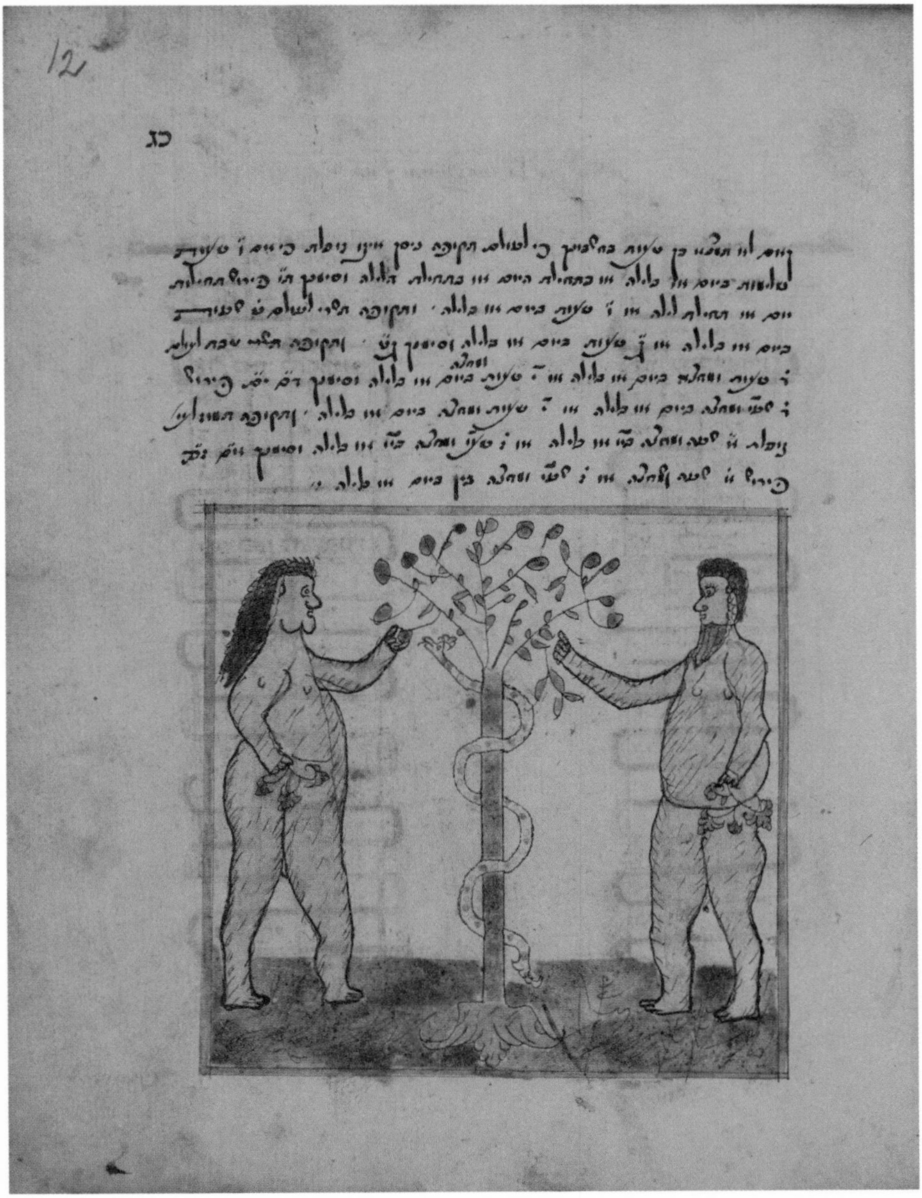

FIG. 4.8. Adam, Eve, and the Serpent. *Sefer evronot*, 1627. Courtesy of the Library of the Jewish Theological Seminary ms 2662, fol. 12r.

FIG. 4.9. Adam, Eve, and the Serpent. *Sefer evronot*, 1631. Courtesy of the Library of the Jewish Theological Seminary ms 2540, fol. 17v.

Who went out with Adam from the Garden? There went out with him from the Garden . . . the rod of the Lord; he (Adam) carried it in his hand . . . it is the rod of Moses, upon him be peace. And what was the secret of the rod? It had many secrets . . . it is said that upon it was written the true (calendar) reckoning and the book of the wars and the book of the signs and the book of astronomy. . . . The three books were preserved until the coming of the apostle and some (parts) of them were with Laban and some with Balaam but from the time of the com-

ing of the Law they became defective until they finally departed from the world. Yet a little of the book of astronomy was left; and the true calculation (of the calendar) as this is (calculated) with us, was handed on.[73]

This Samaritan story preserves the ancient link between Adam, who first learned the secret of calendar lore and began its transmission, and Moses, whom God taught the importance of the phases of the moon for the Jewish calendar.[74] The staff on which the calendar secrets were carved is reminiscent of the carved wood or stone calendars that were prevalent before paper. In *Pirqe de Rabbi Eliezer*, an enigmatic anonymous composition (from the eighth to ninth centuries C.E.), Adam received the laws of the calendar in the Garden of Eden shortly after his creation.[75]

A convergence of influences may have contributed to the emergence of the Adam and Eve images as central to sifre evronot. In pre-Reformation German lands, similar images were ubiquitous in Bibles both Christian and Jewish, both handwritten and printed. Apocryphas (stories outside the biblical canon) concerning the lives of Adam and Eve were very popular, and the iconography that adorned some of these manuscripts is strikingly similar to images found in the sifre evronot.[76]

One additional point should be noted about the Adam, Eve, and serpent iconography: it had a polemical subtext. Paul identified the "old," or first, Adam with fallen humanity. In his view, Adam destroyed the balance in the relationship between God and man and introduced a state of sinfulness and death into the world. Jesus was seen as the counterweight to Adam, come to atone for his sin and to bring eternal life. "For as in Adam all die, so in Christ all will be made alive" (I Corinthians 15:22). In the second century C.E., Irenaeus developed the parallel further, contrasting Eve to Mary. Eve represented the mother of early, corrupted humanity, while Mary, as the mother of Jesus, had brought salvation to all humankind.[77] Finally, the Christian Bible compares and contrasts the Tree of Life and the cross; Acts 23:29, for instance, refers to "those who took him [Jesus] down from the tree [meaning cross]," and other parallels between Eden and Golgotha (where Jesus was crucified) abound.[78]

Contemporary Christian Bibles provided the visual juxtaposition of these polemical narratives and personalities. Typically, the left side of the images depicted the Jewish and the "old," and the right side, the Christian and the "new." One typical title page to a Christian Bible arranged the following three figures

on the left side: God handing the Law to Moses; Adam, Eve and the serpent; and a corpse in a coffin, the figure of Death. Arrayed opposite them on the right side are an Annunciation scene, the Crucifixion, and a man stepping out of the coffin, representing Life. Thus the image of Adam, Eve, and the serpent coiled around the tree is directly juxtaposed with that of the Crucifixion.[79]

The positioning of the Eden scene conspicuously in the center of a Jewish text and at the beginning of Jewish time constituted an implicit rejection of the Christian narrative and proclaimed the continued validity of the Hebrew biblical account. Although not every sefer evronot illustrator made the point explicit, some placed the primordial garden scene next to a chart stating the current year "to the small counting," that is, to the conventional Jewish chronology.[80] Just as the *anno mundi* chronology provided Jews with an alternative to the Christian *anno Domini*, the graphic statement regarding the birth of man and of historical time that was made a part of the Garden of Eden scene provided an alternative narrative to Christian message that was so prevalent in Books of Hours and in Christian Bibles.[81]

.   .   .

Not all the illustrations in manuscript sifre evronot contained weighty polemical or theological statements. Just as colophons and glosses allowed scribes or owners room for personal expression in what would otherwise have been impersonal and mechanical chores of manuscript reproduction, some illustrations were just for fun. These playful elements undoubtedly elicited inner chuckles each time the user came upon them, and like other forms of traditional Jewish literature, such as haggadot, offered an outlet for scribes' sense of humor.[82]

One of the elements of sifre evronot that was commonly enlivened with humorous illustrations was the chart used for double-checking the calculations, or the *panim ahor* (literally "face-back," or what is usually front is now back, a reversal of the natural order of things). Each of the terms are dense and allusive, and in the sifre evronot they are interpreted punningly so that illustrations near the panim ahor chart show a man standing on his head, or more commonly and more ribaldly, a man whose backside greets the viewer.[83] Medieval Christian artists, architects, and sculptors had a long tradition of inserting clever or bawdy humorous elements into their work, and the margins of medieval manuscripts provided a similar creative space for illustrators. These comic offenders often appeared in the most sacred of spaces such as churches and monasteries, or adorned hallowed texts, and they appeared in every European tradition.[84] So common was the slapstick image of the bare behind that one sixteenth-century

FIG. 4.10. *Panim ahor. Sefer evronot*, 1627. Courtesy of the Library of the Jewish Theological Seminary ms 2662, fol. 15r.

Bible printer used it for the opening initial of the Book of John.[85] In addition to visual puns like these, some illustrations played with words. A popular medieval pun on the name Dominican divided the word into *domini canes*, and so illustrated the page with the "dogs of the Lord."[86]

Christian artists sometimes substituted apes or simian figures to subvert the human subject.[87] Some church sculptures featured men with exposed buttocks as a means of giving comic offense; in one, the head protrudes between the legs, much like some *panim ahor* illustrations.[88] (*Panim ahor* illustrations were "verbal puns," in which the picture played on the words, and should not be confused with the very popular medieval motif that portrayed the world upside

FIG. 4.11. Bare-bottomed man defecating. *Sefer evronot*, 1664. Cincinnati, Klau Library, Hebrew Union College–Jewish Institute of Religion ms 906, fol. 61v.

down, *inversus mundi*.) Other examples of clever verbal or visual puns in sifre evronot include a picture of a baby being rocked by its mother in a crib to illustrate the term *molad* (the moon's conjunction, or literally, "birth"); a man smoking a pipe, emitting a cloud of smoke labeled איד (a cloud), playing on the same word used for non-Jewish holidays; and where the text instructed *ve-teda* (and you should know), a master is shown instructing his pupils.[89] Other examples include an ostrich captioned with its Hebrew name *bat ya'anah* (a play on the opening words of some texts, "*ya'an u-ve'ya'an*"); an elephant, captioned in Hebrew *pil* (alluding to charts on the page in which various times "fall," for example, *tequfah nofelet*), and a monkey, or *qof*, a riff on tequfah, which has a similar Hebrew root.[90]

More subtle word- and image-based jokes can be seen as well. For example, some charts feature a serpent's head and tail peeking out at the ends of various lines in the table, giving the impression that the horizontal and vertical lines in the table are formed by the serpent's body wrapped in impossible ways.[91] The serpentine theme continues later in this manuscript: a twisted serpent's body

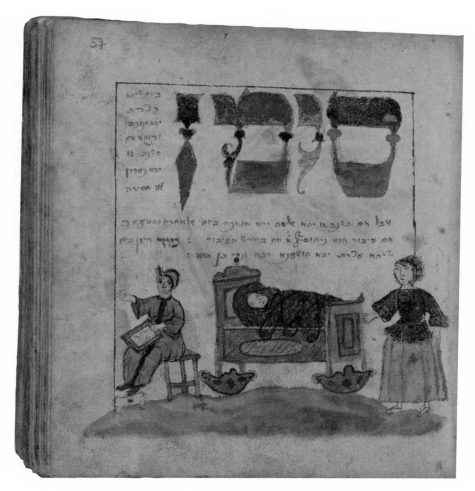

FIG. 4.12. Swaddled baby, wordplay on *molad* (conjunction, or birth of a new moon). *Sefer evronot*, 1716. Reproduced with the permission of the National Library of Israel ms Heb 8° 2380, fol. 57r.

shaped like a pretzel separates two columns in the table used to calculate the conjunctions.[92] Fittingly, that table faces a full-page illustration of Adam, Eve, and the serpent, in which Eve is feeding a fruit from the Tree of Knowledge to the serpent, which is wrapped around the trunk. Although most such imagery alludes generally to the fall into history precipitated by the tasting of the Tree of Knowledge, one manuscript contains a detail that does not appear in other illustrated sifre evronot: a penis has been drawn on the serpent, and it is pointed at Eve. This detail in the illustration alludes to a midrash that explicitly characterized the encounter between Eve and the serpent as sexual.[93] According to

FIG. 4.13. Pipe-smoking man produces cloud, wordplay on *eyd* (also, Christian holidays). *Sefer evronot*, 1716. Reproduced with the permission of the National Library of Israel ms Heb 8° 2380, fol. 163v.

this midrash, the serpent injected his filth into Eve, and this primordial pollution affected all mankind until the giving of the Torah on Mount Sinai, when it departed from the Israelites. If this reading of the illustration is correct, it provides a visual shorthand for a polemical statement about the ontological status of Jews vis-à-vis non-Jews.

·   ·   ·

Even though rabbinic sources were ambivalent about the representation, in any medium, of the heavenly bodies, scribes and illustrators granted the sun, moon, stars, and planets prominent places in illustrated sifre evronot manuscripts, and they appear in printed Jewish calendars as well.[94] Through the medieval and early modern periods, these images imparted profound symbolic meanings. In particular, an entire system of religious identifications was linked to the moon in early modern Christian and Jewish teachings.

Christian theologians and artists staked their own complex web of claims on the symbolism of the celestial orbs. In a painstaking and expertly argued analysis, Eileen Reeves has laid out the complicated and changing notions concerning the moon in Western science, art, and religion.[95] Christianity inherited from Western classical antiquity an image of the moon that embodied the notions of variability, flux, change, and periodicity. Linked to the ebb and flow of the tides, the moon was associated with instability, miasma, and madness, that

FIG. 4.14. Master and disciples, wordplay on *ve-teda* (you should know). *Sefer evronot*, 1716. Reproduced with the permission of the National Library of Israel ms Heb 8° 2380, fol. 106v.

is, with the fleeting and mutable aspects of the material, sublunar world—a negative association in every respect. "The moon, because it has certain blemishes on its body and undergoes eclipse and scatters darkness here and there," represented weak and corruptible human nature. The qualities of the moon always stood in contrast to those of the sun, long associated with the divine qualities of constancy, light, warmth, and sustenance of life. A strong symbolic identification of Jesus with the sun entered Christianity early on and remained a staple over the centuries.[96] The history of the symbolic identity of the moon, however, fluctuated over time. Because of its attributes, the moon was often gendered female in Christian thought, and Christian thinkers originally viewed the moon as the antithesis of Mary, who triumphed over all such defects.

One of the pivotal Christian images, from the Book of Revelations (12:1),

FIG. 4.15. Elephant, marked *pil*, play on the Hebrew root meaning to fall (as in a holiday falling on a certain date). *Sefer evronot*, 1627. Courtesy of the Library of the Jewish Theological Seminary ms 2662, fol. 21v.

depicts a woman who will soon give birth to the child who will rule nations. The woman appears "clothed with the sun, the moon under her feet, and upon her head a crown of twelve stars." Christian exegetes identified the woman as the church itself, or as Mary. In either case, the woman is nourished by the sun, Jesus, while transcending the moon and its negative attributes. Gregory the Great saw the moon beneath the woman's feet as everything the church despised, "fallen, mutable and earthly."[97]

The traditional iconography had been severed from this strain of commentary by the time of Bede, the learned eighth-century monk. Instead of seeing the moon as the embodiment of weakness and flawed humanity, Bede and his successors transformed the moon into a symbol of the church, or of Mary herself. Bede elevated the moon to central importance as a Christian symbol.

> The Moon, on the other hand, was full at sunset for the Creator, Who is justice itself, would never make something in an imperfect state. It appeared, together with the glittering stars, in the midpoint of the east . . . and by its rising, it sanctified the beginning of Easter. For the only paschal rule to observe is that the spring equinox be completed with a full Moon following. . . . For it is fitting that just as the Sun at that point in time first assumed power over the day, and then the Moon and stars power over the night, so now, to connote the joy of our redemption, day should first equal night in length, and then the full Moon should suffuse [the night] with light. This is for the sake of a certain symbolism, because the created Sun . . . signifies the true and eternal light which lighteth every man that cometh into the world, while the Moon and the stars, which shine, not with their own light (as they say) but with light borrowed from the Sun, suggest the body of the church as a whole, and each individual saint. . . . Christ [precedes] the church which cannot shine save through Him. For if anyone were to argue that the full Moon can come before the equinox, he would be stating . . . that the Holy Church existed in its perfection before the Saviour came in the flesh.[98]

If the sun symbolized Christ, and the moon signified the church, the weakness of the moon was transformed into strength.[99] Other Christian thinkers continued to see the feminine principle in the moon, but rather than bearing the stains of mortal female weakness, the moon came to symbolize Mary herself. In this phase of iconography, the moon was depicted as an orb of the purest light—crystalline, radiant, diaphanous. This spotless moon became linked to

the notion of Mary as immaculate, not only in the conception of her son but in her own conception as well.

It is this close affiliation between doctrine, visual perception, and science, Reeves explains, that made Galileo's *Siderius Nuncius (Starry Messenger)* so controversial. Galileo described the moon's surface as "duskish, leaden," and "rough, solid, opaque." His depiction violated cultural suppositions and seemed to threaten the doctrines of the Immaculate Conception along with the entire symbolic identification of Mary and the moon.[100] His description of the lunar substance became a source of conflict between Marian devotees and astronomers. Even Catholics who accepted Galileo's observations as accurate persisted in seeing some type of Christian image in the moon.[101]

Intense preoccupation with symbolic identification of the moon was not unique to premodern Christianity. The moon's secondary status as a luminary, its disappearance and rebirth, those very features that granted the moon its unstable status, were precisely those aspects that caused Jews to identify with it over the centuries. In "The Sanctification of the Moon," a ritual that practicing Jews perform every month, this identification is reinforced and ritualized. The practice dates back to ancient times when the beginning of the new month was observed as a major festival. Sources from the late ancient and early medieval period document the continuity of the practice and its accompanying prayers.[102] The text of the monthly prayer underscored the relationship between God as creator of the moon and as comforter of Israel:

> By His [God's] word, He created the heavens, by the breath of His mouth, all of their hosts. He assigned to them a fixed law and a set time so that they would not alter their heavenly course. They [the heavenly bodies that unswervingly follow their divinely ordained course] are workers of truth whose work is truth. To the moon He said that it should be renewed in brightness and become a crown of glory to those whose wombs are heavy for *they were to be renewed just as it was.*[103]

The formulators of this prayer recognized the symbolism inherent in the moon's periodicity and linked it to the Jewish people's destiny. Although pinpointing the time of the renewal of the moon based on observation had long since been replaced by the use of calculations, rituals related to the new moon persisted.[104] Heavenly fixtures were often called on in biblical and talmudic writing to be enduring witnesses to various treaties and covenants, but the moon was singled out as the symbol for the covenant with the House of David.

FIG. 4.16. Sanctifying the new moon. *Minhogim*, Amsterdam, 1662, fol. 12v. Courtesy of the Library of the Jewish Theological Seminary.

That tradition was so deeply rooted "that Judah the Patriarch asked Hiyya to inform him of the new moon's appearance and its sanctification with the password 'David, King of Israel, lives on,'" a formulation still recited with the blessing of the new moon.[105] Another element of the ritual is the statement, made toward the moon, "Just as I dance before you but cannot touch you, so may my foes be unable to harm me. Fear and dread will befall them, and by means of your great arm [God] they will become mute as stone. David, King of Israel, lives on." This proclamation overtly identified the people of Israel with the moon—and so with the wish that, like the moon, the Jewish people would be able to elude their enemies and ultimately to outlive and triumph over them.[106]

The identification between the Jewish people and the moon entered sifre evronot through a talmudic midrash on the diminution of the moon.[107] "Dur-

ing those three hours the sun and the moon stood in the same window [they were the same size] and they served simultaneously and equally, as is cited in the chapter *elu trefot* [Babylonian Talmud Hullin]. The moon rose and complained, 'It is impossible for two kings to wear the same crown.' To this the Holy One Blessed Be He replied, 'Go, diminish yourself.' The moon remained rejected until Friday, 14 hours."[108] According to this midrash, God felt that He needed to atone for the diminution by eventually restoring the moon to its former glory, closing the circle that paralleled its fate with the now rejected, but soon to be redeemed, people.[109] Significantly, Islam too adopted the lunar crescent as its identifying symbol, similar in function, if not in doctrinal centrality, to the crucifix in Christianity.

·　·　·

A small number of sifre evronot contain illustrations of Moses as lawgiver. Since the rabbinic tradition interprets the very first active commandment as the fixing of the calendar according to the new moon that God showed Moses, it would seem natural for Moses to play a more prominent role in sifre evronot iconography.[110] But the figure of Issachar usurped that role.[111] Moses instead makes a rare appearance in an illustration to a talmudic discussion, cited only in some sifre evronot, as to why certain months could not vary in their number of days between 29 and 30, but must remain fixed. Moses had ascended Mount Sinai on 6 Sivan and remained there for three periods of forty days, until finally descending permanently on Yom Kippur, 10 Tishre. The months from Sivan through Tishre could not vary in length, because the 120 days between Moses' ascent and his final descent were fixed. Some sifre evronot also depict Moses shattering the Tablets of the Law, the event that necessitated his return to get a new set. These illustrations may have been influenced by the illustrations in some mahzorim for the prayer *"Adon imnani"* that show a scene of the giving of the Torah on Mount Sinai.[112] In these illustrations Moses is often depicted with Aaron and the elders while the rest of the people wait at the foot of the mountain.

Scales, particularly the balance, constitute a longstanding and familiar image in Jewish illuminated manuscripts and early printed books. It is interesting to note that although the scales in calendar treatises are symbols of purely mathematical functions, many scribes continued to label them *moznei tzedeq* (scales of justice), a reference to their older iconography.[113]

The balance is the symbol for Libra in the zodiac, a sign that translated perfectly for the month of Tishre with its Day of Atonement, when Jews are judged

FIG. 4.17. Justitia with scales. *Sefer evronot*, 1583. Courtesy of the Library of the Jewish Theological Seminary ms 2547, fol. 71r.

and their deeds weighed in the balance.[114] In medieval mahzorim the balance was also an integral illustration for the special liturgy of Shabbat *sheqalim*, with *sheqel* derived from the root "to weigh." The liturgy includes the reading from Exodus commemorating the practice of collecting a symbolic half-shekel from all Jews by the first of the month of Nissan.[115]

The image of the balance as an illustration of mathematical checks and balances that allow the calculator to confirm his answers goes back to the earliest

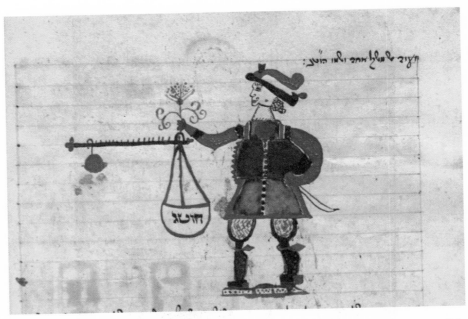

FIG. 4.18. Man carrying scale. *Sefer evronot*, Cincinnati, Klau Library, Hebrew Union College–Jewish Institute of Religion ms 903, fol. 15v.

complete sifre ibbur. Abraham ibn Ezra uses the term *mozna'im* (scales) in his *Sefer ha-ibbur* to introduce a simple table that teaches the principle of places for the ones, tens, and hundreds, as well as the idea of carrying over from one column to the next.[116]

Circular charts, known as volvelles, appeared in virtually all sifre evronot.[117] They organized considerable amounts of information in a compact and accessible form, facilitating rapid calculation. An arrangement of Jewish computus materials in circular form dates to the Geonic period if not earlier; one chart was attributed to R. Nahshon Gaon. Astronomical texts were among the first to feature wheels as instructional tools.[118] So much of the cosmos had been imagined as spherical, including the sun, the moon, the planets, and their orbits, that the tools of astronomical pedagogy such as the armillary sphere, astrolabe, and orrery tended to be comprised of circles, and until Kepler's findings regarding elliptical orbits in the early seventeenth century, the "perfect" form of the circle dominated astronomical discourse.

The first printed astronomy textbooks also included paper wheels. Georg Peurbach's *Theoricae Novae Planetarum* of 1482 contained wheels illustrating Ptolemy's planetary epicycles. His pupil, Johannes Mueller, better known as Re-

FIG. 4.19. Angel holding balance, signifying the divine provenance of ibbur. *Sefer evronot*, 1557. Courtesy of the Library of the Jewish Theological Seminary ms 2548, fol. 16r.

giomontanus, had his own printing press as well as a scientific observatory. He was one of the earliest figures to use printing to disseminate astronomical information. His *Kalendarium* (1474) advanced astronomical knowledge, and its meticulous calendar contained exquisite lunar volvelles.[119]

Creating volvelles required some craftsmanship on the part of the scribes, because a volvelle is composed of several layers of concentric circles arranged in descending size on top of one another. The scribe had to cut each circle to a precise size, position the correct information on each piece, and then attach

FIG. 4.20. Angels holding balance, signifying the divine provenance of ibbur. *Sefer evronot,* 1631. Courtesy of the Library of the Jewish Theological Seminary ms 2540, fol. 11v.

them carefully with a small string knotted at the middle so that each layer could be rotated as needed. Some scribes decorated the volvelles lavishly. Others personalized the wheels by affixing parts of their full name to the stationary base of the circle. This practice enabled the user to determine the beginning and end positions of the circular chart and became something of a convention.[120]

Another very old visual device in sifre evronot is the chart in the shape of a hand, a motif that undoubtedly originated when the fingers and knuckles were used by students as mnemonic devices for studying the computus.[121] Some scribes of sifre evronot further endowed the hand shape with symbolic meaning. One hand, for example, is captioned with the verse: "And Israel saw the great hand."[122]

· · ·

Many illustrated sifre evronot contain scenes of a hunt.[123] Because these are not directly linked to the text, we can surmise that such illustrations migrated into these Jewish manuscripts from Christian Books of Hours. The seasons for hunting various quarry were often set from one Christian holy day to another. Indeed, images of the hunt in all its variations abounded in medieval iconography.[124] They generally depicted images of aristocrats who hunted for sport. Just

FIG. 4.21. Volvelle, *Sefer evronot*, 1779. Cincinnati, Klau Library, Hebrew Union College-Jewish Institute of Religion ms 902, fol. 18r.

as the Labors of the Months—agricultural scenes borrowed directly from non-Jewish calendars—appeared in sifre evronot and Jewish calendars, so too did images of hunting. Medieval Hebrew illuminated manuscripts developed an iconography of the hunt and these entered sifre evronot as well.

In one seventeenth-century sefer evronot hunt scene, a stylishly dressed man shoots pellets at a bird with a gun; a dog attacks another of the birds on top of the same page.[125] In another illustration, a man holding a three-pronged pitchfork in one hand blows a horn, a rider dressed in fine riding outfit and plumed hat rides the horse and holds the reins, while two dogs lead the hunt. A bit further on, there appears a larger image of a man dressed in the same habit,

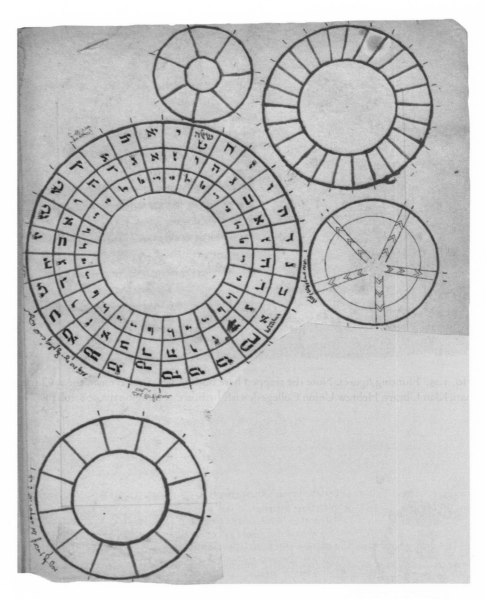

FIG 4.22. Volvelle in preparation, *Sefer evronot*, 1717. Cincinnati, Klau Library, Hebrew Union College–Jewish Institute of Religion ms 903, fol. 47v.

FIG. 4.23. Hunting figures. Note the trapped hare bottom left. *Sefer evronot*, 1664. Cincinnati, Klau Library, Hebrew Union College-Jewish Institute of Religion ms 906, fol. 10v.

FIG. 4.24. Hunter with gun. *Sefer evronot*, 1664. Cincinnati, Klau Library, Hebrew Union College-Jewish Institute of Religion ms 906, fol. 15v.

FIG 4.25. The hunt with hare as quarry, underneath verses of consolation. *Sefer evronot*, 1631. Courtesy of the Library of the Jewish Theological Seminary ms 2540, fol. 38v.

wielding a large pike with his right arm and unsheathed sword in his left; a gazelle and three does appear in the foreground.[126] The hunt scene is reprised in miniature in the columns surrounding the Hebrew charts for the Christian calendar. There the horned man and one dog occupy one small frame, and a dog chases a stag and a doe in the next.[127] No particular style of dress, hunter, or quarry dominates in the sifre evronot, but the presence of the imagery is pronounced. This choice of theme is particularly noteworthy because aristocratic hunting, on horseback and accompanied by hounds, was not a common pastime for European Jews of the early modern era.

Along with almost every other element in sifre evronot, the hunt scenes attest to the layered, intricate, and very complicated process of cultural sharing between Jews and their Christian neighbors. It is not sufficient to point out the obvious fact that Jewish scribes and illustrators of early modern times often consciously modeled their drawings on those found in Christian books, appropriating an iconography that was risibly foreign to common Jewish experience. Instead we must try to understand the likely meaning of such scenes for their creators and users. The hunting scenes, particularly those with hares as the quarry, conveyed a subversive eschatological message to Jewish readers: that

FIG. 4.26. David and Goliath. *Sefer evronot*, 1717. Cincinnati, Klau Library, Hebrew Union College–Jewish Institute of Religion ms 903, fol. 54r.

they would survive and escape the terrible pursuit by their historical foes.[128] Indeed, this message is conveyed explicitly in one seventeenth-century sefer evronot where the hunt appears in three images. In the first, three dogs pursue a stag, and one has caught the stag by his hind leg. Several folios later, the stag has leaped free of his pursuer. In the last of the hunt-related pictures, the stag stands triumphantly alone at the center.[129]

A similar analysis of the meaning of the hunt scenes in Jewish manuscripts can be confirmed by the lavishly and imaginatively illustrated sefer evronot by Pinhas of Halberstadt from the early eighteenth century. Many of Pinhas's illustrations appear to have been copied directly from contemporary Christian models. In the case of the elaborate hunting scene, in which a hound chases a deer while a mounted nobleman shoots a boar, we can see the process by which Pinhas injected new meaning into the borrowed iconography.[130] Pinhas captioned his hunt scene with a verse from Isaiah: "I will rejoice greatly in God, my soul will be joyful with my Lord, for He has clothed me with the *garments of salvation*" (Isaiah 61:10). The verse that follows this one in Isaiah expresses this

notion of eventual triumph even more clearly: "God will cause righteousness and praise to flourish before the nations." Here we have an explicit interpretation of the hunt as the struggle of Jews to elude the snares of their tormentors in this world.

A variation on this theme appears in a few manuscripts as a confrontation between David and Goliath. David, dressed as a peasant lad, gathers stones for his slingshot, while Goliath is clad in scaled armor, holding a long pike and shield in his hands.[131] Garments of privilege and power clothed the aristocratic hunters now; in the messianic future, however, those garments of salvation will clothe the Jews. Other images make similar suggestions, but this one sets forth most directly the intentions of the scribes and artists.[132]

The inclusion of illustrations in concise ibbur treatises marked their development into complete and independent works with all the features that mark an early modern book. The illustration tradition in sifre evronot lasted for over three centuries, complementing the text and providing valuable insights into early modern Ashkenazic culture. It was a culture at once suffused in nostalgia for a lost past, with abiding reverence for its local traditions, and burdened with an acute awareness of its precarious place in the larger Christian world of early modern Europe. By inventing a new genre of text and illustration, the scholars, students, and scribes of evronot not only asserted their mastery over a Jewish tradition; they also provided a creative response and alternative to Christian calendar culture and its iconography.

{ 5 }

Keeping Christian Time in Jewish Calendars

What (I wondered) should we say on St. John's Day if the balance of
the rent were not forthcoming for the landlord?

Memoirs of Ber of Bolechow, 1723–1805

IN the cold winter of fifteenth-century Germany, a Jew presented his Christmas dilemma to a rabbinic scholar. It had been customary to send gifts to the priests and local authorities in honor of New Year's Day. Was a Jew permitted to acknowledge the Christian calendar in that way, given that New Year's marked the eighth day after Christmas? The rabbi reviewed various opinions and noted a useful strategy: if possible, the gift should be sent slightly in advance of New Year's Day. This plan would allow the Jew to circumvent the problem of marking a Christian religious day. If that were not possible, however, the Jew would be permitted to send the New Year's gift on New Year's Day, for the day had acquired a cultural significance independent of its religious aspects, that is, it marked the beginning of a new civil year.

This exchange, preserved in the responsa collection of R. Israel Isserlein (d. 1460), *Terumat ha-deshen*, captures the delicate balancing act required of Jews who lived among Christians in the premodern era. Jews had to weigh the legacy of their religious requirements against the customs of the lords of the land, in a manner that respected the religious and social sensitivities of all parties concerned. The rabbinic scholar considered the cost of delaying the gift ("It might cause hatred") against the prohibition of supporting idolatrous customs. He ultimately decided that it was possible to live amicably with the Christian neighbors with minimal damage to tradition. The language of the responsum itself distilled the ambiguities inherent in the Jewish situation. It referred to some of the Christian holidays in pejorative language: Christmas was called *nittel*, a common Jewish replacement term for that holiday, and New Year's is referred to as Kalend, a reference to Roman pagan festivals.[1]

This tradition of repudiation arose from the need of a minority population

to honor the religious culture of the powerful majority while simultaneously resisting its message. Jewish communal record books often noted special gifts given to powerful Christians annually on the New Year or holidays, in what had become another form of taxation. Even had they wished to remain ignorant of these dates, Jews could not afford to do so.

Calendar literature reflected this central paradox of Jewish existence. It embodied the need to understand, internalize, and instruct in the culture of the other. Yet precisely because it acknowledged the calendar of the other in all its intricacy, the Jewish calendar advanced strategies to counter the power of that culture. Jewish calendars and their literature walked the line between engagement and detachment, between promoting a body of knowledge and simultaneously subverting its message by negating its central teachings and mocking its sacred totems. While Jewish calendars might seem at first glance to reflect and mandate Jewish separation and distinctiveness, a closer inspection reveals a complex story of cultures so deeply intertwined that they could never be completely unraveled.

Jewish calendar literature included so much detailed and nuanced information about the Christian calendar that it could have served Christians quite well in translation. Virtually every European Jewish calendar carried a full Christian calendar in its core section; sifre evronot, too, contained information about how to construct and observe the Christian calendar. The reasons for including this information are obvious: the rhythms of economic activity in European culture were tied to its calendar, not only to the seasons of nature, but also to its feasts and holy days.

As a religious minority, Jews conducted business and pledged to honor tacit or explicit agreements on Christian holidays. A fourteenth-century Jewish money lender recorded in Hebrew the loans that were to be repaid by his Christian clients on "Lorenz tog," "Jorg tog," and other local saints' days.[2] To justify an edict of expulsion of Jews from Tuscany in the sixteenth century, Cosimo, duke of Tuscany, listed alleged violations of their charter: "Jews have made loans on days prohibited by their charters, that is, on *Christian festival and holy days*" [my emphasis].[3] Tuscan Jews were expected to know when these days fell, and to refrain from engaging in commerce with Christians then. One Jewish banker admitted to the charge but claimed he had done so with the express permission of the vicar. He had made very small loans to poor people who needed it for bread, violating those holidays solely out of compassion for the Christian poor who could not afford to lose a day's wages by coming to him on regular working

days. Sixteenth-century Jews in Rome stipulated that they would pay rent by *natale*.[4] Ber of Bolechow, the eighteenth-century merchant and memoirist, recorded rents and debts fixed by Christian partners on religious dates: "What (I wondered) should we say on St. John's Day if the balance of the rent were not forthcoming for the landlord?"[5]

Profound cultural consequences arose from this need to enclose another calendrical system within the pages of the Jewish calendar. The architects of the Christian calendar had specifically designed it to disengage from, to compete with, and ultimately to supersede the Jewish calendar. The story of how the birth, crucifixion, and resurrection of Jesus came to replace the major festivals of the Jewish calendar that commemorated the Exodus from Egypt and the giving of the Law at Sinai is well known. These changes evolved over time, accompanied by dissension and resistance that lingered for centuries. They ensured the social segregation of the two religious communities and produced acute discomfort on both sides.[6]

The Christian Bible is reticent on the question of Jewish calendar observances, and the mandate to separate them rests on two rather obscure statements in the letters of Paul.[7] It was not until the second century that the Church fathers began the task of establishing a truly separate calendar, fixing Sunday as the Lord's Day over the Jewish Sabbath, setting the feast days, and inaugurating the long and bitter controversy over the date of Easter. This centuries-long dispute was crucial to the entire enterprise of the Christian computus. Were it not for the need to elude the Jewish calendar, the Christian calendar could rest comfortably on the system it had inherited from Rome.

At the heart of the Easter dispute was the simple fact that Jesus was a Jew, and his death occurred on a date that could only be affixed to the Jewish calendar, the fourteenth of Nissan. For centuries, some Christians (the Quartodecimans or "advocates of the fourteenth" of Nissan) insisted that this date remain central to Christian observance. Their adherence was not simply a question of the date: Passover itself was still a central holy day for them, a day to commemorate the liberation of the people from bondage, celebrated by the sacrifice of the paschal lamb. Their difference with Jews resided in the symbolism of the lamb. For these Christians, the true Paschal Lamb was Jesus, and his Passion stood at the center of their calendar and of their faith. The date 14 Nissan was vital to their understanding of their religion: in their view, it positioned Christianity above Judaism by claiming Christians as the true chosen people within the Hebrew-biblical framework. The churches that did not want to sever Easter

from its original biblical roots continued to refer to it as Pasch/Pascha, a term closely related to the Hebrew word for Passover, Pesah.

The Western Church gradually distanced itself from this approach, emphasizing the Resurrection over the Passion, and insisting that its proper celebration must always occur on the Lord's Day, Sunday. Embarrassed by the need to rely on the Jews to set the date in Nissan, Christian calculators attacked the Jewish calendar, arguing that Jews no longer ensured that Nissan was the first month after the spring equinox. In the third century, Dionysius, bishop of Alexandria, developed a calendar based on the argument that Christians must find their own, more correct, Nissan. In 325, the Council of Nicea decided that Easter could never be celebrated on the Jewish date of 14 Nissan even if that day were a Sunday and it met all the other criteria. This decision, however, did nothing to resolve the confusion over how to provide a recurring table for Easter dates. For centuries, different centers followed different traditions. So great was the confusion that theologians resorted to telling of miracles that confirmed the schemes of particular computists.[8]

The Christian attempt to establish an Easter calendar totally independent of Jewish influence resulted in a fundamental paradox. As Eviatar Zerubavel noted: "In order to make sure that it would *never* coincide with its original precursor, the Church has committed itself to moving it from one date to another every year. Thus . . . it has only managed to immortalize its awareness of—as well as actual dependence on—the latter, . . . a most ironical reminder of some fundamental Jewish influence."[9]

One would think that once the question of how to calculate Easter was settled, the matter would have been relegated to the memories of a remote past. But in the decades preceding the Gregorian calendar reform of 1582, the question of the Christian Easter and its relationship to the Jewish calendar was raised anew. Pope Leo X sent letters to potential participants in the Lateran Council in 1514 in which he defended the need for calendar reform. He noted that errors in the calculation of Easter gave Jews and heretics reason to ridicule Christians. (In the sixteenth century, regardless of whether it was simply a rhetorical vestige or a true source of anxiety, the church still professed concern lest its calendar fall short in Jewish eyes.[10]) One critic of the Gregorian reform, Ignatius the Nestorian, argued that with this reform Easter would sometimes fall on the same day as celebrations by Jews. He also criticized the calculations in Gregory's compendium because they did not take into account the fact that Jews calculated dates from the previous evening rather than from the day.[11] The

Orthodox patriarch Jeremiah, too, observed that if Passover were to fall on the Friday immediately preceding Easter, Easter would have to be deferred a week, because "It is not to be celebrated the same day that the Jews celebrate."[12] These examples demonstrate how much polemical energy still pulsed beneath the surface of the concise calendar references.

The intense focus on calendar reform in early modern Europe magnified the polemical aspects, and the ancient Jewish traditions of disparagement or outright insult of the opposing calendar provided the vocabulary.[13] Heirs to a legacy of religious animosity and rivalry, early modern Jews embedded sharply polemical references to Christian practices within their calendars. Jewish calendars not only alluded to the relative novelty of the Christian calendar, to its invented and artificial nature, but also criticized, by extension, these inadequacies in the Christian religion vis-à-vis the Jewish.

Although most Jewish calendars and treatises did not specify the theological underpinnings for the Christian holidays, they provided detailed instructions for calculating when they fell. These formed a separate section in evronot variously titled *luah he-haga'ot* (calendar of gentiles) and *luhot she'eno nimolim* (calendar of the uncircumcised). They covered the calculations needed to ascertain the holidays of the fixed, or Christmas, cycle, as well as those that revolved around the moveable, or Easter, cycle. They covered the main saints' days in each month, the "Quatember" calculations, and the differences between Christian denominational calendar systems. All of these features testified to the comprehensive knowledge of the Christian calendar that Jewish publishers and authors provided their customers. The books expressed the hope that every Jew, "from great to small," would be able to compose his own Christian calendar from these instructions.[14]

The Classical Rabbinic Legacy

The centuries-long religious polemic between Jews and Christians gave early modern Jews a rich vocabulary for subverting Christian views and practices. For instance, the Talmud's lesson that "all derision (*leitzanuta*) is forbidden except for derision against idolatry" evolved into a well-defined system in which derogatory terms were substituted for words associated with the idolatrous religion and its sancta.[15] The Talmud even provided helpful examples of wordplay that inverted the meaning of regular terms into demeaning epithets. "If the pagans call it *Bet galya* (House of Revelation), you call it *Bet karya* (House of Con-

cealment); [if they call it] *en kol* (the all seeing eye), [you call it] *en qotz* (eye of the thorn)."[16] Accordingly, the rabbinic appellation for pagan festival days was *yeme eyd*, literally, days of calamity, or *haga*, denoting a pagan festival.[17] The Mishnah and the Talmud prohibited Jews from entering into commercial activities with idolaters on the day or days proximate to the Roman pagan festivals: "Kalenda [the pagan New Year], Saturnalia [days of revelry around December 17], Kratesis [days celebrating conquest]," and other days on which Romans were likely to offer sacrifices to their gods, including days celebrating the birth, ascension, or death of a monarch, were called *yeme eyd*.[18]

The Talmud stated that the days of Kalends and Saturnalia were originally universal festivals instituted by "primordial Adam" and were linked to the winter equinox and the associated shortening and subsequent lengthening of the days—that is, they celebrated nature's rhythms and were not solely an innovation of the pagan culture. But the Talmud concluded that "he [Adam] had fixed them for the sake of Heaven, but the [heathens] appointed them for the sake of idolatry."[19] In other words, that pagans had consecrated certain days "for the sake of idolatry" meant that the days had become tainted with pagan observances and meanings. A Jewish anti-Christian polemicist formulated this idea of contamination of time even more sharply: "The people of She'ol asked R. Nathan, 'Why does it not say "*ki tov* (and it was good)" concerning the second day of creation?' He replied: Because G-d knows the future and what will happen, and he saw that a large number of people will be misled by the water [of baptism] and will be ruined and lost, therefore he did not write *ki tov*, as the waters were created on the second [day]."[20] The calendar of nature was a palimpsest on which layers of meaning could be inscribed. Jews could not simply ignore Christian "inscriptions." They were enjoined to be fully aware of them, and to avoid certain types of contact during times that had been appropriated and designated sacred by non-Jews.

Medieval Jews inherited a set of talmudic injunctions regulating trade with pagans that would have rendered their economic existence in the Christian world impossible had it been closely applied to commerce with Christians. Its strictures against even the most circuitous support of idolatrous festivals, such as engaging in commerce with idolaters before, during and after those days, would have prevented Jews from participating in almost all markets and fairs, their economic lifeline. R. Gershom Me'or Ha-Golah (960–1028) argued that the talmudic prohibition was neglected because "most of the days of the year *are* their holidays."[21] He felt that the Christian calendar overflowed with so many

sacred days that the timescape was completely saturated, and thereby appeared to justify the abandonment of that strategy altogether.[22]

The injunction against conducting commercial activities before, during, and after festival days of idolators caused medieval halakhists great discomfort. In order to reconcile the law with the actual practice of Jews in their time, they either mitigated the idolatrous status of Christianity, or eased the scope of the Jewish prohibition.[23] Historians of medieval halakhah and society generally agree that the Jews of medieval Ashkenaz disregarded the talmudic prohibitions of *yeme eydehem* while the halakhists struggled to justify their conduct.[24] Some rabbis felt so uncomfortable about the flagrant and constant contradiction between customs followed by the people and the stringencies in the Babylonian Talmud that they eschewed altogether the intensive study of *Avodah zarah (Idolatry)*, the tractate containing most of these laws.[25]

The discourse of Jews in the High Middle Ages was full of slighting references to the Christian holidays. Rash"i (1040–1105) referred to Sundays as "calamitous day of the Christian," as well as to "calamitous days of saints," in which he included Christmas and other holidays.[26] A twelfth-century questioner requested a definition of contemporary yeme eyd. In the course of his query he employed several apparently established epithets to translate the mishnaic terms: "Kalenda is *niflatz* ... the days they commemorate for the disciples of the condemned to crucifixion, such as *yakme* [James?]; Matthew; *ti'uv hadia*, and similar abominations."[27] Shlomo Eidelberg identifies *niflatz* as a corruption of *Nouvel-âge*, the celebration of the New Year, and *ti'uv hadia* as an altered form of *ti'uv haria* (disgusting excrement), where *haria* is a play on Maria, a derogatory term for holidays related to Mary.[28] This expression can be found in the medieval compendium of anti-Christian polemics, *Sefer Nizzahon (Nizzahon Vetus)* and was quoted from there by Sebastian Münster and indignantly cited by Luther: "A certain Jewish author ... referred to the Virgin Mary as *Haria*, that is excrement."[29]

R. Samuel ben Meir, a twelfth-century tosafist (Talmud commentator), cited an important ruling in the name of his grandfather, Rash"i: "The law prohibits commerce only on the days that are devoted to the *notzri* (Jesus of Nazareth) such as *nittel* or *qetzah* (Christmas or Easter) (in Sema"g: *qeisah*); but other days of their calamity have no substance."[30] The term nittel for Christmas probably originated as a straight transliteration of *dies natale*.[31] Eventually it took on a pejorative meaning. When spelled with a *tav*, its meaning became "the hanged one," a derogatory reference to Jesus who was crucified.[32] *Qetzah, qesah* or *qei-*

sah, polemical distortions of *Pesah*, meaning thorns, were terms that Jews adopted to avoid using "Pascha"—the word that referred to Easter in Latin and Eastern calendars.[33]

The twelfth-century query cited earlier concluded with the question: "When we purchase fields and vineyards from them, as it states, 'And he writes [the deed] and deposits it in their courts,' are we permitted to have the [Christian] priest write the deed in his script, because they always date their deeds *mi-zman hayava tzleva* (from the year of the one who was condemned to crucifixion), is it prohibited or not; and if there is no mention of idolatry, is it permitted? May the master clarify all these matters."[34] This query may contain the earliest Jewish reference to the question of whether Jews may use the Christian calendar and chronology in their dating of documents, or whether using that chronology, anno Domini, constituted a tacit agreement with the Christian accounting and evaluation of Jesus' life.

The various justifications for rejecting the rabbinic prohibitions were both central to the medieval Jewish legal experts' ontological and practical evaluation of Christians and Christianity and pertinent to the legacy that medieval Ashkenazic culture transmitted to its early modern successors. As we have seen, this Ashkenazic inheritance included a strategy of deriding Christian holy days with a cutting turn of phrase or with clever, disparaging word substitutions.

These legacies were tended and nurtured in sifre evronot and Jewish calendars. But why did these forms of invective persevere into early modern times? The answer lies with the rise of the European calendar itself as the central focus of religious, cultural, and political tension in this period. Even as reformers in German lands demanded an end to the cult of saints and a diminution of related observances, the counter-Reformation church renewed its emphasis on just those beleaguered aspects of the calendar, sowing the seeds for new conflicts.

The tiny but pointed barbs that appear in Jewish calendars and their literature reflect another dimension of Jewish-Christian relations in early modern German lands. Luther and his contemporaries argued to the German princes that toleration of blasphemy directly endangered the welfare of Christians, not just theologically but physically as well. They construed famines, plagues, and wars to be divine punishment for tolerating blasphemy, and indeed, the fear of Jewish blasphemy emerged as a central motif in German Reformation thinking about Jews around the turn of the sixteenth century.[35] Yet blasphemy is a notoriously slippery category; its definition depends on the context for the ut-

terer and the hearer. One man's casual remark is another's grave insult. Any strategy adopted by Jews to resist the implicit lure and explicit overtures of Christian culture could have been interpreted as offensive to Christians. Jews were expected to refrain from mocking beliefs they did not hold to be true, to relate to these Christian beliefs with proper dignity, and to avoid expressing their countervailing opinions in public. When by the sixteenth century live, staged public disputations ceased to characterize Jewish-Christian relations, subtle mockery survived and thrived, representing a new phase in which the resistance to the dominant Christian culture became more a matter of tone than of substance.

The Christian Calendar through Jewish Eyes

Sifre evronot generally divided their exposition of the Christian calendar into two sections. The first provided an introduction to its structure and workings; the second contained a fully laid out Christian calendar. The fixed (Christmas) cycle would be presented in its proper place, with the reader already having been alerted in the introduction that the moveable (Easter) cycle could not be as easily arranged and set forth in perpetuity. While Christmas was celebrated on December 25 every year, the date of Easter, along with the entire cycle that depended on it, varied from year to year. Authors of sifre evronot attempted to teach Jewish readers the difference between the two cycles. As one explained: "The *haga'ot* (Christian holidays) that fall each month remain fixed even in leap years, except for 'Mathäus' as I already mentioned. But the five holidays *Fasnacht* (Shrove Tuesday), *Ostern* (Easter), *Opfahrt* (Ascension), *Pfingsten* (Whitsuntide, Pentecost), and *Leichnum* (Corpus Christi), do not come at the same fixed time of the month and they operate according to other rules, as I will show."[36]

The introduction to the Christian calendar followed the discussion of the Jewish calendar structure, usually with little polemical fanfare. Thus a typical segue: "Until now I have written for you . . . how to calculate the molad . . . and to weigh (check) your calculations on 'scales of justice.' And now I shall also write for you how to know the Christian calendar, and to know how to fix the date of the birth of Jesus, which is their New Year, called in their language *Jahrestag*, as well as the holidays of the saints that occur every year, according to the months of our year."[37]

Occasionally, authors included more pointed remarks that were rooted in old traditions. In a seventeenth-century sefer evronot, the Central European

FIG. 5.1. Squatting figure separates Jewish calendar from Christian. Note the highlighting by the censor (or Christian owner). *Sefer evronot*, 1674. Bayerische Staatsbibliothek München ms Cod. Hebr. 394, fol. 29r.

scribe cited from an "old manuscript" evronot that he attributed to David of Lublin:

> These are the words of David. I found it written that their calendar was originally organized on a perpetual cycle of nineteen years, which is the correct cycle according to the secret of the intercalation. They don't know the reason [why they deviate from it], although the one who fixed their calamitous days did know it, because he was a man of our laws. Some say he was R. Simon Pakuli, who was coerced to provide this order for them against his will, and for the benefit of Israel, as is written in the book *Toledot oto ha-ish* (Narratives of That Man).[38] However, he did not reveal this secret to them, and so I have found in *Yesod olam*.
>
> If you ask their tonsured ones [monks, or perhaps priests] and the learned ones among them concerning the intercalation, and its customs and its order, you will not find the correct explanation among them, for they are not a wise nation. Until here [from David of Lublin], and I will explain in greater detail."[39]

The same scribe wrote an unusually testy characterization after his description of the five moveable feasts: "Behold, before you [I have placed] a précis of the debased and fallen foundations [of their calendar]."[40] But then again, even Venetian printers of Jewish wall calendars, who worked under the watchful eyes of authorities during the Inquisition, printed the moveable cycle of Christian

holidays under the heading *hagim ha-mitmotitim*, which can be translated as unstable holidays, or as holidays that are decaying or declining.[41]

Many scribes of evronot abbreviated the instructions for calculating the Christian calendar, telling the reader, "If you want to know their calamitous days you need to know the last holiday of the past year, on what day [of the week] and the day in the month it occurred."[42] So common was this shortcut of building on a previous year's calendar that a popular eighteenth-century treatise appended to a printed sefer evronot promised to teach each reader "to combine the Christian calendar with our calendar *without having to look at last year's calendar at all*" (my emphasis).[43] A mid-eighteenth-century publisher of a Jewish calendar treatise containing a calendar for fifty years solved the problem of the fixed and moveable Christian holidays by listing the moveable dates at the beginning of each Jewish year's entry, while listing the fixed holidays at the end of the volume in a separate list.[44] Another convenient way to instruct Jews in the Christian calendar tied each of the dates of the moveable cycle to a date in the Jewish calendar.[45] In a manuscript addendum to a printed treatise on the calendar from the late eighteenth century, the scribe sectioned off a separate manuscript addendum with a prominent display title: "Calendar of the Uncircumcised."[46]

The scribes of evronot, and, to a lesser extent, printers of Jewish calendars, employed the contemporary local (non-Jewish) vernacular in their works. They used the same words as their Christian neighbors to denote a Christian holy day or to designate local saints' days. By changing a letter to alter the meaning, they were able to both present and subvert the sacred times of Christians. The two major Christian holidays, Christmas and Easter, each provoked a cluster of pejorative names. Jewish calendar makers referred to Christmas in early modern sifre evronot and calendars as *nittel*.[47] Some German Jewish calendars noted Christmas by inserting *wein nacht* (night of wine) for *Weinacht*, the German word for Christmas.[48] Still others mentioned both names, *nittel* and *wein nacht*, suggesting, wryly, that the authors believed "Christmas" simply meant "night of wine."[49] This plasticity in terminology is seen in a set of manuscript calendars written by the same hand over several years. The author took note of *wei nachten* ויי נאכטן in the year 1739; *wein nachten* וויין נאכטן in 1730, 1734, and 1746; and *wein nacht* וויין נאכט in 1742.[50] There is no consistency; the exact spelling was a matter of indifference, sloppiness, or copying from different models.

Easter (German, *Ostern*) was called *qesah* in most routine descriptions of the Christian moveable calendar.[51] This too was not a matter of absolute con-

sistency, for many scribes of evronot varied the designation within the same manuscript.[52] One evronot writer who had difficulty figuring out why Shrovetide sometimes began on a day other than Tuesday sought out the answer from a priest (Shrove Tuesday was a fast day in the eastern rite, a carnival in the west):

> *Fasnacht* (Shrove Tuesday) and Easter are always set so that at least four and a half weeks elapse between them, in order that they should have at least three meat eating days in each month. I heard from R. Loewe Oppenheim, who heard from his father-in-law Zanvil Bing, *z"l*, who heard from a priest the reason that *Fasnacht* sometimes falls eight days into the month, unlike what is written in our books. The Gentile told him the reason is as follows: If the molad falls before noon, then *Fasnacht* occurs on *Rosh Hodesh* so that they should be able to eat meat one day each month; but if the molad falls after noon, then *Fasnacht* is deferred until the eighth day of the month in order to allow them to eat meat one day each month, for the meat they eat on Tuesday is counted [included] since the *molad* falls after noon. And a word to the wise is sufficient.[53]

Some three-quarters of a century later, when R. Zvi Hirsch Koidonover fled Eastern Europe for Frankfurt, he copied a sefer evronot he found there. It included a similar explanation attributed to a priest. Koidonover transmitted the Oppenheim-Bing tradition concerning Shrovetide which provided a subtext of Christian gluttony for meat as the true reason for a calendrical deviation.[54]

Marian festivals and saints' days comprised another category of significant dates on the Christian calendar. Far from falling into disuse with the waning of the medieval period, these holy days were revived in the early modern period.[55] The Protestant challenge to the culture surrounding the veneration of saints—including pilgrimages to their shrines and the sacralization of their relics—threatened these traditions. In response, the Catholic Church revitalized them, producing stories of new miracles so that long-neglected saints now became the objects of even grander cults. A profusion of new sites of pilgrimage, new forms of Eucharistic devotion, and the Marian cult in Bavaria arose to serve the faithful. Corpus Christi processions grew in grandeur. In southern Germany, pilgrimages and urban processions grew increasingly important, serving to revive enthusiasm for the Catholic Church. (They were soon co-opted by the states,

which saw in this revival a means of strengthening their own identity and sanctifying their claims over their territory.)[56]

Despite Protestant opposition, then, the Marian and saintly cults flourished anew through the eighteenth century. In fact, the cult of Mary intensified in the early modern period to the extent that in some places it threatened to surpass devotion to her son. Several major holidays relate to Mary. March 25 marks the "Annunciation of the Blessed Virgin Mary," the day that Mary was informed that she would be carrying a child as a virgin (Luke 1:26–38). August 15, the Dormition or Assumption of Mary, was the day that Mary was said to have ascended to heaven, and was marked in German Christian and Jewish calendars as Maria Himmelfahrt, the Assumption of Mary. Of all the expressions of Marian piety, this one evoked the strongest anti-Jewish associations from Christians, who had long depicted Jews as harassing and insulting Mary even on her death bed.[57] *Lichtmess* (Candlemas, Feast of Purification), celebrated on February 2, marks the fortieth day after Jesus' birth. A Jewish woman who had given birth to a boy was obligated to bring a sacrifice of purification to the Temple on the fortieth day (Leviticus 12:1). On that day, according to Luke 2:21, Mary not only entered the Temple to purify herself; she presented her son there as well. This holiday was often marked by ceremonies in which candles were blessed and held aloft during a procession. In German lands, the blessed candles were carried from the church to the home, extending the purity and sanctity of the religious space into people's dwellings. (This is the root of the custom of "churching," a ceremony in which medieval women formally left the childbirth bed and reentered society.)

Lichtmess was the day between winter and summer, a time to remove the trappings of darkness and prepare for the light of the new season to come.[58] It also became the day when various negative spirits were purged, and for Jews it acquired more sinister overtones. For example, Lichtmess was the day that Nuremberg expelled its Jews in 1499.

Where Christian society saw an opportunity for anti-Jewish action, Jews responded with polemical derision:

> You may argue that he was not defiled in her womb since Mary had ceased to menstruate and it was the spirit that entered her; subsequently he came out unaccompanied by pain or the defilement of blood. The answer is that you yourselves admit that she brought the sacrifice of a childbearing woman. Now, it is clear that this sacrifice is brought as

a consequence of impurity. . . . Indeed, to this day, they call the day that she came to the Temple and brought her sacrifice, "Light" [*Lichtmess*], and they fast for the forty days that she remained impure from Christmas till "Light" as it is written, "If a woman be delivered and bear a manchild, then she shall be unclean seven days" [Lev. 12:2]. The additional "three and thirty days" [Lev. 12:4] makes forty.[59]

In medieval polemical literature, Jews impugned Mary, denied her status as a virgin, rejected the doctrine of Immaculate Conception, and by extension, Jesus' status as a son of God. The conflict over Christian doctrinal beliefs relating to Mary, most particularly those relating to Mary's status as a virgin, had come under Jewish attack almost since the inception of those doctrines. Christians took particular umbrage at Jewish views of Mary's impure sexuality, because they touched the heart of the Christian ascetic tradition, not to mention central doctrines in Christian faith and its most adored personification of purity.

Jewish calendar literature contracted and enfolded the entire sweep of the Jewish-Christian controversy into its coded words. Several sifre evronot manuscripts designate Mary as *teluya*, for example, in descriptions of Christian holy days devoted to Mary.[60] This feminine form of *talui*, the hanged one, provides an unusual perspective on the Jewish perception of Mary, although it distorted her history. By using the feminine form of a derogatory designation for Jesus, the users portrayed Mary as being just as important as her son. At the same time, however, they were evincing ignorance of or indifference to the fate of Mary, who was of course never crucified.

The choice of the word "virgin" or "woman" to designate Marian holidays on the calendar was fraught with polemical considerations. From the time of the conception of Jesus, many Jewish calendars never referred to Mary as "virgin." (In some printed wall calendars, Mary is referred to throughout as virgin, perhaps in deference to the public nature of this form of calendar.)[61] Other calendar makers seem to have marked their days without much careful attention to the matter.[62]

Most discriminating were the texts of sifre evronot that designated September 8 as *leidat betulah* (Birth of the Virgin); and November 21 as *betulah* (virgin, when Mary entered the Temple at age 3), yet from March 25, the date on the Christian calendar celebrates the Annunciation, identified Mary in one word: *isha* (woman). Since this date marked the time that Mary would have conceived her child, she could no longer be considered a virgin by Jews.[63] These

designations differentiated between the festivals that marked days when Jews could acknowledge that Mary was a virgin, that is, during her birth and childhood, and holidays after the Annunciation, when she was a "woman" and no longer a virgin in their eyes. The three letters that form the Hebrew word *isha* in those evronot manuscripts encompassed Jewish comprehension of and resistance to the claims of Christian religious culture. In fact, "*isha*" may be the shortest polemical text in the entire Jewish-Christian encounter.

Aside from the major holidays, Jewish calendars gave saints' days pride of place in the "gentile" column. An integral part of Christian liturgical calendars, commemorating hundreds of figures over many centuries, saints' days proliferated in Europe to the point where there were many more days devoted to saints than days in the year.[64] Comprehensive Christian calendars overlaid several saints' names for each day.[65] Jewish calendars, by contrast, tended to be extremely selective, listing only the most universally important or locally significant days. Since the observance of these days changed the patterns of daily life for Christians, it was vital for Jewish peddlers and merchants to know their dates. A random sampling of Jewish calendars shows that even the tersest calendars included plenty of entries in this category.

The meaning of a brief notation about a saints' day to a Jew reading it on his calendar in the early modern period can be illuminated with some particular examples. The Catholic Church commemorated on October 21 the death of the martyred virgin Ursula and her eleven thousand virgin companions (the headquarters for the celebration was in Cologne).[66] Ursula's legend arose in the early modern period, and a monastic order, the Ursulines, was founded in 1535.[67] The Ursulines, unlike other orders, were allowed to engage in public displays of devotion, with Ursuline communities attending services in decorous processions outside their convents. One priest praised the Ursuline sisters for "serving as lights in the world," inspiring women and girls with their examples of piety.[68]

With a small exchange of one letter and deletion of a word, however, one late-sixteenth-century sefer evronot transformed the eleven thousand virgins into the "eleven tainted ones (י״א פסולים)." The note clarified: "Our teacher R. Isaac Linz said that one should not write here 'eleven tainted ones' lest a gentile find it. On calendars one writes instead of eleven tainted ones, 'Ursulin.'"[69] Thus the Ursulines become emblematic of the Christian saints and Mary, figures at once awesome for their sanctity and sacrifices in the Christian worldview, and precisely because of that forbidden sanctity, to be resisted in the fiercest terms by Jews. Yet the Jewish aversion to celebrating virgin martyrs is not without

complexity: in many German evronot manuscripts (although nearly nowhere else in Jewish literature), Jephthah's daughter is featured as an iconic figure.[70] That is, even as they recoiled from the claims of the Ursulines, Jews in the early modern period maintained the image of their own Jewish virgin martyr.

The terse comment deriding Ursula also illuminates the relationship between evronot and luhot, between manuscript material that was considered private, safe from the prying eyes of outsiders, and the more public printed material that was fair game for critics such as Hebraist scholars, censors, and Christian rulers. (It is unclear whether the commenter intended to draw a distinction here between manuscript and print, although it is likely.) In another manuscript evronot, the day celebrated as St. Thomas' Day was marked in Hebrew with the word *tum'ot* (טומאות), meaning impure. A censor later outlined the offending words in red ink.[71] No such pejorative reference appears in printed calendars.

Another locus of ambiguous notations comes on the day celebrated by the church as "All Saints' Day." The word in Hebrew used for martyrs was *qedoshim*, holy ones, and the straight translation in evronot and luhot was *kol ha-qedoshim* (all the saints). Many evronot and even printed luhot, however, spelled the word by omitting the Hebrew letter *vav* (an optional letter, aiding in pronunciation when vowel dots were omitted), which left the word open to an alternative pronunciation, *qedeshim*, which means "those given over to unholiness."[72] By omitting the letter the authors left room for the subversive reading, one noted with indignation by later censors.

Similarly, several days were designated *Kreuztag*, celebrating miracles relating to the cross: one of these was September 14, *Kreuztag der erhebung* (Latin: *exaltatio cruces*). The term *kreuz*, however, was always replaced in Jewish calendars by the Hebrew-Yiddish word *tzelem*, meaning simply a form.[73] *Lichtmess* (Candlemas), too, was noted in one evronot with a Hebrew spelling that could be read as "candle-death."[74]

No two Jewish calendars listed the exact same saints' days, since observances varied widely according to locale; a complete list of names that appeared in Jewish sources would be comparable to that of the encyclopedic lists of saints' days for any Christian milieu.[75] The full meaning of the calendar entries can only be grasped in the context of the lived experience of the Jews who dwelled among Christians. Even though many of these special Christian days were fraught with anti-Jewish tension, Jews observed their Christian neighbors celebrating them with magisterial ceremony. Jews recoiled from acknowledging these Christian

holidays, but also struggled to maintain distance from the appealing and persuasive aspects. Consequently, even as Jews repudiated the holidays, they subconsciously adopted some of the practices they saw around them.[76] Jewish calendar literature of this period reflected this cultural tension. Jews absorbed Christian culture deeply, at the same time as they reprised medieval strategies to maintain their own distinctiveness.

The introduction of the Gregorian calendar fueled dissension within the Christian world over the start of the New Year, and this debate found a prominent place in Jewish calendar literature. As one seventeenth-century calendar informed its Jewish users in Yiddish, "The Lutherans count 1676 until Monday 8 Shevat; the Catholics count 1676 until Friday 27 Tevet," and similarly, "The Catholics count 1686 until Tuesday 16 Tevet, from then on 1687; the Lutherans count 1686 until Friday 25 Tevet."[77] In the section titled *inyan he-haga'ot* (matters pertaining to the gentile festivals), the calendar maker also attempted to sort through the confusion over the Julian and Gregorian calendars:

> Here is the order of the Christian calendar, their month-names and festivals as they currently observe them. For in the year [5]343 [1583 C.E.] a controversy erupted among the Christians over the insertion of ten days, and it lasted until [5]460 [1700 C.E.] when they agreed to celebrate their holidays at the same time without some being earlier or later, except for the Northern Kings who until this day refuse to move their calendar back so that all the holidays and months in the north fall ten days later than the rest of the Christians. I present here the dates for the holidays of the rest of the Christians, and from this you can calculate the dates in the north as well, ten days later than those given here.[78]

Central and Eastern European Jewish calendars often included Protestant, Catholic, and Orthodox calendars—for both practical and polemical reasons. Jews were highly mobile; merchants on business trips often needed to refer to several calendars over the course of one journey. At the same time, alerting Jewish readers to the multiplicity of calendars in the Christian world highlighted the stability of the Jewish calendar, which like the Jewish people themselves had endured in the face of multiple and lengthy displacements.[79]

· · ·

Some sifre evronot copied in the early modern period included portions of a somewhat obscure text of Abraham ibn Ezra's *Iggeret ha-Shabbat*.[80] This medi-

eval poem, which opens with the line "I am Sabbath, crown of faith . . . and between God and his children I am a sign of the eternal covenant," was conceived and written for exegetical, rather than polemical, purposes.[81] To readers in the early modern period, the traditional Jewish sabbath could stand as a metaphor for the entire Jewish calendar. Sabbath (and by extension, all Jewish religious observances) signified and sustained the covenant between Israel and God. Consequently, in the sefer evronot (rather than the context within which ibn Ezra created it) the poem could be read as a prideful assertion of the Jewish interpretation of the calendar over and against the Christian.

The anonymous polemic *Nizzahon yashan*, from the late thirteenth or early fourteenth century, set forth the contested nature of the Sabbath:

> Ask the Christians why they do not observe the Sabbath. It was after all on the seventh day that the Lord rested from all his work, and it is written, "Remember the sabbath day to keep it holy. Six days shall you labor and do all your work, but the seventh day is a Sabbath unto the Lord your God . . . for in six days the Lord made heaven and earth . . . and rested on the seventh day, and hallowed it" [Exod. 20:8–11]. Moreover, you must admit that the Sabbath which we observe is the seventh day on which the Lord rested, for this is proven by the fact that the stones of the Sambation River rest, as you know, on our Sabbath. Furthermore, your own words force you to make this admission since you call it *septem die*. Now, *septem* means seventh and *die* means day; thus you call it the seventh day. You might then argue that the one who was hanged changed Sabbath to Sunday, which you call *Dominica*.[82]

The celebration of a "Lord's Day" to commemorate the resurrection of Jesus on the first day of the Jewish week was not initially seen as a contradiction to observing the seventh day as the Jewish Sabbath. Eventually, however, observing both Jewish and Christian practices came to be seen by the young church as an unbearable contradiction, and it downgraded and then prohibited Saturday sabbath observance. Nevertheless, Christians maintained the seven-day week of the Jews rather than the eight-day intervals favored by the Romans.[83]

Controlling the Calendars

The potential for polemical mischief in calendars did not attract the eye of censors when they were first issued in print. Authorities who had the power to

FIG. 5.2. Zodiac and men of four nations. *Sefer evronot,* 1664. Cincinnati, Klau Library, Hebrew Union College–Jewish Institute of Religion ms 906, fol. 68v.

oversee calendar production tended to focus elsewhere. Censorship, then, came to calendars late, and in a desultory manner, if it arrived at all.

At least three authoritative bodies asserted an interest in some aspect of the production and sale of calendars. The most imposing of these was the centralizing state, which appointed commissions ostensibly to monitor the accuracy of information contained in calendars. In fact, the states saw calendars as commodities to be taxed for revenue and their appointed commissions often served as a taxing surrogate for the state. Christian censors of Jewish printed materials constituted a second, and sometimes related, intervening party. Finally, rabbinic oversight of Hebrew printing exerted a restraining force. These authoritative bodies existed in various places where Jewish calendars were printed throughout early modern times.

Because written records from the day have survived, we know precisely how these three authoritative bodies operated and sometimes interacted in eighteenth-century German lands. In many of the German cities where Jewish calendars were printed, local governments exercised some form of control, most often by requiring licenses to print the calendars or by imposing a tax on each copy sold. The calendar would be stamped once the tax was paid, and a person found carrying or displaying a calendar without the required stamp could be fined severely.

The Prussian government provides the most vivid example of the commodification of Jewish calendars by a centralizing authority in the eighteenth century. Starting May 10, 1700, the Prussian Academy of Sciences in Berlin garnered a monopoly over the licensing of calendars, and for over a century, until 1811, this was its sole source of income. No calendars could be printed in Prussia without the Academy's approval; anyone dealing with unauthorized or imported calendars would incur a steep fine. In addition, with the permission and seal of the Academy, "good foreign calendars" could be purchased (usually by collectors) for double the price exclusively through the Academy. This rule covered all calendars, even though, at first, the Academy paid no attention to Jewish calendars.

The renewal of the monopoly in 1725 cited Jewish calendars specifically for the first time, and on March 28, 1726, a special royal order went out to the first fiscal councilor regarding Jewish calendars.[84] The king ordered that printed Jewish calendars as well as foreign, imported Jewish calendars, be approved by the Academy. It was the councilor's mandate to notify the rabbis and lay leaders in Berlin as well as in the provinces, and to work out a mechanism for compli-

ance. The royal order stated that any Jewish calendar brought in without the stamp of the Academy would incur a steep fine of ten to twenty Reichsthaler.

Since Jewish calendars were printed exclusively in Hebrew, the Academy relied on the rabbis to act as their representatives. The Academy's records for 1725 contain a note by Yehiel Michel Hasid (who signed it Michel Levin) in which he affirmed that he had checked the printed calendars and had found nothing untoward.[85] In fact, the production of the Berlin calendars was plagued by difficulties. The calendars depended heavily on Polish models, which meant that they mistakenly noted various market dates and Christian saints' days that were not locally observed. The format was unwieldy, the paper bad, the print poor, and the cost high: six groschen, beyond what most consumers could afford. Moreover, any serious misprint would lead to a total loss for the entire batch. These difficulties led to the calendars being placed under the jurisdiction of the community elders, who prepared an annual preprint before Easter to be checked for corrections. Despite this precaution, the cost of producing the calendars remained too high for any party to realize much profit. (Four million printed Christian calendars netted the Academy 253,333 Reichsthaler, while 6,000 Jewish calendars netted it 380 Reichsthaler.)[86]

Berlin Jews sought many means to circumvent the cumbersome stamp requirement, which they also regarded as an incursion into their internal affairs. Calendars from other places were easy to smuggle in, and some printers simply produced unapproved printings. The earliest calendar published with Academy approval was printed in 1725 (for 1725–1726) by Michael Gottschalk of Frankfurt an der Oder, which was followed by a series of Berlin-based Jewish calendars.[87] (Later, printers in Ellwangen and Frankfurt also printed Jewish calendars, some of which bear the stamp of the calendar tax.[88]) In July 1, 1730, Rabbi Hasid issued a notice to Jews that while the Academy was ordered by royal decree "to allow the Jewish calendar to be printed in their own language, so that it could be used in lands far and near," he had approved an arrangement in which the *Schutzjude* (royally protected Jew) and book printer Aron Moses would be granted a monopoly on printing Jewish calendars, and he cautioned his fellow Jews that no other calendars were to be printed or brought into Prussia. This warning had little effect. For years, Aron Moses petitioned the Academy to protect his monopoly by allowing severe bans to be pronounced against those who violated it, all to no avail.[89] His attempt to control Berlin's Jewish calendars exemplifies the intersection between religious and commercial interests.

Later in the eighteenth century, the Academy added another layer of com-

plication. From 1765, the distribution of the limited number of approved calendars would itself be leased to Jewish bidders. For many years, the amount these bidders paid remained the same, 400 Reichsthaler. The calendars were distributed by a formula that remains impenetrable. Each Prussian Jewish community received a certain allocation, and no record survives regarding whether there were enough for every person who needed one.[90] This system remained in place through most of the eighteenth century. Its existence certainly clarifies for us one of the reasons for the persistence of handwritten Jewish calendars in German lands well through the eighteenth century. Some Jews may simply have had to copy one in case they did not receive (or could not afford) one of the formally allocated calendars.

The Academy's onerous tax system more generally may also explain why some printers used false place names on their Jewish calendars. From 1762–1800, Fürth pocket calendars were marked "Sulzbach," misleading bibliographers until today. Later Fürth pocket calendars, too, were prominently marked that they had been printed "in letters of Sulzbach."[91] Fürth wall calendars, by contrast, never bore false place names, perhaps because their larger format would make the lie more difficult to conceal.

It was not until centralizing German states began to impose taxes, licenses, or stamps as a means of monopolizing the income from calendars that evidence of censorship of Jewish calendars emerged. Around this time, the terms that Jews used to designate Christian holy days finally caught the eyes of Christian censors.

One example of this development occurred in the first half of the eighteenth century, after Sulzbach had emerged as a center for German Jewish printing, with Zalman Frankel as the most important of Sulzbach printers. On July 9, 1722, Count Theodore Eustace appointed Sebastian Kyck, inspector of the regional government, to ascertain that there was no anti-Christian material in the printed Jewish calendars. Kyck took this assignment seriously. Alas, he could not make out the meaning of most of the abbreviations and references; he needed the very people he was assigned to censor to help him determine whether the calendars included insulting or blasphemous terms. He defended this bizarre arrangement by explaining that "in such a calendar there is a '*Mischmasch*' (perhaps the better to conceal Jewish malice); not only Hebrew, rabbinic, and Yiddish, but also all types of abbreviations, characters and single letters that stand in for entire words. [They write thus] only for the purpose of making it more intricate, so that later they would be able to hide behind an in-

terpretation most comfortable for their purposes."[92] Accordingly, Kyck demanded from Frankel "a completely intelligible and sufficient German explanation and translation, to be rendered and delivered in writing, so that the hidden things can be found and brought to light of day as soon as possible."[93]

Once the translation had been prepared, the censor found several objectionable aspects. He concluded that an extraordinarily high number of printing errors had crept in, to the point that the finished product was of unacceptable quality and would actually sow confusion among the Jews. In addition to this sloppiness, which he deplored, Kyck noted at least two potentially offensive references, "words that could at least mean something else, and could possibly be intended to imply something subversive." The first came "in the second Jewish month called *Cheshvan*, whose twenty-first day coincides with our November 1. It says in half-Hebrew/half-German, '*Col hakedoschim*,' or as one can also read it here, '*kdeschim*.' The first means 'All Saints' but that word would have been written with the letter *vav*. If read the second way, it means the opposite, all the whores."[94] Another locus of potentially offensive references in the calendars he inspected concerned sacred days related to Mary. "The days of devotion to the Mother of God were noted solely by the word '*Ischa*,' i.e. woman or wife, and the last day of the Jewish month *Sivan*, which is our July 2, or the visitation of Mary and Elisabeth is called '*ischa Chadoscha*,' new woman or wife's day. The question is whether they intend by the simple word *woman* or *wife* to impugn the virginity of Mary."[95] Finally, "all the apostles' days were noted in a very confusing manner, so that one cannot know whether they contain any hidden messages. For example on Peter Paul day, it says 'Pither Pols or Luls.' Johannes' Day is referred to, as it is by us Germans as well, as 'Kanes or kanis' day. At other times they write out this word clearly, as in last year's calendar on August 29 (1 Iyar) it says clearly יאניז (=Johannis) for the day of John's beheading, but in this year it was left out. Similarly, Thomistag with only one letter inverted could easily turn into something deplorable."[96] The censor concluded that while the large number of additional, nonprovocative errors proved that sloppiness was pervasive throughout the calendar, the Jewish printer could not be exonerated and was strongly urged to proceed more carefully in the future.

Several decades later, a similar charge was raised about Jewish calendars in Altona. In 1769, church officials complained that the Jewish calendar printed in Altona contained several offensive terms for the Christian holidays. On May 12, 1770, the printer was exonerated: "In regards to the clarification by the chief rabbi and the Jewish elders concerning the 1769 and previous years' calendars

printed in Altona, we are satisfied, as it has been clarified from there, that the calendar [under scrutiny] was not printed with their permission, and that the various offensive and mocking terms for various Christian feast days are not their responsibility but that of the author, already deceased."[97]

Christian censors looking at Jewish calendars had little scholarship by Christian Hebraists to support their efforts. Oluf Gerhard Tychsen (1734–1815), a Christian Hebraist and Orientalist who studied Jewish calendar calculation extensively, was one of the very few scholars who collected actual printed calendars. His collection is still in Rostock. While his treatise *Beurteilung* provocatively aims to show that Jews have no fixed system of dating, he apparently did not write about blasphemous or deceptive wordplay in the Jewish calendars themselves.

These brief glimpses into the Jewish calendar's encounter with Christian censorship reinforce our understanding that in the early modern period censorship was sporadic, inconsistent, and of dubious efficacy, at least in the short term. Over time, however, it may have had the intended effect, encouraging printers to avoid risk by suppressing polemically inflected readings.

A final shaping force in the production of Jewish calendars was the rabbinate. For the most part, Jewish calendars did not bear *haskamot* (rabbinic approbations). Those that did appear in calendars were often simply copyright protections given to printers to prevent competition. A typical text from an early eighteenth-century Amsterdam calendar issued by the leaders of the Ashkenazic community "gives permission to Mr. Hayyim Druker to print a calendar for the forthcoming year 5468 [1707–1708]. As he has expended funds on the printing, no person here whether circumcised or uncircumcised may print a calendar for the year 5468, until Mr. Hayyim has sold all his calendars. Under threat of absolute ban."[98]

The occasional slipups reveal the rabbinic vigilance that was necessary to maintain correct calendars. In a 1773 rabbinic message appended to a calendar, we learn that the supervising rabbi checked each calendar at several stages:

I saw that the earlier calendar, called wall calendar, for this year, was first printed correctly, but then it was disfigured by the corrector, who erroneously placed Passover Eve on a Sunday [when Sunday was actually the first day of the holiday] and has *isru hag* [the final day] on [what should be] the eighth day. In order that no mistakes should hap-

pen, I ordered that those calendars should be put away in the *geniza* and others printed in their stead. Those I have seen are all correct and look like this calendar. As evidence, I sign my name here in Fürth, Thursday, Lag b'Omer, 1773, Joseph of Steinhardt.[99]

Two Sulzbach calendars, those of 1759 and 1765, contained a printer's remarks that the rabbis had forbade him to include several blessings and special prayers in the calendars—such as the prayer over the New Moon marking the beginning of a new Jewish month—because these contained divine names that would be profaned when the calendars were discarded. To respond to disappointed customers who found the insertions useful, some printers substituted compendia of laws or customs. The Sulzbach calendar of 1765 included an introduction to koshering meat. Other enterprising printers borrowed a page from their non-Jewish counterparts and included useful charts such as arrival and departure times for mail carriages, and useful travel information.[100] The ironic consequence of rabbinic oversight is that it headed off the tendency to develop calendars into pocket prayer and ritual manuals. Instead, calendar printers who sought to increase the usefulness of their product added more mundane and practical elements, which moved Jewish calendars toward the model of secular almanacs rather than religious books.

The three authoritative bodies that imposed their sensibility on Jewish printed calendars each influenced the development of the medium. State authorities, which claimed general control over the content of calendars, eliminated some of the superstitious material that buyers had come to expect in the hope of helping calendars become instruments of rationalism and enlightenment. Christian censors searched for infractions of polemical correctness, leading printers of Jewish calendars to internalize their rules. And rabbinic monitors checked the pages for accuracy and for Jewish religious content, keeping the calendars more in line with the expectations of both state and church. Significantly, however, none of these parties could be too obstreperous about changes, for if the calendars were not released on time, the result would be a complete loss for all.

The censorship of Jewish calendars in Christian Europe provides a perfect symbolic coda for the cycle of awareness and resistance, embeddedness and differentiation, that characterized Jewish life in early modern Christian Europe. The calendar itself was both a locus and expression of the intertwined religious

cultures whose development was shaped by the other. The Christian calendar was created in light of the Jewish calendar, Jewish scribes and printers developed strategies to resist its power, and the Christians subsequently attempted to penetrate those strategies and eliminate them. When Jewish writers, copyists, and printers inserted their small barbs into those humble forms, they were showing, in an often humorous way, how Jews of the era both absorbed and deflected many aspects of the Christian culture that enveloped them.

Church Time and Market Time

I am a Jew called Simon / I'll travel to Wirtzburg, market bound / And will not pursue any usury / For I deal only in luxury.

Christoff Mandel von Ofen, *Beweisung aus der Juden Gesatz*, 1557

WHEREAS references in Jewish calendars to the Christian ritual year signified a temporary suspension of regular routines, of ominous consequences for Jews if they appeared in Christian spaces, of a contraction of the Jewish world, and a solemn and ugly reminder of their status as a despised minority, the one-word place names that appeared in the same columns of their calendars signaled expansion, opportunity, and a measure of freedom. Local markets and regional fairs were important economic and social events for the participants, the culmination of months of preparation.[1] A different set of rules prevailed during these special mercantile times, rules that loosened the tension between Christians and Jews as both groups pursued economic affairs to their mutual benefit.

The careful marking by Jews of Christian religious dates alongside those of the markets and fairs, both monumental and less significant, provides a concrete demonstration of how deeply Christian religious and economic rhythms were imbricated into the lived experience of European Jews. Jews could not afford to be ignorant of either of these cycles; their livelihoods and sometimes their very lives depended on knowing where they could venture to trade, and when it was safe to appear. Even during these exceptional times, both Christians and Jews drew careful boundaries and set limits on the interactions these opportunities afforded.

In the composition and layout of Jewish calendars, notations about these special days, both Christian and secular, were crowded into the single column reserved for non-Jewish days. Thus the fifth column of many calendars contained juxtapositions such as: "All Saints, All Souls, Berlin, Minden."[2] A Lithuanian Jewish calendar from the early nineteenth century advertised that it

contained "The beginnings of months and holidays according to the Greek [Orthodox] Church and the Roman [Catholic] church in Russia: those that they celebrate together, and those that . . . they celebrate separately, with all the . . . fairs pertaining to them, for these will be very useful for people who depend on the fairs. We have also included the beginning of the months and the holidays of Christians outside our land, such as the Prussian State and the Holy Roman Empire . . . with some of the German holidays for the purpose of the fairs in the region of Saxony."[3]

Both religious holidays and market days imposed distinctive rules of access, of exchange, and of intergroup contact. Christian feast days meant that ordinarily neutral spaces were marked as temporarily holy and were off-limits to those outside the religious community. On those Christian holy days, it was dangerous for Jews to traverse such spaces. Market and fair days, in contrast, loosened the constraints on Jewish mobility. Ferdinand Braudel said of these commercial special days: "Their function was to interrupt the tight circle of everyday exchanges. . . . They could mobilize the economy of a huge region: sometimes the entire business community of Western Europe would meet at them, to take advantage of the liberties and franchises they offered which wiped out for a brief moment the obstacles caused by the numerous taxes and tolls."[4] On market days, Jews could enter spaces that were generally closed off to them and engage in interactions with Christians to whom they would not usually have had access.

Christian Holy Days

The Christian religious calendar provided the primary framework for the rhythms of social life in premodern Europe.[5] While there was plenty of disagreement over fine matters of doctrine, and much regional variation in the manner of celebration and the designation of local feast days, "there was no alternative to the liturgical calendar for reckoning time. . . . Business contracts were marked by it, leases and rents came due on certain feast days, the schedule of courses at the universities followed it, as did the chores of the agricultural season."[6] For Jews living in Christian Europe, there was no refuge from this all-encompassing timescape.

Approximately half of the calendar year was devoted to the Christian religious events. Both the Christmas cycle, with its fixed dates, and the Easter cycle, which varied from year to year, were preceded by weeks of liturgical and spiri-

tual preparation. Each cycle had its particular rituals, and every ritual served to solidify the identity of the community members who participated in it. Many of the rituals originated in the High Middle Ages or even earlier. Modifications over time are easily traced by historians, but in the early modern period most participants believed that they were enacting timeless rites. Historical developments changed but did not eliminate the meaning of these days.

The cult of saints, which was vital for the initial growth of Christianity, spurred an expansion in the Christian ritual calendar.[7] Throughout the medieval period saints became the local representatives of Christ; their graves or relics served as Christian shrines. On the day set aside to mark the memory of a saint, regular business would pause while the entire community took part in the ceremonies marking the day. These included reading about the passion of the saint, pilgrimages to the relics, as well as visits to the cemetery. Both the stories and the processions served to link an entire Christian community—men and women, rich and poor, young and old—in an emotional bond: "The procession represents a liturgical marking-out of space, an identification of individuals and local groups with a certain territory and with the powers who exercise authority over that territory."[8]

In the fifteenth century, some of these practices changed or shifted emphasis. Pilgrimages to stationary shrines (such as relics) gave way to a religiosity centered on a moveable and mutable object, the consecrated Host. Unlike the objects of pilgrimage, the Host could be carried around by the clergy. At first the Host left the church walls with priests in order to visit the sick, to cure the insane, or to bless the crops in the fields on the feast of the Ascension (or on Corpus Christi or Rogation Days).[9] Not only the crops, but also the air, to the four corners of the earth, were blessed in weather rituals, and the Host's powers were invoked against any evils lurking in the atmosphere.

Eventually, as the processions grew in importance and complexity, local lay and ecclesiastical authorities claimed them as a means of marking their status in society and their ranking within the church hierarchy. The processions on the day on which the Host was venerated, Corpus Christi (*Leichnum* in the Judaeo-German), became far more central to religious pageantry in the late Middle Ages as the Host was carried aloft beyond the walls of the church.[10] Church officials, guild members, students, and sometimes the rest of the town claimed their places in the processions. The monstrance containing the Host was carried under a magnificent canopy, preceded, flanked, and followed by many sacred vessels borne by eminent members of the church and town. Tapers, bells,

flags, and chalices were carried along a path bedecked with flowers and greens. The processions would pass all of the significant landmarks in a village: the group would walk around the marketplace, over bridges and roads, to every parish church and then back to the central cathedral, mapping the spaces of the entire community as united and sacred.[11] Similar processions, and ceremonies without the Host, began to replace pilgrimages as a way to mark saints' and other feast days throughout Europe. The rituals united the town and the church, and marked off the entire space under the protection of the sacred powers. Their power of inclusion for Christians, however, became a force of exclusion for Jews.

When Protestantism challenged the Catholic veneration of saints, the culture of the pilgrimages and the memories of the shrines did not disappear. Rather, in some Protestant circles the cult of saints was reaffirmed by works like Foxe's *Book of Martyrs* and Catholics' heightened awareness and use of ritual surrounding the saints. New miracles were attributed to saints at long-established shrines, prompting written and printed works about the miracle that revived the cult. Long-forgotten saints were disinterred and moved to grander quarters.[12] In the face of challenges to adoration of the saints posed by Protestants, Catholic officials mounted new propaganda campaigns. The cults of saints continued with renewed vigor. Needless to say, those left outside the marked circle of sacred belonging felt their exclusion most keenly at such times.[13]

The belief that Jews were capable of malevolent acts against Christians, and that even their gaze sullied the purity of the vulnerable Host as it came into public view, grew stronger through the medieval period. Legislation that circumscribed the movement of Jews while the Host was being borne aloft in public spaces proliferated in many parts of Europe. A thirteenth-century synod in Austria declared: "If it happens that the sacrament of the altar be carried in front of the houses of the Jews, those Jews, having heard the heralding sound [of a bell], should be made by us or by the church's bishops to enter into their houses and close their windows and doors; lest they presume to dispute the Catholic faith with simple folk."[14] In Avignon in the mid-thirteenth century the commune decreed that when "Christ's body [the consecrated Host] be carried to the sick, no Jew or Jewess older than nine years old should stay in the Jewish street in Its presence, but rather go away and hide."[15] In 1364, neighbors denounced a Jewish woman for walking through the town on Ash Wednesday. She was penalized with a double fine. In 1374, a servant denounced a Jewish

woman for walking in the street while Christ's body—the host—was being carried through the town, and "she failed to hide or show it reverence." She, too, was fined.[16]

Carnival plays from Shrove Tuesday (Mardi Gras, German: *Fasnacht*) often made Jews the butt of their humor. In fifteenth-century Nuremberg, Hans Folz's plays derided Jewish beliefs and accused Jews of kidnapping and killing Christian children "to mock the annual birth of Jesus."[17] Holy Week, with its culminating Passion, was an especially dangerous time for Jews. During the weeks leading up to Easter, sermons, fasting, and Passion plays annually moved Christians to relive the pain and suffering of Jesus, and to exact some retribution for it from the local Jews. During this time of the year Christians would accuse Jews of ritually murdering Christian children, of needing Christian blood to bake their matzah, or of desecrating the sacred Host and causing it to suffer and bleed. The roots of the tension at these times lay in antiquity, in the differing interpretations of competing religious communities over the meaning of the Passover sacrifice and Passover rituals.

The expressions of that ancient rivalry mutated over time in intensity, kind, and location. Testimony from the fifteenth and sixteenth centuries confirms that these horrible accusations were linked directly to the seasons of the Christian calendar. In Endingen a ritual murder trial transcript opens: "On the Saturday before Easter Sunday [24 March] in the year of Our Lord [14]70."[18] A play about the Endingen accusation, the *Judenspiel*, was performed annually at Easter for centuries, and the entire story was copied into record books of surrounding communities, which fueled the widespread practice of naming Jews as the ultimate nefarious outsiders.[19] The infamous case in which the entire Jewish community of Trent (in northern Italy) was accused of murdering a Christian boy, Simon, took place "during Easter of 1475."[20] And when in 1504 in the small town of Benzhausen a shepherd found a corpse "on Good Friday," the local Jews were accused of murdering the child "to celebrate Passover."[21]

Accusations by Christians of Host desecration, that is, of attacks by Jews on the Eucharist (as a substitute for the Christ child), also occurred during Holy Week. "In Cologne, a Jew always wanted to . . . mock the Eucharist. One Easter, he went to church in disguise."[22] Another host desecration accusation was leveled against a young Jewish man who had witnessed a Christian procession on Good Friday. According to the legend, he was so taken by its pomp and ceremony that he came close to conversion to Christianity, but then changed his mind. He confessed under torture that when he decided to revert to Judaism, he

had stolen and "tortured" a Host.[23] In Prague, in 1389, a massacre of the Jews began with a tale that "during a procession of Holy Week . . . a Jew threw a little stone at the monstrance carried by the priest not far from the Jewish quarter."[24] The preachers of the city enjoined the Christians to take revenge, and so they did, falling upon all the Jews in the quarter and tearing them apart limb by limb. Such accusations, often attended by violence, were particularly common in years when Easter coincided with Passover.[25]

Through the early modern period, charges like these led to trials, torture, and terrible deaths for the individual Jews so accused, and often resulted in the town's permanent refusal to allow Jews to settle within its limits. Even after the face-to-face confrontations stopped, their memory lived on in stories and plays that commemorated these events and continued to stoke animosity between Christians and Jews.

Other medieval Christian practices lingered into the early modern period. These included the ritual stoning or slapping of Jews, and other means of inflicting physical harm on Jews during this time of the year.[26] David Nirenberg has characterized such violence as that in which "the sacred is physically experienced, relations of power criticized . . . urban space was transformed."[27] The practice of stoning dated to ancient times, and was documented widely throughout medieval Spain, France, and Italy.[28] Regarding the incitement to violence against Jews, one thirteenth-century Muslim polemicist with anti-Christian views observed: "In the remainder of the cities of the Franks [Christians] they have three days in the year that are well known, when the bishops say to the common folk: 'The Jews have stolen your religion and yet the Jews live with you in your own land.' Whereupon the commonfolk and the people of the town rush out together in search of Jews, and when they find one, they kill him. Then they pillage any house that they can."[29] This description by an anti-Christian writer describes (and possibly exaggerates) a well-known annual occurrence of ritual violence. The records of the order of St. Vincent of Châlone-sur-Sâone recorded that "the clergy and the people" stoned the Jews every year on Palm Sunday "because they stoned Jesus."[30] In medieval Béziers, bishops authorized stoning of the Jews in retaliation for the Jewish people's condemnation of Jesus and denial of Mary as Mother of God.[31] One witness in a trial in Girona against a young man accused of stoning Jews testified that "he has seen in the city of Girona, as well as in Barcelona and Valencia, and in other places of Catalonia, that students and adolescents threw rocks upon the Jews . . . on Good Friday . . .

and he thinks that this aforesaid custom and observance has gone on thirty years and more."[32]

This custom was far more widespread in Spain and so deeply entrenched that in some Spanish cities Muslims became stone throwers as well, even though they had no theological justification. In Corfu, public officials led the populace in stoning the Jewish quarter from the ramparts in an attempt to extort protection money from the Jews.[33] In Venice, only certain officials held the right to do the stoning, at a prescribed time during the liturgy. The stones were often thrown in the direction of the Jewish quarter, falling on the gates surrounding it, the houses on the perimeter, or on Jews themselves. In some cases the synagogue and even the Torah scrolls were the objects of Holy Week depredations. The period for the stoning began annually on the Saturday before Palm Sunday, and extended until the second Saturday after Easter, that is, for three consecutive weeks.[34] In some places it was customary to stone the Jews on St. Stephen's day.[35] The violence was accompanied by the pealing of the church bells in some locations. Although limited to certain days and certain acts, ritual violence aimed "to make brutally clear the sharp boundaries, historical and physical, that separated Christian from Jew."[36]

Ritual violence against Jews caused authorities in many places to restrict Jewish mobility during those days, as a way to protect the Jews and diminish opportunities for widespread chaos. A standard clause in the papal bull that delimited the rights of Jews within Christendom, promulgated repeatedly from the twelfth through the fifteenth centuries, forbade Christians to harm Jews "in the celebration of their feasts, by sticks and by stones."[37] Some civil authorities issued ordinances designed to protect the Jews during these dangerous periods. In some places it was customary to station guards near the Jewish quarter in anticipation of the riots.[38] In others, Jews appear to have had their own system of lookouts and shofars that trumpeted the alarm.[39] In southern Italy in the fourteenth century, Jews were ordered to keep their doors and windows shut and not to venture out from Passion Sunday to Easter.[40] In the city of Spoleto, Jews left town during Holy Week to avoid the violence. When the damage to their property reached intolerable proportions, the government issued a warning that the stoning should remain a ritual display.[41]

The canonical and civil laws mandating that Jews remain inside their homes or their quarters for Holy Week became excuses for violence: "When questioned about their intentions, they complained that the Jews, who should have been

shut up in the *call* [Jewish street], were still walking about the city."[42] Even so, such laws were enforced in parts of Europe through the eighteenth century. These days of imposed segregation became known as "days of shutting in." In a curious inversion, Jews in medieval France gave the day a Jewish name, *yom ha-hesger*, or *yom tipol*, and a special Jewish liturgy was composed for it.[43] In these liturgical poems, Jews called out to God from the "prisons" into which they had been enclosed, from the "holes" in which they hid from the implacable crowds.[44] In the same verses that bespoke a sense of despair and suffocation, a transformation occurred, as the poets attempted to turn a day designated for contempt into one that became a token of distinction. One such liturgical poem begins: "Like a princess set away / In her palace on this day."[45] The incidents depicted in the poems span from the thirteenth through the seventeenth centuries (with most occurring during the earlier centuries) and new configurations of the poems appeared in eighteenth-century editions.[46] The Jewish liturgies were often highly polemical and always turned the sense of the day inside out: "The Soul of those broken and tottering, suffering the blazing wrath of the foe, will exalt You / Each one could sling a stone at a hair without missing."[47]

Being subjected to vicious accusations and stoning, and having to stay indoors, were only some of the many negative ways in which Jews experienced Christian time. Moreover, these days compel attention because of the lack of randomness in the violence that occurred. These were repetitive, cyclical, ritualistic enactments of the same drama every year. Consequently, notations on the Jewish calendar of days on the Christian liturgical calendar signaled danger to the Jews who fashioned and owned them.

Markets and Fairs

French cultural historian Jacques le Goff has delineated a basic duality for early modern Christian bourgeois, between "church's time" and "merchant's time."[48] Far from being opposing forces, these spheres often overlapped, a congruence that dated back to ancient times. Religious holidays and commercial activities had always been linked, particularly in agrarian economies where any gathering provided an opportunity to exchange vital commodities, and religious festivals in particular provided people a chance to gather and to conduct business. Indeed, some European markets were founded by monks to serve the multitudes of pilgrims who flocked to shrines on specific days to honor the relics of a saint.[49]

The cycle and timing of European markets and fairs was thus intimately tied to the Christian calendar, and most of the dates for these markets had roots reaching back to the High Middle Ages.[50] The German word *messe* means both market and Mass, and in medieval Europe until the Reformation, the celebration of the Eucharist routinely marked the beginning and end of every market. In Catholic states such as Poland, these observances were deeply entrenched and lasted far longer.[51] The autumn market in Frankfurt am Main began with the Assumption of Mary on August 15 and ended on the day celebrating the birth of Mary, September 8, with each date marked by the tolling of church bells and related observances. The Allerheiligenmarkt (All saints market), noted as *kol ha-qedoshim* on Jewish calendars, lasted fifteen days in the twelfth century. The four market times in early modern Hildesheim were each called by their liturgical names (Fastenmarkt, Ostermarkt, Johannismarkt, and Gallenmarkt).[52] Most European markets retained distinctive Christian names and practices well into the nineteenth century.[53]

This intersection between religious time and commercial opportunity had perturbed rabbinic decisors (interpreters of Jewish law) since pagan times. They decided that "three days prior to the festivals of the pagans it is forbidden to engage in commerce with them."[54] Early rabbinic sources attempted to separate Jews from the rhythms of the pagan calendar, not only by forbidding trade with pagans on their holidays, but also by forbidding trade on the days surrounding pagan festivities. Talmudic sources later found this prohibition onerous and attempted to mitigate its severity by limiting the duration of the prohibition to the days of the festival itself rather than the times that preceded or followed it. The rabbinic rules that were created for interactions with pagans were later adapted for Jewish contacts with Christians, sometimes with difficulty. Some Jews voiced fears that sales taxes collected at fairs would directly benefit local churches.[55]

Christian clergymen also expressed discomfort at the idea of Jews attending Christian fairs and voiced fears of Jewish subversion. Ninth-century Bishop Agobard of Lyons was particularly upset that fairs traditionally set for Saturdays were moved to other days, including Sundays, in order to accommodate Jews.[56] (Still, almost a thousand years later, in a public notice in a local newspaper from 1800, officials of the county of Schramberg changed the date of the St. Nicholas Day Goods and Cattle Market from Saturday, December 6 to Thursday, December 4 "because Jews cannot attend [on Saturday]."[57])

Others were perturbed by the general atmosphere of festive laxity that pre-

vailed throughout the market period. Humbert de Romans, in the mid thirteenth century, complained: "Markets . . . are held on feast days, and men miss thereby the divine office and the sermon and even disobey the precept of hearing Mass, and attend these meetings against the Church's commands. Sometimes, too, they are held in graveyards and other holy places. Frequently you will hear men swearing there: 'By God I will not give you so much for it,' or 'By God I will not take a smaller price,' or 'By God it is not worth so much as that.' Sometimes . . . quarrels happen and violent disputes. . . . Drinking is occasioned."[58] (In Frankfurt, cathedral representatives oversaw the religious proprieties of the market, probably to avoid scenes like these.) Thus, for each religious group, markets were characterized by a relaxation of tension, with an abiding undercurrent of unease. These tensions, which were expressed in various ways, remained a subtext in the economic interactions between Jews and Christians in early modern Europe, even as the markets and fairs grew more distant from their religious moorings.

In almost every document produced about Jews in the records of markets and fairs, Jews were identified and distinguished first and foremost as Jews. In the market register of Hildesheim for the early modern period, all Jewish attendees were recorded first as Jews, then by city of origin, then by name—regardless of their class or standing.[59] In the late seventeenth century, the Leipzig municipality ordinances concerning the fair ordered Jews to carry a *gelbe Flecklein*, yellow sign, which they had to be prepared to show to municipal workers.[60] These signs reveal the lingering and pervasive lower-level discrimination that persisted during the fairs, where, for example, Jews were far more likely than others to be victims of physical violence by disgruntled business partners.[61]

Municipalities had solid economic incentives to maintain this distinction: Jews were taxed and assessed fees at higher rates than peer fair participants. In Hildesheim, local Jews were assessed the fees imposed on foreign fair visitors.[62] Many municipalities taxed the Jews at higher rates on the wares they brought in and the amount that they sold, and they required Jews to purchase special, more expensive, entrance passes.[63] Each Jewish person who entered had to pay a "body tax" or *Leibzoll*.[64] The hundreds of passes specially printed and issued to Jews at every juncture of their travel to the fairs survive as tangible testimony to the extra economic and practical burdens that the various authorities imposed on them.[65] If the municipal authorities found a Jew who had no proof of payment, they fined that person heavily and treated it as a grievous case of tax evasion.

The heavy *Leibzoll* imposed on Jewish men in order to attend the Leipzig fair was halved for women and servants. Some Jews took advantage of this loophole and presented other Jews as their servants to lower the cost of participating in the fair.[66] (This practice became so rampant that in 1717 Leipzig instituted an oath for those who identified themselves as servants. Still, some time later the Leipzig register contained many entries of people who registered as "servants without oath.") The only individuals who were permitted to enter without tax obligations were religious functionaries like rabbis, cantors, and teachers, who were ostensibly attending to provide for the religious needs of the Jews. Court Jews were also exempted from the tax, because organizers knew that their higher social stature made them a draw for the market.[67]

If a Jew happened to die at the fair, additional fees were levied. The municipal statutes of Leipzig proclaimed: "As unbelievers and blasphemers against our exclusive-salvation-giving faith we will not allow them any burial place." Permission to enter Christian space was temporary, and death, with its reminder of permanence, came as an inconvenient violation of this uneasy accommodation. When Glikl's husband Haim became ill during the fair at Leipzig, his terrified friend nursed him carefully. If a Jew were to die at the fair, Glikl wrote, "het ess ihm kol asher lo gekost": it would cost him everything he owned.[68] The brother-in-law of court Jew David Oppenheim had the misfortune to die at the Leipzig fair on January 19, 1697. The nearest place to take the corpse for Jewish burial was Dessau, and payment had to be made for its passage as well. The lack of good channels of communication meant that uncertainty for their well-being reigned until the travelers returned home safely.

The fairs that played such an important role in European and in Jewish economic life often took place in cities that did not regularly admit Jews. Strict barriers against Jewish entry were often loosened or dropped for the duration of the fairs, however, in order to profit from the Jews' attendance. The municipality of Leipzig is paradigmatic: it permitted Jews to enter for the thrice-yearly markets under tightly controlled conditions (hence the detailed registers). For the 1682 fair, for instance, the city created highly restrictive ordinances concerning which Jews could enter the city and under what conditions, as well as the specific commodities that they could trade.[69] A hundred years later, by the mid-1780s, only six Jewish families had permission to live in Leipzig.[70]

Economic incentives encouraged authorities in other cities to open their gates to Jews during the fairs. Even after the Jews in Frankfurt am Main were expelled from Frankfurt during the Fettmilch uprising in 1614, they were never-

theless permitted to enter during the time of the fair.[71] Similar exceptions prevailed in German cities such as Nuremberg and parts of Bavaria, Zurzach in Switzerland (an important Rhine entrepôt), and many others.[72]

Jews were active in European fairs throughout the medieval period. By tradition, participants in fairs agreed to abide by the rules but they otherwise enjoyed a certain "diplomatic immunity." One eleventh-century Holy Roman emperor noted in his grant of an annual fair: "We have also granted . . . an annual fair for three continuous days . . . commanding firmly by imperial power that all men seeking that fair, going and coming for business, shall always have peace."[73] Similarly, in the later twelfth century, in granting a biannual fair at Aachen, Frederick I Barbarossa mandated that "all people coming to, staying at, or going from the fairs shall have peace for their persons and goods."[74] Participants in fairs, having traveled far from their home jurisdictions, were thus guaranteed imperial protection of their persons and goods. In fact, during the High Middle Ages, fairs that drew participants from a broad geographical circle established special overseers for the smooth conduct of the fair and special temporary courts to adjudicate disputes arising from it. By this time, Jews had become fixtures within fair culture. They participated in the Cologne fairs of the eleventh century, the Troyes and Provins fairs in the Champagne, and in Orleans. Jews also dominated the medieval Northern European wine trade.[75]

Despite the disapproval of clergymen on both sides, a general atmosphere of festive laxity prevailed on these special market days. During the fairs, Sunday and other holy days were observed less solemnly than usual. Participants were granted papal privileges exempting them from fasting for the duration of the fair, and guilds freed their members to attend to the needs of visitors from far and near. Merchants rewarded clergymen for their support with religious art objects of gold, silver, and the richest textiles.

Markets and fairs provided an opportunity for people to mingle across classes, across national, religious, and cultural lines. "Fairs meant noise, tumult, music . . . the world turned upside down, disorder, disturbance. Traveling troupes of theatrical, musical, comical performers, the opening and closing processions, the lords and ladies and their retinues who came to be amused and provided a spectacle for the onlookers."[76] People arrived by foot, barrow, wagon, or ship, loaded with provisions, animals for conveyance, and livestock—as well as raw and finished products of every conceivable type—for trade.

Among the Jewish fair participants in Leipzig were numerous artists and entertainers, including musicians, jugglers, dancers, a Jewish man with a mon-

FIG. 6.1. Polish Jews arriving at the Leipzig fair. Georg Opiz, *Die Polacken*. Courtesy of Stadtgeschichtliches Museum Leipzig.

key, and a woman with a *Raritätenkästchen,* a curio chest. Showmen were often accompanied by women who helped stage their shows. A number of fairgoers, men and women, listed themselves as cooks and bakers, apparently to feed the Jewish fairgoers. Because of their exclusion from the guilds, there were few artisans among the Jews, with the exception of a button maker. Poor people came to collect alms. Many visitors brought their servants or sons along; the greater the merchant, the more attendants—such as scribes, secretaries, valets, and

sometimes even personal chefs—accompanied him. Often these were relatives using these designations as covers to enter under a lower tax category. Here and there, Jews appeared in the service of prominent Christians.

This spectacular diversion from the norm affected not only individual participants but families and communities as well. The economic and cultural lifeblood of the region, and more so of its Jews, circulated through these events. Smaller local fairs (*Jahrmärkte* in German) provided vital stimulus for regional economic development, constituting an extremely important distribution network for commodities, wares, and information. By the late seventeenth century, local merchants held over seven hundred local markets and fairs in German lands. From the small regional markets that dominated the medieval economy, several urban fairs grew in importance in the early modern period to become centers of European commerce.

As the axis shifted from north-south trade (Mediterranean to North Italy) to east-west (between the Atlantic states and Poland/Russia), the central German region naturally emerged as a new hub. By the late eighteenth century, the leading Northern European fairs in terms of their scope and importance were those held at Braunschweig, Frankfurt an der Oder, Frankfurt am Main, and preeminently, the thrice-annual fairs at Leipzig. The Frankfurt am Main fair was vital for western and southern German lands, and was renowned for its gold and silver crafts, jewelry, samples of artistic crafts, noble horses, arms and armor, art, and books, as well as for money changing. Jaroslav served as a hub for trade in Polish lands, with the Vistula River as its main transportation and trade artery. Markets were temporary "free zones," like port cities whose culture and temperament opened them to many strands of cultural influence.

Today we can scarcely imagine the central importance of these regularly scheduled events in the cycles and cultures of Jewish life. Even single broadsheet wall calendars, where only the most vital information could be noted, bore the names of the important markets in their appropriate time slots. In fact, no Jewish calendars from the early modern period, including those published in England, in France, and throughout Central and Eastern Europe, omitted the most important markets and fairs from their pages, although the scope and number of such events varied greatly over time and place. Cecil Roth wrote of Anglo-Jewish calendars, "from 1772 at the very latest, Yiddish calendars were issued annually largely for the benefit of the itinerant traders, indicating both Jewish and church festivals; various national holidays, weather, local fairs throughout England, days on which coaches departed from London to various provincial

FIG. 6.2. Cattle and horse market days. Calendar, Hannover, 1853–1854. Courtesy Gross Family Collection, Tel Aviv.

centers."[77] A calendar intended for Sephardic Jews of southern France listed fairs of "Lyons, of Provence, Languedoc and neighboring provinces, the county and duchy of Bourgogne and many others of the realm."[78]

Some early modern European calendars attempted to include all of the markets from Amsterdam to Budweis. Other calendars listed only the most important ones, and moved them down to the very bottom of the page.[79] Regardless of their placement, these lists map out what Braudel called the "catchment area" of a particular slice of economic life. For any city or town, the list of markets and fairs defined how broadly its merchants, wares, and currency circulated. Similarly, for Jewish merchants attending fairs, the scope of commercial and cultural networks that overlapped at these sites can be better assessed by mapping information from calendars.

The register of Jewish visitors at the Leipzig fairs over the course of two centuries is a peerless primary source for research on the economic life of early modern European Jews. The early twentieth-century scholar Max Freudenthal described how his own father and grandfather recalled the frenzied preparations for departure, the long arduous journey with fully packed wagons, the ex-

citement of seeing friends and co-religionists from many parts of Europe, and the triumphant return home when the entire community greeted the travelers to hear how they had fared, hungry for the latest news from around the Jewish world. Freudenthal wrote in 1928 that "so many of us know all about this from personal reminiscences" that he had no need to go into details.[80]

The Leipzig fair eventually exceeded Frankfurt in Jewish attendance. Its easterly location gave it more convenient access to Jews from southeastern German lands and Central Europe—Prague annually sent the largest contingent of Jews from any single location—and from Eastern Europe. In the late eighteenth century, as disadvantages for Jewish travel eased and Poland was partitioned, tens of thousands of Polish Jews visited the Leipzig fair, with one Polish Jew visiting the fair annually for forty years straight (a record).[81] Eastern Europeans sent raw goods and brought home finished products. Many of the metal goods, textiles, and furs that arrived at the fair from Eastern Europe were finished in Leipzig and sold further west.

The fair regulated and punctuated the cycle of life for many Jews. Merchant-class Jews often spent months at a time on the road, returning home only for major holidays and family affairs. They often planned their activities for the year around participation in the major European fairs. In addition to Leipzig, the diarist Glikl noted, "We travelled every year to the Braunschweig fair, twice yearly."[82] Of her husband Hayim she commented, "It was approaching the time of the Frankfurt am Main fair, which my husband of blessed memory, had to attend, as he travelled to every fair."[83]

Because so many merchants traveled from one fair to the next, cities tried to schedule their markets and fairs so they would not overlap with others. A subtle change in one location could have a ripple effect on an entire region's economy.[84] When Frankfurt adopted the Gregorian calendar in 1700, the new date of the Frankfurt fair conflicted with the date of the Leipzig fair, creating a logistical problem for merchants accustomed to attending both. The city council of Leipzig refused to move the fair from its traditional time on the liturgical calendar between Sunday Jubilate and Rogate. In some years, the final day of the Frankfurt fair overlapped with the first day of the Leipzig fair, which meant that most merchants who lived closer to Leipzig did not travel to Frankfurt. In 1726, Frankfurt moved its market back a week, enabling merchants to attend both fairs despite some overlap. Still, this conflict hurt the Frankfurt am Main fair profoundly. Other markets filled the void. Even the market in Frankfurt an der Oder grew in this period from a regional *Jahrmarkt* to an international *Messe*.[85]

Lest the restrictions and taxes on Jewish participation in the markets and fairs be interpreted as a sign that Jews were dispensable supplicants to a Christian-set table, it should be emphasized that Jewish attendance was vital to the success of numerous markets and fairs. In the mid-eighteenth century, 13 percent of the visitors to the Leipzig fair were Jews; by the late eighteenth century that percentage had doubled, so that during the late eighteenth and early nineteenth centuries, approximately one out of four visitors to the Leipzig fairs was a Jew.[86] By the mid-nineteenth century, that number had diminished. In 1840, the last time that a census distinguished between Jews and Christians as market attendees, just 15.7 percent were Jewish. The figures for the pre-Emancipation era, however, do not tell the entire story, because very influential Jewish merchants were not required to pay any tolls, and their attendance does not appear on the registers because they were given free passes. The leverage exerted by these merchants attests to their importance in the eyes of those who orchestrated the fairs. When the Leipzig organizers decided in 1682 not to exempt any Jews from paying the toll, the court Jew and Primas (Jewish lay leader) of Bohemia, Abraham Aron, threatened to stop attending.[87] One attendance list noted that court Jew "David Oppenheimer, Chief Rabbi in Prague, arrived with four people and an outdated pass."[88] Nevertheless, he was let in.

Municipalities understood the economic value of even lower-level Jewish merchants, however, and worked to ensure that the taxation remained at a rate that made Jewish participation profitable for Jews as well as for themselves. Officials of each locale spent a considerable amount of time figuring out how an increase in taxes, by themselves or by others, would affect the attendance of Jews.[89] Polac, the mayor of Frankfurt an der Oder, noted with glee that a rise in the levy at Leipzig resulted in more Jewish merchants from Poland and Lithuania forgoing the Leipzig market and visiting his city's market instead.[90]

Jews also played a central role in extending credit at the fairs. When Maria Teresia expelled the Bohemian Jews in 1745, she dealt a devastating blow to the Leipzig fair, because many of the Jewish businessmen there came from Prague and other parts of Bohemia.

The economic impact of Jewish participation extended all along their travel routes, as Jews paid taxes for passing through towns as well as for food and lodging. Princes or municipalities would mandate the roads to be traveled far in advance so that all travelers to the fair, not only Jews, could be monitored and made to pay the appropriate tolls. The tolls covered the expenses of mounting the fairs and often provided significant income to the hosting municipalities.

Jewish attendance at the fairs suffered in times of poor or dangerous travel conditions. Winter was the harshest season for travel, even for shorter distances. Glikl recalled her terror upon hearing that an icy passage over the Elbe River had given way and plunged two carriages of people into its depths.[91] When disasters such as plagues or wars struck places of Jewish residence, attendance at fairs plummeted. The register reflects events such as the plague of 1680, which killed half the Jews of the Prague ghetto, and the eighteenth-century wars of Prussian expansion (when Prussia attacked Saxony and Leipzig), which kept the number of Jewish attendees far below the norm. Although many of these conditions affected the entire population equally, Jews may have felt more worried about falling into the wrong hands at markets, and may have stayed away in greater numbers than Christians.

Given the role of each traveling Jew as a link to many others, as a bearer of news and agent of commerce, the number of Jewish communities represented at the fairs may be of greater significance than the actual number of individuals attending. These rose from twelve Jewish communities participating in the Leipzig fair in 1675, to over a hundred in 1763, the last year of the Leipzig records.[92] Jews came from many parts of Europe, with especially strong representation from Bohemia, Moravia, Austria–Silesia, and Hungary. The Leipzig register is also a remarkable resource for seeing where Jews settled in remote places, how they adopted family and professional names, and how German Jews distinguished themselves from Polish Jews.

Overall, the Eastern European Jewish presence was stronger than the Western, particularly if we count individuals rather than communities. Jewish owners of large commercial firms traveled alongside small businessmen. Those who did not own their businesses could afford to come because they paid proportionately less tax. They were designated as *mäkler*, or exchange agents. Women attended to conduct their own businesses, with or without their husbands, sometimes accompanied by a son or another male relative.[93]

The Leipzig register demonstrates in exquisite detail how economic activities affected the profile and character of Jewish life in early modern Western Europe. Jews were extremely mobile and highly attuned to the Christian world in which they traveled and traded. Many merchants attended as many fairs as they could, circulating their wares, their ideas, and their culture very broadly.[94] These opportunities to congregate also tore down other barriers: Ashkenazic Jews intermingled with Sephardic Jews; Jews from Western, Central, and Eastern Europe converged; and men and women, humble servants and mighty court

Jews, cattle dealers and noblemen, all attended the fairs together in significant numbers.[95] Thus markets and fairs provided opportunities for pan-European Jewish networking that cut across cultural, geographic, gender, and class lines. Indeed, the fairs provided the perfect venue for Jewish kinship networking. Marriages were brokered between distant and scattered families, turning casual contacts into long-term bonds.

Because the fairs gave Jews an opportunity to assemble from distant points on a regular basis, supracommunal bodies such as the Council of (Four) Lands of Poland began to meet regularly there, to discuss and decide about matters that affected them collectively.[96] Sixteenth-century records indicate that rabbis convened to discuss their collective concerns at the Lublin fairs as well.[97]

The fairs were central to another form of circulation of Jewish culture in early modern Europe: they played a vital role in the exchange necessary to sustain the Jewish book printing trade. Distant partners hammered out their commercial agreements at the fairs, and those who needed *haskamot* (approbations) for their books could often find rabbis there to help them.[98] When a would-be publisher of a new Talmud edition was hoping for the support of David Oppenheim, he found Oppenheim himself at the Leipzig fair.[99]

In markets and fairs Jews found a site for the "fabrication of impressions as well as goods."[100] While almost every other theater of social interaction in early modern Europe excluded Jews or placed them on the periphery, markets and fairs provided an opportunity for Jews and Christians to mingle as merchants, as business contacts, and as human beings. Unlike the caricatured Jewish characters depicted in scripture, in polemics, in Christian churches, and on theater stages, in the commercial marketplace Jews acted as equal partners with access to desirable goods.

The expansion of possibilities that markets and fairs signified for Jews can best be appreciated in the context of the contraction of access and the physical danger signified by Christian holy days. If Jewish life in premodern times sometimes felt like a stifling enclosure, markets and fairs served as windows, allowing fresh ideas and impressions in, and allowing non-Jews to look in at the Jewish culture through a lens that was far less distorting.

{ 7 }

Calendar, Ritual, and the Turn of the Seasons

> Four times a year, at a particular hour and minute, a drop of blood falls
> from heaven into all the household vessels in which drinking water is
> kept. Whoever drinks from this water . . . contracts swelling of the
> body. . . . Neither divine authority nor any sort of philosophical or hu-
> man wisdom teaches such things, nor does plain reason.
>
> *The Tegernsee Haggadah*, ca. 1478–1492

TWO eye-catching tables appear in an illustration to a seventeenth-century
sefer evronot. Each lists four names,—Tishre, Tevet, Nissan, and Tammuz;—beside the names, another list appears, containing the day of the month,
the hour in the day, and the minute in the hour. Beneath them stands a woman,
looking rather alarmed or perplexed, holding what appears to be a plant.[1] This
Jewish woman is preparing for the turn of the seasons; the tables will inform
her of the precise hour of the equinox or solstice, or so she will believe. She has
inherited a practice whose obscure roots reach back to ancient times, its observance inadvertently reinforced by the beliefs and practices of her Christian contemporaries.

Sifre evronot and printed calendars assigned a prominent place to the exact
time of the occurrence of the tequfah, the turn of the seasons.[2] In English the
four seasonal turning points (the two longest and two shortest days of the year)
are called the equinox and the solstice, but in Hebrew calendar literature one
word, tequfah, signified all four. A now extinct and relatively obscure Jewish
practice related to these calendar points was widely observed in the medieval
and early modern periods. This custom of the tequfah sheds further light on
the interplay of the Jewish and Christian cultures during this era and opens a
unique view into the lives of the users of the calendar.[3]

The tequfah custom called for Jews to refrain from drinking or otherwise
ingesting water that had been drawn and left standing uncovered during the
time of the seasonal turning points.[4] This exposed water, the sources taught,

FIG. 7.1. Woman and chart with times of tequfot. *Sefer evronot*, 1674. Bayerische Staatsbibliothek München ms cod. hebr. 394, fol. 14v.

could have been struck or contaminated by harmful substances during this critical time, or in later texts, turned into blood. If drawn water had been left in the open during this vulnerable moment, it had to be discarded. Otherwise, anyone who partook of it could swell up, suffer horribly, and die. Some texts advocated a prophylactic: an iron implement, such as a needle or nail, placed into the water would ward off the evil effect.

The observance of the tequfah figured very prominently in sifre evronot of the early modern period, even though it was a disputed practice whose very place in the canon of Jewish custom was usually accompanied by questions concerning its legitimacy. Its history illuminates the relationship between rabbinic teachings and popular customs, and the place of calendar literature as a force that mediated, or intervened, between them.[5]

While Christians derided the tequfah as a superstitious and bizarre custom, they embraced one manifestly parallel in structure. The Jewish practice bore striking similarity to non-Jewish customs such as the Christian Quatember fast. In addition, the gendered dimensions of the custom offer a glimpse of Jewish women's place in calendar literature.

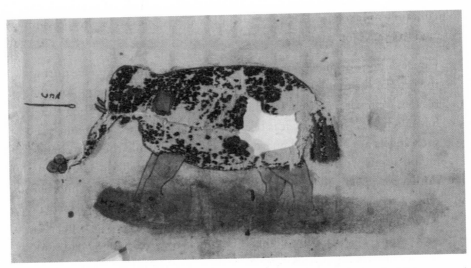

FIG 7.2. Needle, near chart for "fall" (*tapil*) of the tequfah. In a visual pun, the Hebrew word *pil* is elephant. *Sefer evronot*, 1664. Cincinnati, Klau Library, Hebrew Union College–Jewish Institute of Religion ms 906, fol. 36v. The needle protected against noxious tequfah water.

The Danger of Water

One of the earliest mentions of the four tequfot within a Jewish religious context can be found in the liturgical poems of R. Pinhas Ha-Kohen, who flourished in Tiberias in the first half of the eighth century C.E. R. Pinhas was an expert in calculating the calendar and an accomplished liturgical poet who composed poems to be recited at the beginning of each new month.[6] The poems would describe the month in terms of its seasonal and religious attributes. Any fast days and holidays, along with their particular observances, were mentioned within these compressed word tapestries, and special mention was made when a month contained a seasonal turning point. Thus setting out the attributes of the first month, Nissan, he listed it as "head of the four tequfot"; the others follow a similar pattern.[7] R. Pinhas's oeuvre includes fragments of a liturgical poem for "Shabbat tequfot." These fragments contain precious calendrical information, but they do not refer to any particular ritual other than to hint that a public announcement was made on the Sabbath before the tequfah was to occur.[8]

The first reports about the existence of a Jewish custom related to the turn of the seasons testify to its widespread appeal to Jewish masses, to some rabbinic voices that deplored it, and to other rabbis who saw value in it and sought

to maintain it. The first evidence of the practice is preserved in a responsum attributed to Hai Gaon (d. 1038):

> Concerning your query about the popular practice to announce during the time of the tequfah not to drink water; although we don't know the reason, we must pay heed, for this custom did not spread among Israel for naught. . . . [Some say it is because during each one of the four seasons angels are appointed guard over them; and while they are changing positions with the other angels, harm might befall a person.] It is similar to a flesh and blood king who died; when they appoint another king to replace him, they do not know if he will be good or bad. Others say it is a mere sign, they do not wish to begin the new season with water which is something slight. It is similar to what King David said, "Bring him to Gihon," [1 Kings 1:33] meaning may his [Solomon's] reign endure. Here as well, because it is the beginning of the season they instituted this custom.[9]

Another geonic citation concerning the tequfah appears within a discussion of customs related to the departure of the Sabbath. During the holy day the world was at peace and the guardians of the nations were "off duty." It was customary not to drink until the blessing over the departure of the Sabbath and the beginning of the new week was said. "Likewise it is the law at every tequfah, that one does not drink, and the custom has spread to the world, due to the changing of the watch, until each one returns to its station."[10] A fragmented text attributed to R. Hai concerning symbols of the New Year mentioned the tequfah as the start of a new season: "We begin with food and sweets and oils . . . but we don't begin with water, as water is thin and can be found anywhere, it is a substance that has no nutrition, it is a sign of meagerness."[11]

These texts establish several early elements of the custom. Despite its obscure origins, it had at the time of the writing already been accepted as a *minhag* (a religious custom). The first responsa noted that the most common explanation for the custom revolved around the turning of the seasons and the liminal period during the transition. Water symbolized the amorphous flow of time between the seasons, just as it did intervals between kings. They also attributed the spread of the custom to the "common" people; it seems to have been a struggle for rabbinic leaders to find a religious basis to justify it. And finally, the texts testify that the time of the tequfah was publicly announced in order to warn people to refrain from drinking water at that time.[12] Some people suggested

shielding the water with an iron cover; others rejected this as an insufficient antidote to the danger. One responsum juxtaposed the tequfah to a similar liminal period between Sabbath and the weekday, and noted a parallel custom to refrain from drinking during the brief time before the official ceremonial departure of the Sabbath and beginning of the workweek.

A non-Jewish testimony to the custom dates from the same period as its first citation in Jewish sources. A contemporary of Hai Gaon, the great Persian Muslim scholar Abu Rayhan al-Bīrūnī, took great interest in astronomical and calendrical matters, particularly in their comparative dimensions. In his *The Chronology of Ancient Nations* al-Bīrūnī wrote:

> On this rule they [the Jews] have based their calculations for the determination of the tequfoth (which were rendered necessary for this reason, that) the Jewish priests forbade the common people (the laity) to take any food at the hour of the tequfah, maintaining that this would prove injurious to the body. This however is one of the snares and nets which the Rabbis have laid for the people, and by which they have managed to catch them and bring them under their sway.[13]

Al-Bīrūnī's testimony confirms the existence of a widespread custom of observing a fast related to the seasonal points, although he mentions a fast that entailed not eating, rather than not drinking water. He was also the first to articulate the criticism that the rabbis promulgated the fast as a means of exerting power over the ignorant masses. (As seen earlier, in rabbinic sources, it was the masses who introduced the custom and the rabbis who felt pressured to find ways to incorporate it.)

Although the Babylonian geonic citation referred to Jews in the West (the maghrib, western North Africa) who observed the tequfah, by the medieval period the practice had spread into the lore of Jews within Europe, both in Spain and in Western Europe. In medieval Spain it was always accompanied by rabbinic expressions of derision.

Abraham bar Hiyya (1065–1136) in Spain, author of the earliest surviving medieval ibbur, wrote: "The custom practiced in these lands to refrain from drinking water during the tequfah, is nonsense in my eyes, for a person cannot know the hour of the tequfah in his place if he does not know the distance of his place in (longitude) from the east, and this is not possible for all people. If a person had found mention of this matter in the words of the ancients, he would

be obliged to study it and find its meaning, but as it does not appear in their words we should not concern ourselves with it."[14]

A generation later, in his twelfth-century *Sefer ha-ibbur*, Abraham ibn Ezra (ca. 1093–1164) cited the negative geonic opinion concerning the fear of the tequfah and expressed his own disdain for what he considered to be a widespread superstition: "As for those who think that anyone who eats or drinks at the time of the tequfah will be harmed and will swell, it is a mere homily, for the astronomers who knew the true tequfah clearly never mentioned that eating or drinking at the time of the tequfah would be harmful. There is no way through the natural laws that the tequfah could cause any harm. Concerning the homily that Isaac and the daughter of Jephthah were slaughtered there is a secret: for they were not slaughtered as I have explained in my book."[15] Ibn Ezra also cited the responsum of Hai Gaon in a slightly different version:

> The sages of Qairouan already asked R. Hai z"l why they observed the custom not to drink water at the time of the tequfah. He replied that it was *nihush b'alma* (pure superstition) as the tequfah is the beginning of the year, and Jews did not customarily drink water then. They ate everything sweet so that their year should be sweet, and I say, sweet will be the year of the person who serves God every moment. Some of the Geonim say about the tequfah, 'For there should be no divination in Jacob and no magic, but the early sages established this in order to frighten the masses that they should fear God, and the wicked will do no more evil, and they will repent so that God will save them from the four tequfot. For we know that all the words of our sages are truth, either literally, or they have a secret, as I have hinted at some of their secrets in *Sefer ha-yashar*, which is a commentary to the Torah.[16]

For ibn Ezra, the idea of a popular practice based on the harmful effects of the tequfah was inherently ludicrous because most Jews did not even know how to calculate the true tequfah.

In medieval Ashkenazic sources, customs related to the tequfah took a different turn. Jacob bar Samson, disciple of Rashi, cited in his ibbur, *Sefer elqoshi*, biblical "prooftexts" that supplemented and soon supplanted the "natural," causal explanations for the practice. They formed a midrashic gloss on the earlier tradition, and undoubtedly strengthened the observance and meaning of the practice.[17] A century later, the circle of Rabbi Judah Hasid used virtually the same

language.[18] Bar Samson is the earliest source known to date to set the tequfah custom with the biblical homiletical explanation into an ibbur treatise. He assigned a secondary role to the explanation concerning the danger to the world that lurked during liminal times. Tantalizing references exist to other works from this period, now lost, that may have expanded on the role of the tequfot.[19]

In these early sources the malevolent transformation that could occur at the time of the tequfah was still considered a temporary and possibly momentary phenomenon. In a discussion of what constituted a valid break between uttering a blessing over food and its immediate consumption, thirteenth-century *Sefer hasidim*, one of the early and widely respected sources of the custom and its explanation in Ashkenazic circles, noted: "If a person is told 'Do not drink water now for the tequfah is falling, perhaps at this very moment,' and the person has already said the blessing (on partaking of water) he should wait and not speak until he is certain that the tequfah has passed, and then he should drink and not make a new blessing."[20] This source linked the tequfah with other malicious spirits that could contaminate the water. *Sefer hasidim* regarded the tequfah as a momentary strike that conferred danger only during that instant. Once it had passed, the water would be safe to drink again. Over time, however, the perceived period of danger and contamination appears to have expanded from the equinoctial moment to a full day. A fourteenth-century manuscript written in Italy included "the four points in which water turned to blood" among other lists of dangerous days.[21] From a practice to refrain from drinking water, the tequfah evolved into the widespread fear that the affected water would turn into harmful blood, although such a belief had no manifest roots in Jewish sources.

The similarity of the tequfah to certain Christian folk beliefs and practices may have contributed to its persistence. In medieval German folklore, on Midsummer Day, St. John's Day, drops from the bleeding corpse of John the Baptist, which hovered over the earth at that time, could be found on the leaves of *Johanniskraut* (St. John's Wort).[22] The Quatember fasts, also known as the fast of the four seasons, were instituted by the Western church in the eleventh century and marked a spiritual and physical break between seasons, much like the tequfah. Of nebulous origins, they were used through the medieval period to mark civil dates.[23] Both Jews and Christians noticed the similarities and identified the customs with one another. Hebrew sifre evronot identified the Christian Quatember with the Jewish tequfot: "Four tequfot, the Christians call them Quatember in their language."[24] Likewise, Christian sources referred to the

Jewish tequfot as Quatember. "The tequfot, which we call Quatember . . . are observed by the Jews with greatest punctiliousness."[25] Some Jewish writers sought explanations for the tequfot in other traditional Jewish fasts. "One fasts three days, 'Monday, Thursday and Monday' after the holidays in case some sin was committed during the eating and drinking. Some say these are the times when the seasons separate, summer from winter. . . . Some people say that at the time that summer and winter separate, the air is bad, therefore we fast and ask God that the bad air should not harm us."[26]

Medieval Jewish rituals of inversion added layers of meaning to the tequfah. In such rituals, Jewish practices marked sacred Christian texts, observances, or symbols with a mocking or parodic inversion. According to some Jewish sources, Christmas, the holiday that marked the birth of Jesus, fell on tequfat Tevet, the winter solstice. This confirmed its ominous status as a time when evil spirits roamed free.[27] At this time, Jews withdrew from their regular activities and engaged in rituals of mockery.[28]

References to the tequfah custom persisted in medieval Jewish textual sources, although the trail of evidence is scanty and it did not appear to attract much Christian attention until the early modern period. By the late fifteenth century, however, there was an efflorescence, if not in its actual observance, then certainly of interest in the custom, its origins, and its meaning. By then the danger from the tequfah to unprotected water had become an accepted belief; many sources elaborate on its laws and customs. This reawakened attention can be attributed to several early modern currents: the Renaissance interest in unusual natural phenomena, printing and its concomitant dissemination of ideas and texts to wider readership, vernacular translations of Jewish custom books, and a new "ethnographic" strain in Christian anti-Jewish polemics.

Widespread interest in exceptional natural occurrences, fueled by reports that circulated in print in large numbers, contributed to the strengthening of the tequfah custom in the early modern period. Some of these events included the appearance of reddish microbes on food, the spread of red algae in water, and instances of so-called blood rain, the product of a mixture of red Saharan sand and rain. Fewer than ten cases of blood rain were documented in Europe for each of the thirteenth, fourteenth, and fifteenth centuries. In the sixteenth and seventeenth centuries, however, the number increased tenfold, either because it fell more often, or, more likely, because people noticed it more and were more apt to discuss it.[29] Early modern calendars and almanacs regularly re-

ported such paranatural climate events.[30] In German lands in particular, there was a heightened interest in aberrations of nature, which were interpreted as signs of divine fury or benevolence.[31] After a widely reported incident of blood rain in 1503, the artist Albrecht Dürer drew the stain it left on a servant girl's linen shift. To contemporaries, it formed the shape of a crucifix with a human figure on either side. Dürer was deeply impressed by this miracle; he noted that the servant girl "feared that she would die of it."[32] Such incidents and their popular interpretations, extraordinary as they may have been, would have served to corroborate the popular Jewish belief. The testimony of Dürer is particularly valuable, because it shows that such events were interpreted in a religious manner and appear to have left their deepest imprint on women in the household. This may explain why the custom, which was enjoined for all Jews and spread to many Jewish cultures, remained a women's custom, particularly in German lands.

Sifre evronot, custom books, and halakhic codes proliferated in early modern German lands, aided by the relatively new printing technologies. The significance of the tequfah custom was magnified as these pathways of communication multiplied. The medieval *Sefer hasidim*, to take an example of an older work, was printed several times in the sixteenth century: in Bologna in 1538; in Basel in 1580; and in Cracow in 1581. These printings of the book disseminated its brand of Jewish pietism into early modern Ashkenazic Jewry.[33]

In Jewish legal works, the tequfah was mentioned most often within the laws pertaining to the preparation of Passover matzot (unleavened bread). The law required preparing water that had been drawn in advance and allowed to rest overnight (hence the designation *mayim she-lanu*, waters that rested). The stillness of the water would ensure that no leavening would occur when the water was mixed with flour. In the section pertaining to preparation of matzot for Passover, one of the most influential Ashkenazic compendia, that of R. Jacob Moellin (Maharil, 1365–1427), noted:

> Tequfat Nissan sometimes falls on the night of drawing water for the matzot.... Although some say there is no problem with this, that there is no danger in the water except if one drinks it at the moment of the tequfah ... for one who is fulfilling a mitzvah will know no harm, nevertheless, we have not conducted ourselves thus, as one may not rely on a miracle. One should take a new iron nail and hang it with a string or

pulley into the water at the time of the tequfah, as is the custom of the world. One should not just throw it into [the water] for when he has to remove it he will have to put his hand in the water and it will become warmer. It must be a new nail or needle or similar implement, not another iron tool, lest some tiny particle cling to it and enter the water.[34]

The sixteenth-century halakhic code of Joseph Karo, *Shulhan arukh*, which later became the canonical code of Jewish law, incorporated from sources such as Moellin the notion of the tequfah as a potentially dangerous time.[35]

The proliferation of books of customs in Yiddish translation aimed at a popular readership in Western and Central Europe maintained and spread the custom of the tequfah as well. Following the model of Hebrew books on Jewish law and custom, many Yiddish customals (compendia of customs) included a warning about the tequfah in the instructions for preparing the water for matzah baking: "Occasionally, the tequfah occurs during the night of mitzvah water. You must not fear any danger, as it is water in service of a mitzvah. Nevertheless, it cannot hurt to put an iron nail into it."[36]

The emergence of new genres, printing, and translation propelled knowledge of the tequfah practice into the early modern period despite the skeptical voices that had countered it. Although notices of the tequfah custom were widespread in these sources, it was not particularly central to their purpose. The reverse can be said of sifre evronot: the tequfah was the only religious ritual specifically promoted by calendar literature, and the ritual played a central role in their development.

The Tequfah as a Biblical Homily

Sifre evronot written by hand in early modern German lands included medieval explanations for why water turned dangerous during the change of the seasons. They cited what appeared to be the oldest explanation: as the seasons changed, the natural world was left unguarded by protective forces. A typical passage in an early modern sefer evronot states:

Four guardian [angels] watch over the entire world. Each one must stand guard during one tequfah. And between one tequfah and the next, there are moments, like the blink of an eye, during the changing of the guards, instants during which the world stands without its guard-

ian, and the *maziqim* (harmful spirits) roam freely during that time. Anyone who drinks at that moment, takes his life into his hands [lit.: his blood is on his head].[37]

This explanation for the dangerous time was overshadowed by a midrashic-style gloss on the four biblical incidents, first noted in the medieval ibbur of Jacob bar Samson. In the early modern period the text had barely changed from its medieval template:

> I heard another explanation, as to why it [this practice] is directed at each tequfah. Tequfat Tishre: because at that moment Abraham came to slaughter his son Isaac and his knife dripped blood, and at that moment all the water in the world turned into blood, as it still does at that moment, now.
>
> Tequfat Tevet: because Jephthah sacrificed his daughter at that time, and all the water turned into blood.
>
> Tequfat Nissan: because all the waters of Egypt turned to blood, and all the water in the world was affected.
>
> Tequfat Tammuz: because at the moment that God spoke to Moses and to Aaron, "Speak to the rock and it will give its water," what did Moses do? He hit the rock and blood flowed . . . and all the water in the world turned to blood and still [today], at that moment, all the water turns to blood for an instant.[38]

The scribes of early modern sifre evronot granted this explanation the distinction of a set of unique illustrations. Only rarely did they depict the practice itself.[39] Instead they focused on the four dramatic moments in biblical narrative that came to be associated with each tequfah.

For tequfat Tishre, the fall equinox, Abraham was depicted holding a knife over Isaac, in a version of the classical Binding of Isaac scene. For tequfat Tevet, Jephthah was drawn sacrificing his daughter; for tequfat Nissan, Moses and Aaron stood over the Nile, turning it to blood in the first biblical plague; and for tequfat Tammuz, Moses hit the rock and blood flowed from it. Most scribe-illustrators situated the images close to the relevant passages. While some of these motifs, such as Moses, Aaron, and the Sacrifice of Isaac, appeared in illustrated haggadot or mahzorim, their combination, some particular details, and the additional depiction of Jephthah and his daughter were unique to sifre evronot.

FIG. 7.3. Aqeda, Abraham ready to sacrifice Isaac. *Sefer evronot*, 1627. Courtesy of the Library of the Jewish Theological Seminary ms 2662, fol. 18r.

The *aqeda*, the binding and near sacrifice of Isaac by Abraham, the first illustration in the tequfah series, was a long-established and well-researched motif in Jewish and Western art history.[40] In sifre evronot, as in most Jewish depictions and in keeping with the biblical text, Abraham wielded a knife, rather than a sword.[41] According to the midrash, the danger from the tequfah of Tishre arose because Abraham lightly wounded Isaac with his knife. Some *aqeda* images in sifre evronot supported the tequfah narrative with depictions of drops of blood dripping from Abraham's knife.[42] Every formulation of the explanation for the tequfot used the talmudic verb "*tiftef* ha-ma'akhelet dam," the knife

FIG. 7.4. "Abraham our father, peace on him, wanted to sacrifice his son," illustration of tequfot. *Sefer evronot*, 1665–1666. Cincinnati, Klau Library, Hebrew Union College–Jewish Institute of Religion ms 901, fol. 32v.

dripped blood. Abraham, in his zeal, inflicted a wound on Isaac that drew blood before he could withdraw the knife at God's command. "The two of them built the altar, and [Abraham] bound Isaac on the altar and took the knife to slaughter [Isaac], until a quarter of his blood flowed from him."[43] Not every illustration of the Sacrifice of Isaac in sifre evronot contained this feature.[44] Some depicted angels rushing in to protect Isaac from Abraham's fervent desire to inflict a mortal wound by the knife.[45]

For the tequfah of Nissan, Moses was depicted standing over the blood-red

FIG. 7.5. Aqeda, blood dripping from Abraham's knife. *Sefer evronot*, ca. 1625. Courtesy of the Rare Book and Manuscript Library, Columbia University ms X893 Se36, fol. 16r.

Nile, long a standard illustration in haggadot for the first biblical plague in which the waters of the Nile turned into blood. For the tequfah of Tamuz, Moses stood over the rock, which in some cases was colored red (although in the biblical text water, rather than blood, flowed from it).[46]

In the most remarkable of the four drawings, Jephthah stands ready to sacrifice his daughter. This was the only image of the tequfah quartet that did not readily appear in other illustrated Jewish texts. In Christian art, this image of a father prepared to sacrifice a child had long been paired with the Binding of Isaac, and Jephthah's daughter came to signify the sacrifice of cloistered religious women.[47] In some illustrations, Jephthah is dressed as a contemporary

FIG. 7.6. Aqeda, blood dripping from Abraham's knife. *Sefer evronot*, 1716. Reproduced with the permission of the National Library of Israel ms Heb 8° 2380, fol. 80v.

military figure and one eighteenth-century sefer evronot depicts Jephthah's daughter dressed as a fashionable contemporary young woman. Even if the illustrations of Jephthah and his daughter had precedents in Jewish manuscript illustration, however, grouping the series of images as a set was unique to sifre evronot.

It is notable that both the Binding of Isaac as well as the image of Jephthah's cloistered daughter symbolized long-standing polemical disputes between Judaism and Christianity. The Binding of Isaac was a richly allusive scene that recurs in even the earliest examples of Jewish and Christian figurative art. The story of fathers willing to sacrifice their only sons turned the Binding of Isaac into an adumbration of the Passion in Christian homilies and art. Consequently, the story became central to the prefiguration of the Christian Bible in the Hebrew.[48] Christian interpretation drew parallels between the lives of Isaac and

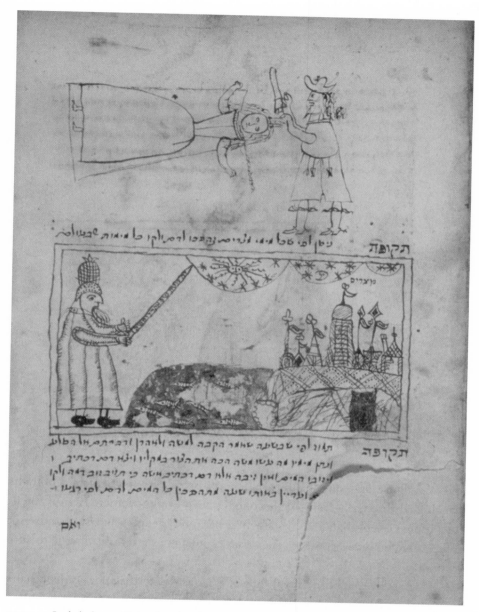

FIG. 7.7. Jephthah sacrificing his daughter (*top*); Moses turning the Nile into blood. *Sefer evronot*, ca. 1625. Courtesy of the Rare Book and Manuscript Library, Columbia University ms X893 Se36, fol. 16v.

FIG. 7.8. Jephthah's daughter. *Sefer evronot*, 1716. Reproduced with the permission of the National Library of Israel ms Heb 8° 2380, fol. 81r.

Jesus: the Annunciation of their births, their miraculous conception, and their bush with thorns (the bush that ensnared the ram came to be seen as parallel to the crown of thorns). In both cases, the life trajectories and denouements resulted from divine intervention.[49] These parallel images became commonplace in Christian art, and where they appear in sifre evronot they can be seen as a response that affirms the Jewish reading of history. For Jews, the Binding of Isaac evoked the divine irrevocable promise to Abraham concerning Jewish destiny. It was linked to the bondage and exodus from Egypt illustrated in the next panels.

Recent scholarship has focused attention on the way medieval Jews and Christians read the story of Jephthah and his daughter in light of Christian monasticism.[50] Elisheva Baumgarten places Jephthah's daughter at the center of the tequfah text and its observance as a women's practice. In her study, the ex-

ample of Jephthah's daughter served as a counterweight to medieval Christian female piety, which centered on celibate virginity within a monastic setting. From the iconographic perspective, this emphasis is not sustained in the early modern period, as all four incidents in the iconography are accorded equal weight, with some illustrators privileging the Binding of Isaac.[51]

The tequfah and its illustrations support the contention that the interplay between Jewish and Christian cultures figured prominently in sifre evronot. But it was not a rigid reenactment of old themes, frozen in time; instead it was a responsive and changing reaction to ongoing mutual perceptions. Cultural contact and Christian influence shaped the illustrations in early modern sifre evronot. The polemical subtext that pervaded the literature of ibbur shaped its iconographic program. It reinforced the message of the priority and importance of the Jewish calendar over its Christian counterpart.

· · ·

The first printers of the ibbur for Jews, Jacob Marcaria and Issachar ibn Susan, included the custom of tequfot prominently in their works. Marcaria's *Sefer evronot* assigned a conspicuous position to the tequfot in the form of an eight-line poem. The poem condensed the biblical explanations for the tequfah and presented them as the "words of the sages."[52] Ibn Susan included a lengthy discussion of the tequfah practice in his *Ibbur shanim*. He strongly criticized the early Sephardic authorities who had questioned the gravity of the threat of the tequfah. He could not accept their facile dismissal of its danger. He tore into Hai Gaon, ibn Ezra, and others who had not endorsed the full severity of its consequences. His words demonstrate how a practice that had been derided among Sephardic rabbis in medieval times was promoted among them in the early modern period:

> I, orphan of orphans, least of the least among the disciples, have difficulty with the words of R. Hai, of blessed memory. If he is correct [that the tequfa practice was merely symbolic of the new season], why did the people not also refrain from drinking water on the New Year, which is the essence of the whole year? [They should have been required to do so] at least at the beginning of the day or at night at the first meal, as it is customary during the tequfah not to drink water even during a meal. The same [question applies to] the three other New Years throughout the year. According to the words of those Geonim, of blessed memory, who say that the early [sages] said these things merely to frighten the

masses . . . this is a great puzzlement. For even the sages of the Talmud and the kabbalists have suffered this [the harmful effect of the tequfah] over many generations since ancient times, all of them have had this frightening voice in their ears, cautious and warning others, sages and plain folk, with proclamations in their synagogues, their communities and among the people. If the matter seemed inherently unclear, would our predecessors not have had some other way to frighten the masses to fear God except for this way? Perhaps . . . with the things they continually preach in their sermons and exaggerate for them? If those blandishments did not cause people to fear God, how much less will they listen because someone tells them, "Whoever drinks water during the tequfah will be harmed." This does not lead to fear of God, not a lot and not a little. . . . Furthermore, one can wonder at the words of R. A[braham] ibn Ezra, of blessed memory, who wrote, "The matter of the swelling up is the prattle of old women," as it is impossible that this fear has become known and spread throughout the world for no reason. . . . Even the books of codifiers and kabbalists, of blessed memory, contain written evidence of this fear.[53]

Ibn Susan rejected the explanation that rabbis promoted the custom as a calculated attempt to intimidate the masses by invoking spurious false consequences (although he himself decorated his tequfah chart with the verse "Fortunate is the person who is always afraid").[54]

In the seventeenth century, the Sephardic rabbi Hezekiah de Silva (1659–1698) described a custom that had expanded geographically to "the entire Jewish dispersion," as well as temporally, to include the entire day or the entire night. De Silva described the public announcement of the custom: "The custom of the people is to declare the times of the tequfah so that the people will be careful not to drink water at that time because of the danger that they would be harmed and would swell up." The custom he described had developed a leniency: the people believed that danger lurked only in unused water, not water that had been boiled or used for salting or pickling. De Silva expressed perplexed anger over ibn Ezra's cavalier dismissal of the danger of the tequfah water as an "old wives' tale." In his view the concern was valid: "We have heard in our own days several cases of those who drank during the time of the tequfah and swelled up, some of them died, others were healed."[55]

The Tequfah through Christian Eyes

Few Christian writers paid notice to the tequfah custom before the eighteenth century. One who did was the late-fifteenth-century Dominican monk Erhard von Pappenheim. In his Latin prologue to a polemical Haggadah translation, von Pappenheim wrote:

> Four times a year, at a particular hour and minute, a drop of blood falls from heaven into all the household vessels in which drinking water is kept; and whoever drinks from this water, in which these drops have fallen, contracts hydropsis or another type of swelling on the body. That is, unless an iron object is first dunked into the water, since once this is done it is no longer able to inflict damage. In their language, [the Jews] call this drop [. . .] 'Tokofah.' They carefully plot the times and minutes when this *tokofah* ought to fall. I cannot cease to be amazed how it can be that they find these fabulous claims, not to say superstitions, so persuasive when, so far as I know, no other race or language or nation knows or is even aware of them. Neither divine authority nor any sort of philosophical or human wisdom teaches such things, nor does plain reason.[56]

Pappenheim did not explain why the water was considered dangerous at these junctures, but he did get the story right: that Jews referred to the blood that dropped into their water as "the tequfah," that they feared falling ill from drinking it, and that they believed the antidote was to thrust a metal object into the water. Most notably, Pappenheim concluded that as a result of this belief, "Jews carefully plot the times and minutes." Here he may have touched on one of the reasons that the custom was tolerated by so many Jewish legal experts despite the lack of any basis: it turned calendrical precision into a matter of life and death.

Pappenheim was not preparing a compendium of harmless Jewish practices, but a polemical treatise about the dangers of Judaism. Later in the passage he continues to ridicule the custom, and more ominously, to link it to the Jewish use of Christian blood in baking matzot. He noted that its inclusion in a work about Passover was appropriate because of the problem with water drawn for the matzah; he went on to charge that the first matzot eaten for Passover were made with Christian blood.

Not all Christian scholars who mentioned the tequfah custom intended to accuse Jews of ritual murder. Sebastian Münster, the first to print the Hebrew ibbur in 1527, observed that Jewish calendars noted the days, hours, and seconds of the tequfot. His remarks were made within the context of a caustic evaluation of the rabbinic calendar. He referred to the Jewish tequfah customs as hallucinations, and reported a Jewish view that each season was ruled over by an angel: during the transfer of the seasons the *shedim*, devils, seized power. They were the ones who harmed the water supply, and those who drank it would contract dropsy.[57]

Jacobus Nigri's *Kalendarium*, published two years after Münster's, also presented the Jewish calendar in a rather derisory tone. Nigri's book followed the structure of the calendar itself, with each Jewish month presented first in Latin, in (a rather atrocious) transliteration; an expanded description of each item followed. He described the tequfah custom only once, under the rubric "Lel hatekupha," or night of the tequfah, within the month of Tishre between Yom Kippur and "Haisinu" [*Ha'azinu*, Deut. 32: 1–52], immediately followed by "suckas" [Tabernacles]. He referred to the tequfah as "what we call *angaria*," a conjunction.[58] After transcribing the exact time of the tequfat Tishre from a Jewish calendar, Nigri described how "the Jews observe a point of time, 'kufa,' when the evil spirits rule in all the waters. . . . Jews observe them because the malignant spirits reign at this time; those who drink submit to dropsy, and applying themselves by reason, they insert the angarias [tequfot] into their diaries [calendars]."[59]

Given the western Christian culture's fascination with blood during medieval times, it is puzzling that the custom of the tequfah and the explanation of the blood event drew little Christian attention then.[60] The delayed interest is even more remarkable given the propensity of Christian writers to misread (sometimes deliberately) Jewish customs—particularly those related to Passover—as spiteful inversions of Christian practices.[61] It was not until the publication of a series of harsh ethnographic works by Christian converts out of Judaism in the early eighteenth century that the tequfah became central to anti-Jewish polemics, a chapter in a protracted onslaught by converts against Jewish daily practices. Although these Christian works supposedly aimed at theological and religious issues, the information conveyed in their work was sociological and domestic.

While manuscript sifre evronot were rarely owned and never written by women (although they may have been intended viewers of the illustrations), to

date no printed Jewish calendars from this period have surfaced that were marketed directly to women. It is only within the works of these converts that (to date) we find evidence of the "missing" calendars, Jewish calendars whose primary users were women. In describing the rituals surrounding the tequfah these authors made an unambiguous case that women were at the forefront of tequfah observance in their kitchens. One mentions "several printed Jewish calendars" in which the observance of the tequfah and its religious justification were taught in Yiddish verse.[62]

The first polemical work to focus exclusively on the tequfah was Paul Wilhelm Hirsch's *Megalleh tekuphoth (Revealer of the Tekufot)*, printed in Berlin in 1717. In the introduction, Hirsch made it perfectly clear that as a convert from Judaism to Christianity, his book would be a bitter diatribe against the blind Jews. He would prove that the blood curse pronounced by the ancestors of the Jews in the Book of Matthew, "His blood be upon us and upon our children" (27:24–25), still caused blood-punishment to come upon them. One of the manifestations of the curse, Hirsch averred, was a form of male menstruation. He claimed to have witnessed it in his own father, a blood flow every four weeks. Some would say this flow was due to hemorrhoids that Jews suffered because they ate unhealthy food. Hirsch refuted this by noting that the Bible prohibited unhealthy foods such as pig and rabbit meat, and yet the Jews bled. As a result of this continuous blood flow, Hirsch concluded, Jews stank. This is the reason, Hirsch wrote, that one could smell a Jew before one saw or heard him.[63]

Given this preamble, drenched with self-hatred and offering tired canards, all of Hirsch's testimony must be regarded as potentially unbalanced or untrue. Hirsch's descriptions of Jewish households reacting to the tequfah should be read with these caveats in mind. Yet like converts who produced similar polemical ethnographies, bits of truth were likely embedded in them. In any case, if for no other reason than that his work was read and copied by others, his account merits analysis.

Hirsch intimated that the term "tekuphah," which was scattered throughout Jewish calendars, included another, more sinister meaning than its etymological definition, a cycle.[64] Hirsch's prooftexts were Yiddish calendars in which the tequfah stories were spun out in rhyme; he cited these at length. Hirsch then retraced the meaning of each set of verses for the Christian reader, with a refutation of what had become the popular Jewish explanation. This he followed by the "true"—that is, Christian—interpretation. Hirsch began with the

first of the four tequphot of the Jewish year, Tishre, in early October, at the start of the Jewish New Year. Jews understand this to be month that Abraham offered Isaac on Mount Moriah. As they present it, Abraham did not just have the knife in his hand to slaughter his son, he actually began to cut, and some drops of blood escaped, when the angel called upon him to stop. He was unable to finish the job. They say that in the month of Tishre these drops of blood spread throughout the world, therefore in this period, one must be careful not to drink any water unless one puts a piece of iron in it.[65]

Hirsch followed his exposition of the first tequfah with a refutation from Jewish exegetical sources that interpreted the biblical text to mean that Abraham withdrew his knife before Isaac's neck had been nicked.[66] He produced midrashim indicating that Isaac's near sacrifice would stand eternally as a merit when Israel sought divine forgiveness.[67] If the transformation of water into blood at this juncture did not result from Abraham's wounding Isaac, Hirsch concluded, "It must necessarily be a different blood that is 'on their head' and a punishment for them."[68]

Hirsch continued in a similar vein through the four tequfot. Concerning tequfat Tevet, he argued, both Jewish and non-Jewish commentators agreed that it was unclear from the text whether Jephthah had actually sacrificed his daughter. "Regardless, I ask the Jews: why should water turn to blood because of it? And why should it harm them? It appears that the text credits him [Jephthah] for keeping his oath, and God rewards him with victories, so why assume that a punishment comes to the world on his account?"[69] Regarding tequfat Nissan, Hirsch claimed that while there was no question according to the biblical text that water turned to blood, it would be preposterous to assume that the Israelites suffered the plagues alongside the Egyptians.[70] And concerning the explanation of Moses hitting the rock for tequfat Tammuz, he argued that even if one were to concede that the rock bled, there could be no reason for water to continue turning to blood forever.

Hirsch described a people obsessed with fear of the harmful blood. "Four times a year, blood comes upon the Jews, not only in their water, but also in their food and drink, and this blood is very harmful to them. The Jews were more fearful of this harmful blood-event (*Blut-Fall*) which comes four times a year into their water, food, and drink, than of the pestilence. They take all measures to prevent it; not only is it distinctly printed in their calendars, four times,

as you can see, but in addition the sexton or cantor must announce it loudly in the synagogue."[71] The example he cited "from this year's calendar" 1715–1716 —"Tequfat Tevet falls four-and-a-half hours into the night of the seventh, on Rosh Hodesh Tevet"—is typical of the way the time of the tequfah was in fact recorded in Jewish calendars in early modern western Europe.[72] The written and public oral announcements constituted proof, in Hirsch's book, that Jews were fixated on the tequfah. Their terror is evident from their announcements in the synagogue on the Shabbat before the event, not only of the hour, but also of the minutes and even seconds of the impending tequfah. It was announced again on the weekday, during the daily prayer that preceded the tequfah, so that both housefather and housemother were reminded.[73]

Hirsch was not content to report on textual and ritual traces of the tequfah practice. He described in vivid detail the frenzy within Jewish households before the advent of that dreaded time.

> As soon as they come home, the women take measures to secure against the blood-event by placing an iron nail, iron knife or fork, or something else made of this material. They place it on a plate or lid with which they cover their food or drink. As long as something iron lay on the covered pots, basins, and other dishes, the tequfah does not harm them at all and the blood does not come into their food or drink. As to the water, it is poured out and the dishes are newly washed and cleaned if anything remained in the house after the tequfah. Since men are not occupied with running the household or the kitchen, it falls solely on the women. They know best how great a supply of food and drink they have on hand. At the same time, the men also remind their wives urgently to be careful of the tequfah. That is how the Jews ensure that their four-times-yearly blood-event does not harm them. If they mistakenly forget it, and someone should eat or drink of the uncovered food, and something of the blood got into it, that person begins to swell up like a drum and dies suddenly.[74]

Hirsch bolstered these domestic, gendered images of the observance of the tequfah, and of the panic that it caused in Jewish households, with a vivid description of the blood that fell into the unprotected food. The noxious blood looked "sometimes like other blood, as if it were wrapped in a blueish membrane with tiny blue veins radiating out from it."[75] He illustrated its arrival with several case histories to which he claimed a personal connection. In the first two

instances he claimed only a tangential relationship to the events. He reminisced: "In my youth I saw in Kremzier, Moravia, three miles from Olmütz, where the bishop has a beautiful castle and garden, a Jewish woman who had settled there when she was expelled from Vienna along with the other Jews [1670]. She suddenly swelled up and died. The old Jews said to one another, 'Sie wäre an der Tekupha gestorben (She died of the tekufah).'"[76] A second incident took place in Keppen, two miles from Frankfurt an der Oder.

> The tequfah fell into a bowl of sweet milk. The Jewish woman wanted to remove the blood from the milk with a spoon to throw it away. That is what she did, but perhaps she did not remove it all. She ate from the left-over milk and let out a great scream. She was not unlike the women in the Old Testament who drink from the bitter accursed water (Numbers 5:27). She was so swollen that the flesh fell off her body in chunks. This can be verified at this moment by a woman who now lives in Berlin. She married an informer (*informatorem*) but before she was baptized she had lived in the same house as that unfortunate Jewish woman. She saw the blood, she stood by the Jewish woman as she skimmed the blood off her milk, and lived through her horrendous death.[77]

The second set of anecdotes that Hirsch cited was based on far more personal memories.

> The first kind I saw with my parents in Prague. They once had an entire pot of goose fat, as Jews until today hold it in esteem, and stored it in abundance, particularly in Bohemia and Moravia. My parents forgot to put the iron nail onto it, and as they wanted to use some of that fat, the tequfah fell into it. In the middle of the fat there appeared from above to below a vein filled with blood as round and the size of a blood spot. The remainder appeared normal and although they could have used the remainder, their fear and terror was so great that they were moved to throw the pot with all the fat into the water.[78]

Here Hirsch appears to be conflating the fear of the tequfah with another obscure custom to refrain from slaughtering geese in the winter months because of a special danger.[79]

In another incident Hirsch reported the fate of the landlady at the "Jewish university," the yeshiva which he attended as a young student, who had forgot-

ten to put a nail in the pot. "She found in the evening in a wooden jug such blood-drops wrapped in a blue membrane, sprouting veins."[80] She punctured the membrane with a needle, and as the blood made its way, she remembered with terror that she had forgotten to protect her food and drink. She threw everything out. A final incident in Hirsch concerned a woman in Kalisch, in Great Poland, who found the blood enclosed in a skin that she was forced to clean away because it was so disgusting. She, together with her husband and children, now lived in Berlin, and had converted to Christianity.[81]

Hirsch's anecdotes, with their vivid imagery, gave the beliefs and practices of the Jews he described a textured realism that no theoretical description could provide. If his depiction contained any truth, then Jews during his day had a vastly expanded fear of the tequfah that made any liquid, including milk and rendered goose fat, vulnerable to it. According to Hirsch, the tequfah became a widespread, deeply entrenched—and gendered—folk practice.

Hirsch's anecdotes add details to the tequfah observance that do not appear in earlier sources. He alleged that the Jews tried to conceal the practice and the true reason behind their fear of the tequfah blood from their Christian neighbors. "They want to keep it hidden, and do not want the truth to come out."[82] One of Hirsch's proofs that Jews deliberately concealed the practice from non-Jews was that Jews did not use it to curse:

> It is remarkable that Jews never swear by the tequfah. When they want to use a strong and terrible curse, they say "You should die an unnatural death, you should collapse; or great misery, rot, rancid air, or the plague should take you, or other such curses." However, the fact that the Hebrews never swear by the tequfah stems from two reasons: it is so terrible they do not even wish it upon their worst enemies. [Alternatively] they are afraid that the curse would revert back onto them. If many of them were to fall victim to the tequfah, then this secret would be exposed.[83]

Approximately a decade after Hirsch's book appeared, two other converts from Judaism to Christianity each made the tequfah central to their anti-Jewish conversionary treatises. One of these, Phillip Nicodemus Leberecht, hoped "thereby to lead the poor misguided Jews not only away from this particular accursed custom, but away from their entire misguided reliance on the unnecessary and superfluous rabbinic teachings as well as from the entire curse of the law."[84] Leberecht had left Judaism when he was thirty-two years old and had

produced the customary anti-Jewish works to attest to the sincerity of his break from his former world.[85] Leberecht aimed to show from the Jews' own writings "that what they consider to be the basis for this custom in holy scripture is in fact nothing but falsehood."[86] Unlike Hirsch, Leberecht admitted that during his entire life among the Jews he had never seen this blood, nor was he ever able to get any Jew to give him a clear, firsthand account of it. Instead, his evidence for its existence rested "in the large Jewish 'Luchos, Calendern' as well as other books."[87]

Lebrecht, like Hirsch, describes a custom that had come to include far more than danger to drawn water. "This blood, annually . . . re-spills, and it appears in various places as testimony to the sacrifice of Isaac: in their cellars and kitchens, in their food and drink."[88] Although Hirsch provided a text from the calendars in Latin characters, Leberecht transcribed the Yiddish in the distinctive typeface used to print that language. The result is nearly identical to the transcription found in Hirsch's *Megalleh tekuphot*. The small differences and strong similarities between the texts lead to the conclusion that both authors were copying independently from Yiddish lukhot. In both texts, the author of the rhymes advertised that his work should be read by young and old, women and girls.[89]

Levi Abraham de Vries, another convert out of Judaism, published a work with the same title as Hirsch's in 1733. He claimed to have been a teacher and circumciser in Amsterdam; he converted to Christianity in the Danish city of Flensburg and three years later published his revelation of the tequfot there.[90] His book is a nearly verbatim copy of Hirsch's. De Vries brazenly lifted every incident from Hirsch's book with a few slight changes of name and place, and he hinted slyly to his theft by saying that the facts could be confirmed by a great "Rabbi Hirsch" who had converted to Christianity and resided in Berlin.[91]

Like Hirsch, de Vries linked the iron nail of the tequfah to "Christ who was nailed through his hands and feet by your ancestors."[92] Jews who thought that the blood did not enter cooked foods would do well to think of Christ on the cross burning with the heat of his love. De Vries painted a scene of neighborly interchange in which Jewish women, embarrassed by the tequfah blood, tried to hide it from their neighbors by saying, "We will not put any nail in our food and drink, and still, no blood will enter it."[93] De Vries warned the Christians that the Jewish women were concealing a small rod or sewing needle in their pots to ward it off.

The tequfah remained a popular topic in certain anti-Jewish scholarly circles.[94] The repetitive nature of subsequent discussions of it betrays the authors'

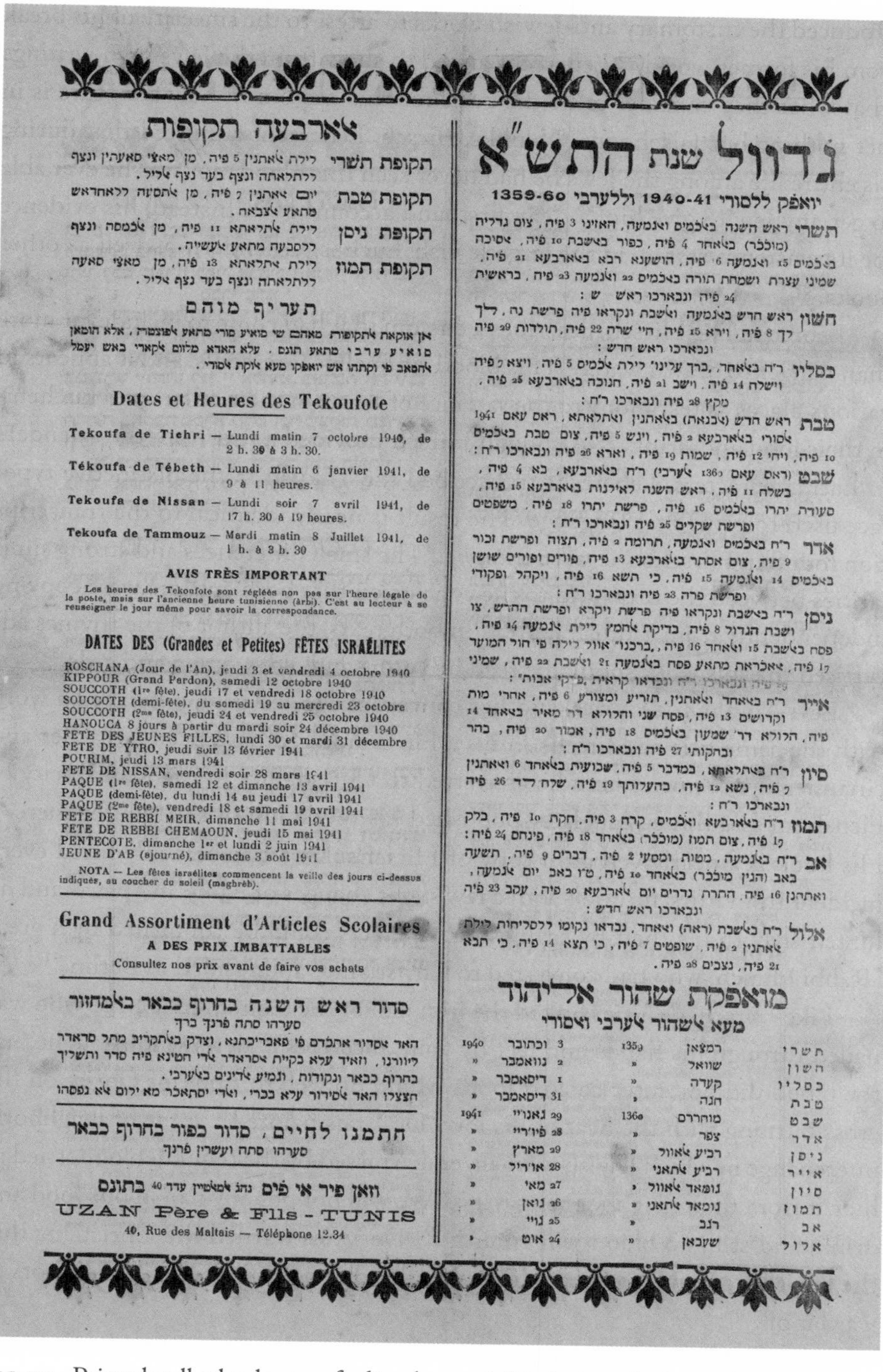

גדול שנת התש"א

יואפק ללסורי 1940-41 וללערבי 1359-60

תשרי ראש השנה באלכמיס ואגמעה, האזינו 3 פיה, צום גדליה (מוכר) באחד 4 פיה, כפור באשבת 10 פיה, אסיכה באלכמיס 15 ואגמעה 16 פיה, הושענא רבא באארבעא 21 פיה, שמיני עצרת ושמחת תורה באלכמיס 22 ואגמעה 23 פיה, בראשית 24 פיה ונבארכו ראש ש :

חשון ראש חרש באגמעה ואשבת ונקראו פיה פרשת נח, לך לך 8 פיה, וירא 15 פיה, חיי שרה 22 פיה, תולדות 29 פיה ונבארכו ראש חדש :

כסליו ר"ח באאחד, „ברך עלינו" לילת אלכמיס 5 פיה, ויצא 7 פיה וישלח 14 פיה, וישב 21 פיה, חנוכה באארבעא 25 פיה, מקץ 28 פיה ונבארכו ר"ח :

טבת ראש חרש (אכנאת) באאתנין ואתלאתא, ראס עאם 1941 אסורי באארבעא 2 פיה, ויגש 5 פיה, צום טבת באלכמיס 10 פיה, ויחי 12 פיה, שמות 19 פיה, וארא 26 פיה ונבארכו ר"ח :

שבט (ראס עאם 1360 אערבי) ר"ח באארבעא, בא 4 פיה, בשלח 11 פיה, ראש השנה לאילנות באארבעא 15 פיה, סעודת יהרו באלכמיס 16 פיה, פרשת יתרו 18 פיה, משפטים ופרשת שקלים 25 פיה ונבארכו ר"ח :

אדר ר"ח באלכמיס ואגמעה, תרומה 2 פיה, תצוה ופרשת זכור 9 פיה, צום אסתר באארבעא 13 פיה, פורים ופורים שושן באלכמיס 14 ואגמעה 15 פיה, כי תשא 16 פיה, ויקהל ופקודי ופרשת פרה 23 פיה ונבארכו ר"ח :

ניסן ר"ח באשבת ונקראו פיה פרשת ויקרא ופרשת החדש, צו ושבת הגדול 8 פיה, בדיקת אחמץ לילת אגמעה 14 פיה, פסח באשבת 15 ואאחד 16 פיה, „ברכנו" אוול לילה פי חול המועד 17 פיה, אאכראת מתאע פסח באגמעה 21 ואשבת 22 פיה, שמיני 29 פיה ונבארכו ר"ח ונבדאו קראית „פרקי אבות" :

אייר ר"ח באאחד ואאתנין, תזריע ומצורע 6 פיה, אחרי מות וקרושים 13 פיה, פסח שני והלולא דר' מאיר באאחד 14 פיה, הלולא דר' שמעון באלכמיס 18 פיה, אמור 20 פיה, בהר ובחקותי 27 פיה ונבארכו ר"ח :

סיון ר"ח באתלאתא, במדבר 5 פיה, שבועות באאחד 6 ואאתנין 7 פיה, נשא 12 פיה, בהעלותך 19 פיה, שלח לך 26 פיה ונבארכו ר"ח :

תמוז ר"ח באארבעא ואלכמיס, קרח 3 פיה, חקת 10 פיה, בלק 17 פיה, צום תמוז (מוכר) באאחד 18 פיה, פינחס 24 פיה :

אב ר"ח באגמעה, מטות ומסעי 2 פיה, דברים 9 פיה, תשעה באב (הגין מוכר) באאחד 10 פיה, ט"ו באב יום אגמעה, ואתחנן 16 פיה, התרת נדרים יום אארבעא 20 פיה, עקב 23 פיה ונבארכו ראש חדש :

אלול ר"ח באשבת (ראה) ואאחד, נבדאו נקומו לרסליחות לילת אאתנין 2 פיה, שופטים 7 פיה, כי תצא 14 פיה, כי תבא 21 פיה, נצבים 28 פיה.

מואפקת שהור אליהוד

מעא אשהור אערבי ואסורי

תשרי	רמצאן	1359	3	וכתובר	1940
חשון	שוואל	»	2	נוואמבר	»
כסליו	קעדה	»	1	דיסאמבר	»
טבת	חגה	»	31	דיסאמבר	»
שבט	מוחרם	1360	29	גאנויי	1941
אדר	צפר	»	28	פיורייי	»
ניסן	רביע אאוול	»	29	מארץ	»
אייר	רביע אתאני	»	28	אוריל	»
סיון	נומאד אאוול	»	27	מאי	»
תמוז	נומאד אתאני	»	26	נואן	»
אב	רגב	»	25	גויי	»
אלול	שעבאן	»	24	אוט	»

ארבעה תקופות

תקופת תשרי לילת אאתנין 5 פיה, מן מאצי סאעתין ונצף ללתלאתה ונצף בער נצף אליל.

תקופת טבת יום אאתנין 7 פיה, מן אתסעה ללאחראש מתאע אצבאח.

תקופת ניסן לילת אתלאתא 11 פיה, מן אכמסה ונצף לרסבעה מתאע אעשייה.

תקופת תמוז לילת אתלאתא 13 פיה, מן מאצי סאעה ללתלאתה ונצף בער נצף אליל.

תעריף מוהם

אן אוקאת אתקופות מאהם שי סואיע פורי מתאע אפוצטה, אלא הומאן סואיע ערבי מתאע תונס. עלא האדא מלזום אקארי באש יעמל אחסאב פי וקתהו אש יואפקו מעא אוקת אסורי.

Dates et Heures des Tekoufote

Tekoufa de Tichri — Lundi matin 7 octobre 1940, de 2 h. 30 à 3 h. 30.

Tékoufa de Tébeth — Lundi matin 6 janvier 1941, de 9 à 11 heures.

Tekoufa de Nissan — Lundi soir 7 avril 1941, de 17 h. 30 à 19 heures.

Tekoufa de Tammouz — Mardi matin 8 Juillet 1941, de 1 h. à 3 h. 30

AVIS TRÈS IMPORTANT

Les heures des Tekoufote sont réglées non pas sur l'heure légale de la poste, mais sur l'ancienne heure tunisienne (àrbi). C'est au lecteur à se renseigner le jour même pour savoir la correspondance.

DATES DES (Grandes et Petites) FÊTES ISRAÉLITES

ROSCHANA (Jour de l'An), jeudi 3 et vendredi 4 octobre 1940
KIPPOUR (Grand Pardon), samedi 12 octobre 1940
SOUCCOTH (1re fête), jeudi 17 et vendredi 18 octobre 1940
SOUCCOTH (demi-fête), du samedi 19 au mercredi 23 octobre
SOUCCOTH (2me fête), jeudi 24 et vendredi 25 octobre 1940
HANOUCA 8 jours à partir du mardi soir 24 décembre 1940
FETE DES JEUNES FILLES, lundi 30 et mardi 31 décembre
FETE DE YTRO, jeudi soir 13 février 1941
POURIM, jeudi 13 mars 1941
FETE DE NISSAN, vendredi soir 28 mars 1941
PAQUE (1re fête), samedi 12 et dimanche 13 avril 1941
PAQUE (demi-fête), du lundi 14 au jeudi 17 avril 1941
PAQUE (2me fête), vendredi 18 et samedi 19 avril 1941
FETE DE REBBI MEIR, dimanche 11 mai 1941
FETE DE REBBI CHEMAOUN, jeudi 15 mai 1941
PENTECOTE, dimanche 1er et lundi 2 juin 1941
JEUNE D'AB (ajourné), dimanche 3 août 1941

NOTA — Les fêtes israélites commencent la veille des jours ci-dessus indiqués, au coucher du soleil (maghrèb).

Grand Assortiment d'Articles Scolaires
A DES PRIX IMBATTABLES
Consultez nos prix avant de faire vos achats

סדור ראש השנה בחרוף כבאר באמחזור
סערהו סתה פרנך ברך
האר אסדיור אתכדם פי פאבריכתנא, וצדק באתקריב מתל סראדר ליוורנו, וזאיד עלא בקיית אסראדר אדי חטינא פיה סדר ותשליך בחרוף כבאר ונקודות, ותמיע אדינים באערבי.
חצלו האר אסידור עלא בכרי, ואדי יסתאכר מא ילום לא נפסהו

תתמנו לחיים, סדור כפור בחרוף כבאר
סערהו סתה ועשרין פרנך

וזאן פיר אי פים נהג אמאטין עדד 40 **בתונס**
UZAN Père & Fils - TUNIS
40, Rue des Maltais — Téléphone 12.34

FIG. 7.9. Printed wall calendar, tequfot listed upper left in Judaeo-Arabic and French. Tunis, 1940. Courtesy Gross Family Collection, Tel Aviv.

impulse to profit from a sensationalist topic that drew many interested readers rather than to provide original insights or information.

Observance of the tequfah custom survived in parts of the Jewish world into modern times.[95] In the West, where it was strongest in the early modern period, it has disappeared with nary a trace. Recovering the practice and the array of voices that attended it in the early modern period, however, opens another perspective into Jewish cultural history encoded within the pages of the calendar. It grants us knowledge of previously unknown layers of meaning that the calendar held for the men and women who used it. The brief notations of seasonal turning points hinted at rituals of water and blood, danger and disease, men in the synagogues rushing to warn their wives in the kitchens, and Christian neighbors observing in mocking wonderment, unaware of the role their own culture played in the scenes that unfolded before them.

Imagining the Beginning of Time: Jewish Chronology

Thus the calendars do not measure time as clocks do; they are monuments of historical consciousness.

Walter Benjamin, *Illuminations*, 1938

JEWISH calendars in early modern Europe opened with the "year from the world's creation" emblazoned on their title pages, reinforcing the impression that they had been calculated and presented in this immutable form over the ages. Who could resist the image of Adam, freshly molded from the Creator's clay, inscribing the first year from the creation, then another, in a chain of seemingly unbroken duration and remarkable precision?

While most early modern Jews accepted the chronology offered by their calendars at face value, the idea of reckoning from the "starting point of creation" was, in fact, a parvenu among Jewish chronological systems. Far from beginning with the stroke of Adam's pen, the anno mundi system was a comparatively recent innovation in Jewish chronology.

The importance of chronology in a culture as historically conscious as that of the Jews can hardly be exaggerated. Cultures rely on their calendars not merely to plot the days, weeks, months, and seasons in their inexorable cycles, but also to create a linear sequential order that reaches back into the past and forward into the future. Calendars situated the users in a particular year within a particular chronological system. This seemingly stable, dependable, and predictable aspect of the calendar, in which one numbered year invariably followed the next, served as a grid on which to plot the entire sweep of past events. Chronology provided the tool without which the calculation and presentation of the past would be impossible.[1]

A rather staggering assortment of different systems had been used to count the years among ancient Israelites and Jews. Multiple and various chronological systems flourished and then fell into disuse, some leaving only faint traces of

FIG 8.1. "Shenat" (In the year), opening word of a chronograph, lettered with whimsical creatures. *Sefer evronot*, 1552. Courtesy of the Library of the Jewish Theological Seminary ms 9487, fol. 1r.

their existence. A number of chronological systems were based on the regnal years of kings: Israelite, Judean, Persian, and Hasmonean.[2] Others counted from historical events such as the Exodus from Egypt or the Destruction of the Temple.[3] The Septuagint, the first "translation" of the Hebrew Bible into Greek, presented a chronology for biblical events (the length of the patriarch's lives, for example) that differed so much from the Hebrew that creation was dated nearly fifteen hundred years earlier than the normative Jewish anno mundi.[4]

Even where there were no great computational and hermeneutical differences, significant variations existed among Jewish sources as to when the chronology began. Was it in Tishre before the world was actually created, so that the *molad tohu* (conjunction of chaos) before the actual moment of creation would be included? Was it sometime thereafter when the celestial luminaries (sun, moon, and stars) were "hung" in the sky, or at the time of Adam's creation? Evidence from the Geonic period indicates that the Jews of Babylonia used a slightly different chronology than those of the Land of Israel.[5]

The most persistent and widespread Jewish chronology in the ancient period, the *minyan shtarot* (Era of Contracts), counted from the victory of Seleucus in the fourth century B.C.E. and remained in use among some Jews at least through the tenth century C.E., and in many parts of the world for far longer.[6] Gravestone inscriptions from southern Israel during the fourth through sixth centuries C.E. counted the year within the sabbatical cycle, and to the Era of the Destruction of the Temple.[7] From the Italian Jewish community at Venossa, surviving tombstone inscriptions from the ninth century C.E. reveal a slow shift in which chronologies were used. All twenty-three surviving inscriptions bear dates to the "*bet ha-miqdash ha-qadosh*," the holy Temple, the Era of Destruction, and just three of these bear an additional dating to the Era from Creation. Because this community was heavily influenced by the culture in the Land of Israel, the inscriptions testify that the Era of Destruction was still the dominant chronology there, with the Creation Era slowly making headway.[8]

Around the tenth to eleventh centuries C.E., Jews in most Western communities adopted and began to use widely the counting that began with creation, anno mundi.[9] The emergence of a widely used "Jewish chronology" was a triumph of imaginative pragmatism whose author(s), time, and methods of institution remain largely unknown. The primary literary source for anno mundi chronology was the rabbinic composition titled *Seder olam*, literally, "Order of the World." Scholars have suggested that this distinctively Jewish chronology was developed as a response to the widespread adoption of Christian chronology, and their temporal congruence makes this a logical explanation; but there is as yet no definitive evidence to support this idea.

Christians, meanwhile, did not count years from the birth of Jesus right away either. They had inherited a rich chronological tradition from the Greeks and Romans before them. Some of these predecessors had incorporated into their universal histories knowledge of biblical or Septuagint chronology.[10] Eu-

sebius's *Chronicle* passed this tradition on to the emperor Constantine, and from there it became the basis for Christian chronologies throughout the medieval period.[11]

The anno domini (year of our Lord) chronology eventually adopted by Western Christians is credited to the learned monk Dionysius Exiguus (ca. 470–ca. 544). Dionysius labored to create a new perpetual calendar to replace the Cyrillic tables he had inherited, because they extended only until the year 531 C.E. The earlier chronologies that had been passed down from the Romans were pegged to the lives of the Roman emperors. But Dionysius balked at incorporating into his perpetual calendar for Christians the names of Roman emperors like Diocletian who were notorious for persecuting them. So although he did provide Roman "checks and balances" for his chronology, such as years of indiction (cycles of taxation), Dionysius essentially marginalized these and all other means of reckoning dates and elevated his new system, which began from the year of the Incarnation as he understood it, to the central position.[12]

Although Dionysius designed it, the spread of the new Christian chronology can be credited to Bede, who incorporated it into his *Ecclesiastical History*. From Bede it entered the Carolingian schools, then slowly spread throughout Western Europe. Its eventual dominance over other chronological systems at about the same time as the Jewish anno mundi system began to be used strengthens the possibility that there may have been a link between the two.

Most of the creators and users of sifre evronot were not concerned with technical chronology, that is, the art and science of pinpointing dates for past events in a coherent and systematic way.[13] Yet chronology was intricately interwoven into every calendrical work. Medieval and early modern Jews inherited the anno mundi chronological tradition, and sifre evronot taught their calculations from that beginning point, so that all Jewish calendar literature remained closely tied to chronology.[14] A sixteenth-century computus guide thus began: "If a person wishes to reckon [the calendar] he must at least know the present year from Creation. And if you do not know, ask. For this chronology is known to almost all Jews, particularly to Torah scholars and to scribes who write contracts."[15]

Chronology provided the key to several strands of culture embedded in early modern calendars. Calendars used chronology to foster the pedagogy of the past, to position other chronological systems in a comparative and often polemical perspective, and to contribute to the search for meaning in time.

Chronographs

Early modern calendars trumpeted "Chronograph from the beginning of the world's creation," telegraphing their authors' or printers' intention that they serve as vehicles of Jewish temporal consciousness.[16] For in addition to guiding their users to march to the cadences of the present time, sifre evronot and Jewish calendars reflected a collective historical past. As they propelled the commemoration of events from ancient times into the present by displaying the cycle of annual religious observances, calendars also presented historical information that did not pertain directly to religious ritual or natural rhythms. Sifre evronot and calendars typically contained a prominently placed list of notable events from the time of creation until the current year. These registers, called chronographs (originally the drum on which a stylus recorded intervals of time), listed dates and events in brief, crisp entries devoid of nuance, narrative, complexity, or interpretation.[17]

After an opening declaration that announced the current year in anno mundi chronology: "_____ years since the creation of the world," chronographs typically compressed the significant events of the next several thousand years into a few lines. A sample chronograph from 1585 C.E. thus situated the user within the anno mundi chronology: "5345 years since the creation of the world," then listed the number of years since

> the flood . . . our ancestors arrival in Egypt . . . the birth of Moses our master, of blessed memory . . . the exodus from Egypt . . . entry of our ancestors into Eretz Israel . . . to the building of the first Temple . . . to the exile of the Ten Tribes . . . to the destruction of the first Temple . . . the building of the second Temple . . . the kingdom of the Greeks . . . the Era of Contracts . . . the end of prophecy . . . the reign of Herod . . . the destruction of our splendiferous house [the second Temple] may it be rebuilt speedily in our days . . . to the completion of the Mishnah . . . the completion of the Jerusalem Talmud . . . the completion of the Babylonian Talmud . . . the completion of the Code of Maimonides, of blessed memory . . . to the exile from France.[18]

Until this point in the text, chronographs were very similar to one another. Deceptively simple, the chronology in these brief texts derived from a reservoir of chronological sources, and so they vary only subtly in detail, emphasis, and de-

gree of congruence to one another. Innumerable exemplars circulated in sifre evronot and calendars throughout Europe. The printer or editor had only to adjust the number of years by one in order to revise the material for the coming year.

The earliest surviving Hebrew chronological text from which the chronographs drew was *Seder olam*, which likely dates to the third century C.E.[19] A later text, dubbed the "Small *seder olam*" (*Seder olam zuta*) overlapped, contradicted, and extended the earlier work.[20] It too served the early modern chronographers.

Chronographs that employed *Seder olam* in their opening strata expanded their reach through the early modern period with the addition of fragments from the "chain of tradition" genre, which consisted primarily of notable events in rabbinic literary history, such as the year of Maimonides' completion of his Code, which appears in the earlier quoted example. Compilers of chronographs drew on medieval chronicles like Abraham ibn Daud's twelfth-century *Sefer ha-qabbalah*, as well as sixteenth-century additions to the genre such as Gedaliah ibn Yahia's *Shalshelet ha-qabbalah* (*Chain of Tradition*) and Abraham Zacuto's *Sefer yuhasin* (*Book of Geneology*).[21] Calendar makers borrowed from all these works, patching, grafting, cutting, and pasting to form new conventions that appeared to users to be seamlessly integrated into familiar forms.

Each of these diverse strands was included in chronographs for different reasons and from various sources. Elements that appeared to be of vague general or universal historical interest may have been incorporated in order to advance a polemical point. Entries that announced somewhere in the middle of the list of events the beginning of the Christian calendar, and in some cases the Muslim, subtly reminded Jewish users of the priority of "Jewish" time. They silently proclaimed that Jewish history had begun to unfold long before these rival religions came into being; indeed, that time began with creation and had developed according to a divine plan ever since. Many of the elements in ibbur literature that were intended to help Jews make sense of the Christian calendar emphasized its dependence on the Jewish. Even when presenting "facts" such as the year of events of universal significance, calendar makers often used the calendar as a forum for promoting the Jewish version of history over those of other religions (which they frequently disparaged).

Some entries in Jewish chronographs reflected the Renaissance interest in universal history. Jewish chronicles such as David Ganz's *Tzemah David* (*Sprout of David*, 1592), Elijah Capsali's *Seder Eliyahu zuta: Toldot ha-ottomanim*

u-venezia (*History of the Ottomans and of Venice*, mid-sixteenth century, although unpublished until the nineteenth century), and Joseph Ha-kohen's *Divrey ha-yamim le-malkhey Tzarefat u-bet Ottoman ha-togar* (*History of the French and Ottoman Kings*, 1553), recorded historical events that had no specific connections to Jewish communities.[22] Other entries were borrowed from the chronologies or dynastic histories in local non-Jewish calendars. Thus the same chronograph that opened with a list of biblical events since creation could conclude with a dynastic history of local kings and princes.

The simple style and fluid organizational scheme of chronographs made them accessible even to minimally educated users. Compilers and printers included historical tables and brief chronologies in virtually every type of calendar; in the early modern period these became ubiquitous and accessible history lessons.[23] The reworked fragments from *Seder olam* that appeared around the regular calendar entries became a powerful tool for preserving and communicating the pedagogy of the past.

The last lines of chronographs incorporated local and recent events such as expulsions, salvations, fires, wars, and plagues. These presented the greatest challenge to the calendar makers, because so many recent events competed for inclusion in this space that careful editing and compression were required. The inherent brevity of the form demanded that "Each successive generation had to sift out, from all the ingredients constantly deposited by an expanding . . . culture, those portions of the past for which it had particular use."[24] Crises of local life loomed large in communal consciousness; the need to memorialize victims and celebrate narrow escapes was ever present. Printed broadsheets could speed the news and could serve as a short-term reminder, but enshrining an event in the calendar was manifestly a step beyond. This minute portion of calendar space was a most valuable and ever shifting site for retaining a precious few events in the communal memory. By situating events from relatively recent times along the diachronic continuum from Creation, calendar makers imbued these events with greater dignity and validity. At the same time, those of the remote past became much more concrete and real in the popular imagination than if they had remained isolated from recent events.

Chronographs disseminated both a fixed view of the distant past shared by all users and a flexible model for adding events of the recent past into the grid. While most chronographs were extremely terse and formulaic, others testified to the individual proclivities and worldviews of the authors. Since they were constructed from diffuse and often conflicting views of Jewish chronology, their

place in Jewish calendars serves more as a reminder of the process than as a precise determination of any date for past events. Many chronographs were highly idiosyncratic, tailored to a specific community, tempered by the redactor's sense of which events merited inclusion. For example, in the sixteenth century, Ashkenazic sifre evronot and calendars included an expulsion from Bohemia in 1542 at the end of their chronograph; several decades later, many completely obliterated the Bohemian reference and substituted notices of the depredations of 1648–1649.[25] Yshak de Cordova printed his multiyear calendar with a chronograph noting the "Anhos mas memorables" (most memorable years) from creation through the expulsion from Spain. The very last item he entered into his record was "the arrival of the Portuguese Hebrews in Holland," which had happened more than a century before his calendar was published.[26] Mardochée Venture's *Calendrier Hébraïque*, directed to the Sephardic community in eighteenth-century France and virtually devoid of Hebrew characters, included many of the standard ancient events in his "Supputation pour l'année presente de la création du monde" (computation for the world's year of creation) including the "beginning of the vulgar year" (the Christian calendar), as well as the onset of the "belief of the Turks" (the Muslim calendar). The comparatively recent chronology is devoid of the tragic dates of expulsion and persecution, marking only the recapture of the Holy Land by the Turks and the invention of printing.[27]

This aspect of Jewish calendars may be characterized as "the social circulation of the past." Flowing through any given society are a variety of competing or complementary sets of memories; no single set of such memories remains rigidly fixed. As Daniel Wolf observes, "Notions of the past developed within any historical culture are not simply abstract ideas but part of the mental and verbal specie . . . passing among contemporaries through speech, writing and other means."[28] In early modern Jewish society, these means for "circulating the past" included ballads, narrative chronicles, synagogue poetry—and abbreviated chronologies within calendars.[29]

Here Issachar ibn Susan's sixteenth-century report of the often obscure process of creating chronographs, integrating them into calendars, and distributing those calendars provides a valuable perspective:

This year, 5306 [1546 C.E.] the sage R. Hayim Haver sent from Damascus, his place of residence, here to Safed, a *luah* [calendar or broadsheet] to the congregation, for this year, to be hung in the synagogue of the

Sicilian congregation, as was the custom of his father R. Isaac, of blessed memory. [The calendar] declares: "The year 5306 from Creation is the year ... to the Flood, ... to the birth of Abraham, ... to the generation of Babel, ... to the covenant between the parts, ... to the birth of Isaac our patriarch, ... to the binding [of Isaac]; ... to the birth of Jacob our patriarch, ... to the exodus from Egypt and the giving of the Torah, ... to the sabbaticals that were counted in the First Temple period, may it be rebuilt in our days, ... to the building of the first temple, ... to the exile of the children of Gad and Reuben, ... to the destruction of the First Temple, may it be rebuilt in our days, ... to the building of the second Temple, ... to the "Contracts," ... to the destruction of the second Temple, may it be rebuilt in our days. This year follows the sabbatical according to Maimonides, the Mishnah, and the Jerusalem and Babylonian Talmud; it is 55 years since the expulsion from Spain. May the Lord return the remnants of his people and rebuild his Temple, swiftly.[30]

Ibn Susan described a tradition then in its second generation in which the year's chronology would be calculated by the sages in Syria and sent to their colleagues in Safed. In this particular chronology the event that followed the canonization of the Babylonian Talmud (by nearly a millennium) was the expulsion of the Jews from Spain, a traumatic event that directly affected many of the Jews in the Ottoman Empire, some of whom were still living when ibn Susan wrote this.

Famous rabbinic arguments—such as those over the start of the year, the duration of the bondage in Egypt, and the longevity of the Temples—were nowhere to be found in the simple but effective lists and charts that came to be an integral part of calendars. In an age that advanced new forms of historical culture in narrative histories, antiquarian scholarship, philological and archaeological studies, historical dramas, and ballads about the past, calendars winnowed, diluted, and mediated the mass of material for the common reader. The scholars compared histories and synchronized chronologies while calendars presented this information to the masses in a pared-down and predigested form.[31]

Chronographs appended to calendars were an intermediate step between inchoate memories and serious history. Aside from professional scholars, most people did not read history every day, but not a day would pass on which they would not consult their calendars. While centralizing states used calendars and

almanacs to advance new political agendas and reformed religions, creating a sense of social solidarity based on new configurations of the past, Jewish calendars propelled ideas of the past into the present with remarkable purpose.

Anniversaries and Holidays

The past both distant and recent was also represented on calendar pages through anniversary events—events whose date recurred each year. These events would not bear a year but simply a day within the month. Like the fixed cycle of the Christian calendar, recurring feasts and fasts on the Jewish calendar, such as Passover or the Day of Atonement, came on the same date each year and determined the ritual character of a season. Even so, this aspect of calendars was not rigid; new days celebrating salvations or mourning calamities were continually added, and sometimes later deleted, from the calendar. Some days that were observed as feasts or fasts found a place within the core of the calendar, the columnar center which guided users' daily observances. The process of adding to biblically mandated days of observance had been occurring since ancient times, and Jewish calendars in the early modern period listed historical occurrences based on ancient sources that had no practical import. These lessons about the past were commonly clustered at the bottom of the month's page. A mid-eighteenth-century Fürth calendar for 1756–1757 [5517], for instance, listed the following events to be remembered during the month of Tevet:

> On Rosh Hodesh Tevet, Noah saw the peaks of the mountains peeking out of the water; on this day the Jews separated from their pagan wives whom they married in Babylonia; on the sixth, Ezekiel prophesied about the destruction of the Temple; on the eighth the Torah was written in Greek by the seventy elders under the direction of Ptolemy; the ninth is a fast day and one does not know what happened on that day.[32] The gloss of Mhr"A [Rabbi Abraham ben Avigdor] of Prague adds that Ezra the scribe and Nehemiah died on that day; on 10 Tevet, Nebuchadnezzar, King of Babylonia laid siege to the city of Jerusalem.[33]

This historical material was derived from diverse texts including some with roots reaching to antiquity. *Megillat ta'anit*, written during the era of the Second Temple, listed days of salvation for Israel on which one could not fast nor eulo-

gize the dead.[34] It was eventually complemented by a later "continuation," *Megillat ta'anit batra (Later megillat ta'anit).*[35] While the two texts were unrelated and opposite in nature—the *Later megillat ta'anit* is a list of calamitous days in Jewish history when fasting was recommended—they came to be linked in the common perception. The supplement, a lachrymose list of fast days, had many variants and was copied often in medieval sources, but it is unclear whether its material was ever presented in medieval calendars. In the early modern period, however, its circulation as a printed work may have fostered interest and awareness of it. The original *Megillat ta'anit*, by contrast, was printed first in Mantua, 1513, then reprinted some twenty-five times through the nineteenth century. Sixteenth-century Jewish chroniclers such as Zacuto (in his *Yuhasin*) cited it often. Its format made it a good fit for calendar makers who propelled its lessons of the ancient past into renewed circulation in the early modern period.

Local fasts and second Purims were noted in both pocket and wall calendars. For example, the nineteenth day of Adar and the twenty-seventh of Elul were designated *Ta'anis Frankfurt* (Fast day of Frankfurt), to commemorate the expulsion of the Jews in 1614 during the Fettmilch uprising.[36] Appearing a scant decade after the event, a wall calendar from Hanau for 1625–1626 noted the fast day, although it did not yet note "Purim Vints," which came to be celebrated the following day.[37] These dates continued to be marked in calendars and remembered for centuries, sometimes inconsistently. The Frankfurt Fast and its second Purim appeared on many calendars from German lands.[38] The makers of calendars from other parts of the Jewish world were also interested in their own locally rooted observances.[39] Polish calendars marked the date 20 Sivan to commemorate the destruction of many Jewish communities during the Chmielnicki uprising.[40] The 1814 Jewish calendar for Lunéville (although not the one for 1812) marked Ta'anit Metz (the Fast of Metz) on 25 Tevet, a designation that appeared on subsequent French Jewish calendars through the mid-nineteenth century.[41] These calendar notations allow scholars today to take measure, albeit crudely, of the influence of an event on Jewish collective memory.[42]

Moreover, since fasts and Purims appeared on calendars destined for points far beyond the directly affected locale, calendars stimulated awareness and memory of these events beyond their place of immediate concern. Local fasts and Purims formed an integral part of Jewish self-perception in a non-Jewish world, even while their very placement in calendars may have been shaped by the Christian tendency to crowd the calendar with secondary observances.

Jewish and Universal History

Anniversary events that migrated into Jewish calendars from non-Jewish ones allow us to delve into yet another dimension of early modern calendars: their inclusion of events from a world in which Jews were the most marginal of players, and in which their existence was hardly ever noted. The *Seder olam* chronography could not have formed the basis for the later opening of the chronographies to non-Jewish notices. Although it was based on the biblical narrative and began with world (albeit biblical) history, the *Seder olam* gradually focused exclusively on Jewish history. Its universal impulse ended with ancient events. In the sixteenth-century, works like the *Tzemah David* by David Gans divided their chronicles between Jewish and universal, or sacred and secular, history.[43] Thus the same Jewish calendar that introduced a "chronograph from Creation" would include a section on the local political leaders and their important anniversary days. Alongside Jewish feast, fast, and historical dates, a calendar would include in its non-Jewish segment the birthdays, ascent to throne days, or death dates of local rulers. For example: "January 4, Phillip Ernst Fürst Hohenlohe Schillingsfürst 93 years; [January] 18, Johann Aloisius Fürst von Oettingen, 50 yrs; [January] 20, Karole, king of Naples and Sicily 40 years; [January] 24, Friedrich king of Prussia and Kurfürst of Brandenburg, 44 years; [January] 29, Christian, crown prince of Denmark, 9 years."[44] Similarly a luah of 1754–1755 closed its December section with a list that included (in Yiddish, of course): "29 December, "Elizabeth, great czarina of Russia, 45 years; 8 December, Franciscus Stephan, Roman Emperor, 46 years." The inclusion of some of these anniversaries may have been mandated for all calendars. Others may simply have resulted from an ambitious printer's or editor's desire to expand the material in his product. Either way, they exemplify the kinds of cultural documentation and engagement that had taken place on the pages of the Jewish calendars since their inception.[45]

Symmetry in History and the Secrets of Time

Medieval and early modern practitioners of chronology in any form searched for hidden patterns and secret codes that would provide the key to the most elusive puzzle of time: its end. The assumption that such an end was inevitable and possibly imminent infused history with retrospective meaning, turning events into portents and annalists into calculators. No aspect of chronology was

spared the fate of serving as an interpretive tool. The Jewish and Christian perceptions of historical time as a finite line that began at one point, creation, and ended with another, redemption, fueled the search to know the endpoint. As Gerson Cohen has argued in his meticulous deconstruction of a medieval chronology, symmetry provided the consolation of history.[46] It confirmed to its authors and interpreters that historical time was shaped by a divine plan, that both good times and bad were preordained. For Jewish chronographers, this notion was embedded in biblical texts. It intensified in the Second Temple period, was elaborated in rabbinic texts, and waxed and waned at various other historical junctures.[47]

Calendars played a significant role in supporting and maintaining the belief and influence of meaning within historical time. One calendar manual published in the sixteenth century explained the interpretation of chronology as follows: "To know the workings of chronology and to understand somewhat the verses in the prophecy of Daniel, to fortify weak hands and to strengthen weak knees; not, God forbid, to calculate the end but to open with good portents and messages, may God in his mercy fulfill them and send his anointed one to redeem us."[48]

While calendars rarely carried overt advertisements for specific messianic predictions, they carried ardent messages of consolation and hope; they taught and maintained the hermeneutical rules by which the signs of time could be interpreted and manipulated to yield meaning. Calendar makers interlaced the number of the years and cycles with a rich array of prooftexts, biblical and rabbinic, famous and obscure. Verses from the Bible, from prophecies of consolation, and from the Book of Daniel became standard embellishments of calendars.

Calendars used various techniques to telegraph homiletical messages about the history concealed in their numerical codes. For instance, manuscripts that displayed information in checkerboard-pattern charts, with squares alternating between colored and plain, would affix a little ditty that ended, "God will take us out of darkness to light."[49] Another method was the chronogram, in which the letters used to designate a particular year or cycle were formed into a word that carried symbolic meaning. These messages stimulated hope that the year or the cycle would be particularly propitious. The chronograms could be created out of letters related to the solar cycle, the lunar cycle, the sabbatical cycle, or the year, since most chronographs situated the users within each of these scales of time.

אלי׳ עלה אל השמים באש

FIG. 8.2. Elijah, figure of messianic consolation, ascends to heaven in fire. *Sefer evronot*, 1716. Reproduced with the permission of the National Library of Israel ms Heb 8° 2380, fol. 57v.

A noted medieval example of this is the 256th nineteen-year lunar cycle to the Era from Creation (covering the period from 1085 c.e.). Its chronogram, *ran"u* (רנ"ו), led contemporaries to hope for salvation and comfort according to the prophecy of the prophet Jeremiah: "Cry out in joy (*ranu*) for Jacob, shout at the crossroads of the nations!" (Jeremiah 31:6).[50] Hebrew chroniclers of the Crusades noted the high messianic hopes that Jews had pinned onto that cycle and the portent of redemption contained in its anagram. Indeed, both Shlomo bar Shimshon and Eliezer bar Nathan opened their chronicles by contrasting the messianic hopes for that period with the grim reality: it had turned into a

period of "sorrow and sighing, weeping and crying."[51] Another Hebrew Crusade chronicle simply and sadly noted about the year, "From the Era of the Destruction."[52]

Sabbatical and jubilee cycles formed another popular basis for medieval counting of the cycles of time. The week, the seven-year sabbatical, and the seven-times-seven-year jubilee cycles were closely identified with the concept of liberation in Jewish sources since ancient times. The seventh day represented freedom from creative labor; the sabbatical liberated the earth from exploitation by man (by letting the fields rest); and the jubilee, which entailed the manumission of slaves, meant freedom from human exploitation of other humans.[53] Some medieval calculators of the end time included sabbatical cycles within their calculations. Menahem Tziyon, a medieval commentator and kabbalist, wrote in his commentary on a biblical cantillation point *pazer gadol*: "When Israel was dispersed into exile, a great dispersion (*pazer gadol*) ensued, and the sabbaticals and jubilees were abolished; a corresponding diminution took place above, on account of our sins, from the day our city was destroyed and our Holy Temple ruined. If the inquirer were to ask, 'When is the end of time, the time of the ingathering of the dispersed and the assembling of the scattered of Israel?' The reply would come as a voice from Heaven: 'When the earth will requite her sabbaths.'"[54] The place of the year within the sabbatical cycle was often noted in calendar chronographs.

As calendars and their literature expanded from manuscript to printed form, chronograms and other coded language about meaningful numbers were used more extensively. In fact, chronograms decorated the title pages of many printed Hebrew books, so as to become the standard means of indicating the year of printing.[55] Both printed and manuscript calendar texts adorned their title pages (or crowned the top of the calendar if it was a broadsheet) with biblical verses that either played on the year or cycle number or simply sent the user a consoling and uplifting message. The earliest surviving printed Jewish broadsheet calendar, that of 1495–1496, is crowned by the verse: "And those redeemed by God will return." Its brief chronograph ends with the destruction of the Temple, "may it be speedily rebuilt in our days," followed by additional consolatory words from the holiday liturgy: "Our Father, our King, renew a good year for us; Our Father, our King, cause our salvation to arise imminently." A thirty-year calendar published in Constantinople in 1510 ends its chronograph with a wish for redemption: "He will gather the dispersed, gather in the dispersed of Israel, and a redeemer shall come to Zion." Printed wall calendars from the six-

teenth and seventeenth centuries, too, displayed eschatological chronograms embedded in prominent headlines at the top of the page. A calendar for 1738–1739 used an eschatological chronogram for the anno mundi year [5]499: *yifdeh* (He will redeem).[56]

Such overt references to the end of time on the face of calendars did not escape the keen eyes of contemporaries. Azariah de Rossi, a sixteenth-century humanist and Hebraist scholar with a profound interest in chronology, noted: "It is as though the authority of the calendar in its entirety is only valid as long as our storm-swept community is in exile and disdained in her affliction and sorrow. You will therefore acknowledge the superior wisdom of our rabbis whose souls are at rest, and the extent to which they have helped us in these oppressive times. For when they realized that we are unable to have what we desire, they taught us to desire that which we can attain."[57]

De Rossi's dispassionate study of Jewish chronology was unique in the early modern period. Various motivations have been attributed to de Rossi: that he undermined rabbinic chronology in order to discourage calculations of the end with their inevitable disappointments; that he intended to undermine a Christian apocalypticism that was based on Jewish chronological schemes; or simply that he was a true humanist participating in one of the most compelling intellectual pursuits of his age. His essay on chronology opened with a seemingly modest agenda: "Now . . . I should like to examine and investigate the number of years that we count from the time of creation."[58] And yet he shocked his contemporaries by holding up to the light of analysis the many problems and inconsistencies in the prevailing Jewish chronology, concluding that "the age of the world as we computed it . . . is open to doubt. . . . The age of the universe must also in all truth be greater than that which we reckon."[59] De Rossi was the first Jew since the time of the widespread adoption of the "Creation era" to argue that it was a construct rather than a historical fact. Yet despite his repeated assertions that this tool of rabbinic chronology was a useful convention that ought to be maintained regardless of its historical or scientific accuracy, Jews of his own time rejected or ignored his work.

Messianic speculation was more intensive in some periods than others. Reading the signposts of time continued to be an activity pursued with urgency among early modern Jews, with speculators about the end of time abounding during the sixteenth and seventeenth centuries.[60] The travails of Polish Jews in the mid-seventeenth century sparked a profound search for redemptive meaning. Kabbalah disseminator Isaiah Horowitz, author of the *Shne luhot ha-brit*,

predicted 1647–1648 as the year of redemption based on the numerical value (*gematria*) of a word in the verse, "In this הזאת [408] year of jubilee you shall return every man to his possession" (Lev. 25:13). Yom Tov Lipmann Heller initially made the same prediction, and Shabtai Cohen, in *Megillat eivah*, implied that this year, which had been anticipated with joy, had now turned into a year of sorrow. In his sermon preached in the summer of 1647–1648, Israel ben Benjamin of Belżyce referred to the year as one "of messianic birthpangs," because the Hebrew term *hevlei mashiah* is numerically equivalent to 408 (1648 C.E.).[61]

Adherents of the seventeenth-century Sabbatian messianic movement operated with a keen sense that chronology could be used as a hermeneutic tool in the creation of a redemptive history. Many printed works from the height of the movement highlighted the anno mundi year 5426 (1665–1666) with a chronogram from the verse "Behold I will save [Hebrew: *moshi'a*]," because the numeric value of *moshi'a* is 5426.[62] A calendar tells the tale of one enthusiastic adherent of Sabbatai's, Solomon de Oliveyra, a Sephardic rabbi in Amsterdam, who left a trail of prayers, hymns, and letters extolling the newly announced messiah when the movement was at its height. After news of the apostasy of Sabbatai broke out in 1666, Oliveyra published a calendar whose chronograph included a unique entry in the medieval section titled "David Al Roy was made a messiah in . . ." The final entry is lengthier than the others and tells a tale of dashed hopes: "Sabbatai Zevi arose in Smyrna as Messiah Son of David, and Nathan Benjamin Ashkenazi in Gaza as a prophet heralding the redemption one year and several months prior to this year, 1666/67. The season of reaping has passed . . . and we have not been redeemed. Redeem us, Lord of our Salvation, redeem and save us."[63] Even among nineteenth-century traditionalists who awaited the year 1840 en masse, chronology served as a handmaiden in the search for symmetry in history.[64]

Chronographs, as abbreviated history lessons, conveyed many messages to early modern readers who scanned them to read the obligations for the coming day or week. Even though they could have imparted only fleeting impressions, the fact that they were seen over and over again would have given them considerable power. The very name of the chronographs' most important source, *Seder olam* (even if it did not appear on the chronograph itself), implied that there was an order to time in the world. The final passage in *Seder olam* confirmed this message: "'This is the book of the history of man.' To teach us that God showed Adam each generation and its leaders, each generation and its prophets, each generation and its commentators, each generation and its sages . . . the

number of their names, the accounting of their days, the reckoning of their hours, the total of their footsteps, as the verse says: 'For You count my footfalls, etc.'" *Seder olam* taught that the entire course of earthly time had been shaped by the Divine into perfectly symmetrical intervals, as in the ten generations from Adam to Noah and the ten from Noah to Abraham, as well as in cyclical recurrences, such as the destruction of the First and Second Temples, commemorated on the same day of the week. "Fifty-two years after the destruction of the Temple, R. Jose said: 'A positive merit is unfolded on a day of merit and a negative [action] on a negative day.' Thus we find that when the First Temple was destroyed, it was *motz'ei shabbat* and *motz'ei shevi'it* and the watch of Jehoyariv, and the Ninth of Av. And so for the [destruction of the] Second [Temple]."[65]

Readers of the calendar who were even slightly familiar with the resonant message of *Seder olam* would know of its insistence on the symmetry of history, a sign that everything that happened in the world was preordained. It provided the framework for placing tragic events within the perspective of a divine time scale. Along with the many messages of consolation adorning Jewish calendars, chronographs served to fortify Jewish spirits against the often harsh vicissitudes of their condition as exiles. Just as the verses crowning the printed wall calendars or embedded in the year's highlighted anagram transmitted messages of solace and teleological meaning regarding the punishments of time, so too did the chronographs.

The inclusion of chronographs in Jewish calendars made these calendars far more than temporal manuals for ritual observances. Chronographs provided the framework for placing current events and individual lives within a vast time scale and a collective perspective. These supplements were meant to instill a sense of the great sweep and grandeur of Jewish history, the rise and fall of the nation over many eras, and a message of hope for the future. They served no practical purpose, but for their producers and users, they transformed calendars from portable, convenient markers of local events into perpetual witnesses to the Jewish passage through time.

Epilogue

> While the chief rabbi was flatly denied permission to publish a weekly
> newsletter, he was allowed to put out a Jewish calendar. This calendar
> was a most valuable reference work that enabled practicing Jews to cel-
> ebrate the holy days at the appropriate time. . . . Duly inspected by the
> censor, it was the only Jewish publication to be approved since the Ar-
> mistice. It was in the fall of 1940.
>
> Renée Poznanski, *Jews in France during World War II*, 1999

WE have seen that the Jewish calendar, far from being an obscure and
static component of Jewish culture, remained a vital and dynamic locus
of Jewish creativity through the early modern period. By the late eighteenth
century, Jews in Western Europe no longer cultivated manuscript sifre evronot.
And as a result of the combination of external censorship and internal recon-
figuration, calendar literature no longer served to channel Jewish polemical resentment of the Christian temporal order. But this is far from the end of the
story. A cultural history of the Jewish calendar in the nineteenth and twentieth
centuries would provide just as rich and colorful a story as that of its predecessors, for Jews maintained a dynamic and ongoing engagement with their repre-
sentations of time.

The insistent calls to secularize aspects of European life and to integrate
Jews into European society presented new challenges to the separate calendar
system for Jews within the Christian world in the later eighteenth century. The
rhetoric of modernization called on Jews to integrate into the majority societies
and to erase or diminish markers of religious and cultural distinction. Virtually
no area of Jewish culture emerged from this turning point in history without
a sustained critique by modernizers—except, remarkably, the Jewish calendar.
Although many Jews diluted or ignored aspects of traditional calendar-related
observances, the system of Jewish calendar calculation never became the focus
of a thorough reappraisal.

The sole attempt by a modernizer to subject the traditional calendar to

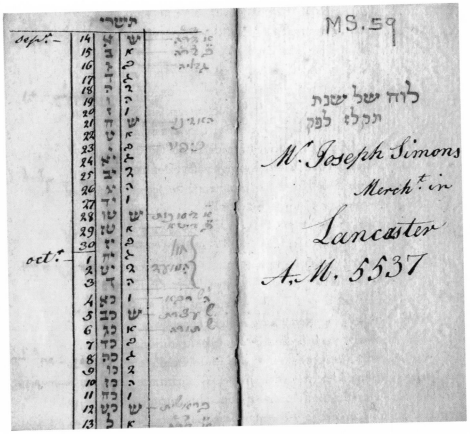

FIG. 9.1. Lancaster calendar for the year of the American Revolution, 1776–1777. Courtesy of the Library at the Herbert D. Katz Center for Advanced Judaic Studies, University of Pennsylvania ms 59, verso of cover and 1r.

rationalist analysis was that of enlightener and Kantian philosopher Lazarus Bendavid (1762–1832). Bendavid devoted an entire work to the Jewish calendar and its traditional chronology, belittling the Jewish claim to an original divinely ordained system of calculation.[1] It was simply not credible, he argued, that Jews just happened upon the same precise elements of time in their calculations as did the ancient Persians, Greeks, and Babylonians.[2] Bendavid historicized the traditional Jewish chronology as a relatively recent invention and averred that students of the Bible alone would never be able to satisfactorily answer the question of when historical time began.[3]

Bendavid's polemic was distinctive for the attention he paid to a subject neglected by most other Jews of his time, as well as for its mocking and scornful

tone. Bendavid's dismissive treatise provoked an angry traditionalist response from rabbi, scholar, and mathematician Meyer Moses Kornick.[4] The exchange between Bendavid and Kornick concerning the value of the Jewish calendar and chronology was one of the sharpest to take place in the modern era.[5] But the calendrical system remained remarkably impervious to foundational challenges, suggesting some limits of the modernizing enterprise. No modern Jewish ideology advocated the total abandonment of the Jewish calendar in favor of the Western civil calendar. For all his sarcasm, Bendavid did not advocate in his treatise the abandonment of a distinctive Jewish calendar. And despite the tendentiousness of some of Kornick's arguments, he seems to have intuited the centrality of the calendar to Jewish identity.

Galician enlightener Joseph Perl (1773–1839) approached the calendar far more subtly than did Bendavid. In fact, Perl's appropriation of the traditional calendar for promoting his program of enlightenment may be regarded as a true turning point in the development of Jewish calendars in Europe. In Perl's model, the core of the calendar remained intact, even as it was relegated to secondary status behind the supplementary material that advanced his ideas. Perl exploited the familiarity and ordinariness of the traditional calendar to disguise an ambitious maskilic agenda.[6] Perl was undoubtedly emulating the huge industry in "Volkskalender" all over Europe. Although the results of his venture were slow to materialize, and Perl abandoned his calendars after three years, his model ultimately succeeded. Calendar-based almanacs and yearbooks became one of the most popular media for disseminating a variety of messages and ideologies among European Jews.

Another intriguing attempt to detach a traditional form from the calendar and expand it for new purposes was that of Leopold Zunz, one of the founding fathers of academic Jewish scholarship.[7] Zunz gradually removed the chronograph from its place within the Jewish calendar and developed it into a vehicle for shaping a new form of Jewish historical memory. His first installment was appended to a calendar in 1847; it was followed by two additional pieces, with a full, freestanding booklet completed in 1872. The genre that he developed from this marginal segment within the calendar was a list of death dates of Jewish notables interspersed with the anniversaries of various persecutions and expulsions of Jews. Zunz intended his compilation to serve as a didactic tool for disseminating knowledge of Jewish history. He did include some figures outside the Jewish world, but his true innovation was the chronological system he used to create this list: Zunz organized his collection of events exclusively according

FIG. 9.2. Zodiac man and a bloodletting table, Calendar, Sulzbach, 1789. Courtesy Gross Family Collection, Tel Aviv. Note chronograph at top.

to the Gregorian calendar, completely effacing the Jewish chronology.[8] In this way he inscribed Jewish memory into the history of the larger European world, a symbolic expression of the alignment that Jews hoped to achieve as they entered European society.

Through the nineteenth and twentieth centuries, Jewish calendars expanded far beyond their original formats. Calendars, along with the almanacs and yearbooks that evolved out of them, emerged as literary and cultural omni-

buses in the nineteenth century. Their only serious rival as a medium of popular culture was the periodical press. The single-leaf broadsheets and compressed pocket calendars of the early modern period might not have recognized their nineteenth-century successors. Jewish almanacs and yearbooks exploited the familiar dependence on the calendar to become social, cultural, and economic guidebooks. The traditional luah (calendar), for instance, evolved into a Jewish Volkskalender, a transformation that is seen in one typical series and which encapsulates the trajectory of modern Jewish history and culture.[9] The sequence begins with the published document standing as a full-service traditional luah to which additional materials were appended. Fifteen years later, a reversal had occurred: the series had become a Jewish literary almanac to which a luah was appended. With each successive issue, the luah and the Jewish chronograph can be seen receding farther from the beginning of the volume. Ten years into its existence, the same calendar series that had begun its chronograph with years to the "Jewish chronology" provided an alternative date to creation according to Lutheran chronologist Seth Calvisius. Popular calendars and almanacs have been printed by Jews of every ideological and denominational stripe into the present time, reflecting every movement and major event in Jewish history. Sephardim and Ashkenazim, Hasidim and their opponents, Zionists and diaspora nationalists all printed calendars, as did Jews under the Nazi regime during the Holocaust. Jewish calendars have been printed in every corner of the globe, in dozens of languages.

Editors and printers have used calendars to strengthen Jewish political identities, as well as to educate, agitate, and advertise. Advertisements containing detailed information about the goods and services of Jewish-owned businesses allowed the calendars to continue their function of maintaining commercial networks among geographically dispersed Jews. From automobiles to toothpaste, every sort of commodity was advertised in their pages. Tailors and shopkeepers, matchmakers and booksellers, all found a place in ubiquitous calendars. Yet despite their close reflection of the timebound elements reflected in their pages, the core of the calendar remained timeless. Easily overlooked but abundantly preserved, calendars have served as mirrors and agents of change, as indexes of acculturation, and as matchless reflections of the Jewish experience over time.

ABBREVIATIONS

A.D.   anno Domini
A.M.   anno mundi
B.C.E. before the Common Era
BT   Babylonian Talmud
C.E.   Common Era
R.   Rabbi

NOTES

Introduction

1. Tychsen, *Bützowische*, 74. I thank Michael Silber for this reference.
2. Geertz, *Interpretation of Cultures*, 89.

1. Calendar and the Cultural Meaning of Time

1. For a cultural history of the week, see Zerubavel, *The Seven Day Circle*; for a similar history of the hour, see Dohrn-van Rossum, *History of the Hour*.
2. The actual lunation period (from the time of one new moon to the next) varies slightly each month, so a calendar that determined months based on observing the actual new moon (as did the Jewish calendar in ancient times) would have months that varied in length. The present Jewish calendar is based on a widely accepted mean value of the moon's lunations, 29.5306 days (29 days, 12 hours, 44 minutes, and 3 seconds).
3. Stern, "Fictitious Calendars," 104.
4. North, "The Western Calendar," 106.
5. On the origin and meaning of the term computus, see Wallis, *Bede*, xviii–xxx, 425–426.
6. Dohrn-van Rossum, *History of the Hour*, 40.
7. Schwartz, *Christliche und jüdische Ostertafeln*.
8. Cited in J. R. Marcus, *Jew in the Medieval World*, 117.
9. Johannes Kepler, "Ein Gespräch von der Reformation des alten Calendars," in *Joannis Kepleri Opera Omnia* (1863) 4:37. This work is cited and translated in "Bibliography on the Computus and the Calculation of Easter Sunday," http://www.phys.uu.nl/~vgent/easter/easter_text6a.htm (last accessed October 11, 2010).
10. Thurston, "Easter Controversy."
11. Jones, "The 'Lost' Sirmond Manuscript," 204.
12. Wallis, *Bede*, xxiii.
13. Ibid., 27.
14. Ibid., lxxii–lxxix.
15. Borst, *Der Karolingische Reichskalender, Der Streit um den karolingischen Kalender, Schriften zur Komputistik*.
16. Jones, "Early Medieval," 21.
17. Stevens, "Introduction to the Computus of Hraban," in his *Cycles of Time*, 167.
18. Dowd, "Astronomy." Grosseteste determined anew the lengths of years and lunations, since "Scriptures say that Christ was born on the winter solstice, but . . . now Christmas precedes the solstice by about as many days as centuries since his birth" (294). The moon's age is equally significant for calculating Easter, but Grosseteste never advocated a full reform of the calendar and did not suggest changing the date for Easter.
19. Incorporating the technical advances made by scientists or astronomers to correct an existing calendar sometimes took centuries. See Robbins, "Studies," 123.

20. As late as 1034 c.e., the name of the priestly group whose turn it was to officiate was still announced in some congregations. They had once served as human calendrical devices for numbering the Sabbaths. See Joseph Baumgarten, *Studies in Qumran Law*, 117.

21. See, e.g., the laws of intercalation in Mishnah Sanhedrin 1:2; Arachin 2:2, and Tosefta Sanhedrin, chapter 2; Stern, *Calendar*, 155–180.

22. Langermann, "Eimatai." This void is being filled with scholarship on the Qumran calendars and the *Book of Jubilees*. See James M. Scott, *On Earth as in Heaven* (Leiden: Brill, 2005); Jonathan Ben-Dov, *Head of all Years* (Leiden: Brill, 2008), as well as the work of Stern, *Calendar*.

23. A work attributed to Nahshon Gaon (d. ca. 889), *Ibbur qatzuv* or *Iggul d' R. Nahshon*, is often cited in ibburim. Its original form has not survived.

24. For a brief overview of science in the early Islamic calendar see Ilyas, "Lunar Crescent," 425–431.

25. Cited in Langermann, "Eimatai."

26. See the characterization of Qaraites in Rustow, *Heresy*, xviii.

27. Goldstein, "Astronomy and the Jewish Community in Early Islam," 32; Al-Qirqisani, *Yaqub al-Qirqisani on Jewish Sects*, 114–115. On the link between Qaraite and rabbinic Jewish calendars, see Rustow, *Heresy*, 15–20; 57–65; Astren, *Karaite Judaism*, 73, 169, 226.

28. *Pirqe de Rabbi Eliezer*, ed. Börner-Klein, 72–79. Beller, "Ancient," dates *Pirqe de Rabbi Eliezer* to the early Islamic period. On the date of the Baraita de Shmuel, see Goldstein, "Astronomy," 22. Goldstein dates the text to the late eighth century c.e.

29. Stern, "Fictitious Calendars," 104.

30. Bornstein, "Mahloqet." See also Brody, *The Geonim*, 118–121, and literature cited there; as well as Lasker and Lasker, "Tav-resh-mem-bet halaqim," 119–128.

31. For other works of Sa'adiah related to astronomy, see Goldstein, "Astronomy."

32. Obermann, introduction to *Maimonides*, xlii, n. 28.

33. Rustow, *Heresy*, 19, 59–60. Empirical methods of calculation (by observation) were not completely abandoned by rabbinic Jews until sometime after the Sa'adiah controversy. On the scroll of the Palestinian gaon, Evyatar ha-kohen, see pp. 337–338. In the late eleventh century, Evyatar rested an argument for the revival of the authority of his office on the exclusive monopoly over the secret of intercalation, which he claimed had been transmitted in an unbroken chain from Moses.

34. Geniza fragments confirm that other works preceded bar Hiyya's. See Gandz, introduction to *Maimonides*.

35. Ibn Ezra's *Sefer ibbur* apparently represents only half of the work that Abraham ibn Ezra intended to complete. See Spiegel, *Amudim*, 2:564. For a brief introduction to bar Hiyya's oeuvre as a translator from Arabic to Latin in twelfth-century Barcelona, see Levey, "The Encyclopedia," 257–258.

36. Langermann, *Jews and the Sciences*, 10–16.

37. Bar Hiyya, *Sefer ha-Ibbur*, ed. Filipowski, title page.

38. Sela, *Abraham ibn Ezra*, 101.

39. Ibid., 99, 205.

40. Bar Hiyya, *Sefer ha-Ibbur*, ed. Filipowski, title page.

41. On his scientific oeuvre, see Sela, *Abraham ibn Ezra*.

42. Ibn Ezra, *Liber de Rationibus Tabularum*, ed. Vallicrosa, 99.
43. Obermann, introduction to *Maimonides*, xxxiv.
44. Ibid., xliv.
45. On Arab translators and their role in the transmission of astronomical knowledge, see Saliba, *A History of Arabic Astronomy*.
46. On esotericism in medieval Jewish writing, see Obermann, introduction to Maimonides, xxxvii; for sources regarding the esotericism of the ibbur, see Kasher, *Humash*, introduction to vol. 13, pp. 15–19; Halbertal, *Concealment and Revelation*, 176, n.7.
47. Langermann, "Sefer huqot shamayim," 91.
48. Ibn Ezra, *Sefer ha-ibbur*, ed. Sh. Z. H. Halberstam, "Sod ha-ibbur," 7a. He writes "I will reveal that secret in the second chapter," on page 1a.
49. Maimonides, "Sanctification," 11:4; Beller, "Ancient," on Maimonides' "secret."
50. Ibn Ezra, *Sefer ha-ibbur*, ed. Bakal, 56: "Asher tiqen hibbur be-seder ha-ibbur le-mevin im talmid." Similarly, see Ibn Ezra, *Sefer ha-ibbur*, ed. Bakal, 49: "This is the method of calculation that the young students learn in their books."
51. "Derekh," Ibn Ezra, *Sefer ha-ibbur*, ed. Bakal, 57; "ve-hakhmei ha-ibbur hishtabshu" (and the wise men of the calendar stumbled), 71. He attributed a tradition concerning the nineteen-year cycle to the descendants of King David as transmitted by Rabban Gamliel (64).
52. Halbertal, *Concealment and Revelation*, 39–42.
53. Ibn Ezra, *Sefer ha-ibbur*, ed. Halberstam, 4a–b.
54. Ibid., vii, n.1. The title of the work was *Seder ha-ibbur*; one section within it was titled "sod ha-ibbur," 7a.
55. Ibn Ezra, *Sefer ha-ibbur*, ed. Halberstam, 8a.
56. Ibn Ezra, *Sefer ha-ibbur*, ed. Bakal, 7b.
57. 2 Chronicles 30. On this episode see Chavel, "The Second Passover."
58. Ibn Ezra, *Sefer ha-ibbur*, ed. Bakal, 82, 91. Among the instruments that ibn Ezra regarded as essential to calculations was a measuring device that he called *keli ha-nehoshet*, the astrolabe.
59. BT Berakhot 58b.
60. Ibn Ezra, *Sefer ha-ibbur*, ed. Halberstam, 8a–b.
61. Ibn Ezra, *Sefer ha-ibbur*, ed. Bakal, 8b.
62. On tequfat *R. Ada*, see Bornstein, "Mahloqet R. Sa'adiah," appendix 6; on the *Baraita de R. Shmuel*, see Stern, "Fictitious Calendars," 105–124.
63. Ibn Ezra, *Sefer ha-ibbur*, ed. Halberstam, 9a.
64. Ibn Ezra, *Sefer ha-ibbur*, ed. Bakal, 82.
65. *Bereshit rabba* 6.3; BT, Hulin 60b; *Pirqe de Rabbi Eliezer*, chs. 6 and 51; Stern, "Fictitious Calendars," 115.
66. Sela, "Abraham bar Hiyya's Astrological Work."
67. Neugebauer, "Astronomical Commentary to Maimonides."
68. Obermann, "Supplementation."
69. Bar Hiyya, *Sefer ha-ibbur*, ed. Filipowski, 100.
70. Ibid.
71. Ibid.
72. Ibid., 109–110.
73. Ibid., 110.

74. Ibid., 112. Toward the end of his disquisition on the Christian calendar, bar Hiyya remarked that he would not expand on "the computus of gentiles for which we have no practical use."

75. Ibn Ezra, *Sefer ha-ibbur*, ed. Bakal, 60.

76. Sela, *Abraham ibn Ezra*, 41.

77. Maimonides later argued that the two sources complemented one another, for the members of the court could use their knowledge of the calculations to verify the testimony of the eyewitnesses. Obermann, "Supplementation," xvii.

78. Compare the passage from the memoir of Judah Leib Katzenelson of Bobruisk (1846–1917): "The gabbai, R. Judah b. Rabbi Jehiel . . . was well educated and a bibliophile. Once he came over to me while I was studying Maimonides' 'Laws of the Sanctification of the New Moon.' Seeing me doing calculations with pencil and paper in front of me . . ." Cited in Zalkin, "Scientific Literature," 250.

79. The Institute of Microfilmed Hebrew Manuscripts, National Library of Israel, has filmed and catalogued close to 90 percent of extant Hebrew manuscripts, by its account. (The contents of even one significant undocumented library could skew these numbers significantly, and the vulnerabilities of Hebrew manuscripts must be taken into account as well.) Its holdings allow us to make a tentative assessment of the circulation and demand for the sifre ibbur of bar Hiyya and ibn Ezra. Of nineteen manuscripts titled *Sefer ha-ibbur* dating from the thirteenth until the seventeenth centuries, fifteen are bar Hiyya's, three are ibn Ezra's, and one is of unknown authorship. Italian scribes produced the earliest surviving copies: six were produced between the thirteenth and fifteenth centuries by Italian hands. Of those, five were bar Hiyya's and one ibn Ezra's. Of the seven ibburim of Sephardic (or in some cases possibly Provençal) provenance from the same period, four were bar Hiyya's, and three, ibn Ezra's. Four manuscripts from this period are of Byzantine provenance, all of bar Hiyya's ibbur. Only one of the manuscripts from before the late fifteenth to early sixteenth centuries is of Ashkenazic provenance.

80. This trajectory is roughly consonant with that outlined in Elbaum, "Influences."

81. Rome, Vatican, Biblioteca Apostolica ms ebr. 299/6. The secret of the intercalation appears on fols. 73r–76r.

82. Italian Jews may have transmitted Byzantine calendar traditions to Western Europe. Sarfatti, in "An Introduction," argues that Shabbetai Donnolo, the tenth-century southern Italian author of *Hakhemoni*, was probably the author of the *Baraita de mazalot*.

83. The Worms Mahzor, Jerusalem, National Library of Israel ms 4° 781/1–2, completed in 1272 and 1280, was intended as a guide for the cantor, based primarily on the liturgy of Eretz Israel. See Beit-Arié, ed., *Worms Mahzor*.

84. My discussion of the development of the mahzor in medieval Ashkenaz is based directly on Grossman, *Hakhmei Tzarefat*. German *mahzorim* made for the cantor contained many liturgical poems and were created in an unusually large format. See Narkiss, *Hebrew Illuminated Manuscripts*, 32.

85. Yahalom, *Mahazor Eretz-Yisra'el*, 18–21.

86. Grossman, *Hakhmei Tzarefat*, 402.

87. Ibid., 418–423.

88. Ibid., 419. The *Sefer elqoshi* only survives in fragments. The most significant—Oxford, Bodleian Library ms Opp. 317—contains chapters 24–39 of "*Sod ha-ibbur*." This is apparently the last portion of the compilation, because it closed with "*nishlam sod ha-ibbur* (the secret of the intercalation is completed)." Grossman located additional fragments in ms Sassoon/Klagsbald 535.

89. The section that follows it in the Oxford, Bodleian Library ms Opp. 317, contains a calendar beginning in 1123 c.e.

90. Both bar Hiyya and bar Samson believed that the stars influenced human affairs, but that Jews were exempt from this influence. Prayer and repentance could in any case disrupt the control of the constellations.

91. Grossman, *Hakhmei Tzarefat*, 422–423. Grossman notes that bar Samson's use of this tradition suggests that during the Sa'adiah—ben Meir controversy, ben Meir was adhering to an authentic tradition, not an invented one.

92. Soloveitchik, "Halakhah, Hermeneutics," 278–286.

93. Freudenthal, "Science in the Medieval Jewish Culture."

94. Israeli, *Liber Jesod Olam*.

95. Langermann, *Jews and the Sciences*, I:8.

96. Ibid., I:9.

97. Abudarham, *Perush seder tefillot* (Lisbon, 1489), n.p. After its publication in pre-expulsion Portugal, Abudarham's commentary was published in Constantinople in 1513, Venice in 1546 and 1566, and in many subsequent editions.

98. Oxford, Bodleian Library ms Opp. 317, fol. 110v, contains a chronograph "from creation of the world until today which is five thousand and seventy five years according to the counting from creation [1315 c.e.]."

99. Paris, Bibliothèque Nationale ms 644, fol. 183v.

שמות החדשים
למה נקרא שמו ניסן שנעשו בו ניסים לישראל
אייר מפני שכל העולם כולו תלויים בו באויר
סיון שבו נעשו סימן למקום
תמוז שבו תמו דור המבול
אב שהוא אב לפורענות

100. Parma, Biblioteca Palatina ms 2467/3, fols. 32a–60b. The section is titled *Seder sod ha-ibbur* (the order of the secret of intercalation); it closes with *nishlam sod ha-ibbur* (the secret of intercalation is complete). It bears no colophon but uses the year 1410 c.e, fol. 46b, as the basis for calculation. It was written in Italy in a Sephardic hand, which perhaps indicates that Italy was a transmission point for this literature.

101. Cambridge University Library ms Add., 3127–3129.

102. For the complete Christian calendar, see fols. 346r–350v; the other elements are described in fol. 335r. Fol. 339v contains the same information linked to the dates of the Christian calendar. This manuscript was in use for at least a century and a half after its completion, because it includes calculations for the years 1421–1424, 1436, and 1531–1542 c.e.

103. See, e.g., Paris, Bibliothèque Nationale ms 644; London, British Library ms Add. 26970/4, fols. 182r–183v; Zurich, Zentralbibliothek ms Heid. 145/2, fols. 22r–v; 45r–

52v; 53v, 167r; 171r; Oxford, Bodleian Library ms Mich. 74; Cambridge, Trinity College ms F 1221; Oxford, Bodleian Library ms Opp. 614, fols. 48a–55b.

104. Ta-Shma, "The 'Open' Book," 5–16; Matt, *Zohar*, introduction.

2. The Politics of Time in Early Modern Europe

1. Davis, *Society and Culture*, 198.
2. Capp, *Astrology*, 25.
3. In the late fifth century, as the Christian calendar stabilized around the nineteen-year cycle, a nineteen-verse poem was composed that gave the dates of the full moon and a number that could be used to calculate the 14 Nisan, the *ferial regular*. Jones, "Legend," 199.
4. Krünitz, *Oekonomisch=technologische*, 525. Krünitz cites the example found in the prayer book by Martin Luther, *Ein Betbüchlein mit eyn Kalender und Passional hübsch zugericht* (Wittenberg, 1530). On top of the calendar, the following is written: "Auf dass die jungen Kinder den Kalender auswendig an den Fingern lernen, haben wir hiebei den Cisio-Janus in seinen Versen gesetzt." Krünitz, *Oekonomisch=technologische*, 529n.
5. Krünitz, *Oekonomisch=technologische*, 525, dates the use of *cisiojanus* poems to the tenth or eleventh century. According to one definition, these poems were "a medieval composition of 24 hexametrical verses with a syllable for each day in the year. [Their] purpose is to memorize the most important feasts. The name is taken from the incipit Cisio Janus Epy (Circumcision, January, Epiphany, etc). [They] originated in North Germany in the twelfth century but spread to France only in the late fifteenth century with calendars in Books of Hours." www.chd.dk/cals/cisiojan.html (accessed September 15, 2010).
6. Brévart, "The German *Volkskalender*," 315.
7. Krünitz, *Oekonomisch=technologische*, cites the example of the reformer Melanchton who prepared a superior version of the mnemonic verse.
8. Thorndike, "Computus," 224.
9. Wallis, *Bede*, 138.
10. Ibid., 345. Calculating systems based on the hand, *computus manualis*, were common in Jewish computus manuscripts as well; see Chapter 4.
11. Ibid., 139.
12. For a digital reproduction of this calendar in the back of a Psalter, see New York Public Library, Online Gallery of Images, digital id. 427584.
13. Wieck, *Time Sanctified*, 34, 157.
14. Krünitz, *Oekonomisch=technologische*, 518.
15. Ibid., 530. Golden numbers indicated the occurrences of the new moon; adding fourteen days led to the date of the full moon. These were used to determine the date of Easter. The golden numbers, along with the dominical letters, appear in the first column of the calendars in Books of Hours.
16. For related compendia, see Brévart, "The German *Volkskalender*," 338–342.
17. Ibid.
18. Sommer, *The Kalender of Shepherdes*.
19. Davis, *Society and Culture*, 205.

20. Rohner, *Kalendergeschichte*, 50; Riehl, "Volkskalender"; Bollème, *Les almanachs populaires*, 14.

21. Rohner, *Kalendergeschichte*, 69.

22. Capp, *Astrology*, 23.

23. Krünitz, *Oekonomisch=technologische*, 535, where the author notes: "In Paris alone some 120 calendar editions are published each year, then bought in the same quantities the next year, because of new art, new information. For similar numbers of French almanacs, see Bollème, *Les almanachs populaires*, foreword.

24. See Heller, *Printing the Talmud*, 33, for a German calendar used as "binder's waste."

25. Krünitz, *Oekonomisch=technologische*.

26. Ibid., 539. Krünitz complained that although such information was long known to be useless, "When the respected Sturm of Altdorf published his calendar without this, no one wanted to buy it. The old rule still stands: the world wants to be deceived!"

27. Sommer, *Kalender of Shepherdes*, 56, 61–70.

28. Neugebauer-Wolk, "Der Bauernkalender," 75–111.

29. Krünitz, *Oekonomisch=technologische*, 537.

30. Rohner, *Kalendergeschichte*, 73.

31. Fricke, "Denkmäler."

32. See Rich, "The Brest Union," 46–61.

33. On the meaning of this phrase, see the possibilities explored in Kay, "Unwintering January (Dante, *Paradiso*, 27.142–143)."

34. Ziggelaar, "Papal Bull," 222, notes that the introduction to the papal bull promulgating the change refers specifically to the Council of Trent, although Tridentine documents never explicitly mention calendar reform.

35. On the papal bull "Inter gravissimas," and its promulgation, see ibid.

36. Chapman, "Politics of Time," 4.

37. Ziggelaar, "Papal Bull," 228; Frick, "Bells," 50.

38. Hoskin, "The Reception," 257.

39. Ibid., 260.

40. Bogucka, "Space and Time," 50 n.34.

41. Rich, "The Brest Union," 49–50.

42. Gingerich, "The Civil Reception," 265.

43. Frick, "Bells," 30.

44. Voigt, *Calendarische*, n.p.

45. See Albert Parry, "The Soviet Calendar," *Journal of Calendar Reform* 10 (1940):65–69, and other articles in that journal.

46. Hoskin, "The Reception," 259, cites Reverend Peirson Lloyd: "It might have given a handle to inculcate the doctrine of his infallibility, since he could correct the calendar."

47. Edgerton, "The Calendar Year."

48. Woolf, *Social Circulation*, 11.

49. Cressy, "The Protestant Calendar," 35, 51–52.

50. On England's calendar culture see, e.g., Poole, *Time's Alteration*; Cressy, *Bonfires*; Hutton, *The Rise and Fall* and *Stations of the Sun*; as well as Collinson, *Birthpangs of Protestant England*.

51. Cressy, "The Protestant Calendar," 31–52. John Selden, *De Anno Civili et Calendario*

Veteris Ecclesiae seu Reipublicae Judaicae (1644), presented the Jewish precedent as a model during the English struggle to find a balance between civil and religious law (as well as among calendar systems). Selden was the first Western scholar to study the differences between Qaraites and rabbanites over the calendar. On this controversy see Ankori, *Karaites*, 292–353; Ziskind, *John Selden*, 17.

52. Cressy, "The Protestant Calendar," 31–32.
53. Poole, *Time's Alteration*, 74.
54. Ibid., 84.
55. Ibid., 123.
56. This discussion is based on ibid., 121–141.
57. Robert of Leicester (d. 1348) wrote a treatise in 1294 on the computus of the Hebrews. See Thorndike, "Computus," 225.
58. Cited in Poole, *Time's Alteration*, 74.
59. Ibid., 75.
60. Ibid., 107, 109.
61. I owe the formulation "bouleversement des habitudes" to Gaspard, "Les Almanachs," 144. For a penetrating sociological analysis of the French calendar reform, see Zerubavel, "The French Republican Calendar."
62. *Calendrier pour l'année sextile* (1794), 6.
63. Ibid.: "Le temps ouvre un nouveau livre à l'histoire."
64. The Froeschlé-Chopards' "Une double image" contrasts the failure of the revolutionary calendar with the successful French rationalization of weights and measurements using the metric system.
65. For the mechanics of the French Revolutionary calendar, see Reingold, Dershowitz, and Clamen, "Calendrical Calculations," 393–396.
66. Shaw, "Reactions," 10.
67. See, e.g., *Le calendrier républicain: Ballet qui doit être exécuté a la suite de l'engagement des citoyennes, sans-culottide nationale* (Bordeaux: Delormel, ca. 1800).
68. Shaw, "Reactions," 4. The author of an introduction to the French revolutionary calendar compared the sweeping changes it introduced to the transition in Jewish chronology from the Seleucid era to the anno mundi chronology. See *Calendrier*, 1794, 10.
69. Thomas, *Le temps des foires*.
70. Among the intended customers of a concordance of the French Republican and Gregorian calendars were French agents in other countries whose unpleasant task it was to instruct foreign business and diplomatic corps regarding the new calendar. See *Concordance des calendriers*, v.
71. The French revolutionary calendar went into effect on November 24, 1793. It began from September 22, 1792, the day after the republic was established. See Reingold, Dershowitz, and Clamen, "Calendrical Calculations," 393.

3. The Jewish Calendar in the Age of Print

1. Fowler, "The Formation," 185–188.
2. Katz, "Mahloqet ha-semikha," 232.
3. Da Costa, *Examination*, 300–301.
4. Fishman, *Shaking the Pillars*, 137.

5. Ibid., 135, 140.

6. Nieto, *Matteh Dan*. Nieto wrote another work devoted completely to the Jewish calendar, *Pascalogia*.

7. Dane, *The Myth*, introduction. For classical Jewish texts, see Heller, *Printing the Talmud*, 345–355.

8. Crick and Walsham, *Uses of Script and Print*, 4 (see also 1–26); Hindman, *Printing the Written Word*, introduction.

9. McKitterick, *Print, Manuscript*, 22–52.

10. This format was also adopted by Elia Levita for his *Tishby*.

11. Münster, *Kalendarium Hebraicum*; Bloch, "Erasmus and the Froben Press"; Jardine, *Erasmus, Man of Letters*. On the printing in Basel of scholarly works in classical languages, see Bietenholz, "Édition et Réforme," 239–268; Bernoulli, *Basler Büchermarkt*.

12. Münster, *Kalendarium Hebraicum*, 1–4.

13. Zimmer, "Jewish and Christian," 69–88, esp. 86 n.2. For Münster's sources, see Weinberg, "Invention and Convention," 319–322.

14. See, e.g., the epistolary exchange between R. Sholomo Azubi and Nicolas-Claude Fabri de Peiresc (1580–1637). Peiresc asked about the Jews' method of calculating their New Year, and Azubi's response constitutes the longest surviving letter in the correspondence. Miller, "Mechanics," 74, 86.

15. *Sefer evronot* (Riva di Trento: Jacob Marcaria, 1561). The sales pitch on the title page plays on the title itself: "וקנה ספר עברונות כל בני עבר" (Buy this sefer evronot, children of Ever). I thank Sharon Koren for the suggestion that Marcaria may have turned away from the term *ibbur* because its use in qabbalistic literature would have misled potential readers about the nature of the book. For more on the use of ibbur versus evronot, see Idel, "The Secret of Impregnation," 353–354.

16. Title page: "בקיצור הפלא ופלא". On the role of printing in consolidating texts that had circulated in various configurations in the medieval period, see the comments of Matt, *Zohar*, 1:xvi; as well as Milikowsky, "Further on Editing Rabbinic Texts," 137–149. For a different printed collection of ibbur texts, see Yosef ben Shem Tov, *Sefer she'erit Yosef*.

17. On the Hebrew press in Riva, see Joseph Jacobs, "Riva di Trento," *Jewish Encyclopedia*; Carmoly, *Annalen*; Bloch, *Hebrew Printing in Riva di Trento*; and Bloch, "A Hitherto Unrecorded Hebrew Publication."

18. Ibn Susan, *Tiqqun Issachar*, and *Sefer ibbur shanim u-tequfot*. For a bibliographical description of the 1578 edition, see Hill, *Hebraica: Manuscripts and Early Printed Books*, no. 45. On ibn Susan see David, *To Come to the Land*, 152–153.

19. Kohen based his work on that of Yosef ben Shem Tov; hence the title *She'erit Yosef*.

20. In the preceding five years, 1558–1563, a number of previously unprinted qabbalistic works, including two editions of the Zohar, the archetypical esoteric text, were brought to print. See Tishby, "The Controversy."

21. Ibn Susan self-identified as "the maghrebi"; he was known to others by that designation as well. Aaron Ashkenazi, who saw the manuscript of *Tiqqun Issachar* in 1554, referred to ibn Susan in his approbation as "he-hakham ha-ne'erav me-benei ha-ma'arav," a Hebrew wordplay on "maghrebi."

22. Ibn Susan, *Sefer ibbur shanim*, v.

23. On the controversy, see Katz, "The Dispute," 137–139.

24. Ibn Susan, *Sefer ibbur shanim*, 3v.

25. Ibid., introduction, 1v.

26. Ibn Susan, *Sefer ibbur shanim*, 5r.; see also Isaac ben Moses, known as Eshtori ha-Parhi, *Kaftor va-ferah* (completed in 1322; published in 1549 in Venice).

27. *Tiqqun Issachar*, title page: "This is a book on the ibbur and tequfot which return eternally, from the year 5324 [1564 C.E.], printed at the order of Solomon."

28. Ibn Susan, *Sefer ibbur shanim*, 2r. Ibn Susan requested that anyone who copied his charts reprint this warning about the lacunae in the early edition.

29. Ibid., 10r.

30. Ibid., 10r.

31. Ibid., 10v.

32. Yosef ben Shem Tov, *She'erit Yosef*, introduction, n.p.

33. Ibid.

34. The catalogue of the National Library of Israel, Jerusalem, not only attributes all editions titled *Sefer evronot* to Belin; it also accuses Jacob Marcaria of deliberately failing to credit Belin as the author. See also Fishoff, *Written in the Stars*, 72, and *Jüdische Handschriften*, 168. The Offenbach, 1722 ed., states: "הח"ר אליעזר בלין אשכנזי נדפס כבר מועתק מהחיבור של".

35. On the Belin (sometimes Balint, Blyn) family in the sixteenth century, see Zimmer, *Fiery Embers*, 43 n.2. In Eidelberg, *R. Juspa*, the name Isaac Belin occurs in the *Sefer minhagim* of Worms for 1666, p. 31, and in the *pinqas* (communal record book) of the community (1658), 107. No conclusions can be drawn regarding the identity of "Eliezer Belin" without further confirmation.

36. The 1615 edition is rare. My citation from the introduction is from a microfilm of the copy in the Oxford, Bodleian Library, Opp. 4° 1387. The edition of 1691 (Frankfurt an der Oder) contains the same message in the introduction: without a sefer evronot it would be impossible to fulfill the mitzvah of *qiddush ha-hodesh*.

37. Introduction to the Lublin, 1640 edition, from the microfilmed copy held in the Bodleian Library (Steinschneider, Cat. Bodl. 2:958–959): "Reprinted here in Lublin, under King Wladislav in the press established by Zvi z"l bar Abraham Kalonymos Yafeh zt"l."

38. *Sefer evronot* (1691).

39. Shifra Baruchson-Arbib, in her census of Italian Jewish libraries, *Books and Readers*, 166, counted five copies of ibn Susan's *Sefer ibbur shanim*. Counting any one title may be misleading, because there are many additional works related to ibbur listed generically, and Baruchson-Arbib has classified them with scientific works. Examples include *Tekhuna ve-toldedot ha-ibbur*; *moladot*; *pinqas moladot*; *seder moladot*; *mafteah moladot*; *sefer al luah moladot*, *Sefer lilmod la'asot luhot ha-shanah*; *sefer luhot*; and *qetav yad mar'eh la'asot luhot*.

40. Ibn Susan, *Sefer ibbur shanim*, 3b. "Through the year 6000 A.M." refers to the widely held belief among Jews that the world would last six thousand years. The locus classicus is in BT Sanhedrin 97a–b.

41. Finzi's *Luhot* was published in Mantua by Abraham Conat in 1475. On this printer, see Colorni, "Abraham Conat."

42. Bloch, "Zacuto," 59.

43. This calendar, a unicum, is in the Library of the Jewish Theological Seminary. For a

more detailed description see Goff, *Incunabula*, Hebr. 3; *Gesamtkatalog der Wiegend-rucke*, Add. 1514/20; Offenberg, *Hebrew Incunabula*, 7, no. 5; Habermann, *Ha-madpisim*, 46.

44. On printing and the introduction of errors into astronomical works, see Johns, *The Nature of the Book*, 543–621.

45. Feiner, *Jewish Enlightenment*, 382 n.10.

46. Zunz, "Verfassen und übersetzen," 50–67; Berger, "An Invitation," 35.

47. Heller, "Ambrosius Froben, Israel Zifroni," 137–148.

48. Wall calendar (Venice: Juan da Gara, 1598–1599 [שנ"ט]). Valmadonna 7392. Zafroni referred to himself as המגיה.

49. Wall calendar (Venice: Juan da Gara, 1599–1600 [ש"ס]).

50. Wall calendar (Venice: Juan da Gara, 1600–1601 [שס"א]). Valmadonna 4773/C6.

51. Wall calendar (Venice: Juan da Gara, 1601–1602 [שס"ב]). Valmadonna 4954/C7. In this calendar the chronograph appears to be more prominent; perhaps that is the innovation of the year.

52. Wall calendar (Venice: Juan da Gara, 1604–1605 [שס"ה]). Valmadonna 4955/C8.

53. Wall calendar (Venice: Juan da Gara, 1604–1605 [שס"ה]). Valmadonna 4955/C8.

54. Wall calendar (Venice: Juan da Gara, 1608–1609 [שס"ט]). Valmadonna 4956/C10.

55. Wall calendar (Venice: Juan da Gara, 1610–1611 [ש"ע]). Valmadonna 4771/12.

56. On this printer, see Rosenfeld, "Zebi Hirsch ben Chaim aus Fürth," 34–40. See, e.g., the 1742–1743 calendar, which bears the father's imprint.

57. For Fürth, for example, there is an unbroken chain of calendars from 1737 through 1877. See Rosenfeld, "Taschenkalender," 26. On the collection of Olaf Tychsen, see Süß and Tröger, *Die Judaica und Hebraica*, 3–4. The Valmadonna Trust collection contains an almost complete series of calendars published in Mantua from the mid-sixteenth century, with many examples as well from sixteenth- and seventeenth-century Venice.

58. On German genizot, see Timm and Süss, *Yiddish Literature in a Franconian Genizah*; Süß, "Zur literaturgeschichtlichen," 81–83. The genizah of Veitshöchheim contained approximately 70 pocket calendars and 20 wall calendars. Rosenfeld, *Jewish printing in Wilhermsdorf*, notes genizot from Reckendorf, 160 no. 148, and from Westheim, 218 no. 209. For the later eighteenth century, the Hechingen genizah contained an entire series of calendars, in both pocket and wall format. The wall calendars date from 1777–1778 until 1818–1819. See Hüttenmeister and Kohring, "Funde" 230, 232.

59. Rosenfeld, "Wandkalender."

60. Rosenfeld, "Ein jüdischer." Rosenfeld provides a facsimile of the early seventeenth-century Hanau calendar as well as a facsimile of a Sulzbach wall calendar from 1723.

61. The earliest surviving wall calendar from Fürth is from 1740. The auction catalogue of Kestenbaum & Company for the March 11, 2003 auction, lot nos. 61, 36, reproduces wall calendars from Jessnitz, 1740 and 1748; and Altona, 1748 and 1749. I thank the staff for allowing me to examine the calendars prior to the sale.

62. The brief chronographs and times of local prayers were included in Fürth wall calendars only after 1807.

63. Mosche Rosenfeld, in his "Taschenkalender," 35, notes that weather predictions were sporadic and arbitrary and eventually disappeared. Like other supplemental elements, they move the calendar into the realm of farmer's almanacs, and were generally removed as calendar publishers moved on to other interests. On bloodletting, see the

1778 Fürth calendars, which include "whether it is propitious or not to let blood, day by day": Rosenfeld, "Taschenkalender," 27. On page 31 of this work, Rosenfeld describes an 1805 calendar in which the days marked with ° are bad for bloodletting. For a fifteenth-century reference to a table of days on which "the wise men of the gentiles" prohibited bloodletting, see Gold, *A Sign and a Witness*, 164, from a northern Italian Hebrew medical treatise. On propitious days for commercial activities, deliveries, travel, and moving, see Rosenfeld, "Taschenkalender," 34. After 1794, this feature disappeared from the Fürth calendars.

64. Peterson, "Hof-Og." The Altona calendars, published by the Danish government in German from 1743–1848, included weather, sunrise and sunset times, postage charts, along with political information such as the royal and state notables and new laws.

65. The New York Public Library, Dorot Jewish Division ms Heb. 268.

66. Manuscript pocket calendars existed long before printed ones, of course. See, for example, the description of a fourteenth-century English pocket calendar or almanac that contains very similar information to that found in much later examples, in Alexander and Binski, *Age of Chivalry*, 288, no. 222.

67. New York, Library of the Jewish Theological Seminary ms (NS) C110, spanning the years 1831–1875.

68. Sarna, "An Eighteenth Century," 25–27.

69. The University of Pennsylvania Center for Advanced Judaic Studies, in Philadelphia, holds a small collection of eighteenth-century manuscript Jewish calendars: see especially ms 58, Luah le-shenot 5516–19 (1756–1759); Rare ms 59, 1776–1777 Luah shel shenat 5537 (1777); and ms 61, Luah shel shenat 5542 (1781–1782). I thank Arthur Kiron for his gracious and knowledgeable help with these.

70. University of Pennsylvania Center for Advanced Judaic Studies ms 60, Luah shel shenat 5541 [1781].

71. Rosenbloom, *A Biographical Dictionary*, 35–36; Jacob R. Marcus, *The Concise Dictionary*, 1:142.

72. The original calendar was published by Proops. The businessman who transformed it is not identified; his partner was Kalman Eschwe. He recorded expenses such as repairs, taxes, and maintenance items. In the spring of 1800 the partnership fell apart.

4. A New Jewish Book in Christian Europe

1. Berlin, Staatsbibliothek ms or. oct. 3150, fol. 78r. On the scribe Yuda Reutlingen Mehler, see Bloch, "Ein vielbegehrter Rabbiner."

2. Zimmer, *Rabbi Hayim*, 5–43, and *Fiery Embers*, 220–237.

3. Reiner, "Aliyat ha-qehillah ha-gedolah."

4. Zimmer, *Fiery Embers*, 32. The portion of the citation in brackets is deleted here; cf. Zimmer's "R. David b. Isaac of Fulda," 230 n.38.

5. Zimmer, *Fiery Embers*, 31 n.11, and "R. David b. Isaac of Fulda," 229 n.35.

6. Zimmer, *Fiery Embers*, 33. The forgotten ritual that R. David recovered is the subject of Ivan Marcus, *Rituals of Childhood*.

7. Zimmer, *Fiery Embers*, 32 n.21.

8. For a sixteenth-century example, see New York, Library of the Jewish Theological Seminary ms 2634, fol. 11r.

9. Munich, Bayerische Staatsbibliothek Cod. Hebr. 394, fol. 53r.

10. New York, Library of the Jewish Theological Seminary ms 2540, fol. 73v.

11. Berlin, Staatsbibliothek ms or. oct. 3150, fol. 45v: "Until here I found in an ancient evronot written in the year [5]312 to the small counting [1552 C.E.]." The passage he cited rejected the computus of Nahshon Gaon as inaccurate, cited that of the tosafist R. Samson of Sens approvingly, and dismissed that of his brother R. Isaac bar Abraham as overly stringent.

12. New York, Yeshiva University, Mendel Gottesman Library ms 1083, fol. 1r. Because the Jews were expelled from Nuremberg in 1499, we have a *terminus ad quem* for the date of Neimark's source. On Samuel Schlettstadt, a fourteenth-century Alsatian rabbinic scholar, see Yuval, *Hakhamim be-doram*, 276, 295.

13. Oxford, Bodleian Library ms Opp. 700, fol. 59v.

14. Beit-Arié, *Unveiled Faces*, 61–62, contrasts Latin book production with the absence of institutional, ecclesiastical, or commercial frameworks for copying Hebrew texts.

15. Strasbourg, Bibliothèque Nationale et Universitaire ms 3931, owner's inscription and colophon.

16. For a parallel phenomenon in communal records, see Litt, "Pinkassei Kahal."

17. Elijah b. Moses Troitlein of Worms completed the Sotheby sefer evronot in 1552–1557, and another sefer evronot during the same period: Leiden, Bibliotheek der Rijksuniversiteit Cod. Or. 4736. The Sotheby manuscript contains approximately twice the number of folios and illustrations.

18. Budapest, Magyar tudomanyos akademia ms Kaufmann A 515.

19. The scribe of New York, Jewish Theological Seminary Library ms 10572, claimed that he made an exact copy of a printed evronot. The New York Public Library, Dorot Jewish Division copy of Meldola, *Sefer mo'ed David* contains an extensive manuscript supplement by Hirtz Reinganum of Frankfurt am Main, a hybrid of print and script.

20. Cincinnati, Klau Library, Hebrew Union College ms 899, fol. 2v: "סליק הקדמה" Prague, Jewish Museum ms 61, fol. 2r.

21. See, e.g., Jerusalem, National Library of Israel ms Heb 8° 3416, fol. 20r, in which the scribe and a woman (his wife?) hold a frame for the colophon.

22. Itzik Kreilsheim, Prague, Jewish Museum ms 61, fol. 39r.

23. Stevens, *Cycles of Time*, 288, describes the Fulda scriptorium of Hraban Maurus. Hraban gave the *annus praesens* of his computus and detailed examples of how to apply it to the year in which he wrote it, 820 C.E.

24. Oxford, Bodleian Library ms Opp. 701, fols. 1r–58v. Loanz is referred to in the inscription as Elijah ba'al shem. See Theodore Friedman, "Elijah ben Moses Loanz," *Encyclopedia Judaica*. I thank Elhanan Reiner for bringing this manuscript to my attention.

25. Oxford, Bodleian Library ms Opp. 701, fols. 2r, 58v. The year 1552 is the template year for many sifre evronot. See, e.g., Budapest, Magyar tudomanyos akademia ms Kaufmann 515, fol. 31; Munich, Bayerische Staatsbibliothek cod. hebr. 394, fol. 91, image 200 (1566); Leiden, Bibliotheek der Rijksuniversiteit cod. or. 4736 (1557).

26. On Wolf of Moravia, see Cincinnati, Hebrew Union College, Klau Library ms 906, fol. 77v; possibly identical to "Wolf Bukh of Moravia," mentioned in Oxford, Bodleian Library ms Opp. 332, fol. 179v. On Yehiel of Guenzberg, see Oxford, Bodleian Library ms Opp. 701, fol. 14v; Oxford, Bodleian Library ms Mich. 152, fol. 184r (ms is dated, or copied from one dated 1552, Frankfurt). Budapest, Magyar tudomanyos akademia ms

Kaufmann 515, fol. 32, was in the possession of a Frankfurt family for several generations; Budapest, Magyar tudomanyos akademia ms Kaufmann 520, fol. 159; Oxford, Bodleian Opp. 698, fol. 47r; Oxford, Bodleian ms Opp. 700, fol. 12r. On Naftali Hertz Treves (likely the father of Jonathan), see Zimmer, *Fiery Embers*, 244–246. Treves settled in Worms and later served as cantor in Frankfurt. On Zeqlein of Metz, see Oxford, Bodleian Library ms Opp. 698, fol. 47r. And on Samuel of Schweinfurt, see Oxford, Bodleian Library ms Opp. 700, fol. 1v.

27. The Sotheby evronot was written by "I, Elijah son of R. Moses Troitle z"l," fol. 21v. Nathan Shapira of Horodna and Posen was author of *Mavo she'arim,* a commentary on the classical rabbinical work *Sha'are dura.*

28. Zimmer, *Fiery Embers,* 180.

29. Sifre evronot that cite Aqiva of Frankfurt as a source include Cincinnati, Hebrew Union College, Klau Library ms 906, fol. 77r; Oxford, Bodleian Library ms Opp. 332, fol. 181r; New York, Jewish Theological Seminary Library ms 2662, fol. 57v; New York, Jewish Theological Seminary Library ms 2547, fol. 116v.

30. Dietz, *Jewish Community of Frankfurt,* 119, 164. Aqiva came to Frankfurt from Prague in the 1530s. He married Ella, daughter of Simon Guenzberg. See Gans, *Sefer tzemah David,* 144; Rohrbacher, "Medinat Schwaben," 86–88. One of his brothers-in-law migrated to Safed, suggesting the possibility of cultural contact with figures such as ibn Susan. Oxford, Bodleian Library ms Opp. 700, fol. 59r, contains the following note in the margin: "Here is a sign concerning the Frankfurt fair, the spring fair: The fair always begins on the second day (Monday), always before Palm Sunday. This I found in the sefer evronot in the community of Frankfurt, by the great sage R. Shimon" (likely a reference to Simon Guenzberg).

31. On yeshiva students as manuscript copyists see Reiner, "A Biography."

32. E.g., New York, Jewish Theological Seminary Library ms 2578, fol. 32r: "I heard in the name of our master R. Aqiva that he found in the book *Shalshelet ha-qabbalah* that the nations also intercalate in the years 3, 6, 8, 11, 14, 17, 19."

33. Oxford, Bodleian Library ms Opp. 700, fol. 59v.

34. New York, Library of the Jewish Theological Seminary ms 9487, fol. 3r; Jerusalem, National Library of Israel ms Heb 8° 3416, fol. 2v. Although BT Rosh hashanah 25a attributes the tradition to R. Gamliel, some mss say R. Simon ben Gamliel.

35. Jerusalem, National Library of Israel ms 8° 2380, fol. 3r.

36. On a circle of manuscript illuminators in the first half of the eighteenth century in Hamburg-Altona, see Fishof, *Jüdische;* on *seder brakhot,* see Fishof, *Grace after Meals,* introduction.

37. Loanz copied his sefer evronot "word for word." Oxford, Bodleian Library ms Opp. 701, fol. 1v.

38. Jerusalem, National Library of Israel ms 8° 2380, fol. 2r. The translation of the verse in Exodus, cited in Rashi at that place, follows the midrashic interpretation (Mekhilta, chapter 3, Lauterbach ed., p. 25; BT Shabbat 133b); this is the meaning that Pinhas of Halberstadt intended. It forms the basis of the concept *hiddur mitzvah,* the adornment of rituals by beautifying the instruments used to perform them.

39. BT Rosh Hashanah 24b; BT Avodah zarah, 43a–b.

40. These motifs have generated a considerable body of scholarly analysis. See, e.g., Levine, "Figural Art," 19; Friedman, "The Meaning of the Zodiac," 51 n.1.

41. For some early modern examples, see *Shulkhan arukh*, Yoreh de'ah, 141, par. 4; Abraham di Boton, *Lehem rav*, no. 15. For other scholarship on this question see Bland, *The Artless Jew*; Cohen, *Jewish Icons*; Mann, *Jewish Texts*; and Gutmann, *No Graven Images*. Cincinnati, Klau Library, Hebrew Union College ms 902, fol. 14r, contains drawings of the moon in its various configurations.

42. Narkiss, *Hebrew*, 32.

43. Ibid., 33. Although *qinot* were rarely illustrated, one *qinah* for *Tish'a be-Av* contains a lament by personifications of every sign of the zodiac. See England, "Mosaics," 189–214, 202; Goldschmidt, *Seder ha-qinot*.

44. On "Gates of Mercy," see, e.g., New York Public Library, Dorot Jewish Division, *Mahzor*, fol. 353v. Online digital image id no. 404991, *"sha'arei rahamim."*

45. Copyists configured the text around the charts and illustrations. For a finished example of a meticulously configured manuscript, see ms Yeshiva Ahavas Torah Baranovich, auction 11, item 297. Cincinnati, Klau Library, Hebrew Union College ms 899 is another example of an expertly written manuscript that bears virtually no figural drawings. The unfinished Klau Library Hebrew Union College ms 903 provides insight into the actual process of laying out the pages and tables for the manuscript and to the working methods of the evronot scribes. It, too, is beautifully decorated but does not contain many of the standard illustrations. In New York, Columbia University ms x 893 Se36, the scribe carefully glued a new page over one with errors. Rather than crossing out or erasing them, he began anew. I thank Jennifer Lee, of the Rare Book collection, for having that page opened for me expeditiously.

46. Blank leaves or unused space provided scribes with a canvas for whimsical doodling or serious practice: see, e.g., Cincinnati, Klau Library, Hebrew Union College ms 901, fol. 30r. On the common tendency to make use of the space in these ways, see Goddard, "Probationes Pennae," 242–267; Bischoff, *Mittelalterliche Studien*, 74–87.

47. The source for the formulation of the opening text in many evronot appears to be Coucy, *Sefer mitzvot gadol, mitzvot aseh*, 46–47. Kasher, *Humash*, 13:4 cites the code *Halakhot gedolot*, which counts *qiddush ha-hodesh* and calculating the tequfot as two separate mitzvot.

48. Oxford, Bodleian Library ms Opp. 702, fol. 1r: "This sefer evronot I have written in 1692, here in the community of Lissa in the yeshiva and midrash of the great sage R. Isaac b. Elijah.

49. Budapest, Magyar tudomanyos akademia ms Kaufmann A 515, fol. 33.

50. Cosgrove and Daniels, *The Iconography of Landscape*, introduction.

51. Berger, "An Invitation," 36–42.

52. E.g., New York, Columbia University ms x893 Se36, title page; Cincinnati, Klau Library, Hebrew Union College ms 899, title page, fols. 13–16; Klau Library, Hebrew Union College ms 901, fol. 1r.

53. Berlin, Staatsbibliothek ms or. 3150.

54. See Cincinnati, Klau Library, Hebrew Union College ms 902, where the title page portal appears to be a gateway to the heavens; the effect is even more pronounced in the title page to the second section. The portal to the first section is flanked by Moses on the left and Aaron on the right. The divine finger in the heavens points to the moon, and Moses' elongated index finger echoes it. Fol. 15r also depicts the portal as

an entryway into heaven, with R. Samuel and his calculations on the right, R. Ada and his computus on the left.

55. Robbins, "Studies," 63.

56. Goldberg, *The Sacred Portal*, 67–70.

57. Cincinnati, Klau Library, Hebrew Union College ms 903, fol. 1r, depicts roundels with figures of David and Solomon beneath the portal.

58. Roth, "A Masterpiece," 359; Nordström, "Temple Miniatures," 39–81. On the calendar and Temple in messianic yearning in Jewish late antiquity, see Hirshman, "Yearning for Intimacy."

59. Cincinnati, Klau Library, Hebrew Union College ms 901, fol. 35r.

60. [זה הלציי״ב] "פתחו לי שערי צדק אבא בם אודה י-ה" New York, Library of the Jewish Theological Seminary ms 2572. Since these verses had no connection to the calendar, they would have originated from another genre.

61. On the *luah arba she'arim*, see Stern, *Calendar and Community*, 193. The four "gates" correspond to the four days of the week on which the year can begin (three are eliminated because of the deferral *lo adu rosh*). The seven-portal calendar tables, configured for when molad Tishre falls on each of the seven days of the week, appeared less frequently; see, e.g., Klau Library, Hebrew Union College ms 901, fol. 42a: "With the aid of the Creator of the mountains, I begin to write the seven portals," followed by an elaborately illuminated portal; similarly Cincinnati, Klau Library, Hebrew Union College ms 901, fol. 44a; Oxford, Bodleian Library ms Opp. 700, fol. 34v. See also decorated portals in Jerusalem, National Library of Israel ms 8° 2380, fols. 45v, 47r, 46r.

62. Examples include New York, Columbia University ms X893 Se36, fol. 4r; Oxford, Bodleian Library ms Opp. 701, fol. 4v; and Berlin, Preussische Staatsbibliothek ms or. oct. 3150, fol. 7r. In Cincinnati, Klau Library, Hebrew Union College ms 901, fol. 2b, the ladder hovers, the figure of Issachar is not on the ladder, and he is not holding an hourglass. The hourglass may refer to the division of the hour into 1,080 parts as the specific knowledge Issachar brought. On hourglasses in sixteenth-century German art, see Balmer, "Operation of Sand Clocks," 615–632. A Jewish communal ordinance from Nikolsburg, Moravia, required every teacher to have a *zand sha'a* (sand clock) in order to allocate the right amount of attention to each pupil. Assaf, *Meqorot*, 1:479.

63. A number of biblical figures mediated astronomical or astrological knowledge. Adam heads the list, which includes Enoch, Nimrod, and Abraham. For Nimrod, see Obrist, "Les vents," 57–76. On the association with Issachar, see Stern, *Calendar and Community*, 178–179, 214.

64. Heck, *L'échelle*; Cahn, "Ascending," 2:697–724.

65. Houtman, "What Did Jacob See," 337–351, on the possible meanings of *sullam*.

66. For figures descending head first, see, e.g., Heck, *L'échelle*, plates 7, 8, and 26, with examples from the twelfth through fourteenth centuries. In addition, see Oxford, Bodleian Library ms Opp. 700, fol. 2r., where Issachar on the ladder is captioned "Issachar ascended to the heights," and beneath that, "1,080 parts to the hour," signifying one of the elements essential for calculation of the ibbur. Cf. Jerusalem, National Library of Israel ms 8° 2380, fol. 10r, where an angel comes down to Issachar who is standing on the ladder, linking this scene to a second title illustration, fol. 3r.

67. Jerusalem, National Library of Israel ms 8° 2380, fol. 57v, contains a full page illustration labeled "Elijah ascends to heaven in fire," but it is not linked to the earlier depiction of Issachar.

68. Jacob bar Samson, *Sefer elqoshi*, attributed the development of the fixed calendar to "bene Issachar." See Oxford, Bodleian Library ms Opp. 317, fols. 94r–v.

69. וכן תניא בברייתא דשמואל ירחנאי כשעלה יששכר לרקיע קבע אלף ופי׳ חלקים בשעה
ועוד תנן ומבני יששכר יודעי בינה לעתים עתים ר״ת עיבור, תקופה, יתרון, מולד

70. Cahn, "Ascending," 721, notes that in Christian iconography Jacob's ladder prefigured the Cross, or Christ himself, bridging heaven and earth. Given the polemical subtext of sifre evronot, this image may have been intended as a subtle subversion of the Christian interpretation.

71. For a similar scene in an earlier Hebrew manuscript, see London, British Library ms Add. 11639, fol. 520v, reproduced in Epstein, *Dreams*, 83. Here Eve stands on the left, Adam on the right, with the serpent entwined around the tree. All three hold the fruit of the tree, and the serpent has a human face, a common representation in Christian art. Other examples in sifre evronot include Cincinnati, Klau Library, Hebrew Union College ms 901, fol. 26a; Cincinnati, Klau Library, Hebrew Union College ms 906 fol. 23v–24r (damaged); Columbia University ms Se 36 X893, fol. 19v; New York, Jewish Theological Seminary Library ms 2662, fol. 23r; Berlin, Staatsbibliothek ms 3150, fol. 10r; Berlin, Staatsbibliothek ms or. quart. 692, fol. 18r; and New York, Jewish Theological Seminary Library ms 2540, fol. 17v.

72. E.g., Reinitzer, *Biblia Deutsch*, 67, image 28, entry 41, reproduced from the Luther Bible printed in Augsburg: Guenther Zainer, 1475; title page, upper left, from the Wittenberg: Lufft, 1541 Bible.

73. Bowman, "Malef," 9–10.

74. Exodus 12:2, commentary of Rashi ad loc.

75. *Pirqe de Rabbi Eliezer*, trans. and ed. Friedlander, 52.

76. Stone, *History*; de Jonge and Tromp, *The Life*. Note the discussion of Christian influence on the *Pirqe de Rabbi Eliezer*, 8. Similar iconography is on view in Murdoch and Tasioulas, *The Apocryphal Lives*, title page.

77. Baggely, *Festival Icons*, 9.

78. Davies, "The Evocative Symbolism," 34. For parallels between Eden and the church, see Pearsall and Salter, *Landscapes and Seasons*, 69.

79. Reinitzer, *Biblia Deutsch*, 217.

80. Jerusalem, National Library of Israel ms 8° 2380 fol. 29v.

81. See, e.g., Luther Bible, Lübeck: Dietz, 1533, reproduced in Reinitzer, *Biblia Deutsch*, 167.

82. Some scribes illustrated bitter herbs in the Passover haggadah by having a man point to his wife with the text "this bitter herb," a veiled reference to "I have found woman more bitter than death," e.g., British Library ms or. 1404, fol. 18r. *The First Cincinnati Haggadah*, fol. 11b, portrays the last of the four sons, the one "who does know how to ask," as a jester, and illustrates the haggadah's advice "to open for him" by having another man literally hold his mouth open and pour words into it. See Roth, "A Masterpiece," 358, 507, for scribal flights of whimsy.

83. Berlin, Staadtsbibliothek ms or. oct. 3150, fol. 22r, contains both these illustrations.

In Oxford, Bodleian Library ms Opp. 701, fol. 17r, an animal (fox?) is depicted with its head turned backward touching its tail. In Jerusalem, National Library of +Israel ms Heb 8° 3416, fol. 16v, a face is drawn that can be seen in one way when the page is held straight and another when it is upside down. Goddard, "Probationes Pennae," 248 n.15, notes the association between bare bottoms and the figure of Folly. Clark, *Thinking with Demons*, 13, notes that according to a German proverb, a figure gazing backward at the world through its legs catches sight of the devil.

84. Mellinkoff, *Outcasts*, esp. ch. 10, "Vulgar Gestures and Indecent Exposure."

85. Reinitzer, *Biblia Deutsch*, 90. This was Erasmus's Latin translation of the Bible, intended for scholars.

86. Benton, *Medieval Mischief*, 45, image I.66, shows Dominican monks represented as dogs in the fresco "Triumph of the Church" by Andrea da Firenze.

87. Camille, *Image*, 45.

88. Benton, *Medieval Mischief*, 1, 116–118, figs. III.37–III.41; 128, figs. III.50–III.51; for the head protruding between the legs, 69, fig. III.50.

89. On the *molad*, see Jerusalem, National Library of Israel ms 8° 2380, fol. 12v. On the smoke (and non-Jewish holidays) motif, see Jerusalem, National Library of Israel ms 8° 2380, fol. 163v. Regarding *ve-teda*, see Jerusalem, National Library of Israel ms 8° 2380, fol. 106v.

90. For puns on the Hebrew word for elephant, see New York, Jewish Theological Seminary Library ms 2662, fol. 21v. Similarly, Oxford, Bodleian Library ms Opp. 700, fol. 12r, depicts an elephant, labeled in Hebrew letters הֶעלפֿנד. There the play on words is clearer. For adding fractions, the reader is instructed to *tapil*, a play on the Hebrew *pil*, elephant (the last three references are from Straus, "Calculating"). Jerusalem, National Library of Israel ms Heb. 8° 3416, fol. 8v, contains an ostrich holding the key, but the illustration is missing a key of its own: it is completely detached from the text and has no caption.

91. Berlin, Staatsbibliothek ms or. oct. 3150, fol. 65a.

92. Ibid., table on fol. 17v.

93. Berlin, Staatsbibliothek ms or. oct. 3150, fol. 18r; the motif of Eve's sin is alluded to in BT Shabbat 146a.

94. Sources and examples include lunar chart, Cincinnati, Klau Library, Hebrew Union College ms 902, fol. 14r (15r contains same for sun); Cincinnati, Klau Library, Hebrew Union College ms 902, fol. 28r, chart of "the six angels who are appointed over the seven planets and over the zodiac"; Cincinnati, Klau Library, Hebrew Union College ms 902, fol. 29r, windmill house with seven windows for the seven planets. The moon is often depicted as a crescent with a face protruding. See, e.g., Cincinnati, Klau Library, Hebrew Union College ms 901, fol. 15r, cartouche containing both sun and moon with faces; Cincinnati, Klau Library, Hebrew Union College ms 902, fol. 11v, anthropomorphic sun and moon; New York, Library of the Jewish Theological Seminary ms 2662, fol. 15r (original foliation), sun and moon with man's face protruding from moon; Library of the Jewish Theological Seminary ms 2540, fol. 10v. For *qiddush levana*, see *Minhagim* (Amsterdam, 1662), 12v; Kirchner, *Juedisches Ceremoniel* (1734), 74–78.

95. Reeves, *Painting the Heavens*, 138–183.
96. Linked to the verse in Malachi 4:2.
97. Reeves, *Painting the Heavens*, 139.
98. Wallis, *Bede*, 25–26. Wallis cites earlier analogies between the moon and the church, such as those of Isidore and Ambrose, 26 n.39.
99. Johannes Lucidus, the sixteenth-century author of an important treatise devoted to establishing the date of the Crucifixion, noted that the incarnation took place at the time of a full moon. Reeves, *Painting the Heavens*, 128–133.
100. The preceding description is based on ibid., 138.
101. Father Maelcote, the first Jesuit to confirm Galileo's description, saw rosary beads in the shadows of the moon. See ibid., 152.
102. *Masekhet sofrim*, ch. 19, 329–333, contains the *qiddush levana* text. Genizah fragments contain a prayer, *qedushat ha-yom*, declaring the moon's sanctity, concluding with the blessing "Blessed art Thou, who sanctify Israel and the new month." Fleischer, *Tefilla*, 62, 66; Fleischer, "Berurim"; Hoffman, *Covenant of Blood*, 176–177.
103. Translation based on Hoffman, *Covenant of Blood*, 177. My emphasis.
104. Brody, *The Geonim*, 119.
105. England, "Mosaics," 201. Talmudic citation, BT Rosh Hashanah 25a.
106. Isserles, commentary to *Orah Hayim* 426:2; *Magen Avraham*, 426:11; *Megillah* 3a and Tosafot, on the phrase that begins with the word "Hayshinan."
107. E.g., Berlin Staatsbibliothek ms 3150, fol. 20v.
108. Cincinnati, Klau Library, Hebrew Union College ms 901, fols. 6r–6v. Several versions of this midrash survive. The one referred to in this text is from BT Hullin 60b; other significant variants include Genesis Rabbah 6.3; *Pirqe de Rabbi Eliezer*, chs. 6 and 51. See Stern, "Fictitious Calendars," 115 n.26 on the verse in Isaiah implying that the moon will return to a state of equality with the sun.
109. The close identification between Israel and the moon endures today in some Jewish circles. "Like the Jewish people, the moon goes through stages. It waxes and it declines. Like Israel, it becomes full and it later becomes diminished, but even then, it comes back. The moon symbolizes that in moments of the most intense darkness, when all hope seems to be lost, the Jewish people, as a nation and as individuals—will come back . . . the moon was a mirror of themselves." Feinstein, *Jewish Calendar*, 16–17.
110. See Exodus 12:2 and rabbinic interpretations there. For a collection of midrashic sources that place Enoch and then Moses at the crux of the transmission of the ibbur, see Kasher, *Humash*, 13:5–8. Illustration of Moses, Braginsky ms 247 fol. 70r.
111. For an exception, see Cincinnati, Klau Library, Hebrew Union College ms 902, title page. Moses, identifiable by the rays emanating from his head, points his finger in an echo of the divine finger shown directly above his. The verse from Exodus 12:2 is explicit here: "And God spoke to Moses and Aaron in the Land of Egypt to say: This month is for you the first of the months."
112. Berlin, Staatsbibliothek, Orientabteilung ms 3150, fol. 9r; similarly, Cincinnati, Klau Library, Hebrew Union College ms 901, fols. 5r–v.
113. For examples, see Berlin, Staatsbibliothek ms or. oct. 3150, fol. 16r; and Cincinnati, Klau Library, Hebrew Union College ms 899, fol. 7, *moznei tzedek, boge"d u-ba*. Cincin-

nati, Klau Library, Hebrew Union College ms 901 fol. 15r, depicts a balance, *moznei tzedek*, linked to a cartouche containing the sun and the moon. Cincinnati, Klau Library, Hebrew Union College ms 903, fol. 14v. For more on the *hutag* scale, see Cincinnati, Klau Library, Hebrew Union College ms 901, fol. 15v; ms Cincinnati, Klau Library, Hebrew Union College ms 903, fol. 15v.

114. For depictions of balance scales in Jewish zodiacs, see Fishof, *Written in the Stars.*

115. Wischnitzer, "The Moneychanger."

116. Ibn Ezra, *Sefer ha-ibbur*, ed. Bakal, 49. See fig. 4.6.

117. Examples of volvelles include Cincinnati, Klau Library, Hebrew Union College ms 902, fols. 18r, 24r; Berlin, Staatsbibliothek ms or. oct. 3150, fol. 33r. Cincinnati, Klau Library, Hebrew Union College ms 903, fol. 47v, shows a volvelle in the process of preparation.

118. Helfand, *Reinventing the Wheel*, 10; and Helfand's catalogue to accompany the exhibit *The Magnificent Art of Circular Charting* (The Grolier Club, New York City, 2004, co-curated by Helfand), have been my primary sources of information about this form of chart.

119. Helfand, *Reinventing the Wheel*, 18. Reproductions are from the 1476 edition of *Kalendarium*, 31, fig. 29.

120. On the art of creating concentric "dials," see Stirrup, *Horometria.*

121. On hand imagery and its relationship to memory, see Sherman and Lukehart, *Writing on Hands.*

122. Cincinnati, Klau Library, Hebrew Union College ms 902, fol. 20r.

123. E.g., Oxford, Bodleian Library ms Opp. 700. On fol. 9v, three dogs chase a stag, and one of them has caught the stag by the hind legs; on fol. 19v, the stag leaps free, and by fol. 34r, the stag stands alone in the center of the image. The stag could be a play on the author's name, Tzvi Hirsch. See also *Jüdische Handschriften*, 165.

124. On the iconography of the hunt see Almond, "The Hunting Year," 30–36; Almond, *Medieval Hunting*; Cummins, *The Hound and the Hawk*; Randall, *Images in the Margins*; and Thomas et al., *The Hunting Book.*

125. Cincinnati, Klau Library, Hebrew Union College ms 906 fol. 16v.

126. Berlin, Staatsbibliothek ms or. oct. 3150, fol. 32v.

127. Ibid., fol. 64v.

128. Epstein, *Dreams of Subversion*, 16–38, focuses on the hare in hunt scenes; it is linked to the *yaknehaz (jag den has)* pun. On other quarry, such as gazelles, see 21–22, 131 n.42. Jewish sources about the ethical dimensions of hunting for sport are ambivalent. See Midrash Rabbah, Leviticus 13:3; Meir b. Barukh Rothenburg (d. 1293), *Sha'arei Teshuvot Maharam*, ed. Moses Bloch (Berlin, 1891; repr Jerusalem 1968), vol. 1, ch. 1, par 27: "Those who hunt animals with dogs will not have a share ... in the world to come." I thank Sharon Mintz for this reference.

129. Oxford, Bodleian Library ms Opp. 700, fols. 9v, 19r, 34r.

130. National Library of Israel ms 8° 2380, fol. 61r.

131. Cincinnati, Klau Library, Hebrew Union College ms 903, fol. 54r; similarly, New York, Columbia University ms X893 Se36, fol. 32r.

132. The verses from Isaiah appear in the brief notation for the *haftara* reading cycle in most sifre evronot, a notation that links the images to the text.

5. Keeping Christian Time in Jewish Calendars

1. Isserlein, *Sefer Terumat ha-deshen*, no. 195. The copy I examined in the YIVO Institute for Jewish Research has the offending terms blocked out, either as an act of censorship or self-censorship, adding another layer to the Jewish-Christian interaction.

2. Toch, "Geld und Kredit," appendix, e.g., lines 12, 13, 29, 36. I thank Ivan Marcus for bringing this source to my attention.

3. Siegmund, *The Medici State*, 172, from the edict of expulsion, September 26, 1570.

4. Stow, *Theater of Acculturation*, 74.

5. Ber of Bolechow, *Memoirs*, 107, 162.

6. Zerubavel, "Easter and Passover," 284–289.

7. In his Letter to the Galatians, 4:10, Paul upbraided them: "You observe days and months and times and years." It is unclear whether he was referring to pagan or Jewish times. In his Letter to the Colossians, 2:16, Paul wrote more clearly that once they had embraced Christianity, "Let no man therefore judge you in meat, or in drink, or in respect of an holyday, or of the new moon, or of the sabbath days." See Pederson, "The Ecclesiastical Calendar," 22.

8. My account is based primarily on that in Wallis, *Bede*, xxxv–xxxvii.

9. Zerubavel, "Easter and Passover," 288.

10. North, "The Western Calendar," 97.

11. Ziggelaar, "The Papal Bull," 216.

12. Rich, "The Brest Union," 50.

13. Frank Talmage, in his introduction to Muelhausen, *Sefer nizzahon*, 20, claims that some anti-Christian polemical works were written in 354 paragraphs, the number of days in the lunar year, as a subtle rebuke to the solar-based Christian calendar of 365 days. Neither Joseph Official's *Sefer Yosef ha-meqaneh* nor the anonymous *Sefer nizzahon yashan* contain exactly 354 paragraphs in the editions I checked. The reason given in the introduction to Lipman's *Nizzahon*, "to hint that all days of the year all Jews must be punctilious in their faith," does not necessarily support this claim.

14. E.g., New York, Jewish Theological Seminary Library ms 9085, fol. 26v: "Everything you need to connect the Christian calendar to our calendar."

15. BT Sanhedrin 63b; BT Megilla, 25b. Merhavia, *Ha-Talmud*, 277 nn. 147, 148, cites the translation of this passage in the writ of Gregory IX in the Paris disputation of 1239. There, *leitzanuta* is translated as blasphemy.

16. BT Avodah zarah, 46a.

17. See a discussion of the alternative meanings: *eyd* as days of witness, when spelled with ayin; as calamity when inverted and spelled with aleph (Avodah zarah 1 n.1). Ta-Shma suggested that it is probably a play on the Roman "ides." In his sixteenth-century guide to expurgating Jewish books, Catholic censor Domenico Gerosolimitano ruled that references in Jewish works "mentioning holidays, festivals, and holy days of ours in a disgraceful manner, such as *lifne eydehem* or that it is forbidden for Israelites to do business with them on those days, should be erased completely." Raz-Krakotzkin, *The Censor*, 123.

18. Avodah zarah, 1b, 8a. (Mishnah and Bab. Talmud).

19. Ibid., 8a.

20. Official, *Sefer Yosef ha-meqaneh*, 30, par. 2.

21. Ta-Shma, *Halakha, minhag*, 244 ("רוב ימות השנה יום אידם הם").

22. Ibid., 245, which argues that R. Gershom did not mean the literal proliferation of individual days, but the "conversion" of the timescape into a predominantly Christian one. It is unclear whether R. Gershom referred to the proliferation of saints' days or to the extreme talmudic opinion that maximized the number of days on which trade with idolators was prohibited, to three days before and three days after the festival, and then included Sunday as a festival, thus creating a ban on commerce with gentiles "on all the days of the year." In printed Babylonian Talmuds, Avodah zarah, 7b, Sunday is referred to as יום א'; while manuscript editions use יום נוצרים or יום נוצרי. Hayes, *Between*, n.34. See Rashi on that passage: "ד"ה יום א': הרי כל השבת כולה." In antiquity, Christians referred to Sunday as *dies dominica*, the Lord's Day, a day marking the commemoration of the Resurrection. See the comments of Eidelberg, *Be-netive Ashkenaz*, 315, on various levels of Christian observance of Sunday.

23. Blidstein, *Rabbinic Legislation*, ch. 4, maintains that the roots of medieval leniency are already apparent in the talmudic discussions, although he does not extend his analysis to Christianity.

24. Katz, *Exclusiveness and Tolerance*; Halbertal, *Beyn Torah*; Soloveichik, *Yenam*; Ta-Shma, *Halakha, minhag*; Kanarfogel, "Halakha and Metziut," and sources cited there.

25. Grossman, *Hakhmei Ashkenaz*, 290; Soloveichik, *Ha-yayin*, 133–136, 321.

26. Ta-Shma, *Halakha, minhag*, 246 n.19.

27. Ibid., 256.

28. Eidelberg, *Be-netive Ashkenaz*, 315.

29. Berger, *The Jewish-Christian Debate*, 302; Burnett, "Spokesmen for Judaism," 49.

30. Ta-Shma, *Halakha, minhag*, 245:

"מן הדין אין איסור אלא ביום איד שעושין בשביל הנוצרי כגון ניטל או קצח [בסמ"ג: קיס"ח], אבל שאר איד שלהם אינם תופסים בהם ממשות."

31. Ibid., 246 n.19.

32. See Deut. 21:23 *"qilelat eloqim talui"* and some of its Jewish exegesis.

33. Eidelberg, *Be-netive*, 315, locates an additional variant to קיס"ח: כס"ח; קצח או; see his etymological explanation there.

34. Cited in Ta-Shma, *Halakha, minhag*, 259.

35. Arnoldi, *Pro Iudaeis*, 26–28.

36. Hamelburg, *Quntres*, 39b.

גם החגאות הנופלים בכל חדש וחדש אינם משתנים רק כל כך ימים שנופלת החגה
במשך ימי החדש בפשוטה סך כך משך ימים נופלת החגה בחדשה בעיבור השנה
חוץ (ממטיז) כנ"ל. וחמישה חגאות (פאזינכט אוסטרן אופהרט פפינגשטן לייכנום)
אינם בכלל שאר החגאות בקביעתן תוך ימי החודש והם על ענין וכללים שונים בפני עצמם

37. See, e.g., New York, Jewish Theological Seminary Library ms 2634, fol. 72r:

עד כאן כתבתי לך . . . לחשוב המולד . . . ולשקלו במאזני צדק . . . והנה אכתוב לך גם
כן לידע לוח של נוצרים ולידי' יום קביעות של תולדות יש"ו שהוא ר"ה שלהם הנקרא בל"א יארשטג
והחוגות הקדשים שבכל שנה ושנה לפי חדשי השנה שלנו

In other manuscripts, e.g., Munich, Bayerische Staatsbibliothek Cod. hebr. 394, fol. 91r, image 200, the New Year is more correctly identified as the date of Jesus' circumcision.

38. The reference is to a version of *Toledot Yeshu*, a Jewish subversive account of the life of Jesus that circulated in many versions in the vernacular.

39. New York, Yeshiva University, Mendel Gottesman Library ms 1083, fol. 100v:

ואלה דברי דוד מצאתי כתוב שנסדר להם בראשונה כדי שיחזור להם

חלילה בכל מחזור י"ט שהוא המחזור הנכון לפי סוד העיבור

והם אינם יודעים טעם זה אע"פ שממסדר אידיהם ידע

זה כי הוא היה מאנשי תורותינו וי"א שהוא הי' ר' שמעון הפקולי שהוכרח לסדר להם כן

על כרחו ולטובת ישראל כמו שכתוב בס' תולדות אותו האיש אבל לא גלה להם סוד זה

מצאתי ביסוד עולם ואם תשאל לגלחיהם והמשכילים שבהם על אודות העיבור ומנהגו והסדר שלו

וכן

לא תמצא בפיהם נכונה כי לא עם בינות הוא ע"כ [מדוד לובלין] ואני אבאר באריכות

רב בסמוך עכ"ד

40. New York, Yeshiva University, Mendel Gottesman Library ms 1083, fol. 102r:

הוא ניסן וקובעין בו קיסה הרי לפניך תמצית יסודם ההרוס והנפול

Similarly, Prague, Jewish Museum ms 61 fol. 33v:

לפי מנהג חשבונם הכשל

41. Wall calendar, Venice, Juan de Gara, 1598/99, Valmadonna no. 4486/2 (similarly 1601–1602 and other years); wall calendar, Mantua, 1594/95, Gross collection 075.011.018.

42. E.g., New York, Columbia University ms X893 Se36, fol. 43v.

43. Hamelburg, *Quntres*, 39b. "עתה אסדר לך סי' וכלל כדי שתוכל כל שנה לחבר

לוח הנוצרים עם לוח שלנו ואינך צריך להסתכל ולראות בלוח של אשתקד כלל"

Hamelburg published his treatise *Noten yeshua* to supplement what had by then become the standard text of Ashkenazic sifre evronot.

44. Venture, *Calendrier*, 96: "Table des principales Fêtes des chrétiens qui se trouvent dans les mois de l'année sans jamais varier."

45. Yeshiva Ahavas Torah Baranovich ms evronot, fol. 27r:

לעולם פאזנכט ביום ג' אחר ר"ח אדר או ואדר . . . בדרך קצרה סימני והנה אפרש לך

46. "לוחות שאינו נמולים". This is the title of New York Public Library, Dorot Jewish Division manuscript notes by Hirtz Reinganum of Frankfurt am Main to David Meldola, *Sefer Mo'ed David*. Amsterdam: David Atthias, 1740.

47. The scribe of Oxford, Bodleian Library ms Opp. 701, fol. 54v, used the spelling ניתל, which unambiguously means "the hanged one." New York, Jewish Theological Seminary Library ms 2566, fol. 41r, designates ניטיל; similarly, New York, Yeshiva Ahavas Torah Baranovich, fol. 28r. The sole mention of the Christian calendar in Philadelphia, Center for Advanced Judaic Studies ms 61 is December 25, ניטל. On the term *nittel* in Jewish popular culture see Shapiro, "Torah Study," 334–349; Landman, "Jewish Attitudes," 49; Zimmels, *Ashkenazim and Sephardim*, 158–160.

48. Calendar of Lunéville, 1812, 1814: ויין נאכט [wein nacht]; wall calendar, Altona, 1747/8 and Altona 1748/9, where December 25 is ויין נאכטן [wein nachten].

49. New York, Jewish Theological Seminary Library ms 2634, fol. 76v: ניטל הנקרא ווין נכט. A Jessnitz wall calendar for 1740 uses the term ויין נאכטן for December 25.

50. New York Public Library, Dorot Jewish Division ms Heb. 268.

51. For examples see New York, Library of the Jewish Theological Seminary ms 2566, fol. 34v:

    פלים זונטג איז אלי צייט דען לעצטין זונטג פור קסח (Palm Sunday). And similarly, קעלטה טרכט איז אלי צייט דען צוויטן ורייטוג נוך קסח

52. The scribe of Yeshiva Ahavas Torah Baranovich evronot used *ostern* in a list of the moveable feasts (fol. 27r) but qesah (קיסח), fol. 29v, when he laid out the Christian calendar. Oxford, Bodleian Library ms Opp. 701, uses qetzah in fol. 54v, but "ostern" in fol. 58r. New York, Jewish Theological Seminary Library ms 2634, fol. 78r, lists "Mess Licht" rather than the usual "Lichtmess" (in Hebrew characters).

53. New York, Jewish Theological Seminary Library ms 2634, fols. 77a–77b:

    לעולם קובעין ואזנכט ואושטרן שיהיו ד' שבעות שיוכלו לאכל בשר
    ג' ימי' לכל הפחות בכל חודש וחודש. שמעתי מהר"ר ליוא אופנהיים
    ש"י איך ששמע מחמיו זנוויל בינג ז"ל איך ששמע מגלה אחד הטעם
    למה לפעמים ואזנכט עד ח' ימים בחודש מה שאין כן נמצא בספרינו. ואמר
    לו הגוי הטעם כך שאם חל המולד קודם חצות אזי חל ואזנאכט בר"ח
    מפני שיוכלו לאכל בשר יו' א' בכל חודש אבל אם חל המולד אחר חצות
    אז נדחה ואזנאכט עד יום ח' בחודש והטעם כדי שיוכלו לאכול בשר יו'
    א' בכל חודש כי מה שאכלו בשר ביו' ג' נחשב אחר המולד והמולד אחר חצי וד"ל.

54. Oxford, Bodleian Library ms Opp. 700; similarly, Munich, Bayerische Staatsbibliothek cod. hebr. 394, fol. 95r, image 208 where the chain of attribution extends from Loewe Oppenheim to his father-in-law to [unclear] from Mainz.

55. Soergel, *Wondrous*; Sargent, "Religion and Society"; Zika, "Hosts, Processions."

56. Soergel, *Wondrous*, 3–9.

57. Shoemaker, "Let Us Go," 790. I thank Kristin Peterson for this reference.

58. Baumgarten, *Mothers and Children*, 220 n.101.

59. Berger, *The Jewish-Christian Debate*, par. 6, p. 5; p. 44 in English translation.

60. Oxford, Bodleian Library ms Heb. d. 11, fols. 2v–3r; Munich, Bayerische Staatsbibliothek Cod. hebr. 394, fol. 92r, image 202, תלוייה בקלייבן "teluya bekleiben" (lit. the hanged one (f.) is chosen) for Annunciation; similarly fol. 93v, image 205.

61. Wall calendar, Altona, 1747/8. The word *isha* does not appear. Rather November 22 and December 8 are marked בתולה [betula]; July 2 is בתולה היימזוכן [betula heimsuchen]; and September 8 appears as לידת בתולה [leydat betula]. See Calendar of Lunéville, 1812, 1814, note בתולה [betula], for all days related to Mary (November 21, December 8, March 25, July 2, and August 15).

62. See New York Public Library, Dorot Jewish Division ms Heb. 268. For the year 1733–1734, November 21, December 8, March 25, and May 17 are all marked *isha*; July 2 is *isha hadasha*; August 15 is shown as *isha* and September 8 is *isha ahrona*. In the 1739–1740 calendar, December 8, May 15, July 2, August 15, and September 8 are marked *isha*. Neither *isha* nor *betula* appears in 1742; while in the 1746 calendar, September 8,

August 5, and August 15 are all marked בתולה (betula); no holidays are designated *isha* that year. Compare to "Lady day" in English calendars, see, e.g., Forster, *Circle*. April 30, 1734, is also marked as צלם טג (tzelem tag) and May 7, as כל הצלמי' (kol hat-zelamim); in addition, in the later calendar, May 8, 1739, is כל הצלמים (kol hatzelamim) and September 14, 1739, appears as צלם טג (tzelem tag).

63. New York, Jewish Theological Seminary Library ms 10572. The scribe claimed that the manuscript was an exact copy of the evronot printed in Offenbach that also included the entire Christian calendar (fol. 27a). The printed text (p. 40r), however, contains no mention of Mary for the months September and November, and designates August 15, March 25, and December 8 *isha*.

64. Eisner, *Kalendarium*, 64, exemplifies the embeddedness and centrality of the saints' days. New Year is noted as "Circumcisio Domini," and Roman feast days were incorporated into the Christian calendar as saints' days.

65. For a sense of the profusion of saints' days, see Forster, *Circle*; Sellner, *Immerwährender*.

66. Timm, "Die 'Fabel,'" 142 n.136, cites *Sefer ha-zikhronot*, Oxford, Bodleian Library ms Heb. d. 11. Fols. 2v-3r contain a Christian calendar from the second half of the fourteenth century. In addition to well-known holidays, it includes holy days centered near the city of Cologne (Kunibert, Severin, Elftausend Jungfrauen [Ursula]) or in the archbishopric (Gertrud, Lambert, Servatius, Viktor van Xanten) or those that were represented by an order in the city (Caecilia, Laurentius, Mauritius, Pantaleon).

67. On the founding and development of the Ursuline order, see Culpepper, "Our Particular Cloister." New convents of the order were founded through the sixteenth and seventeenth centuries.

68. Ibid., 1025.

69. Derisive reference to the myth of the eleven thousand virgins can be found in medieval manuscripts such as the fourteenth-century Oxford, Bodleian Library ms Heb. d. 11, fol. 3r: "Eleven thousand tainted ones" י״א אלפים פסולות. Early modern examples appear in New York, Jewish Theological Seminary Library ms 2634, fol. 84, s.v. October; similarly Munich, Bayerische Staatsbibliothek Cod. hebr. 394, fol. 94r, image 206. The dysphemism is based on the exchange of one letter from פסולה to בתולה.

> י״א פסולים. מהר״ר אייזיק לינז אמר שאין כותבין כאן י״א פסולי׳ שמא ימצאנו גוי וכתו׳ בלוחות
> במקום י״א פסולי׳ [אורזלין]

as well as on the change of the grammatically correct betulot, for virgins, to the masculine ending pesulim. This is a hybrid notation (betulim), along with the definition, Ursel. Similarly, eleven betulim (י״א בתולים) in Leiden, Bibliotheek der Rijksuniversiteit, Cod. Or. 4736, fol. 77r; Budapest, Kaufmann ms 515, fol. 144. New York, Library of the Jewish Theological Seminary ms 2566, fol. 39v, simply notes here, "Ursel" [אורזל]. Budapest, Kaufmann ms 515, fol. 137, cautioned the next copyist not to inscribe a day for Peter in the calendar (פיטריז הלוי אין כותבין אותו בלוח), and referred to John the Baptist, fol. 144, in prominent letters, as John the Apostate (יהניש המשומד).

70. Baumgarten, "Remember." Oxford, Bodleian Library ms Heb. d. 11, which contains the notation of the Ursulines as tainted ones, also contains the story of Jephthah's daughter; in addition, see Yassif, *Sefer*, 209–210.

71. Munich, Bayerische Staatsbibliothek cod. hebr. 394, fol. 29v, image 65. To sound like

"Thomas," the word for impurity is pluralized and in Ashkenazic pronunciation. Idol worship is called *tuma* in Tosefta Avodah zarah 7:2.

72. The term *qedeshim* in the Bible refers to male prostitutes. It later came to denote unsavory people. It was used in the liturgical poetry of Eretz Israel in the eighth century to denote non-Jews or Amalekites, Elizur, *Piyute*, 8, 232; Elizur, *Lama tzamnu?* 18. By the twelfth century it was used as a dysphemism for Christian saints. Tosafot to BT AZ 2a, s.v. *assur las'et: de-rov eydeyhem min ha-qedeshim hem.* A Jessnitz wall calendar, 1740, contains a usual mix of Christian holidays and market place names "כל הקדשים כל הנשמות. ברלין. מינדן. בועזר." Note the defective spelling *qdshim*. By reverse token, Catholic censors objected to Jews' referring to anyone Jewish who lived "after the coming of our Lord . . . [as a] saint or a *tzaddiq*, or . . . refer[ring] to a [Jewish] congregation as a holy assembly." Raz-Krakotzkin, *Censor*, 123. New York, Columbia University ms X893 Se36, fol. 51r spells קל, meaning the "slight" saints.

73. Thus on a wall calendar for Altona, 1747–1748, September 14 is צלם טאג. New York, Jewish Theological Seminary Library ms 2566, fol. 35r, notes כל הצלמים יום צלם.

74. Oxford, Bodleian Library ms Opp. 701, fol. 54v.

75. The printed wall calendar of 1769–1770, Italian names, n.p. (Jewish Theological Seminary Library C28), col. 6, has Christian (Italian) month names followed by holidays and saints' days.

מלאכים שומרים יום ב ד בו א תשרי

פראנסיסקו יום ד ד בו ג תשרי.

The Fürth wall calendar of 1807 lists for September 21, מטיז, Matthäus, one of the apostles; for September 29, מיכעלי, meaning Archangel Michael; for October 18, לוקוס, that is, Luke, an evangelist; and for October 21, Ursula. October 25, marked קרישפינן, commemorates the martyrdom of the brothers Crispinus and Crispianus; October 28, זימן יודן, similarly marks the martyrdom of Simon the Zealot and Judas Thaddäus, the apostle; November 7 appears as לינהרט, for Leonhard (a good day for curing diseases including syphilis); November 11 is shown as מרטינא, for Martini. For an example of an encyclopedic list, see Sellner, *Immer-währender*; Wieck, *Time Sanctified.*

76. Horowitz, "Processions, Piety."

77. Rosenfeld, *Jewish Printing in Wilhermsdorf*, 26, no. 20, pocket calendar, 1676/7, title page; similarly, 40, no. 31, pocket calendar, 1686/7. By 1717–1718 the calendar no longer contains this note; see Calendar for 1717/8, 90, no. 77.

78. Hamelburg, *Quntres noten yeshua*, 39a–b.

ענין החגאות

הא לך סדר חדשי נוצרים

בשמותיה' וחגיהם לפי מה שנוהגין עתה כי בשנת שמ"ג לפ"ק

הית' מחלקת בין הנוצרים בקדימה ואיחור י' ימים זה מזה

בקביעת חדשיהם וחגיהם עד שנת ת"ס לפ"ק

שהשוו עצמם לעשות חגיהם וחדשיה' כאחד בלי שום קדימה ואיחור זה מזה

חוץ ממלכי צפון' שעוד היום רוצים ליסוג אחור

וכל חגי וחדשי צפוניים יפולו עשרה ימים אחר חגי וחדשי שאר הנוצרים

וממנו תדע ג"כ נפילת חגי וחדשי צפוניים והנוטים אחריהם שהם עשרה ימים מאוחרים לאלו

79. Many Jewish calendars situated the users in more than two time cycles. In addition to those aligning Jewish with Christian and Muslim time, calendars in Western Europe after 1583 showed Catholic and Protestant dates, and those that covered Eastern Europe included the Orthodox Christian calendar as well. For an early example of a Jewish-Christian-Muslim calendar, see the Constantinople calendar of 1510, intended primarily for Jews in the Ottoman Empire. See further Rivkind, "Luah Qushta"; Hacker, "Qroniqot hadashot." For a later example, see Vilna-Horodna calendar, 1825/6 and 1826/7:

לוח משנת תקפ"ו עם כל המועדים והצומות . . . גם זמן קדוש לבנה
גם ראשי חדשים וחגים כמנהג גריכישע קירכע ורומישי קירכע דיירי
מדינת רוסיא אשר המה כעת חוגגים ביחד ואותם שהגריכישע קירכע
חוגגים לבדם סימנם (מג"ק) מנהג גריכישע קירכע. ואותם שהרומישי
קירכע חוגגים לבדם סימנם (מר"ק) מנהג רומישי קירכע עם כל
העניויים והירידים השייכים להם אשר המה תועלת להמחכים
לימי השווקים (ירידים). עוד נוסף בו ראשי חדשים וחגים של
נוצרים חוץ למדינתנו כמו מדינת פרייסן וקיסר רומי וסימנם
(ח"נ) עם איזה חגים מאשכנזים לתועלת הירידים במדינת (זאקסין).

80. See, e.g., Munich, Bayerische Staatsbibliothek Cod. hebr. 394, unpag., image 7; New York, Jewish Theological Seminary Library ms 2634, fols. 3a–5a: "This is the Sabbath letter of Rabbi ibn Ezra." On the *iggeret*, see Sela, *Abraham ibn Ezra*, 49–57.

81. אני שבת עטרת דת . . . ובן [כך] השם ובין בניו אני אות ברית עולם The poem refers to an exegetical polemic over the meaning of Genesis 1:5 about when the day begins.

82. Berger, *The Jewish-Christian Debate*, 45, par. 8. The Sambatyon is a legendary river blocking access to the Ten Lost Tribes by throwing up a torrent of stones. It rests only on the Sabbath, hence the name, meaning Sabbath River. On the Sambatyon as a polemical subject in the seventeenth century, see Carlebach, "The Last Deception," 133–134.

83. Zerubavel, *Seven Day Circle*, 21–22. Sifre evronot that included ibn Ezra's poem alerted their readers to the polemical aspects of the Sabbath day.

84. The Jewish calendar for the previous year, 1723–1724, for example, printed in Frankfurt an der Oder and used by the Jews in Berlin, bore no stamp of approval whatsoever, not even a rabbinic note of approbation. It appears that the license did not bear upon Jewish calendars until 1725.

85. Meisel, "Berliner Judenkalender."

86. Ibid., 280.

87. Ibid.

88. Hüttenmeister, "Die Genisot," 213–214.

89. Steinschneider, "Hebräische Drucke," 3, no. 2, pp. 262–274.

90. Meisel, "Berliner Judenkalender," 285, provides a table of the distributions.

91. Rosenfeld, "Taschenkalender," 28.

92. Weinberg, "Der Sulzbacher Wandkalender," 89: "In solchen Calender gleich als in einen Mischmasch (umb vielleicht hierdurch die Jüdische tücke desto besser zu bergen) nicht nur hebraïsch, Rabinisch, Jüdischteutsch sondern auch allerhand abbrevia-

turen, characteres und einzle Buchstaben für gantze Wörter mit Fleiss gesetzt, umb nur die Sache desto intricater zu machen und sich hernach hinter eine auslegung zu stecken welche Ihnen am bequembsten ist."

93. Ibid., 90.

94. Ibid.: "In den zweyten Monat der Juden, Gesvan genannt, d. 21. tag so auf unsern 1. November trifft, findet sich halb hebraïsch und halb teutsch Col hakedoschim oder wie mans auch lesen kan hackdeschim, welches erste Alle Heiligen bedeutet, doch müste noch in solchen Wort der Buchstab ו sich finden. Lisset man aber auf die andre oder letzte art, so heisset es stracks dass contravium nemblich alles leichtfertige Huren Gesind; wie den auch solches wort Hackdeschim in 2 Kings 23:7."

95. Ibid., 91. Manuscript evidence indicates that such a polemical intention was indeed present.

96. Ibid. Thomas was spelled in Hebrew letters to imply *tuma*, impurity.

97. Marwedel, *Die Privilegien*, 324, doc. 89, dated May 12, 1770. See also Arnheim, "Hebrew Prints," 8.

98.

הסכמה

אלופי קציני מנהיגי קהילתנו ק״ק אשכנזי יצ״ו נתתו [!] רשות להנ״ל
כמר חיים דרוקר לדפוס לוח של שנת תס״ח הבע״ל ומאחר שהוציא
הוצאות על הדפוס לא ידפיס שום אדם פה לוח של שנת תס״ח הן ע״י
נימולים או אינו נימולים עד שכבר מכר כמר חיים הנ״ל לוחות שלו
בגזירת חרם גמור הנוקב רמ״ח איברים והשומע יזכה לרב טוב. נאום הצעיר
יהודה ליב בן א״א מ״ו מוהר״ר אפרים אשר אנשיל ז״ל מהמבורג
היום יום ו׳ ח״י שבט תסז״ל בק״ק אמשדרדם

99. Rosenfeld, "Wandkalender," 27.

100. Süß, "Zur literaturgeschichtlichen," 81. Cf. Rosenfeld, "Taschenkalender," 26.

6. Church Time and Market Time

1. Frequent small local markets and periodic large fairs varied tremendously in terms of products, scope, and duration. For an overview, see Braudel, *Civilization*, 2:28–82.

2. Jessnitz, wall calendar, 1740.

3. Calendars, Vilna and Horodna, 1825/26 and 1826/27.

4. Braudel, *Civilization*, 2:82.

5. For a review of the liturgical year see Muir, *Ritual*, 55–80.

6. Ibid., 60.

7. Brown, *The Cult of the Saints*.

8. Zika, "Hosts, Processions," 44.

9. Ibid., 34.

10. Ibid., 38; Rubin, *Corpus Christi*.

11. Zika, "Hosts, Processions," 40.

12. On the revival of saint adoration as a reaction to Protestantism, see Soergel, *Wondrous in His Saints*.

13. When the Jews of Carpentras were confined to a walled quarter in the fifteenth cen-

tury, they asked for and received assurance that church processions would no longer pass through the Jewish quarter. Einbinder, "Hebrew Poems," 131.

14. Rubin, *Gentile Tales*, 29.
15. Ibid., 30.
16. Ibid.
17. Hsia, *Myth*, 63.
18. Ibid., 18.
19. Ibid., 37, 41.
20. Ibid., 43, and see Hsia, *Trent 1475*.
21. Hsia, *Myth*, 92.
22. Ibid., 55.
23. Ibid., 68.
24. Rubin, *Gentile Tales*, 135.
25. See, e.g., ibid., 41 (St-Jean-en-Grève, 1290), 65 (Pulkau, 1338).
26. The ritual slap, *Colaphus Judaeorum*, was documented in pre-twelfth-century Toulouse. On at least one occasion it was delivered with such force that it killed the Jew. See Zuckerman, "Nasi"; Mentgen, "Der Würfelzoll," 12–24; Malkiel, "Jewish-Christian," 66, 77.
27. Nirenberg, *Communities*, 201.
28. Roth, "Eastertide," 361.
29. Cohen, *Under Crescent*, 191, quoting the Egyptian polemicist Ahmad ibn Idris al-Qarāfi.
30. On the images of Jews stoning Jesus, see Mentgen, "Der Würfelzoll," 18. Bächtold-Stäubli, *Handwörterbuch*, 4:830, records a Christian folk belief that Jews buried their dead with stones in the casket in order to stone Jesus if they met him on the way to the next world. For a similar belief that emerged in the eighteenth century, see Carlebach, *Divided Souls*, 211.
31. Both instances in Roth, "Eastertide," 361–362.
32. Nirenberg, *Communities*, 203.
33. Roth, "Eastertide," 363.
34. Mentgen, "Der Würfelzoll," 15.
35. Ibid., 18–19.
36. Nirenberg, *Communities*, 217.
37. This was the *Constitutio pro Judaeis*. See Roth, "Eastertide," 365.
38. Nirenberg, *Communities*, 205; Einbinder, "Hebrew Poems, 122.
39. Einbinder, "Hebrew Poems," 122.
40. Roth, "Eastertide," 361.
41. Einbinder, "Hebrew Poems," 132.
42. Nirenberg, *Communities*, 209 n.38.
43. The word *tipol* refers to the reading of the song of Moses upon crossing the Sea (Exodus 15:16): "There shall fall upon them (*tipol*) fear and dread; by the greatness of Your arm they shall be silent as a stone." See Roth, "Eastertide," 368.
44. Einbinder, "Hebrew Poems," 122.
45. Roth, "Eastertide," 367. Roth first published the poem in 1934; I have not seen that version. See Einbinder, "Hebrew Poems," 112 n.2.

46. Einbinder, "Hebrew Poems," 118. Einbinder notes (128) that the seventeenth-century law confining the Jews to their quarter every night for the entire year dated the seasons from St. Michael's Day in late September to Easter, and from Easter to St. Michael's Day.

47. Ibid., 122.

48. Le Goff, "Merchant's Time and Church's Time," 29–42. While Le Goff uses these terms to denote conflicting ideas concerning the value of time, see p. 35 where he defines merchant's time in similar fashion to the meaning ascribed to it here. See also Zerubavel, *Hidden Rhythms*.

49. Isherwood, "Entertainment," 24, and Braudel, *Civilization*.

50. On the origins and rise of European fairs and their relationship to the Christian ritual calendar, see Jarnut, "Die Anfänge," 1–12; on the concept of the "agro-liturgical" year, see Fenske, *Marktkultur*, 45 n.17.

51. Grochulska, "Jarmarki."

52. Fenske, *Marktkultur*, 33.

53. Lerner, "Messe und Klerus," 33–37.

54. Mishnah and Babylonian Talmud Avodah zara, 2a.

55. Baron, *A Social and Religious History of the Jews*, 4:325.

56. On Agobard see ibid., 4:263 n.67.

57. Rose, *Portraits*, 33.

58. Cave and Coulson, *A Source Book for Medieval Economic History*, 113; Arkenberg, *Internet Medieval Sourcebook*.

59. Fenske, *Marktkutur*, 275.

60. Hasse, *Geschichte*, 300, in paragraph 6 of the ordinance.

61. Fenske, *Marktkultur*, 272 n.82.

62. Ibid., 56–57.

63. Blaschke, "Der Übergang," 263.

64. Freudenthal's *Leipziger Messgäste* is based on a register of this Leibzoll.

65. For examples of these passes from the eighteenth century, see Rose, *Portraits*, 48–49; Wiesemann, *Genizah*, 201, no. 111. For a nineteenth-century pass no longer bearing the inscription "Jude," see the one attached to the page for the year 1844 in the New York, Jewish Theological Seminary Library ms calendar C110.

66. The body tax for Jews to enter the Leipzig fair stood at 10 *taler*, 4 *groschen* for Jewish men in the early eighteenth century, a considerable sum.

67. The family of Glikl of Hameln, whose husband Hayim signed himself Goldschmidt or Heine Goldschmiedt in the registers, appears several times. He visited both the Easter and Michaelis fairs when possible. After his death in 1689, she appears alone as his widow. Freudenthal, *Leipziger messgäste*, 7–8 n.2.

68. Glikl, *Zikhroynes*, 199.

69. Reinhold, *Polen/Littauen*, 9; Hasse, *Geschichte*, 300.

70. Reinhold, *Polen/Littauen*, 9.

71. Ulmer, *Turmoil, Trauma*, 47.

72. The Zurzach market attracted Jews from the German lands, France, Holland, Austria, and Bohemia. The closest Jewish communities were those in Lengnau and Endigen. See Guggenheim-Grünberg, "Die Juden," notes, section 2, p. 13.

73. Emperor Conrad, Grant of a Market and Fair at Donauwörth, 1030. Heinrich Gengler, *Codex Juris Municipalis Germaniae* (Erlangen: F. Enke, 1867), 806, in Arkenberg, *Internet Medieval Source Book.*

74. "No merchant, nor any other person, may take a merchant to court for the payment of any debt during these fairs, nor take him there for any business that was conducted before the fairs began; but if anything be done amiss during the fairs, let it be made good according to justice during the fairs. Moreover, the first fair shall begin on Quadragesima Sunday, which is six weeks before Easter, and it shall last for fifteen days. The second fair shall begin eight days before the feast of St. Michael and shall continue for eight days after that feast. And all people coming to, staying at, or going from the fairs shall have peace for their persons and goods." See Cave and Coulson, *A Source Book for Medieval Economic History*, 120–122, in Arkenberg, *Internet Medieval Sourcebook.*

75. Soloveitchik, *Yenam.*

76. Braudel, *Civilization and Capitalism*, 2:85; Isherwood, "Entertainment," 24–28.

77. Roth, *Essays and Portraits*, 132.

78. See, e.g., Venture, *Calendrier hebraïque*, 182, 194.

79. See, e.g., Rosenfeld, "Taschenkalender," 35.

80. Freudenthal, *Leipziger messgäste*, 7.

81. Reinhold, *Polen/Littauen*, 67–75.

82. Glikl, *Zikhroynes*, 416.

83. Ibid., 216, similarly, 304.

84. Fenske, *Marktkultur*, 45.

85. Kaufhold, "Messen und Wirtschaftsausstellungen," 248.

86. Reinhold, *Polen/Litauen*, 9. In 1754, out of 6,736 *Messfremden*, foreign visitors, to the Leipzig fairs, 884 were Jews, approximately 13 percent. In 1799, among 9,220 outsiders coming to the three Leipzig fairs, 2,486 were Jews. See also Braudel, who provides a sweeping overview of the rise and decline of various European regions and their markets.

87. Freudenthal, *Leipziger messgäste*, 10 n.1. On this court Jew see Eidelberg, "Abraham Aaron."

88. Freudenthal, "Zum Jubiläum," 141: "mit 4 Personen hat einen alten Pass, der noch nicht zum Vorschein gekommen."

89. Rose, *Portraits*, 32, cites the example from the 1780s in which a district authority from Schwarzwald petitioned the mayor of Rottweil to rescind a tax increase on Jews for fear that it would cause the Jews to stop coming to the region. The mayor acceded to the request.

90. Reinhold, *Polen/Litauen*, 14.

91. Glikl, *Zikhroynes*, 202–203. In her old age, as her financial circumstances worsened, Glikl recalled, "I suffered terribly: in the heat of summer and in the rain and snow of winter, I travelled to the fairs and stood days on end in my stall in winter season" (496–497).

92. Freudenthal, *Leipziger messgäste*, 16.

93. Ibid. R. Meir (Maharam) Padua exhorted the men of Cassel to stop their wives from traveling alone to markets and fairs, where people tended to get drunk. Padau, *Sefer*

she'elot, no. 26. Joel Sirkes noted that wives of ignorant Jews (*amei ha-aretz*) traveled in carriages driven by non-Jews, with only small children as guardians. Sirkes, *Bayit ḥadash*; R. Asher, *Arba turim*, Even ha-ezer, par. 22. I thank Debra Kaplan for these references.

94. In addition to attending the Leipzig fair, Glikl and her family members traveled regularly to the fairs at Braunschweig (Glikl, *Zikhroynes*, 397, 523), Frankfurt am Main, and Frankfurt an der Oder (405). "He travelled to every fair," she wrote of her husband, Hayim (217). "This happened before the fair at Frankfurt am Main; my husband had to travel there, as he attended every fair." (305) They were reluctant to miss any opportunity to attend, because each visit meant profit for the family, chances for new connections, and collection of outstanding debts.

95. In 1800, almost 12 percent of the total number of visitors—and 35 percent of the Jewish visitors—to the Leipzig fairs came from Poland; the next largest group was from Galician Brody.

96. The only surviving pages of the Council are dated to the Jaroslav fairs of the later seventeenth century. See facsimile in Halperin, *Pinqas*, xxxi.

97. Ibid., xxxviii.

98. In the 1570s, Basel printer Ambrosius Froben contracted with Frankfurt Jew Simon zum Gembs to produce and sell 1,100 sets of the Talmud, to be delivered at the Frankfurt fair over three years. When the Catholic Imperial authorities sought to question Froben, they picked him up for questioning at the fair. See Burnett, "German Jewish Printing," 511–513.

99. Freudenthal, "Zum Jubiläum," 134–143.

100. Agnew, *Worlds Apart*, 152.

7. Calendar, Ritual, and the Turn of the Seasons

1. Munich, Bayerische Staatsbibliothek ms cod. hebr. 394A, fol. 14v. Perhaps she is holding St. John's Wort?

2. For wall calendars, see Constantinople: Soncino Press, 1547/48, which lists the tequfot and the zodiac signs prominently in a separate column; Sabionetta, 1560/61 lists the tequfot of Samuel and R. Ada separately; Venice: Juan da Gara, 1599 lists tequfot according to R. Ada, Samuel, and "*le-yod'ei ha-itim* (for those who know the times)." Valmadonna Trust Collection, German-Jewish calendar fragment for 1735/36, is illustrated with four men holding shields, each inscribed with the hour of the tequfah; Sulzbach, 1803/04, lists them prominently, bottom right. Fürth, 1817/18, lists the times of the tequfot prominently, top right.

3. Ta-Shma, "Issur"; Baumgarten, "Remember"; Klein, "Ha-sakanah." Tequfot were calculated mathematically and were not necessarily congruent with the actual equinox and solstice.

4. Some sifre evronot refer to *nequdot ha-tequfot* (literally, seasonal points); see, e.g., New York, Jewish Theological Seminary Library ms 2572, fol. 16r.

5. Freiman, "Tarbut," 1–7. The development of the tequfah custom fits well into his thesis about the popular origins of certain Jewish customs.

6. My discussion of R. Pinhas is based on Elizur, *Piyute*.

7. Ibid., 690.

יהי ראש ארבע תקופות להבן: Nissan, 690
כי תקופה שניה בו: Tamuz, 698
רון תקופה שלישית לועד בו: Tishre, 707
טבת תקופתו חשבתי בלי עוד ליסרי: Tevet, 715

8. Ibid., 641–644. See also the Qalir poems: "Adar arba tequfot," in Fleischer, *Ha-yotzrot be-hithavutan*, 107–109; Spiegel, *Avot ha-piyut*, ed. Schmelzer, "Or hama u-levana," *Le-tequfot*, 136.

9. *Teshuvot ha-geonim*, ed. Mussafia, 9, no. 14. According to Ta-Shma, "Issur," 22, the portion enclosed in brackets is not of Geonic origin but was interpolated later.

10. *Teshuvot ha-geonim*, ed. Leiter, no. 80.

11. *Sefer hemdah genuzah*, 29b, no. 166. These attributes of water are mentioned in BT Brakhot, 35b; BT Sukkah, 48b.

12. Abudarham provides this description: "On the Sabbath prior to a fast, [except Tisha b'Av, Yom Kippur and Esther] after the reading of the prophetic portion . . . the cantor announces to the public the day on which the fast will fall. He says, "Listen my Jewish brothers: the following fast falls on the following day. May God turn it into a day of rejoicing as he promised in his consolations, let us say amen." Cited in Sperber, *Minhage Yisrael*, 1:169–177.

13. Al-Bīrūnī, *Chronology*, 162–163; Goldstein, "Astronomy and the Jewish Community," 28. Al-Bīrūnī's anti-rabbinic slant may indicate that his source was a Qaraite Jew. Al-Bīrūnī observed that "the Jews maintain too, that at the hour of the Moleds of the months the water becomes turbid"; and he criticized them for "not reckon[ing] the year with mathematical accuracy," with regard to the seasonal turning points.

14. Bar Hiyya, *Sefer ha-ibbur*, ed. Filipowski, 86.

15. Ibn Ezra, *Sefer ha-ibbur*, ed. Bakal, 82.

16. Ibid. In Abudarham's fourteenth-century liturgical compilation, *Perush* (1566), "Sha'ar ha-tequfot," 122r, based on the liturgy of Judah ben Yaqar (twelfth century), the same geonic citations appear as in ibn Ezra, however the tequfot are listed in a different order.

17. For two recensions of this text see Oxford, Bodleian Library ms Opp. 317, fol. 90r; Oxford, Bodleian Library ms Opp. 614, fol. 50v.

18. Dan, "Qeta mi-*Sefer ha-kavod*," 118–120; English trans., Baumgarten, "Remember," 193–194.

19. Emanuel, *Shivre luhot*, 253 n.139, discusses the authorship of a treatise titled *Sod ha-ibbur* by R. Elhanan, a tosafist whose identity is unclear. An excerpt from it is cited in *Minhat Yehudah al ha-Torah*, a tosafist Bible commentary composed by R. Judah b. Eliezer/Eleazar in 1313, on Gen. 21:4, s.v. "la-mo'ed asher dibber oto." I thank Ephraim Kanarfogel for this reference.

20. *Sefer hasidim*, ed. Margaliot, par. 851:

אם אמרו לאדם אל תשתה עתה מים כי התקופה נופלת ושמא עתה עת נפילתה וכבר בירך ימתין ואל ידבר עד שידע בטוב שעברה התקופה ואז ישתה ואל יברך פעם שניה.

21. Valmadonna Trust collection ms 267 (Richler catalogue no. 219), fol. 86v.

22. Trachtenberg, *Jewish Magic*, 257.

23. Gumbert-Hepp, *Computus Magistri Jacobi*, 108–111.

24. Budapest, Magyar tudomanyos academia ms Kaufmann A515, fol. 160:

ארבע תקופות הנוצרים נקראים בלשונם קוטמבר.

25. Krünitz, *Oekonomisch*, 32: 512–513.

26. Tyrnau, *Minhagim*, 33a:

עטליכע זאגן אין דען דעם ציטן שייד זיך זומר אונ׳ ווינדר פון אננדר אונ׳ די לופט
זיין ביז דרום פאשטן מיר אונ׳ בעטן גאט דאז דאז אונז קיין ביזר לופט אן וועהן.

27. Lieberman, "Nittel," 134–137. Some sifre evronot also noted the congruence of Christmas and tequfat Tevet, e.g., Budapest, Magyar tudomanyos academia ms Kaufmann A 520: "ניטל חל בליל תקו׳ טבת. כך מצאתי".

28. Shapiro, "Torah Study."

29. Jaritz and Winiwarter, "Perception of Nature," 100.

30. Rohner, *Kalendergeschichte*, 127–128.

31. Jaritz and Winiwarter, "Perception of Nature," 99, compare reports in Protestant Germany with Catholic France and conclude that it took Catholic culture far longer to relinquish the notion that miracles were carried out in the realm of saints.

32. Russell, *The World of Dürer*, 66.

33. Fram, "German Pietism," 54.

34. Moellin, *Sefer Maharil, Minhagim*, 34, par. 7. Moellin cited Abraham Klausner to the effect that one must be concerned with the tequfah only with regard to water from a river, but not if the water came from a protected urban source. See Spitzer's editorial comments ad loc.

35. "One should not spill out the *mayim she-lanu* because of a death or the falling of the tequfah. In any case it is better to put an iron in them in the first instance." *Orah Hayim*, 455, par. 1.

36. *Minhogim oyf teitsh*, n.p.

אונטר ווילן איז דיא תקופה בייא דער נכט פון מצוה וושיר.דא דארפשטו דיך פור קיין סכנה
פורכטן דא ווייל עש מצוה וושיר איז. דוך שאט עס ניט וען מן איין נייא אייזין נאגיל דריין טוט.

37. New York, Columbia University ms X893 Se36, fol. 16r. This explanation has roots in talmudic sources: BT Avodah zarah, 30b, refers to practices that expose a person to "danger." One of them is drinking water left uncovered overnight. I thank David Kraemer for alerting me to this connection. In the same Talmudic discussion, the language *me tiftif* is used; the root recurs in the tequfah passages.

38. New York, Columbia University ms X893 Se36, fol. 16r.

39. Ms Sotheby, and Oxford, Bodleian Library ms Opp. 701, depict a young man or woman discarding water from a bucket that had apparently been left "unprotected" during the change of tequfot. I thank David Wachtel and Sharon Mintz for bringing the Sotheby manuscript to my attention.

40. The earliest known Jewish depiction is the mosaic in a mid-third-century synagogue in Dura Europos. Another early and well-known example comes from the early sixth-century synagogue at Bet Alpha. See, e.g., Poseq, "Toward a Semiotic Approach," 34, fig. 5.

41. Christian illustrators tended to depict Abraham holding a sword; Jewish illustrators, a knife. Kogman-Appel, "Sephardic Picture Cycles," 461.

42. Berlin, Staatsbibliothek ms 3150, fol. 19r; New York, Columbia University ms X893 Se36, fol. 16r.

43. *Midrash Tanhuma* cited in Elbaum, "From Sermon," 106; on the significance of the knife, see p. 103. For a midrash that Abraham actually sacrificed Isaac, see Spiegel, "Perur," 549.

44. Two manuscripts with similar illustration patterns contain virtually identical *aqeda* scenes; see New York, Library of the Jewish Theological Seminary ms 2662 (ca. 1627) and New York, Library of the Jewish Theological Seminary ms 2540 (ca. 1631). Either ms 2540 was copied from ms 2662 or they both used the same model. In both, the *aqeda* scene appears later in the manuscript than the corresponding text. Both begin from the right side with an image of the lads and their donkey waiting in the distance; in both, Abraham holds the knife far above Isaac with no drops of blood on it, and both have the ram in its thicket off to the left.

45. In New York, Jewish Theological Seminary Library ms 2540, fol. 11v, an angel appears from heaven. In Cincinnati, Hebrew Union College Klau Library ms 901, fol. 32v, the *aqeda* scene bears the inscription, "Abraham our father, peace on him, wanted to sacrifice his son." Abraham's knife does not drip blood, and Isaac lies bound on a raised altar with an angel hovering over him.

46. On the discrepancies between the text and the explanations in the midrash see Baumgarten, "Remember," 194.

47. Drewer, "Jephthah."

48. Woerden, "Iconography." Smith, "Iconography of the Sacrifice," 159, cites Ambrose, I cap. viii: "Isaac ergo Christi passuri est typus."

49. Note also Poseq, "Toward a Semiotic Approach," 33, on the Annunciation of Isaac's birth and the Sacrifice of Isaac in a mid-sixth-century mosaic from a church in Ravenna.

50. Berman, "Medieval Monasticism"; Baumgarten, "Remember," and sources cited there.

51. Cincinnati, Hebrew Union College ms 901, fol. 32v, contains only the Binding of Isaac among tequfah illustrations.

52. On the poem, see Carlebach, "Water into Blood."

53. Ibn Susan, *Sefer ibbur shanim*, 132r.

54. Ibid.

55. De Silva, *Sefer peri hadash*, commentary to *Shulkhan arukh, Orah haim*, Hilkhot rosh hodesh, 428.

56. The citation is from Munich, Bayersiche Staatsbibliothek ms cod. hebr. 200, and the translation is from the forthcoming book, *The Tegernsee Haggadah*, eds. David Stern, Sarit Shalev-Eyni, and Christoph Markschies, with a translation of the Latin prologue by Erik Koenke (College Park: Penn State University Press, 2011). I thank David Stern for sharing this research with me prior to its publication.

57. Münster, *Kalendarium Hebraicum*, 48: "Atque hic egregie delyraut Iudaei, fabulantes quod per singulas tkuphas soli specialis deputetur angelus & director: & in illo momento quo sol ipse priorem compleuit tkupham & sequentem inchoat, priusque unus director alteri locum cesserit, שדים id est, daemones omnem possunt in aqua exercere tyrannidem: non secus quam cum imperator quispiam moritur, minores domini in-

terim grassantur in hostes suos, donec alius instituatur rex, qui eos a sua praesump-
tione possit coercere. Vnde icunt quod si quis in illos momento uel tantillum biberet
aquae, hydropisim uel aliam grauem infirmitatem euadere non posset. Hinc est quod
illarum quatuor tkupharum initia tam superstitiose custodiunt, & לוחות suis id est,
Kalendariorum tabulis diligentur inscribunt, non modo horam, ueram & momentum
ipsum observantes, ne potum a diabolo maledictum in ea hora sumant. Sed facessant
hae nugae. Est tkuphae primae & alius usus." See also the remarks of Weinberg, "Invention and Convention," 324.

58. HaTkupha Lel .i. Angaria fit nocte in quinta feria & die undecima hora nona huius
mensis, habent enim quator Kuphas quas nos angarias vocitamus, in tempore pares
quia iuxta solis cursum perpendunt, circa quas Iudaeorum festa minime mensuranda
scias. Sed omnia solennitatem capita a lũa pendere, has propter maturitaté frugum
arborumq; fructus, illa, ob statũ festorũ ordiné: observant iudaei punctũ kuue, plus
spiritus malignos in cunctis tunc temporis regnare undis, bibiturũ intercutis morbũ
subire, ob quã causã affectandi studio, angarias suis diarijs inserunt.

59. Nigri, *Kalendarium*, n.p.

60. On the centrality of blood in late medieval Christian society, see Bynum, *Wonderful
Blood*. For a medieval Jewish blood custom that disappeared precisely because of its
vulnerability to polemical manipulation, see Gross, "The Blood Libel," 171–174.

61. Yuval, *Two Nations*, 205–254.

62. Hirsch, in his *Megalleh tekuphot*, cited an entire tequfah cycle from "einigen gedruck-
ten jüdischen Calendern" (some printed Jewish calendars). The actual calendars from
which Hirsch and de Vries quoted have yet to be located, but this would not be the
first case of a Yiddish text preserved in Christian sources.

63. Ibid., iii. On the origins of this charge see Resnick, "Medieval Roots," 257–261. It was
recycled in Heinrich Kornmann, *Opera Curiosa* (Frankfurt: Gensch, 1694), 1:128–129,
which was perhaps a source for Hirsch.

64. Hirsch, *Megalleh tekuphot*, 4: "Allein die Tekupah, davon hin und wider in einigen
jüdischen Calendern zu finden ist / hat eine gantz andere Bedeutung."

65. Ibid., 15–16.

66.

רש"י. אל תשלח. לשחוט. אמר לו א"כ לחנם באתי לכאן אעשה בו חבלה
ואוציא ממנו מעט דם אמר לו אל תעש לו אל תעש לו מאומה אל תעש בו מום.

67.

מ"א: יראה עקידה זו לסלח לישראל בכל שנה ולהצילם מן הפורענות כדי שיאמר
להם בכל דורות הבאים בהר ה' יראה אפרו של יצחק צבור ועומד לכפרה.

68. Hirsch, *Megalleh tekuphot*, 16.

69. Ibid., 17–18.

70. Ibid., 19.

71. Ibid., 24–25.

72. תקופת טבת נופלת ארבע שעות ומחצה תוך ליל ז' בר"ח טבת.

73. Hirsch, *Megalleh tekuphot*, 26–27.

74. Ibid., 27.

75. Ibid., 30.

76. Ibid., 28.
77. Ibid., 28–29.
78. Ibid., 31.
79. Trachtenberg, *Jewish Magic*, 258.
80. Hirsch, *Megalleh tekuphot*, 31.
81. Ibid.
82. Ibid., 23.
83. Ibid., 29.
84. Leberecht, *Machmath Hatekuphoth*, 4.
85. On this phenomenon see Carlebach, *Divided Souls*, 170–199; and Leberecht's own *Geistlich-todten Juden* (Magdeburg, 1725); *Tariack mitsvoth* (Hamburg, 1734).
86. Leberecht, *Machmath Hatekuphoth*, 4.
87. Ibid., 3–4, 6.
88. Ibid., 7.
89. Ibid., 8. There is no emphasis on the Jephthah's daughter passage.
90. De Vries, *Entdeckung derer Tekuphoth*.
91. Ibid., 35.
92. Ibid., 47.
93. Ibid., 48.
94. In 1734, Gustav Georg Zeltner, sponsor of Leberecht's book, sponsored a second work on the subject by Carl Friedrich Lochner. See Zeltner, *Genaue Untersuchung*.
95. For examples from North Africa, see Shkalim et al., *Mosaic*, 113–116; Mishael, *Beyn Afganistan*, 180. Printed wall calendar Tunis, 1940/41, Gross collection 075.011.022, devotes a quarter of the entire space to the exact time of the tequfot in Judaeo-Arabic and in French.

8. Imagining the Beginning of Time

1. Grafton, *Joseph Scaliger*, 2:7.
2. I Kings 6:1 provides a useful example of biblical chronology: "It was in the four hundred and eightieth year after the children of Israel had left Egypt, in the fourth year, in the month of Ziv, the second month, of Solomon's reign over Israel he [began to] build the house of the Lord."
3. The Era of Contracts dates from 312 B.C.E.; the Era to the Destruction begins in 381 of the Era of Contracts and in 69 C.E. (The Era of the Destruction of the Temple started the year on the Ninth of Av.) The Babylonian Talmud discusses the quandary of people compelled to date documents to one Era while their own reckoning system only knew another. BT Avodah zarah, 9a.
4. The translators may have relied on earlier world chronicles written by Hellenistic Jews; see Wacholder, "Biblical Chronology," 452–458. The standard Jewish A.M. reckoning posits 3761 B.C.E. as the year of creation, while that of the Septuagint is close to 5000 B.C.E.
5. Jaffe, *Qorot*, 198–199; Bornstein, "Mahloqet," 121–128; and Akavia, "Sefer meyuhad," 121, regarding a genizah document about the ibbur dated to *shtarot* (Era of Contracts), and to *bereshit* (Era of Creation).
6. For examples see the colophon "I, Isaac ben Abraham ha-Levy wrote and inserted

vowel and masorah points with the Lord's help in 1418, Era of Contracts," Jerusalem, Jewish National Library ms 8°2238, fol. 33v. In the margin, another (later) hand added: "In the Era from Creation, 4866 [1106 C.E.]." In Yemen, the Era of Contracts was in use through the nineteenth century.

7. Sukenik, "Matzevot," 83–88. The tombstone inscriptions from Zo'ar, south of the Dead Sea, dating from the fourth through sixth centuries C.E., each note the year in the sabbatical cycle and the year to the Era of the Destruction of the Temple.

8. Cassutto, "Ha-qetovot ha-ivriot," 106–107, 110, 112.

9. On the adoption of Jewish A.M. dating see Sidersky, "L'Origine," 325–329. See further BT Avodah zarah, 9a–10b (Soncino ed. transl. Mishkon, Neziqin 4:47). In one statement, Maimonides employed three different eras: "In the year 1107 from the destruction of the Temple, 1487 of the Seleucid era, 4936 from the Creation." See *Mishneh Torah*, Zera'im, Hilkhot shemittah ve-yovel, 10:4.

10. Wacholder, "Biblical Chronology."

11. Mosshammer, The *"Chronicle"* of Eusebius.

12. Pederson, "Ecclesiastical Calendar," 49–50.

13. One way to create a universal baseline for dating events across nations and cultures was to find an astronomical event such as a notable conjunction or eclipse and coordinate it with historical events. See Goldstein, "Astronomy," 31; Sibony, "Le calendrier juif," 154 (on an attempt to correlate astronomical with biblical events); and Grafton, "Invention," 16 (on an attempt to invent a source linking an eclipse to the Crucifixion).

14. E.g., New York, Columbia University ms X893 Se36, fol. 4v, citing R. Samuel of Schweinfurth: "Even if you do not know the molad of this cycle, of this year, and of this month, and you want to figure out the molad of the year you are in, do the following: *add the years that have passed from the creation of the world*, until the year for which you want to find the molad . . . add to it *bahara"d* as that was the molad of chaos (*tohu*), the New Year before the creation of the world.

15. Ibn Susan, *Tiqqun Issachar*, 4a.

16. *Chroniq min tehillat briat olam*. See, e.g., facsimiles in Rosenfeld, "Taschenkalender," 27.

17. For a similar characterization, see Shatzmiller, "Provençal Chronography," 43–61.

18. *Sefer evronot*, Cincinnati, Klau Library, Hebrew Union College ms 900, fol. 3v. The expulsions from France (along with those from Spain and Portugal) appeared regularly within chronographs. Cf. Einbinder, "Recall from Exile."

19. Milikowsky, "*Seder 'Olam* and Jewish Chronography," 122, asserts that its anonymous author(s) never intended that it become the basis for a practical system of chronology. BT Avodah zarah, 9b, citation of a Baraita (pre-200 C.E. rabbinic source), which refers to an Era from Creation, is the only mention in the Talmud and the earliest mention of a creation era anywhere. See Encyclopaedia Judaica 16 (1983): 1264–1265; Goldberg, *La clepsydre* 1:265–330.

20. *Seder olam zuta*, ed. Neubauer, has never been thoroughly studied. It originated between the sixth and ninth centuries.

21. Zacuto, *Sefer yuhasin*; ibn Yahia, *Shalshelet ha-qabbalah*. Renewed interest in this genre in the early modern period stimulated the printing of older chronological works. *Seder olam* and *Seder olam zuta* were among the most frequently printed Jewish "historical works" in the early modern period.

22. Bonfil, "How Golden," 90–96, argues that the political and military themes, along with a renewed interest in antiquity, resonated with interests of Renaissance period readers. See also Breuer, "Modernism and Traditionalism," 67–79.

23. Woolf, *Social Circulation*, 321.

24. Eisenstein, "Clio and Chronos," 53.

25. The chronographs in Leiden, Bibliotheek der Rijksuniversiteit ms Cod. Or. 4736, date the current year [5]317 A.M. (1556–1557 C.E.) It ends: "62 years since the expulsion from Naples; 15 years since the expulsion from Bohemia." Similarly, Munich, Bayerische Staatsbibliothek ms Cod. Hebr. 394, begins "[5]326 A.M. = 1565/66 C.E." Budapest, Magyar tudomanyos akademia ms Kaufmann A 515, fol. 9, begins its chronograph "[5]359 A.M. [1598/99 C.E.]," and ends, "65 years since expulsion from Naples; 18 years since exile from Bohemia." (The copyist updated the first entry in the chronograph to reflect the year of writing, but apparently did not bother to update the entries that followed.) Budapest, Magyar tudomanyos akademia ms Kaufmann A 511, in its chronograph until [5]422 A.M. [1661/62 C.E.] ends: "389 years since the beginning of the Austrian Empire; 271 since the expulsion from France; 170 since the expulsion from Portugal; 14 since the great destruction in the Ukraine; 13 since the destruction in Helm and its region."

26. *Calendario de Ros-Hodes* (1704).

27. Venture, *Calendrier*, 1. Venture promoted an enlightened sensibility in that his chronology refrained from dwelling on bitter past experiences of Jews in the Christian world.

28. Woolf, *Social Circulation*, 10.

29. Ibid., 321.

30. Ibn Susan, *Tiqqun Issachar*, 7b.

31. On the role of printing in the resolution of similar contradictions in scientific sources, see Eisenstein, *Printing Revolution*, 79.

32. In some piyyutim Ezekiel is linked to the tenth of Tevet. See, e.g., Elizur, *Lama tzamnu?* 103.

33. Rosenfeld, "Taschenkalender," 35. The date for when the "Torah was written in Greek by the seventy elders" is taken from the list in *Megillat ta'anit batra*. See ibid., 70: "On the eighth of Tevet the Torah was written in the days of King Ptolemy the Greek, and darkness came over the world for three days." This date for the "ninth day" is taken from the *Megillat ta'anit batra* verbatim; on its meaning, see Leiman, "Scroll." R. Abraham ben Avigdor wrote a gloss to the Turim, first published in 1540 in Prague and Augsburg. (Most of his dates are taken from the Tur, which cites *Halakhot gedolot*.)

34. Noam, *Megillat ta'anit*.

35. Elizur, *Lama tzamnu?* contains a comparison of all relevant manuscripts.

36. On the uprising, see Baron, *Social and Religious*, 14:194–197; and Friedrichs, "Politics or Pogrom?" Jewish primary sources include Abraham Heln's "Megillas Vints," a Yiddish historical *lid* (ballad) preserved in Wagenseil, *Belehrung*, 119–149; and the contemporary account of Nördlingen, *Yosif omets*, nos. 953–958, 1107–1109. See Ulmer, *Turmoil, Trauma*; and on the literary genre of historical *lider*, Turniansky, "The Events."

37. Rosenfeld, "Ein jüdischer Wandkalender," 32.

38. In New York Public Library, Dorot Jewish Division ms Heb. 268, the calendar for

1734, 20 Adar is marked *Purim Vints* (where it is spelled ווינץ); 27 Elul of that year is marked *Ta'anis Frankfurt* תענית פ״פ. In the calendar for 1742 (where it is spelled פינץ), the Purim falls out on a Shabbat but is deferred to Sunday. Within that series, the Purim is not noted in the calendars for the years 1730, 1739, or 1746.

39. Simonsen, "Freud und Leid," 527 n.2, lists one local Purim for Tripoli on 15 Shevat that he attributes to "an old calendar in his possession," but he does not specify a place of publication or date for the calendar.

40. David Wachtel, "The Ritual and Liturgical Commemoration of Two Medieval Persecutions," master's thesis, Columbia University, 1995; Shmeruk, *Ha-qeri'a le-navi*, 18. A fast on that date was believed by some medieval rabbis to have been mandated by R. Jacob Tam to commemorate the martyrdom of the Jews of Blois in 1171. During the seventeenth-century persecution of Polish Jews, the date was reactivated.

41. New York, Library of the Jewish Theological Seminary, collection labeled Luhot/Tzarefat.

42. On local Purims, see Zunz, *Die Ritus*, 2:127–130; Steinschneider, "Purim und Parodie," 47; and Yerushalmi, *Zakhor*, 46–52.

43. Breuer, "Modernism and Traditionalism"; Bell, "Jewish and Christian Historiography."

44. Rosenfeld, "Taschenkalender," 35. Similarly, the calendar for 1801–1802 printed by Moshe Witzenhausen, Kassel, listed in Yiddish the dates of birth and accession of the princely house of Hesse-Kassel.

45. A bizarre genre of "mock Jewish chronicles," subtly anti-Jewish political "chronicles" written by eighteenth-century lawyer Christoph Gottlieb Richter, mimicked the terse, pseudo-biblical style of authentic Jewish chronicles because they were the "shortest and oldest of all." See Cerman, "Maria Theresia," 6.

46. Cohen, *Critical Edition*, 190. See the critique of Cohen in Krakowski, "Literary Character."

47. Biblical texts often cited include Psalms 90:15: "Gladden us according to the days you have tormented us"; Psalms 90:4: "For a thousand years in Your sight are like one day gone by." Daniel's vision of the Four Kingdoms provided another template for the interpretation of time.

48. Yosef ben Shem Tov, *Sefer she'erit Yosef*, eighth portal.

49. Munich, Bayerische Staatsbibliothek Cod. Hebr. 394, fol. 66v; similarly, Leiden-Bibliotheek der Rijksuniversiteit Cod. Or. 4736, fol. 27v.

50. The verse begins with the Hebrew word *ranu*, and ends: "Redeem your people, the remnant of Israel."

51. Eidelberg, *Jews and the Crusaders*, 21, 79.

52. Ibid., 99.

53. On ancient sevenfold counting systems, see Elior, *Three Temples*; and Wacholder, "Chronomessianism"; for medieval counting systems, see Idel, "Ha-yovel be-mistiqa yehudit," 80.

54. Yuval, *Hakhamim be-doram*, 292.

55. Heller, *Studies*, 54–71.

56. New York, Dorot Jewish Division, New York Public Library ms Heb. 268, 1738–1739.

57. Cited in Weinberg, "Invention and Convention," 325.

58. De Rossi, *Light*, 405. Weinberg's introduction to ibid., xxv–xxx, and her translation and annotation to de Rossi's chapter 29, form the basis for my discussion of de Rossi.

59. De Rossi, *Light*, 425.

60. Silver, *Messianic Speculation*, 116–118.

61. Saperstein, *Jewish Preaching*, 289, n.1.

62. Scholem, *Sabbatai Sevi*, 524–525.

63. Oliveyra, *Miqra'ei*.

64. Morgenstern, *Hastening Redemption*, 23–50.

65. *Seder olam*, ch. 30, 478–479.

Epilogue

1. Bendavid, *Zur Berechnung*.

2. Ibid., 6.

3. Ibid., 15. Bendavid also belittled the Christian chronology, accusing Christians of manipulating the years so that Christ should appear near the four-thousandth year from creation, a method he characterized as "der Beweis nach dem Bedarf."

4. Kornick, *Davar be-itto*. Kornick's *System der Zeitrechnung* (Berlin, 1825), a concordance of Julian, Gregorian, Jewish, and Islamic calendars, was highly regarded in its time and formed the basis for Jahn's *Tafeln*.

5. For an expanded treatment of the Bendavid-Kornick exchange, see Carlebach, "When Does."

6. Mahler, *Hasidism*, 149–168; Perl, *Tzir ne'eman*. I thank Nancy Sinkoff for sharing with me her copy of the first year's calendar, which does not bear a title.

7. Schorsch's "History as Consolation" has fully treated Zunz's work.

8. Meyer Kayserling, a nineteenth-century rabbi and historian, followed Zunz with his own list of Sterbetage, but he returned his to the pages of a calendar. See *Illustrierte Israelitische Volkskalender f.d. J.* 5602 (Prague: N.p., 1891), 57–96.

9. *Volks-Kalender und Jahrbuch für Israeliten*. I follow the calendar from its inception in 1842 through mid-1865; imprint varies.

GLOSSARY

anno Domini: year of our Lord, used to indicate dates within Christian and Western culture

anno mundi: year to creation of the world, used to indicate dates within the Jewish chronological system

dehiyya, dehiyyot (pl.): rule(s) for deferring the declaration of a New Moon for the first calendar month

gaon, geonim (pl.), geonic: relating to the period from approximately the mid-eighth through the early eleventh centuries C.E., when Jewish scholars known as geonim headed academies in Persia and greatly influenced their times

genizah, genizot (pl.): storage collection(s) of old texts

haggadah, haggadot (pl.): liturgical compendium or compendia recited on Passover night at the seder

ibbur, ibburim (pl.): computus, the rules for calculating the calendar, also used for a leap month

intercalation: addition of an interval (such as a leap day or month) to bring calendrical cycles into alignment

luah, luhot (pl.): calendar(s)

mahzor, mahzorim (pl.): cycle(s); liturgical compendium or compendia

megillah, megillot (pl.): scroll(s)

minyan shtarot: Era of Contracts. A chronological system related to the Seleucid dynasty in use among Jews.

molad: conjunction of the moon

panim ahor: literally, facing back. A method of checking mathematical calculations.

parshat sheqalim: one of four special portions read from the Torah (Numbers 30:11–16) concerning the census of the Israelites taken by counting their donated shekels. Represented in some manuscripts by a balance on which money was weighed.

qehillah, qehillot (pl.): Jewish community(ies)

qeviot: abbreviated codes for determining the character of a year

qiddush ha-hodesh: sanctification of a new month

Sefer evronot, sifre evronot (pl.): title of early modern Jewish calendar manuals

Sefer ibbur: title of medieval Jewish calendar manual

sod ha-ibbur: In antiquity, the council that determined the calendar. In medieval and early modern usage, the "secret of intercalation," formulae used to determine the Jewish calendar.

tequfah, tequfot (pl.): the seasonal points, including both equinoxes and solstices

BIBLIOGRAPHY

Manuscripts

Sifre evronot

Note: *Sefer evronot* (Book of intercalation) is a generic title for an anonymous composition. I have provided names of scribes and other identifying details where possible.
Where I have examined only a microfilm, I provide the number. IMHM stands for the Institute of Microfilmed Hebrew Manuscripts, Jewish National Library, Jerusalem.

BERLIN

Staatsbibliothek, Preussischer Kulturbesitz. Orientabteilung ms or. oct. 3150. Scribe: Yuda b. Samuel Reutlingen Mehler. Bingen, 1648–1651.

Staatsbibliothek, Preussischer Kulturbesitz. Orientabteilung ms or. quart. 692.

BUDAPEST

Magyar tudomanyos akademia ms Kaufmann A 511 (IMHM F15164). Scribe: Moses b. Jacob of Moravia. ca. 1662.

Magyar tudomanyos akademia ms Kaufmann A 515 (IMHM F15167). Sixteenth century.

Magyar tudomanyos akademia ms Kaufmann A 520 (IMHM F15170).

CINCINNATI

Klau Library, Hebrew Union College ms 444 (First Cincinnati Haggadah). Scribe: Meir Jaffe. Late fifteenth century.

Klau Library, Hebrew Union College ms 899. Scribe: Yaakov bar Yozef Sega"l. Eastern Europe, 1682.

Klau Library, Hebrew Union College ms 900. ca. 1577–1585.

Klau Library, Hebrew Union College ms 901. 1665–1666.

Klau Library, Hebrew Union College ms 902. Scribe: Moses ben Jacob Abraham Wiener of Gehaus, 1779.

Klau Library, Hebrew Union College ms 903. 1717.

Klau Library, Hebrew Union College ms 906. Scribe: Zechariah Shimon bar Yaakov Warburg, 1664.

JERUSALEM

National Library of Israel ms 8° 2380. Scribe: Pinhas ben Abraham Sega"l of Halberstadt. Halberstadt, 1716.

National Library of Israel ms 8° 3247. Scribe: Asher b. Shmuel HaKohen, 1619.

National Library of Israel ms 8° 3416. Scribe: Reuven bar Eliezer Lipman of Elsi (Alsace?), 1709.

LEIDEN

Bibliotheek der Rijksuniversiteit Cod. Or. 4736 (IMHM F 19187). Scribe: Elijah bar Moses Troitlein of Worms, 1557.

LONDON

British Library ms Add. 26970/4 (IMHM F 05634).

Valmadonna Trust Library ms 267 (Richler catalogue, no. 219).

MUNICH

Bayerische Staatsbibliothek Cod. hebr. 394. Two separate sifre evronot are bound in this volume. Ms 394A: fol. 1r–47v. Scribe: R. Hirsch ben Haggai Hanokh Hanau of Heidelberg, 1674. Ms 394B: scribe unknown, loose fol. Image 8, fols. 48r–109r, 1566.

Digital copy online at Digital Collections, Munich Digitization Center (www.digital-collections.de): urn:nbn:de:bvb:12-bsb00021775–9

NEW YORK

Library of the Jewish Theological Seminary ms 2540.1. 1631.

Library of the Jewish Theological Seminary ms 2547. Scribe: Seligman Leitershofen, 1583. Copied from a manuscript dated 1552.

Library of the Jewish Theological Seminary ms 2548. ca. 1557.

Library of the Jewish Theological Seminary ms 2566. ca. 1661.

Library of the Jewish Theological Seminary ms 2572. Scribe: Anshel Oppenheim. Oettingen, 1703.

Library of the Jewish Theological Seminary ms 2578. 1668.

Library of the Jewish Theological Seminary ms 2634. Scribe: Kalonymus bar Yehuda z″l called Kalman Ransbach, 1577.

Library of the Jewish Theological Seminary ms 2662. Scribe: Eleazar ben Joseph of Fulda, 1627.

Library of the Jewish Theological Seminary ms 9085. Based on a printed 1756 edition.

Library of the Jewish Theological Seminary ms 9487. Scribe: Shlomo ben Shimon Ulma of Günzberg, 1552.

Library of the Jewish Theological Seminary ms 10572. Holesov, 1756. Based on the printed edition.

Rare Book and Manuscript Library, Columbia University ms X893 Se36. ca. 1625.

Sotheby's Important Judaica: Including Property of the Jewish Community of Amsterdam (NIHS). New York: Sotheby's, 2006. Lot 178. 1557.

Yeshiva Ahavas Torah Baranovich. Central European provenance. Auction 11, item 297. Late sixteenth century.

Yeshiva University Mendel Gottesman Library ms 1083. Scribe: Moses ben Benjamin Neimark, 1665.

OXFORD

Oxford University, Bodleian Library ms Mich. 152 (Neubauer 1776/2, IMHM F18068). Scribe: Judah bar Joseph Oppenheim. Frankfurt, 1552.

Oxford University, Bodleian Library ms Opp. 332 (Neubauer 861/5, IMHM F21622).
Oxford University, Bodleian Library ms Opp. 698 (Neubauer 2074, IMHM F19359). 1606.
Oxford University, Bodleian Library ms Opp. 700 (Neubauer 2058, JTSL reel 491). Scribe: Zvi Hirsch b. Aharon Shmuel Koidonover. Frankfurt, ca. 1671.
Oxford University, Bodleian Library ms Opp. 701 (Neubauer 2056, JTSL reel 491, IMHM F19341). Scribe: Elijah ben Moses Loanz, 1586.
Oxford University, Bodleian Library ms Opp. 702 (Neubauer 2057, JTS reel 491). Lissa, ca. 1690–1692. Includes commentary "Divre David," likely by David Oppenheim.

PARIS

Bibliothèque Nationale ms heb. 644 (IMHM F11540).

PRAGUE

Jewish Museum ms 61 (IMHM F46603), early eighteenth century.

ROME

Rome, Vatican, Biblioteca Apostolica ms ebr. 299/6 (IMHM F8701).

STRASBOURG

Bibliothèque Nationale et Universitaire ms 3931 (IMHM F2754).

ZURICH

Zurich, Zentralbibliothek ms Heid. 145/2.

Other Manuscripts

CAMBRIDGE

Cambridge University Library ms Add. 3127–29 (IMHM F 17556/PH 2331). The manuscript was started in 1399 by one scribe and completed by Jacob bar Yedidya z"l in 1414.
Trinity College ms F 1221 (IMHM F 12168).

JERUSALEM

Jewish National Library ms 8°2238 (IMHM B 23) Bible fragment. Scribe: Isaac ben Abraham, 1106.

LONDON

British Library ms or. 1404.

MUNICH

Bayerische Staatsbibliothek Cod. hebr. 154. Wall calendar for 5296 [1535/6]. Scribe: Meshullam of Volterra. Digital copy online at Digital Collections, Munich Digitization Center (www.digital-collections.de): urn:nbn:de:bvb:12-bsb00034259-9.
Bayerische Staatsbibliothek Cod. hebr. 200. Tegernsee Haggadah. ca. 1478–1492.

NEW YORK

Library of the Jewish Theological Seminary ms 2223. Haggadah attributed to Yonah Rappa, also titled *Pilpul zeman, zemanim, zemanehem.*

Library of the Jewish Theological Seminary ms 2226. "Haggadah attributed to Yonah Rappa," Also titled *Pilpul zeman, zemanim, zemanehem.*

Library of the Jewish Theological Seminary ms 2254. "Haggadah attributed to Yonah Rappa," Also titled *Pilpul zeman, zemanim, zemanehem.*

Library of the Jewish Theological Seminary ms 2582. Aviad Sar Shalom Basilea. *Niyyar ha-yamim.*

Library of the Jewish Theological Seminary ms 2588. Aviad Sar Shalom Basilea. *Niyyar ha-yamim* (holograph).

Library of the Jewish Theological Seminary ms 2652. Sefer she'erit Yosef. Yosef ben Shem Tov ben Yehoshua Hai.

Library of the Jewish Theological Seminary ms 8943. Sefer she'erit Yosef. Yosef ben Shem Tov ben Yehoshua Hai.

Library of the Jewish Theological Seminary ms 10696. Sefer she'erit Yosef. Yosef ben Shem Tov ben Yehoshua Hai.

Library of the Jewish Theological Seminary ms C110. Calendar, nineteenth century.

New York Public Library, Dorot Jewish Division. Hirtz Reinganum of Frankfurt am Main. Dated March 27, 1791. Manuscript notes to David Meldola, *Sefer Mo'ed David,* Amsterdam: David Atthias, 1740.

New York Public Library, Dorot Jewish Division ms Heb. 268. Five pocket calendars: 1729–1730; 1734–1735; 1738–1739; 1741–1742; 1745–1746.

Rare Book and Manuscript Library, Columbia University ms X86 C12. *Calendario de todos Ros Hodes Fiestas y Ayunas del Año.*

OXFORD

Oxford University, Bodleian Library ms Heb. d. 11 (Neubauer 2797/2). *Sefer ha-zikhronot.* Luah, fols. 2v–3r; 365. Fourteenth century.

Oxford University, Bodleian Library ms Mich. 74 (Neubauer 1171 IMHM F 16630). Scribe: Isaac b. R. Eliezer, for patron R. Shemarya ben R. Menachem מצולפכא (possibly Sulzbach or Sulzberg).

Oxford University, Bodleian Library ms Opp. 317 (Neubauer 692/6).

Oxford, Bodleian Library ms Opp. 614 (Neubauer 2275/5, IMHM F20967). Early fourteenth century.

PARMA

Biblioteca Palatina ms 2467/3 (IMHM F 13471).

PHILADELPHIA

Center for Advanced Judaic Studies, University of Pennsylvania ms 58. Luah le-shenat 5516–5519. 1756–1759.

Center for Advanced Judaic Studies, University of Pennsylvania ms 59. Luah shel shenat 5537 [1776/77], written for the owner: Mr. Joseph Simons, merchant in Lancaster, Pennsylvania.

Center for Advanced Judaic Studies, University of Pennsylvania ms 60. Luah shel shnat 5541 [1780/81] Jewish calendar adapted from pocket-sized non-Jewish almanac. Collage.

Center for Advanced Judaic Studies, University of Pennsylvania ms 61. Luah shel shenat 5542 [1781–1782].

Printed Material

PRINTED CALENDARS:

Altona, Wall calendar, 1747/48.

Altona, Wall calendar, 1748/49.

Barco, Italy: Soncino, 1496–1497. (The year printed in large letters at the top is רנ"ג [1493], an error.) New York, Library of the Jewish Theological Seminary.

Constantinople, 1510. 20-year calendar. New York, Library of the Jewish Theological Seminary.

Constantinople, Soncino Press 1547/48 (Valmadonna 1813.1).

Fürth, 1807.

Fürth, 1817/18 wall calendars (Valmadonna 8830/A23).

German-Jewish calendar fragment for 1735/36 (Valmadonna 3685/A29).

Jessnitz, Wall calendar, 1740.

JTS C28 printed wall calendar 1769/70, n.p. (Italian?).

JTS uncat. Hebrew Almanac, 1577. Italian broadsheet luah.

Lunéville, 1812, 1814.

Sabionetta 1560/61 wall calendar (Valmadonna 4952/5).

Sulzbach, 1802/03 (Valmadonna 8814/22).

Venice, Juan da Gara, 1599 (Valmadonna 4486/2).

Vilna and Horodna, 1825/26; 1826/27 (Yivo Institute).

'Abodah Zarah. Babylonian Talmud, tractate. Trans. and annot. A. Mishcon. London: Soncino Press, 1935.

Abudarham, David ben Joseph. *Perush seder tefillot.* Lisbon: Eliezer Toledano, 1489; Venice, 1566.

Agnew, Jean-Christophe. *Worlds Apart: The Market and the Theater in Anglo-American Thought, 1550–1750.* Cambridge, Eng.: Cambridge University Press, 1986.

Akavia, A. A. "Sefer meyuhad le-inyenei ha-ibbur." *Sinai* 30 (1952): 118–137.

Al-Bīrūnī, Muḥammad ibn Aḥmad. *The Chronology of Ancient Nations (Athar-ul-Bakiya).* Trans and ed. C. Edward Sachau. London: W. H. Allen, 1879.

Alexander, Jonathan, and Paul Binski, eds. *Age of Chivalry: Art in Plantagenet England, 1200–1400.* London: Royal Academy of Arts, 1987.

Almond, Richard. "The Hunting Year." *History Today* 55, no. 8 (2005): 30–36.

———. *Medieval Hunting.* Stroud, Eng.: Sutton, 2003.

Ankori, Zvi. *Karaites in Byzantium.* New York: Columbia University Press, 1959.

Arkenberg, Jerome S. *Internet Medieval Sourcebook.* www.fordham.edu/halsall/sbook.html (last accessed October 11, 2010).

Arnheim, Arthur. "Hebrew Prints and Censorship in Altona." *Studies in Bibliography and Booklore* 21 (2001): 3–9.

Arnoldi, Udo. *Pro Iudaeis: Die Gutachten der hallischen Theologen im 18. Jahrhundert zu Fragen der Judentoleranz.* Berlin: Institut Kirche und Judentum, 1993.

Asher, Jacob ben. *Arba turim.* Any standard edition.

Assaf, Simcha. *Meqorot le-toledot ha-hinukh be-Yisrael,* ed. Shmuel Glick. 4 vols. New York and Jerusalem: Jewish Theological Seminary, 2002.

Astren, Fred. *Karaite Judaism and Historical Understanding.* Columbia: University of South Carolina Press, 2004.

Bächtold-Stäubli, Hans. *Handwörterbuch des deutschen Aberglaubens.* Berlin and Leipzig: Walter de Gruyter, 1927.

Baggely, John. *Festival Icons for the Christian Year.* London: Mowbray, 2000.

Balmer, R. T. "The Operation of Sand Clocks and Their Medieval Development." *Technology and Culture* 19 (1978): 615–632.

Bar Hiyya, Abraham. *Sefer ha-ibbur.* Ed. Herschell Filipowski. London: Longman, Brown, Green and Longmans, 1851.

Baron, Salo W. *A Social and Religious History of the Jews.* 2d ed. New York: Columbia University Press, 1952–1993. 20 vols.

Baruchson-Arbib, Shifra. *Books and Readers: Reading Culture among Italian Jews in the Late Renaissance.* (Hebrew). Ramat-Gan: Bar-Ilan University, 1993.

Baumgarten, Elisheva. *Mothers and Children: Jewish Family Life in Medieval Europe.* Princeton, N.J.: Princeton University Press, 2004.

———. "'Remember That Glorious Girl': Jephthah's Daughter in Medieval Jewish Culture." *Jewish Quarterly Review* 97, no. 2 (2007): 180–209.

Baumgarten, Joseph. *Studies in Qumran Law.* Leiden: E. J. Brill, 1977.

Beit-Arié, Malachi. *Unveiled Faces of Hebrew Books: The Evolution of Manuscript Production—Progression or Regression?* Jerusalem: Magnes Press, 2003.

———, ed. *Worms Mahzor: Ms. Jewish National and University Library Heb. 4° 781/1.* Vaduz [Liechtenstein]: Cyelar Establishment; and Jerusalem: The Jewish National and University Library, 1985.

Bell, Dean Phillip. "Jewish and Christian Historiography in the Sixteenth Century: A Comparison of Sebastian Münster and David Gans." Pp. 141–158 in J. Harold Ellens et al., eds., *God's Word for Our World: Studies in Honor of Simon John de Vries.* vol. 2. London: T & T Clark International, 2004.

———. *Jews in the Early Modern World: Continuity and Transformation.* Lanham: Rowman & Littlefield, 2008.

Beller, Eliyahu. "Ancient Jewish Mathematical Astronomy." *Archive for the History of Exact Sciences* 38 (1988): 51–66.

Bendavid, Lazarus. *Zur Berechnung und Geschichte des jüdischen Kalendar: Aus den Quellen geschöpft.* Berlin: Nicholaischen Buchhandlung, 1817.

Benjamin, Walter. *Illuminations.* Trans. Harry Zohn, ed. Hannah Arendt. New York: Schocken, 1969.

Benton, Janetta Rebold. *Medieval Mischief: Wit and Humour in the Art of the Middle Ages.* Stroud, Eng.: Sutton, 2004.

Berger, David. *The Jewish-Christian Debate in the High Middle Ages: A Critical Edition of the Nizzahon Vetus with Introduction, Translation, and Commentary.* Philadelphia: Jewish Publication Society of America, 1979.

Berger, Shlomo. "An Invitation to Buy and Read: Paratexts of Yiddish Books in Amsterdam, 1650–1800." *Book History* 7 (2004): 31–61.

Berman, Joshua. "Medieval Monasticism and the Evolution of Jewish Interpretation of the Story of Jephtha's Daughter." *Jewish Quarterly Review* 95 (2005): 228–256.

Bernoulli, C. C. *Basler Büchermarkt bis zum Anfang des 17. Jahrhunderts.* Strasbourg: Paul Heitz, 1895; repr. Naarden: A. W. van Bekhoven, 1984.

Ber of Bolechow. *The Memoirs of Ber of Bolechow (1723–1805).* Trans. Mark Vishnitzer. London: Oxford University Press, 1922.

Bietenholz, P. G. "Édition et Réforme à Bâle (1517–1565)." Pp. 239–268 in J. F. Gilmont, ed., *La Réforme et le Livre: l'Europe de l'imprimé (1517–v. 1570).* Paris: Cerf, 1990.

Bischoff, Bernhardt. *Mittelalterliche Studien: Ausgewählte Aufsätze zur Schriftkunde und Literaturgeschichte.* Stuttgart: Hiersemann, 1996.

Bland, Kalman P. *The Artless Jew: Medieval and Modern Affirmations and Denials of the Visual.* Princeton, N.J.: Princeton University Press, 2001.

Blaschke, Karlheinz. "Der Übergang von der Warenmesse zur Mustermess im 19. Jahrhundert." Pp. 263–280 in Rainer Koch, ed., *Brücke zwischen den Völkern—Zur Geschichte der Frankfurter Messe*, vol. 1. 3 vols. Frankfurt am Main: Historisches Museum, 1991.

Blidstein, Gerald. "Rabbinic Legislation on Idolatry: Tractate Abodah Zarah, Chapter I." Ph.D. diss., Yeshiva University, 1968.

Bloch, Eileen. "Erasmus and the Froben Press: The Making of an Editor." *Library Quarterly* 35, no. 2 (Apr. 1965): 109–120.

Bloch, Joshua. *Hebrew Printing in Riva di Trento.* New York: New York Public Library, 1933.

———. "A Hitherto Unrecorded Hebrew Publication from Riva di Trento." *Jewish Quarterly Review*, n.s. 26 (1935): 129–132.

———. "Zacuto and His *Almanach Perpetuum.*" Pp. 59–62 in Charles Berlin, ed., *Hebrew Printing and Bibliography: Studies . . . Reprinted from the Publications of the New York Public Library.* New York: New York Public Library and Ktav, 1976.

Bloch, Phillip. "Ein vielbegehrter Rabbiner des Rheingaues, Juda Mehler Reutlingen." In *Beiträge zur Geschichte der deutschen Juden: Festschrift zum siebzigsten Geburtstage Martin Philippsons.* Leipzig: Gustav Fock, 1916.

Bogucka, Maria. "Space and Time as Factors Shaping Polish Mentality from the Sixteenth until the Eighteenth Century." *Acta Poloniae Historica* 66 (1992): 39–52.

Bollème, Geneviève. *Les almanachs populaires aux xviie et xviiie siècles: Essai d'histoire sociale.* Paris: Mouton, 1969.

Bonfil, Roberto. "How Golden Was the Age of the Renaissance in Jewish History?" in supp. 27, "Essays in Jewish Historiography" *History and Theory* (1988): 78–102.

Bornstein, Hayim Yechiel. "Mahloqet Rav Sa'adiah Gaon u-ven Meir bi-keviat shenot, 682–684: Pereq me-qorot seder ha-ibbur be-Yisrael." Pp. 19–189 in *Sefer Yovel le-N. Sokolov.* Warsaw: Schuldberg, 1904.

Borst, Arno, ed. *Der Karolingische Reichskalender und seine Überlieferung bis ins 12. Jahrhundert.* 3 vols. Hannover: Hahnsche Buchhandlung, 2001.

———. *Schriften zur Komputistik im Frankenreich von 721 bis 818.* 3 vols. (Monumenta Germaniae Historica, Quellen zur Geistesgeschichte des Mittelalters, vol. 21.) Hannover: Hahnsche Buchhandlung, 2006.

———. *Der Streit um den karolingischen Kalender.* (Monumenta Germaniae Historica, Studien und Texte, 36.) Hannover: Hahnsche Buchhandlung, 2004.

Bowman, John. "The Malef." *Abr-Nahrain* 20 (1981–1982): 1–19.

Braudel, Fernand. *Civilization and Capitalism, Fifteenth–Eighteenth Century*, vol. 2: *The Wheels of Commerce*, trans. Siân Reynolds. New York: Harper & Row, 1982.

Breuer, Mordechai. "Modernism and Traditionalism in Sixteenth-Century Jewish Historiography: A Study of David Gans' *Tzemach David.*" Pp. 67–79 in Bernard Dov Cooperman, ed., *Jewish Thought in the Sixteenth Century.* Cambridge: Harvard University Press, 1983.

Brévart, François B. "The German *Volkskalendar* of the Fifteenth Century." *Speculum* 63 (1988): 312–342.

Brody, Robert. *The Geonim of Babylonia and the Shaping of Medieval Jewish Culture.* New Haven: Yale University Press, 1998.

Brown, Peter. *The Cult of the Saints: Its Rise and Function in Latin Christianity.* Chicago: University of Chicago Press, 1981.

Burnett, Stephen. "German Jewish Printing in the Reformation Era (1530–1633)." Pp. 503–527 in Dean Phillip Bell and Stephen Burnett, eds., *Jews, Judaism and the Reformation in Sixteenth-Century Germany.* Leiden: Brill, 2006.

———. "'Spokesmen for Judaism': Medieval Jewish Polemicists and Their Christian Readers in the Reformation Era." Pp. 41–51 in *Reuchlin und seine Erben*, ed. Peter Schäfer and I. Wandrey. (Pforzheimer Reuchlinschriften 11.) Stuttgart: Jan Thorbecke, 2005.

Bynum, Caroline Walker. *Wonderful Blood: Theology and Practice in Late Medieval Northern Germany and Beyond.* Philadelphia: University of Pennsylvania Press, 2007.

Cahn, W. "Ascending to and Descending from Heaven: Ladder Themes in Early Medieval Art." *Santi e demoni nell'alto medioevo occidentale (secoli V–XI)*, April 7–13, 1988. (Settimane di studio del Centro italiano di studi sull'alto medioevo 36.) 2 vols. Spoleto: Presso la Sede del Centro, 1989.

Calendario de Ros-Hodes, fiestas y ayunos, que los Hebreos celebran cada Año Desde el Año de 5465. à la criacion del Mundo, hasta 5469. Que corresponde con el vulgar del año 1705 hasta 1709. A costa de Yshak de Cordova. Amsterdam: H. Ackerman y W. Groenevelt, [1704].

Calendrier pour l'année sextile. New York: Parisot et Ducros, 1794.

Camille, Michael. *Image on the Edge: The Margins of Medieval Art.* Cambridge: Harvard University Press, 1992.

Capp, Bernard. *Astrology and the Popular Press: English Almanacs, 1500–1800.* London: Faber and Faber, 1979.

Carlebach, Elisheva. *Divided Souls: Converts from Judaism in Germany, 1500–1750.* New Haven: Yale University Press, 2001.

———. "The Last Deception: Failed Messiahs and Jewish Conversion in Early Modern German Lands." Pp. 125–138 in Matt Goldish and Richard Popkin, eds. *Millenarianism and Messianism in Early Modern European Culture*, vol. 1: *Jewish Messianism in the Early Modern World.* Dordrecht: Kluwer Academic, 2001.

———. "Water into Blood: Custom, Calendar, and an Unknown Yiddish Book for Women. Pp. 59–71 in Marion A. Kaplan and Deborah Dash Moore, eds., *Gender and Jewish History.* Bloomington: Indiana University Press, 2010.

———. "When Does the Modern Period of the Jewish Calendar Begin?" Pp. 43–54 in

Mediating Modernity: Challenges and Trends in the Jewish Encounter with the Modern World, ed. Lauren Strauss and Michael Brenner. Detroit: Wayne State University Press, 2008.

Carmoly, Eliakim. *Annalen der Hebraischer Typographie in Riva di Trento.* Frankfurt: G. Hess, 1868.

Cassutto, Moshe D. "Ha-qetovot ha-ivriot shel ha-meah ha-teshi'it be-Venossa." *Kedem* 2 (1945): 99–120.

Cave, Roy C., and Herbert H. Coulson. *A Source Book for Medieval Economic History.* Milwaukee: Bruce Publishing, 1936; reprint, New York: Biblo & Tannen, 1965.

Cerman, Ivo. "Maria Theresia in the Mirror of Contemporary Mock Jewish Chronicles." *Judaica Bohemiae* 38 (2002): 5–47.

Chapman, Alison A. "The Politics of Time in Edmund Spenser's English Calendar." *Studies in English Literature, 1500–1900* 42, no. 1 (2002): 1–24.

Chavel, Simeon. "The Second Passover, Pilgrimage, and the Centralized Cult." *Harvard Theological Review* 102, no. 1 (2009): 1–24.

Cipolla, Carlo M. *Clocks and Culture: 1300–1700.* New York: Norton, 1977.

Clark, Stuart. *Thinking with Demons: The Idea of Witchcraft in Early Modern Europe.* Oxford, Eng.: Oxford University Press, 1997.

Cohen, Gerson. *A Critical Edition with a Translation and Notes of the "Book of Tradition" (Sefer ha-qabbalah) by Abraham Ibn Daud.* Philadelphia: Jewish Publication Society, 1967.

Cohen, Mark R. *Under Crescent and Cross: The Jews in the Middle Ages.* Princeton, N.J.: Princeton University Press, 1994.

Cohen, Richard. *Jewish Icons: Art and Society in Modern Europe.* Berkeley: University of California Press, 1998.

Collinson, Patrick. *The Birthpangs of Protestant England: Religious and Cultural Change in the Sixteenth and Seventeenth Centuries.* Basingstoke, Eng.: Palgrave Macmillan, 1988.

Colorni, Vittore. "Abraham Conat, primo stampatore di opere ebraiche in Mantova e la cronologia delle sue edizioni." *La Bibliofilía* 83, no. 2 (1981): 113–128.

Concordance des calendriers grégorien et républicain. Paris: R. Clavreuil, 1963.

Cordova, Yshak de. *Calendario,* Amsterdam, 1704.

Cosgrove, Denis, and Stephen Daniels. *The Iconography of Landscape.* Cambridge, Eng.: Cambridge University Press, 1988.

Coucy, Moses. *Sefer mitzvot gadol.* Venice, 1547; reprint Jerusalem: Hotza'at he-semag, 1961.

Cressy, David. *Bonfires and Bells: National Memory and the Protestant Calendar in Elizabethan and Stuart England.* Berkeley: University of California Press, 1989.

———. "The Protestant Calendar and the Vocabulary of Celebration in Early Modern England." *Journal of British Studies* 29 (1990): 31–52.

Crick, Julia, and Alexandra Walsham. *The Uses of Script and Print, 1300–1700.* Cambridge, Eng.: Cambridge University Press, 2004.

Culpepper, Danielle. "'Our Particular Cloister': Ursulines and Female Education in Seventeenth-Century Parma and Piacenza." *Sixteenth Century Journal* 36, no. 4 (2005): 1017–1037.

Cummins, John. *The Hound and the Hawk: The Art of Medieval Hunting.* London: Weidenfeld and Nicolson, 1988.

Da Costa, Uriel. *Examination of the Pharisaic Traditions.* Trans. and ed. H. P. Salomon and I. S. D. Sassoon. Leiden, Neth.: Brill, 1993.

Dan, Joseph. "Qeta mi-*Sefer ha-kavod* le-Rabbi Yehudah he-hasid." *Sinai* 71 (1972): 118–120.

Dane, Joseph. *The Myth of Print Culture: Essays on Evidence, Textuality, and Bibliographical Method.* Toronto: University of Toronto Press, 2003.

David, Abraham. *To Come to the Land: Immigration and Settlement in Sixteenth-Century Eretz-Israel.* Trans. Dena Ordan. Tuscaloosa: University of Alabama Press, 1999.

Davies, Douglas. "The Evocative Symbolism of Trees." In *The Iconography of Landscape: Essays on the Symbolic Representation, Design and Use of Past Environments.* Ed. Denis Cosgrove and Stephen Daniels. Cambridge Studies in Historical Geography 9. Cambridge, Eng.: Cambridge University Press, 1988.

Davis, Natalie Zemon. *Society and Culture in Early Modern France: Eight Essays.* Stanford, Calif.: Stanford University Press, 1975.

De' Rossi, Azariah. *The Light of the Eyes.* Trans. from the Hebrew with introduction and annotations by Joanna Weinberg. New Haven: Yale University Press, 2001.

———. *Matzref le-kesef.* Edinburgh: N.p., 1854; repr. Jerusalem: N.p., 1970.

De Silva, Hezekiah. *Sefer Pri Hadash.* Amsterdam: Netanel Foa, 1706.

Dietz, Alexander. *The Jewish Community of Frankfurt: A Genealogical Study, 1349–1849.* Cornwall, Eng.: Vanderher Publications, 1988.

Dohrn-van Rossum, Gerhard. *History of the Hour: Clocks and Modern Temporal Orders.* Trans. Thomas Dunlap. Chicago: University of Chicago Press, 1996.

Dowd, Matthew F. "Astronomy and Compotus at Oxford University in the Early Thirteenth Century: The Works of Robert Grosseteste." Ph.D. diss., University of Notre Dame, Indiana, 2003.

Drewer, Lois. "Jephthah and His Daughter in Medieval Art: Ambiguities of Heroism and Sacrifice." Pp. 35–59 in Colum Hourihane, ed., *Insights and Interpretations: Studies in Celebration of the Eighty-fifth Anniversary of the Index of Christian Art.* Princeton, N.J.: Index of Christian Art, with Princeton University Press, 2002.

Edgerton, William L. "The Calendar Year in Sixteenth-Century Printing." *Journal of English and Germanic Philology* 59 (1960): 439–449.

Eidelberg, Shlomo. "Abraham Aaron: A Court-Jew of the Seventeenth Century." *Michael* 2 (1973): 9–15.

———. *Be-netive Ashkenaz.* Brooklyn, N.Y.: Sepher-Hermon Press, 2001.

———. *The Jews and the Crusaders: The Hebrew Chronicles of the First and Second Crusades.* Madison: University of Wisconsin Press, 1977; repr. Hoboken: Ktav, 1996.

———. *R. Juspa, Shammash of Warmaisa (Worms).* Jerusalem: Magnes Press, 1991.

Einbinder, Susan L. "Hebrew Poems for the Day of Shutting In: Problems and Methods." *Revue des études juives* 163, nos. 1–2 (Jan.–June 2004): 111–135.

———. "Recall from Exile: Literature, Memory and Medieval French Jews." *Jewish Studies Quarterly* 15, no. 3 (2008): 225–240.

Eisenstein, Elizabeth. "Clio and Chronos: An Essay on the Making and Breaking of History-Book Time." *History and Theory* supp. 6: History and the Concept of Time (1966): 36–64.

———. *The Printing Revolution in Early Modern Europe.* Cambridge, Eng.: Cambridge University Press, 1983.

Eisner, Sigmund, ed. *The Kalendarium of Nicholas of Lynn*. Athens: University of Georgia Press, 1980.

Elbaum, Jacob. "From Sermon to Story: The Transformation of the Akeda." *Prooftexts* 6, no. 2 (1986): 97–116.

———. "Influences of Spanish Jewish Culture on the Jews of Ashkenaz and Poland in the Fifteenth and Sixteenth Centuries." (Hebrew). Pp. 95–120 in Joseph Dan ed., *Tarbut ve-historiyah: Le-zikhro shel Prof. Ino Sciaky*. Jerusalem: Misgav Yerushalaim, 1987.

Elior, Rachel. *The Three Temples: On the Emergence of Jewish Mysticism*. Trans. D. Louvish. Oxford, Eng.: Littman Library of Jewish Civilization, 2004.

Elizur, Shulamit. *Lama tzamnu? Megillat Ta'anit Batra u-reshimot tzomot ha-qerovot la*. Jerusalem: World Union of Jewish Studies, 2007.

———. *Piyute Rabi Pinhas Ha-kohen*. Jerusalem: World Union of Jewish Studies, 2004.

Emanuel, Simha. *Shivre luhot: Sefarim avudim shel ba'ale ha-tosafot*. Jerusalem: Magnes Press, 2006.

England, Yaffa. "Mosaics as Midrash: The Zodiacs of the Ancient Synagogues and the Conflict between Judaism and Christianity." *Review of Rabbinic Judaism* 6 (2003): 189–214.

Epstein, Marc M. *Dreams of Subversion in Medieval Jewish Art and Literature*. University Park: Pennsylvania State University Press, 1997.

Feiner, Shmuel. *The Jewish Enlightenment*. Trans. Chaya Naor. Philadelphia: University of Pennsylvania Press, 2004.

Feinstein, David. *The Jewish Calendar: Its Structure and Laws*. New York: Mesorah, 2004.

Fenske, Michaela. *Marktkultur in der Frühen Neuzeit*. Cologne: Böhlau Verlag, 2006.

Fishman, Talya. *Shaking the Pillars of Exile: 'Voice of a Fool,' an Early Modern Jewish Critique of Rabbinic Culture*. Stanford, Calif.: Stanford University Press, 1997.

Fishof, Iris. Introduction to *Grace after meals and Other Benedictions: Facsimile of Cod. Hebr. XXXII in the Royal Library, Copenhagen*. 2 vols. Copenhagen: Forlaget Old Manuscripts, 1983.

———. *Jüdische Buchmalerei in Hamburg und Altona: Zur Geschichte der Illumination hebräischer Handschriften im 18. Jahr hundert*. Hamburg: Christians Verlag, 1999.

Fishof, Iris, with Ariel Cohen and Moshe Idel. *Written in the Stars: Art and Symbolism of the Zodiac*. Jerusalem: The Israel Museum, 2001.

Fleischer, Ezra. "Berurim be-va'ayat yihudam ha-liturgi shel piyyute qiddush yerahim." *Tarbits* 42 (1973): 337–363.

———. *Ha-yotzrot be-hithavutam ve-hitpathutam*. Jerusalem: Hotza'at sefarim a. sh. Y. L. Magnes, 1984.

———. *Tefillah u-minhage tefillah eretz yisraeli'im be-tequfat ha-genizah*. Jerusalem: Hotza'at sefarim a. sh. Y. L. Magnes, 1988.

Forster, Thomas. *Circle of the Seasons, and Perpetual Key to the Calendar and Almanack: To Which Is Added the Circle of the Hours, and the History of the Days of the Week: Being a Compendious Illustration of the History, Antiquities, and Natural Phenomena, of Each Day in the Year*. London: Thomas Hookham, 1828.

Fowler, Alastair. "The Formation of Genres in the Renaissance and After." *New Literary History* 34 (2003): 185–200.

Fram, Edward. "German Pietism and Sixteenth- and Early Seventeenth-Century Polish Rabbinic Culture." *Jewish Quarterly Review* 96, no. 1 (2005): 50–59.

Freiman, Eli. "Tarbut ve-hevra yehudit be-Ashkenaz be-reshit ha-et ha-hadashah." Ph.D. diss., Hebrew University, Jerusalem, 2007.

Freudenthal, Gad. "Science in the Medieval Jewish Culture of Southern France." *History of Science* 33 (1995): 23–58.

Freudenthal, Max. *Leipziger messgäste; die jüdischen Besucher der Leipziger Messen in den Jahren 1675 bis 1764.* Frankfurt am Main: J. Kauffmann, 1928.

———. "Zum Jubiläum des ersten Talmuddrucks in Deutschland." *Monatsschrift für Geschichte und Wissenschaft des Judentums* 42 (1898): 134–143.

Frick, David. "The Bells of Vilnius: Keeping Time in a City of Many Calendars." Pp. 23–59 in Glenn Burger et al., eds., *Making Contact: Maps, Identity, and Travel.* Edmonton: University of Alberta Press, 2003.

Fricke, Hermann. "Denkmäler heimatlicher Volkskultur: Zur Geschichte des Berlinisch-Brandenburgischen Kalenderdruckes." *Der Bär von Berlin: Jahrbuch des Vereins für die Geschichte Berlins* 15 (1966): 44–70.

Friedman, Mira. "The Meaning of the Zodiac in Synagogues in the Land of Israel during the Byzantine Period." *Ars Judaica* 1 (2005): 51–62.

Friedrichs, Christopher. "Politics or Pogrom? The Fettmilch Uprising in German and Jewish History." *Central European History* 19 (1986): 186–228.

Froeschlé-Chopard, Marie-Hélène, and Michel Froeschlé-Chopard. "Une double image de la révolution: Le calendrier et le mètre." *Annales Historiques de la revolution française* 279 (1990): 75–88.

Gans, David. *Sefer tzemah David.* Ed. Mordechai Breuer. Jerusalem: Magnes, 1983.

Gaspard, Claire. "Les Almanachs de l'an II: Quoi de neuf en dehors du calendrier?" *Annales historiques de la revolution française* 264 (1986): 141–159.

Geertz, Clifford. *The Interpretation of Cultures: Selected Essays.* New York: Basic Books, 1973.

Gesamtkatalog der Wiegendrucke. Leipzig: Komission für den Gesamtkatalog der Wiegendrucke, 1925–1940.

Gingerich, Owen. "The Civil Reception of the Gregorian Calendar." Pp. 265–277 in G. V. Coyne, M. A. Hoskin, and O. Pederson, eds., *Gregorian Reform of the Calendar: Proceedings of the Vatican Conference to Commemorate Its 400th Anniversary, 1582–1982.* Citta del Vaticano: Pontifica Academia Scientiarum, 1983.

Glikl. *Zikhroynes, 1691–1719.* Edited and translated from the Yiddish by Chava Turniansky. Jerusalem: The Zalman Shazar Center and the Dinur Center, 2006.

Goddard, Stephen H. "Probationes Pennae: Some Sixteenth-Century Doodles on the Theme of Folly Attributed to the Antwerp Humanist Pieter Gillis and His Colleagues." *Renaissance Quarterly* 41 (1988): 242–267.

Goff, Fredrick Richmond. *Incunabula in American Libraries: A Third Census.* New York: Bibliographical Society of America, 1964.

Gold, Leonard Singer. *A Sign and a Witness: Two Thousand Years of Hebrew Books and Illuminated Manuscripts.* New York: New York Public Library, 1988.

Goldberg, Bernard. *The Sacred Portal: A Primary Symbol in Ancient Judaic Art.* Detroit: Wayne State University Press, 1966.

Goldberg, Sylvie Anne. *La clepsydre.* 2 vols. Paris: Albin Michel, 2000–2004.

Goldin, Judah, trans. *The Fathers According to R. Nathan.* New Haven: Yale University Press, 1955, 1990.

Goldschmidt, Daniel. *Seder ha-qinot le-Tish'ah be-'Av: ke-minhag Folin u-qehilot ha-ashkenazim be-'Erets Yisra'el.* Jerusalem: Mossad Harav Kook, 1968.

Goldstein, Bernard R. "Astronomy and the Jewish Community in Early Islam." *Aleph* 1 (2001): 17–49.

Grafton, Anthony. "Invention of Traditions and Traditions of Invention in Renaissance Europe: The Strange Case of Annius of Viterbo." Pp. 8–39 in Anthony Grafton and Ann Blair, eds., *The Transmission of Culture in Early Modern Europe.* Philadelphia: University of Pennsylvania Press, 1990.

———. *Joseph Scaliger: A Study in the History of Classical Scholarship.* Oxford, Eng.: Clarendon Press, 1983; vol. 2, 1993.

Grochulska, Barbara. "Jarmarki w Handlu Polskim w Drugiej Polowie XVIII Wieku," *Przeglad Historyczny* 64 (1973): 793–821.

Gross, Abraham. "The Blood Libel and the Blood of Circumcision: An Ashkenazic Custom That Disappeared in the Middle Ages." *Jewish Quarterly Review* n.s. 86 (1995): 171–174.

Grossman, Avraham. *Hakhmei Ashkenaz ha-rishonim: Korotehem, darkam be-hanhagat ha-tzibur, yetziratam ha-ruhanit me-reshit yishuvam ve-ad le-gezerot 1096 (The Early Sages of Ashkenaz).* Jerusalem: Magnes Press, 1981.

———. *Hakhmei Tzarefat harishonim: Korotehem, darkam be-hanhagat ha-tzibur, yetziratam ha-ruhanit (The Early Sages of France: Their Lives, Leadership, and Works).* Jerusalem: Magnes Press, 1995.

Guggenheim-Grünberg, Florence. "Die Juden in der Schweiz." *Beiträge zur Geschichte und Volkskunde der Juden in der Schweiz,* no. 7. Zürich: Verlag Jüdische Buch-Gemeinde, 1961.

Gumbert-Hepp, Marijke. *Computus Magistri Jacobi: Een schoolbook voor tijdrekenkunde uit 1436.* Hilversum, Neth.: Uitgeverij Verloren, 1987.

Gutmann, Joseph, ed. *No Graven Images: Studies in Art and the Hebrew Bible.* New York: Ktav, 1971.

Habermann, Abraham M. *Ha-madpisim bene Soncino.* Vienna: D. Frankel, 1933.

Hachlili, Rachel. "The Zodiac in Ancient Jewish Art: Representation and Significance." *Bulletin of the American Schools of Oriental Research* 228 (1977): 61–77.

Hacker, Yosef. "Qroniqot hadashot al gerush ha-yehudim mi-sefarad: Sibot ve-totza'ot." *Zion* 44 (1979): 201–228.

Halbertal, Moshe. *Beyn Torah le-hokhmah: Rabi Menahem ha-Me'iri u-va'ale ha-halakhah ha-Maimonim be-Provans.* Jerusalem: Magnes Press, 2000.

———. *Concealment and Revelation: Esotericism in Jewish Thought and Its Philosophical Implications.* Trans. Jackie Feldman. Princeton, N.J.: Princeton University Press, 2008.

———. *Seter ve-galui: Ha-sod u-segulotav ba-masoret ha-yehudit be-yemei ha-beinayim.* Jerusalem: Ornah Hess, 1999.

Halperin, Israel. *Pinqas va'ad arba aratzot: 1580–1792.* Jerusalem: Mossad Bialik, 1990.

Hamelburg, Meir ben Natan Yehoshua. *Quntres noten yeshua,* appended to Eliezer Belin Ashkenazi, ed. *Sefer evronot, tequfot u-moladot.* Offenbach, Ger.: Be-defus Bona Ventura de la noi, 1722.

Hasse, Ernst. *Geschichte der Leipzige Messe.* Leipzig, 1885; repr. Leipzig: Zentral-Antiquariat der Deutschen Demokratischen Republik, 1963.

Hayes, Christine. *Between the Babylonian and Palestinian Talmuds: Accounting for Halakhic*

Difference in Selected Sugyot from Tractate Avodah Zarah. New York: Oxford University Press, 1997.

Heck, Christian. *L'échelle céleste dans l'art du moyen âge: Une image de la quête du ciel*. Paris: Flammarion, 1997.

Helfand, Jessica. *Reinventing the Wheel: Volvelles, Equatoria, Planispheres, Fact-Finders, Gestational Charts . . .* New York: Princeton Architectural Press, 2002.

Heller, Marvin J. "Ambrosius Froben, Israel Zifroni, and Hebrew Printing in Freiburg am Breisgau." *Gutenberg-Jahrbuch* 80 (2005): 137–148. Repr. pp. 131–150 in *Studies in the Making of the Early Hebrew Book*. Leiden: Brill, 2008.

———. *Printing the Talmud: A History of the Individual Treatises Printed from 1700 to 1750*. Leiden: Brill, 1999.

———. *Studies in the Making of the Early Hebrew Book*. Leiden: Brill, 2008.

Hill, Brad Sabin. *Hebraica: Manuscripts and Early Printed Books in the Library of the Valmadonna Trust*. London: Valmadonna Trust Library, 1989.

Hindman, Sandra, ed. *Printing the Written Word: The Social History of Books, circa 1450–1520*. Ithaca, N.Y.: Cornell University Press, 1991.

Hirsch, Paul Wilhelm. *Sefer Megalleh tekuphot: Das ist Entdeckung derer Tekuphoth oder das schädliche Blut, welches über die Juden viermahl des Jahres kommet laut ihrer eigenen לוחות oder Calender*. Berlin: Johann Christoph Pape, 1717.

Hirschman, Marc. "Yearning for Intimacy: *Pesikta d'Rav Kahana* and the Temple." Pp. 135–146 in Deborah A. Green and Laura S. Lieber, eds., *The Shapes of Culture and the Religious Imagination: Essays in Honour of Michael Fishbane*. Oxford, Eng.: Oxford University Press, 2009.

Hoffman, Lawrence. *Covenant of Blood: Circumcision and Gender in Rabbinic Judaism*. Chicago: University of Chicago Press, 1996.

Horowitz, Elliott S. "Processions, Piety, and Jewish Ceremonies." Pp. 231–247 in Robert C. Davis and Benjamin Ravid, *The Jews of Early Modern Venice*. Baltimore: Johns Hopkins University Press, 2001.

———. "The Rite to be Reckless: On the Perpetration and Interpretation of Purim Violence." *Poetics Today* 15, no. 1 (1994): 9–54.

Hoskin, Michael. "The Reception of the Calendar by Other Churches." Pp. 255–264 in G. V. Coyne, M. A. Hoskin, and O. Pederson, eds. *Gregorian Reform of the Calendar: Proceedings of the Vatican Conference to Commemorate Its 400th Anniversary, 1582–1982*. Vatican City: Pontifica Academia Scientiarum, 1983.

Houtman, C. "What Did Jacob See in His Dream at Bethel? Some Remarks on Genesis XXVIII 10–22." *Vetus Testamentum* 27 (1977): 337–351.

Hsia, R. Po-Chia. *The Myth of Ritual Murder: Jews and Magic in Reformation Germany*. New Haven: Yale University Press, 1988.

———. *Trent, 1475: Stories of a Ritual Murder*. New Haven: Yale University Press, 1992.

Hüttenmeister, Frowald. "Die Genisot als Geschichtsquelle." Pp. 207–218 in *Jüdisches Leben auf dem Lande: Studien zur deutsch-jüdischen Geschichte*, ed. Monika Richarz und Reinhard Rürup. Tübingen: Mohr Siebeck, 1997.

Hüttenmeister, Frowald, and Heinrich Kohring, "Funde aus der Hechinger "Genisa." *Zeitschrift für Hohenzollerische Geschichte* 21 (1985): 215–234.

Hutton, Ronald. *The Rise and Fall of Merry England: The Ritual Year, 1400–1700*. Oxford, Eng.: Oxford University Press, 1994.

————. *Stations of the Sun: A History of the Ritual Year in Britain.* Oxford, Eng.: Oxford University Press, 1996.

Ibn Ezra, Abraham. "Iggeret ha-shabbat." In Nathan ben Shmuel ha-rofe, *Mivhar ha-ma'amarim,* ed. Avraham Barukh Piperno. Leghorn, Italy: M. Ottolenghi, 1830.

————. *Liber de Rationibus Tabularum.* Trans. and ed. José M. Millás Vallicrosa as *El Libro de los Fundamentos de las Tablas Astronómicas de R. Abraham ibn Ezra.* Madrid: Consejo Superior de Investigaciones Científicas, Instituto Arias Montano, 1947.

————. *Sefer ha-ibbur.* Ed. Sh. Z. H. Halberstam. Lyck, Poland: Meqize Nirdamim, 1874.

Ibn Yahia Gediliah. *Shalshelet ha-qabbalah.* Venice: Juan de Gara, 1587.

Idel, Moshe. "Ha-yovel be-mistiqa yehudit." In Yosef Kaplan, ed. *Shilhe me'ot: Qitsam shel 'idanim.* Jerusalem: Merkaz Shazar, 2005.

————. "The Secret of Impregnation as Metempsychosis in Kabbalah." *Verwandlungen: Archaeologie der literarischen Kommunikation* 9 (2006): 341–379.

Ilyas, Mohammad. "Lunar Crescent Visibility Criterion and Islamic Calendar." *Quarterly Journal of the Royal Astronomical Society* 35 (1994): 425–461.

Isherwood, Robert M. "Entertainment in the Parisian Fairs in the Eighteenth Century." *Journal of Modern History* 53 (1981): 24–48.

Israeli, Isaac. *Liber Jesod Olam,* ed. B. Goldberg and L. Rosenkrantz, 2 vols. Berlin: Berolini, 1846–1848.

Isserlein, Israel. *Sefer terumat ha-deshen.* Venice: Daniel Bomberg, 1519.

Jaffe, Zvi Hirsch. *Qorot heshbon ha-'ibbur.* Jerusalem: Darom, 1931.

Jahn, G. A. *Tafeln zur gegenseitigen Verwandlung jüdischer und christlicher Zeitangabe vom Jahre 4118 (358) bis 5810 (2050).* Leipzig: N.p., 1856.

Jardine, Lisa. *Erasmus, Man of Letters: The Construction of Charisma in Print.* Princeton, N.J.: Princeton University Press, 1993.

Jaritz, Gerhard, and Verena Winiwarter. "On the Perception of Nature in a Renaissance Society." Pp. 91–111 in Mikuláš Teich, Roy Porter, and Bo Gustafsson, eds., *Nature and Society in Historical Context.* New York: Cambridge University Press, 1997.

Jarnut, Jörg. "Die Anfänge des europäischen Messewesens." Pp. 1–12 in *Brücke zwischen den Völkern—Zur Geschichte der Frankfurter Messe,* vol. 1, ed. Rainer Koch. 3 vols. Frankfurt am Main: Dezernat für Kultur und Freizeit, 1991.

Jewish Theological Seminary. *Precious Possessions: Treasures from the Library of the Jewish Theological Seminary.* Exhibition, May 14, 2001–Aug. 20, 2001.

Johns, Adrian. *The Nature of the Book: Print and Knowledge in the Making.* Chicago: University of Chicago Press, 1998.

Jones, Charles W. "An Early Medieval Licensing Examination." *History of Education Quarterly* 3 (1963): 19–29.

————. "A Legend of St Pachomius." *Speculum* 18 (1943): 198–210.

————. "The 'Lost' Sirmond Manuscript of Bede's Computus." *English Historical Review* 52 (1937): 204–219.

Jonge, Marinus de, and Johannes Tromp. *The Life of Adam and Eve and Related Literature.* Sheffield, Eng.: Academic Press, 1997.

Jüdische Handschriften: Jüdische Kultur im Spiegel der Berliner Sammlung. Berlin: Staatsbibliothek zu Berlin-Preussischen Kulturbesitz, 2002.

Kanarfogel, Ephraim. "Halakha and *Metziut* (Realia) in Medieval Ashkenaz: Surveying the Parameters and Defining the Limits." *Jewish Law Annual* 14 (2003): 193–224.

Kasher, Menachem M. *Humash torah shelemah*, vol. 13. New York: N.p., 1954.

Katz, Jacob. *Exclusiveness and Tolerance: Studies in Jewish-Gentile Relations in Medieval and Modern Times*. London: Oxford University Press, 1961.

———. "Mahloqet ha-semikhah bein R. Ya'akov Berav ve-ha-Ralbakh." In *Halakha ve-qabbalah*. Jerusalem: Magnes Press, 1986. (In English: "The Dispute between Jacob Berab and Levi ben Habib over Renewing Ordination," trans. Roberta Bell-Kliger, *Binah*, 1:119–141.)

Kaufhold, Karl Heinrich. "Messen und Wirtschaftsausstellungen von 1650 bis 1914." Pp. 239–294 in Peter Johanek and Heinz Stoob, eds., *Europäische messen und Märktesysteme in mittelalter und Neuzeit*. Cologne: Böhlau Verlag, 1996.

Kay, Richard. "Unwintering January (Dante, *Paradiso*, 27.142–143)." *MLN* 118 (2003): 237–244.

Kirchner, Paul Christian. *Juedisches Ceremoniel oder Beschreibung derjenigen Gebräuche*. Nuremberg: P. C. Monath, 1734.

Klein, Avraham Yehudah. "Ha-sakanah lishtot mayim be-she'at ha-tequfah ve-ha-segullah lehishamer memenah be-sifrut ha-halakha." Pp. 86–100 in *Jubilee Volume in Honor of Professor B. Heller*, ed. Alexander Scheiber. Budapest: N.p., 1941.

Kogman-Appel, Katrin. "Sephardic Picture Cycles and the Rabbinic Tradition: Continuity and Innovation in Jewish Iconography." *Zeitschrift für Kunstgeschichte* 60, no. 4(1997): 451–481.

Kornick, Meyer Moses. *Davar be-itto*. Breslau, Ger.: Leib Sulzbach, 1817.

Krakowski, Eve. "On the Literary Character of Abraham ibn Daud's Sefer ha-qabbalah." *European Journal of Jewish Studies* 1, no. 1 (2007): 219–247.

Krünitz, Johann Georg. *Oekonomisch=technologische Encyclopädie*, 2d ed. Berlin: Joachim Pauli, 1793. Vol. 32, 443–604 (s.v. "Kalender"). Vol. 28, 611 (s.v. "tekupha").

Landman, Leo. "Jewish Attitudes towards Gambling, II" *Jewish Quarterly Review* 58 (1967): 34–62.

Langermann, Y. Tzvi. "Eimatai nosad ha-luah ha-ivri?" *Asufot* 1 (1987): 159–168.

———. *The Jews and the Sciences in the Middle Ages*. Aldershot, Eng.: Ashgate, 1999.

———. "'Sefer huqot shamayim' le-Rabi Yehudah ben Asher." Pp. 91–92 in Avraham David, ed., *Mi-ginzei ha-makhon le-tatzlumei kitvei yad ha-ivri'im*. Jerusalem: Jewish National and University Library, 1995.

Lasker, Arnold A., and Daniel J. Lasker. "Behold, a Moon Is Born! How the Jewish Calendar Works." *Conservative Judaism* 41, no. 4 (1989): 5–19.

———. "Tav-resh-mem-bet halaqim: Od al mahloqet Rav Sa'adiah Gaon u-ven Meir." *Tarbits* 60 (1991): 119–128.

Leberecht, Phillip Nicodemus. *Machmath Hatekuphoth, Das ist: Von denen so genannten vier Bluts-Tropffen, welche Jährlichen viermahl zu einem gewissen Zeichen und ewigen Denckmahle unter denen Juden vom Himmel hernieder fallen sollen, so aber in diesen wenigen Bogen aus Göttl. Heil. Schrifft und aus ihren eigenen Schrifften wiederleget wird*. Leipzig: Heinrich Christoph Takken, 1728.

Le Goff, Jacques. "Merchant's Time and Church's Time in the Middle Ages." Pp. 29–42 in *Time, Work and Culture in the Middle Ages*, trans. Arthur Goldhammer. Chicago: Chicago University Press, 1980.

Leiman, S. Z. "The Scroll of Fasts: The Ninth of Tebeth." *Jewish Quarterly Review* 74, no. 2 (1983): 174–195.

Lerner, Franz. "Messe und Klerus. Zum kirchlichen und marktwirtschaftlichen Geflecht eines Begriffes." Pp. 33–37 in *Brücke zwischen den Völkern—Zur Geschichte der Frankfurter Messe*, vol. 2, ed. Rainer Koch. 3 vols. Frankfurt am Main: N.p., 1991.

Levey, Martin. "The Encyclopedia of Abraham Savasorda: A Departure in Mathematical Methodology." *Isis* 43 (1952): 257–264.

Levine, Lee. "Figural Art in Ancient Judaism." *Ars Judaica* 1 (2005): 9–26.

Levita, Elia. *Tishby*. Isny, Ger.: Paul Fagius, 1541.

Lieberman, Yosef. "Be-inyan lel hagam ha-niqra 'Nittel.'" *Moriah* 14 (1986): 131–141.

Litt, Stefan. "Pinkassei Kahal aschkenasischer Gemeinden, 1500–1800: Eine Gesamtsicht." *Simon Dubnow Institut Jahrbuch* 6 (2007): 511–538.

Mahler, Raphael. *Hasidism and the Jewish Enlightenment: Their Confrontation in Galicia and Poland in the First Half of the Nineteenth Century*. Trans. from Yiddish by Eugene Orenstein, trans. from Hebrew by Aaron Klein and Jenny Machlowitz Klein. Philadelphia: Jewish Publication Society, 1985.

Maimonides, Moses. "Sanctification of the New Moon." Trans. from the Hebrew by Solomon Gandz; supplementation and intro. by Julian Obermann; astronomical commentary. In Yale Judaica series, vol. 11: *The Code of Maimonides*, book 3, treatise 8. New Haven: Yale University Press, 1956.

Malkiel, David. "Jewish-Christian Relations in Europe, 840–1096." *Journal of Medieval History* 29 (2003): 55–83.

Mann, Vivian. *Jewish Texts on the Visual Arts*. Cambridge, Eng.: Cambridge University Press, 2000.

Marcus, Ivan G. *Rituals of Childhood: Jewish Acculturation in Medieval Europe*. New Haven, Yale University Press, 1996.

Marcus, Jacob R., ed. *The Concise Dictionary of American Jewish Biography*. 2 vols. Brooklyn, N.Y.: Carlson Publishing, 1994.

———. *The Jew in the Medieval World: A Source Book, 315–1791*. New York: Hebrew Union College Press, 1938; revised ed. 1999.

Marwedel, Günter. *Die Privilegien der Juden in Altona*. Hamburg: Hans Christian Verlag, 1976.

Masekhet Sofrim. Ed. Michael Higger. New York: Hotsa'at de-ve-rabanan, 1937.

Matt, Daniel C. *The Zohar: Pritzker edition*, vol. 1. Stanford, Calif.: Stanford University Press, 2004.

McKitterick, David. *Print, Manuscript, and the Search for Order*. Cambridge, Eng.: Cambridge University Press, 2003.

Meisel, Josef. "Der Berliner Judenkalender und die Kalendergelder." *Monatsschrift für Geschichte und Wissenschaft des Judentums* 71 [n.s. 35] (1927): 274–288.

Meldola, David ben Refael. *Sefer mo'ed David: Kollel kol inyene ha-mahzor ve-ha-moladot ibbur shanim u-tequfotehem im luhotehem*, 2d ed. Amsterdam: Be-vet u-be-defus Avraham ben Refael Atias, 1739–1740.

Mellinkoff, Ruth. *Outcasts: Signs of Otherness in Northern European Art of the Late Middle Ages*. Berkeley: University of California Press, 1993.

Mentgen, Gerd. "Der Würfelzoll und andere Antijüdische Schikanen in Mittelalter und Früher Nuezeit." *Zeitschrift für Historische Forschung* 22 (1995): 1–48.

Merhavia, Chen. *Ha-talmud be-re'i ha-natzrut: Ha-yahas le-sifrut Yisra'el shele-ahar ha-miqra ba-olam ha-notzri bi-yeme-ha-benayim (500–1248)*. Jerusalem: Mossad Bialik, 1970.

Milikowsky, Chaim. "Further on Editing Rabbinic Texts." *Jewish Quarterly Review* 90 (1990): 137–149.

———. "*Seder 'Olam* and Jewish Chronography in the Hellenistic and Roman Periods." *Proceedings of the American Academy for Jewish Research* 52 (1985): 115–139.

Miller, Peter N. "The Mechanics of Christian-Jewish Intellectual Collaboration in Seventeenth-Century Provence." Pp. 71–101 in Allison P. Coudert and Jeffrey Shoulson, eds., *Hebraica Veritas? Christian Hebraists and the Study of Judaism in Early Modern Europe.* Philadelphia: University of Pennsylvania Press, 2004.

Minhagim. Amsterdam: N.p., 1662.

Minhogim oyf teitsch. Frankfurt am Main: Leyzer Flohrsheim, 1706–1707.

Mishael, Israel. *Beyn Afganistan le-Erets-Yisrael.* Jerusalem: Va'ad adat hasefaradim, 1981.

Moellin, Jacob. *Sefer Maharil, Minhagim.* Ed. Shlomo Spitzer. Jerusalem: Makhon Yerushalayim, 1989.

Morgenstern, Arie. *Hastening Redemption: Messianism and the Resettlement of the Land of Israel.* Trans. Joel Linsider. Oxford, Eng.: Oxford University Press, 2006.

Mosshammer, Alden. *The "Chronicle" of Eusebius and Greek Chronographic Tradition.* Lewisburg, Pa.: Bucknell University Press, 1979.

Muir, Edward. *Ritual in Early Modern Europe.* Cambridge, Eng.: Cambridge University Press, 1997.

Münster, Sebastian. *Kalendarium Hebraicum. Opera Sebastiani Munsteri ex Hebraeorum penetralibus iam recés in lucem aeditum: Quod nó tam Hebraice studiosis quam Historiographis & Astronomiae peritis subservire poterit.* Basel: Froben, 1527. (Additional Hebrew title: *Hokhmat ha-mazalot ba-tequfot, u-me'ubarot, ve-ha-qeviot.*)

Murdoch, Brian, and J. A. Tasioulas, eds. *The Apocryphal Lives of Adam and Eve: Edited from the Auchinleck Manuscript and from Trinity College, Oxford, Ms. 57.* Exeter, Eng.: University of Exeter Press, 2002.

Narkiss, Bezalel. *Hebrew Illuminated Manuscripts.* Jerusalem: Keter Publishing House, 1969.

Neugebauer, Otto. "Astronomical Commentary to Maimonides." Yale Judaica series, vol. 11: *The Code of Maimonides, Book 3, Treatise 8.* New Haven: Yale University Press, 1956.

Neugebauer-Wolk, Monika. "Der Bauernkalendar des Jacobiners Friedrich Christoph Cotta: Realität und Idylle der mainzer Republik." *Jahrbuch des Instituts für deutsche Geschichte* 14 (1985): 75–111.

Nieto, David. *Ha-Kuzari ha-sheni, hu Matteh Dan.* Ed. Y. L. Ha-kohen Maimon. Jerusalem: Mossad Ha-rav Kook, 1958.

———. *Matteh Dan ve-kuzari heleq sheni.* London: T. Ilive, 1714.

———. *Pascalogia o vero discorso della pasca.* Cologne: N.p., 1702.

Nigri, Jacobus. *Kalendarium Jacobi Nigri ex Campidonio artium magistri cum u[v]anæ Iudæorŭ expectationis refutatione, & ad bellŭ in omne genus infideliŭ gerendŭ exhortatione annexa.* Vienna: Hieronymus Vietor, 1529.

Nirenberg, David. *Communities of Violence: Persecution of Minorities in the Middle Ages.* Princeton, N.J.: Princeton University Press, 1996.

Nischan, Bodo. "Demarcating Boundaries: Lutheran Pericopic Sermons in the Age of Confessionalization." *Archiv für Reformationsgeschichte* 88 (1997): 199–216.

Noam, Vered. *Megillat Ta'anit: Hanusahim-pesharam-toldoteihem.* Jerusalem: Yad Yitzhak ben Zvi, 2003.

Nördlingen, Yuzpa Hahn. *Yosif omets.* Frankfurt am Main: N.p., 1723.

Nordström, Carl-Otto. "The Temple Miniatures in the Peter Comestor Manuscript at Madrid." Pp. 39–81 in Joseph Gutmann, ed., *No Graven Images: Studies in Art and the Hebrew Bible.* New York: Ktav, 1971.

North, J. D. "The Western Calendar—'Intolerabilis, Horribilis, et Derisibilis'; Four Centuries of Discontent." Pp. 75–113 in G. V. Coyne, M. A. Hoskin, and O. Pederson, eds., *Gregorian Reform of the Calendar: Proceedings of the Vatican Conference to Commemorate Its 400th Anniversary, 1582–1982.* Vatican City: Pontifica Academia Scientiarum, 1983.

Obermann, Julian. "Supplementation and Introduction" to Moses Maimonides, "Sanctification of the New Moon," in Yale Judaica series, vol. 11: *The Code of Maimonides, Book 3, Treatise 8.* New Haven: Yale University Press, 1956.

Obrist, Barbara. "Les vents dans l' *Astronomie de Nemrot.*" *Astronomie et sciences humaines* 6 (1994): 57–76.

Offenberg, Adri. K. *Hebrew Incunabula in Public Collections.* Nieuwkoop, Neth.: De Graaf, 1990.

Official, Joseph b. Nathan. *Sefer Yosef ha-meqaneh.* Ed. Judah Rosenthal. Jerusalem: Mekitze nirdamim, 1970.

Oliveyra, Solomon de. *Miqra'ei qodesh.* Amsterdam, 1666. New York, Columbia University ms X893 Ab71., printed book with ms notes.

Padua, Meir. *Sefer she'elot u-teshuvot Mahari Mintz u-Maharam Padovah.* Jerusalem: N.p., 1964.

Parry, Albert. "The Soviet Calendar." *Journal of Calendar Reform* 10 (1940): 65–69.

Pearsall, Derek, and Elizabeth Salter. *Landscapes and Seasons of the Medieval World.* Toronto: University of Toronto Press, 1973.

Pederson, Olaf. "The Ecclesiastical Calendar and the Life of the Church." Pp. 17–74 in G. V. Coyne, M. A. Hoskin, and O. Pederson, eds. *Gregorian Reform of the Calendar: Proceedings of the Vatican Conference to Commemorate Its 400th Anniversary, 1582–1982.* Vatican City: Pontifica Academia Scientiarum, 1983.

Perl, Joseph. *Tzir Ne'eman.* Tarnopol: N.p., 1813–1815.

Peterson, Niels. "Hof-og Statskalenderen" [Royal and State calendars], *Arkiv* 2 (1968): 39–61.

Pirqe de Rabbi Eliezer. Ed. Dagmar Börner-Klein, based on the Venice and Warsaw 1852 eds. with German trans. Berlin: De Gruyter, 2004.

———. English trans. Gerald Friedlander. London, 1916; repr. New York: Hermon Press, 1965.

———. Facsimile copy of notes made by C. M. Horowitz (Jerusalem: Makor, 1972), based on the 1544 Venice edition.

Poole, Robert. *Time's Alteration: Calendar Reform in Early Modern England.* London: UCL Press, 1998.

Poseq, Avigdor Poseq, "Toward a Semiotic Approach to Jewish Art." *Ars Judaica* 1 (2005): 27–50.

Prescott, Anne Lake. "Refusing Translation: The Gregorian Calendar and Early Modern English Writers." *Yearbook of English Studies* 36 (2006): 1–11.

Qirqisani, Yaqub al-. *Yaqub al-Qirqisani on Jewish Sects and Christianity.* Trans. and introduction by Bruno Chiesa and Wilfrid Lockwood. Frankfurt: Verlag Peter Lang, 1984.

Quad, Mattias. *Die Jahr Blum.* Cologne: Verlag Johann Bussemechers, 1595.

Randall, Lillian M. C. *Images in the Margins of Gothic Manuscripts.* Berkeley: University of California Press, 1966.

Raz-Krakotzkin, Amnon. *The Censor, the Editor, and the Text: The Catholic Church and the Shaping of the Jewish Canon in the Sixteenth Century.* Trans. Jackie Feldman. Philadelphia: University of Pennsylvania Press, 2007.

Reeves, Eileen. *Painting the Heavens: Art and Science in the Age of Galileo.* Princeton, N.J.: Princeton University Press, 1997.

Reiner, Elchanan. "Aliyat 'ha-quehilla ha-gedola' al shorshei ha-kehilla ha-yehudit ha-ironit be-folin be-et ha-hadasha ha-muqdemet." *Gal-Ed* 20 (2005): 13–37.

———. "A Biography of an Agent of Culture: Eleazar Altschul of Prague and His Literary Activity." Pp. 229–247 in Michael Graetz, ed., *Schöpferische Momente des europäischen Judentums in der frühen Neuzeit.* Heidelberg: Universitätsverlag C. Winter, 2000.

Reingold, Edward M., Nachum Dershowitz, and Stewart M. Clamen. "Calendrical Calculations, II: Three Historical Calendars." *Software—Practice and Experience* 23 (1993): 383–404.

Reinhold, Josef. *Polen/Litauen auf den Leipziger messen des 18. Jahrhunderts.* Weimar: Verlag Hermann Böhlaus Nachfolger, 1971.

Reinitzer, Heimo. *Biblia Deutsch: Luthers Bibelübersetzung und ihre Tradition.* Wolfenbüttel, Ger.: Herzog August Bibliothek, 1983.

Resnick, Irven. "Medieval Roots of the Myth of Jewish Male Menses." *Harvard Theological Review* 93 (2000): 241–263.

Rich, Vera. "The Brest Union and Calendar Reform." *Ukrainian Review* [Great Britain] 43 (1996): 46–61.

Riehl, Wilhem Heinrich. "Volkskalender im achtzehnten Jahrhundert." In *Kulturstudien aus drei Jahrhunderten.* Stuttgart: N.p., 1910.

Rivkind, Yizhak. "Luah Qushta bilti noda, mi-shenat 1510 al esrim shana." *'Alim le-bibliografiya ve-qorot Yisrael* (ed. David Fraenkel) 2 (1935): 16–20.

Robbins, Ellen. "Studies in the Pre-History of the Jewish Calendar." Ph.D. diss., New York University, 1989.

Rohner, Ludwig. *Kalendergeschichte und Kalender.* Wiesbaden: Akademische Verlagsgesellschaft Athenaion, 1978.

Rohrbacher, Stefan. "Medinat Schwaben: Jüdisches Leben in einer süddeutschen Landschaft in der Frühneuzeit." In Rolf Kiessling and Sabine Ullman, eds., *Judengemeinden in Schwaben im Kontext des Alten Reiches.* Berlin: Akademie Verlag, 1999.

Rose, Emily C. *Portraits of Our Past: Jews of the German Countryside.* Philadelphia: Jewish Publication Society, 2001.

Rosenbloom, Joseph R. *A Biographical Dictionary of Early American Jews.* Lexington: University of Kentucky Press, 1960.

Rosenfeld, Mosche N. "Ein jüdischer Wandkalender für das Jahr 5386 (1625–1626)." *Nachrichten für den jüdischen Bürger Fürths, Israelitische Kultusgemeinde Fürth* (September 1990): 31–32.

———. "Fürther jüdischer Kalender: Teil 1: Taschenkalender." *Nachrichten für den jüdischen Bürger Fürths, Israelitische Kultusgemeinde Fürth* (September 1989): 26–36.

———. "Fürther jüdischer Kalender: Teil 2: Wandkalender." *Nachrichten für den jüdischen Bürger Fürths, Israelitische Kultusgemeinde Fürth* (September 1990): 26–30.

———. *Jewish Printing in Wilhermsdorf: A Concise Bibliography of Hebrew and Yiddish Pub-*

lications, *Printed in Wilhermsdorf between 1670 and 1739, Showing Aspects of Jewish life in Mittelfranken Three Centuries Ago Based on Public and Private Collections and Genizah Discoveries.* London: M. N. Rosenfeld, 1995.

———. "Zebi Hirsch ben Chaim aus Fürth—Autor und Buchdrucker; ein Beitrag zum 300jährigen Fürther jüdischen Buchdruck." *Israelitische Kultusgemeinde Fürth: Nachrichten* (September 1991): 34–40.

Roth, Cecil. "The Eastertide Stoning of the Jews and Its Liturgical Echoes." *Jewish Quarterly Review* 35 (1945): 361–370.

———. *Essays and Portraits in Anglo-Jewish History.* Philadelphia: Jewish Publication Society, 1962.

———. "A Masterpiece of Medieval Spanish Jewish Art: The Kennicott Bible." In Joseph Gutmann, ed., *No Graven Images: Studies in Art and the Hebrew Bible.* New York: Ktav, 1971.

Rubin, Miri. *Corpus Christi: The Eucharist in Late Medieval Culture.* Cambridge, Eng.: Cambridge University Press, 1991.

———. *Gentile Tales: The Narrative Assault on Late Medieval Jews.* New Haven: Yale University Press, 1999.

Russell, Francis, et al., eds. *The World of Dürer, 1471–1528.* New York: Time, 1967.

Rustow, Marina. *Heresy and the Politics of Community: The Jews of the Fatimid Caliphate.* Ithaca, N.Y.: Cornell University Press, 2008.

Saliba, George. *A History of Arabic Astronomy: Planetary Theories during the Golden Age of Islam.* New York: NYU Press, 1994.

Saperstein, Marc. *Jewish Preaching, 1200–1800: An Anthology.* New Haven: Yale University Press, 1989.

Sarfatti, Gad B. "An Introduction to Baraitha de-mazzalot." (Hebrew). *Shenaton Bar Ilan* 3 (1965): 56–82.

Sargent, Steven. "Religion and Society in Late Medieval Bavaria: The Cult of Saint Leonard, 1258–1500." Ph.D. diss., University of Pennsylvania, 1982.

Sarna, Jonathan. "An Eighteenth Century Hebrew Lu'ah from Pennsylvania." *American Jewish Archives Journal* 57 (2005): 25–27.

Scholem, Gershom. *Sabbatai Sevi: The Mystical Messiah, 1626–1676.* Trans. R. J. Twi Werblowsky. Princeton, N.J.: Princeton University Press, 1973.

Schorsch, Ismar. "History as Consolation." *Leo Baeck Institute Year Book* 37 (1992): 33–43. Repr. in his *From Text to Context: The Turn to History in Modern Judaism,* 334–344. Hanover, N.H.: Brandeis University Press, 1994.

Schwartz, Eduard. *Christliche und jüdische Ostertafeln.* Berlin: Weidmannsche buchhandlung, 1905.

Seder olam zuta. Pp. 68–73 in Adolph Neubauer, ed., *Medieval Jewish Chronicles,* vol. 2. Oxford, Eng.: Clarendon Press, 1887–1895.

Seethaler, Josef. "Das Wiener Kalenderwesen des 15. Bis 17. Jahrhunderts." *Jahrbuch des Vereins für Geschichte der Stadt Wien* 41 (1985): 62–112.

Sefer evronot printed editions:
1. Riva di Trento, 1561. Ed. Jacob Marcaria.
2. Lublin, 1615. Ed. Eliezer Belin.
3. Lublin, 1640. Bodleian: Opp. 4° 1387 [1]. I have only been able to examine a microfilm copy of the title page of this volume.

    4. Frankfurt an der Oder, 1691. Johann Christoph Beckmann.

    5. Offenbach, 1722. Be-defus Bona Ventura de la noi.

    6. Zolkiew, 1756.

    7. Zolkiew, 1770.

    8. *Sefer ha-evronot.* Zolkiew, 1805.

Sefer hasidim. Ed. R. Margaliot. Jerusalem: Mosad ha-Rav Kuk, 1957.

Sefer hemdah genuzah, ve-hu teshuvot ha-geonim. Eds. Zev Wolfenson and Shlomo Zalman Schneurson. Jerusalem: N.p., 1966.

Sela, Shlomo. "Abraham bar Hiyya's Astrological Work and Thought." *Jewish Studies Quarterly* 13 (2006): 128–158.

———. *Abraham ibn Ezra and the Rise of Medieval Hebrew Science.* Leiden: Brill, 2003.

Selden, John. *De anno civili et calendario veteris ecclesiæ seu Reipublicæ judaicæ, dissertatio.* London: Richardus Bishopius, 1644.

Sellner, Albert Christian. *Immer-währender Heiligen Kalender.* Frankfurt am Main: Eichborn Verlag, 1993.

Shapiro, Marc. "Torah Study on Christmas Eve." *Journal of Jewish Thought and Philosophy* 8 (1999): 319–353.

Shatzmiller, Joseph. "Provençal Chronography in the Lost Pamphlet by Shemtov Schanzolo." (Hebrew). *Proceedings of the American Academy for Jewish Research* 52 (1985): 43–61.

Shaw, Matthew. "Reactions to the French Republican Calendar." *French History* 15 (2001): 4–25.

Sherman, Claire, and Peter M. Lukehart, eds. *Writing on Hands: Memory and Knowledge in Early Modern Europe.* Carlisle, Pa: Folger Library/Trout Gallery, 2000.

Shkalim, Esther, Diana Schiowitz, Frieda R. F. Horwitz. *A Mosaic of Israel's Traditions: Holidays, Feasts, Fasts.* Trans. Chuck Becher. Jerusalem: Devora, 2006.

Shmeruk, Chone. *Ha-qeri'a le-navi: Mehqare historiyah ve-sifrut.* Ed. Israel Bartal. Jerusalem: Merkaz Zalman Shazar le-toldot Yisrael, 1999.

Shoemaker, Stephen J. "'Let Us Go and Burn Her Body': The Image of Jews in the Early Dormition Traditions." *Church History* 68 (1999): 775–823.

Sibony, Moïse. "Le calendrier juif et ses problêmes." *Revue des études juives* 136 (1977): 139–154.

Sidersky, D. "L'Origine de l'ère juive de la crèation du monde." *Journal Asiatique* 227 (1935): 325–329.

Siegmund, Stefanie B. *The Medici State and the Ghetto of Florence: The Construction of an Early Modern Jewish Community.* Stanford, Calif.: Stanford University Press, 2006.

Silver, Abba Hillel. *A History of Messianic Speculation in Israel, from the First through the Seventeenth Centuries.* New York: Macmillan, 1927.

Simonsen, David. "Freud und Leid. Locale Fest- und Fasttage im Anschluss an Zunzens Fastentabelle." *MGWJ* n.s. 2 (1894): 524–527.

Sirkes, Joel. *Bayit hadash.* (Commentary to *Arba' ah turim* of Jacob ben Asher.) Königsberg: Gruber and Longrien, 1860–1866.

Smith, Alison Moore. "The Iconography of the Sacrifice of Isaac in Early Christian Art." *American Journal of Archaeology* 26, 2 (1922): 159–173.

Soergel, Phillip M. *Wondrous in His Saints: Counter Reformation Propaganda in Bavaria.* Berkeley: University of California Press, 1993.

Solomon, Yehezqel. "'Nittel' ba-meqorot." *Or Yisrael* 2 (Kislev 1996): 133–135.

Soloveitchik, Haym. "Halakhah, Hermeneutics, and Martyrdom in Medieval Ashkenaz, II." *Jewish Quarterly Review* 94 (2004): 278–299.

———. *Ha-yayin be-yeme ha-benayim. Yeyn nesekh: Pereq be-toldot ha-halakha be-Ashkenaz.* Jerusalem: Mercaz Shazar, 2008.

———. *Yenam: Sahar be-yenam shel goyim, 'al gilgulah shel halakhah be-'olam ha-ma'aseh.* Tel Aviv: Am Oved, 2003. (In English: *The Jewish Wine Trade and the Origins of Jewish Moneylending,* forthcoming, Portland: Littman Library.)

Sommer, H. Oskar, ed. *The Kalender of Shepherdes: The Edition of Paris 1503 in Photographic Facsimile a Faithful Reprint of R. Pynson's Edition of London 1506.* London: Kegan Paul, Trench, Trübner & Co., 1892.

Sperber, Daniel. *Minhage Yisrael: Meqorot ve-toladot,* vol. 1. Jerusalem: Mosad ha-Rav Kuk, 1989.

Spiegel, Shalom. *Avot ha-piyut: Meqorot u-mehqarim le-toldot ha-piyut be-eretz Yisrael.* Ed. Menahem Hayyim Schmelzer. New York: Bet ha-midrash le-rabbanim be-Amerikah, 1996.

———. "Perur me-aggadot ha-aqeda." Pp. 553–566 in *Abraham Weiss Jubilee Volume.* New York: N.p., 1964.

Spiegel, Yaakov. *Amudim be-toledot ha-sefer ha-ivri.* 2 vols. Ramat Gan: Bar Ilan University Press, 2005.

Steinschneider, Moritz. "Hebräische Drucke in Deutschland: Berlin 1733–1762." *Zeitschrift für die Geschichte der Juden in Deutschland* 3, no. 2 (1889): 262–274; 5, no. 2 (1892): 185–186.

———. "Purim und Parodie." *Israelitische Letterbode* 7:1–13; 9:45–58; *Monatsschrift für Geschichte und Wissenschaft des Judentums* 46 (1902): 275–280, 372–376, 473–478, 567–582; 47 (1903): 84–89, 169–180, 279–286, 360–370, 468–474; 48 (1904): 242–247, 504–509.

Stern, David, Sarit Shalev-Eyni, and Christoph Markschies, eds. *The Tegernsee Haggadah.* Prologue trans. Erik Koenke. University Park: Penn State University Press, forthcoming.

Stern, Sacha. *Calendar and Community: A History of the Jewish Calendar, Second Century BCE–Tenth Century CE.* Oxford, Eng.: Oxford University Press, 2001.

———. "Fictitious Calendars: Early Rabbinic Notions of Time, Astronomy, and Reality." *Jewish Quarterly Review* 87 (1996): 103–129.

Stevens, Wesley. *Cycles of Time and Scientific Learning in Medieval Europe.* Hampshire, Eng.: Aldershot; Brookfield, Vt.: Variorum, 1995.

Stirrup, Thomas. *Horometria; or, The Compleat Diallist Wherein the Whole Mystery of the Art of Dialling Is Plainly Taught Several Ways. . . .* London: R. & W. Leybourn for Thomas Pierrepont, 1659.

Stone, Michael. *A History of the Literature of Adam and Eve.* Atlanta: Scholars Press, 1992.

Stowe, Kenneth. *Theater of Acculturation: The Roman Ghetto in the Sixteenth Century.* Seattle: University of Washington Press, 2001.

Straus, Joshua P. "Calculating Celestial Cycles, Courses and Conjunctions: An Introduction to Sifrei Evronot (Books of Intercalations)." Senior project, Program in Asian and Near Eastern Languages and Literatures, Washington University in St. Louis, 2006.

Sukenik. E. L. "Matzevot yehudiot me-Zo'ar." *Kedem: Studies in Jewish Archaeology* 2 (1945): 83–88.

Susan, Issachar ben Mordechai ibn. *Sefer ibbur shanim u-tequfot.* (2d ed. of *Tiqqun Issachar.*)
Venice: Giovanni di Gara, 1578–1579.

———. *Tiqqun Issachar.* Constantinople [Salonika?]: N.p., 1564.

Süß, Hermann. "Zur literaturgeschichtlichen Bedeutung der Veitshöchheimer Genisa."
Pp. 78–83 in Ulrich Wagner, ed., *Zeugnisse jüdischer Geschichte in Unterfranken.* Würzburg: Ferdinand Schöningh, 1987.

Süß, Hermann, and Heike Tröger. *Die Judaica und Hebraica der Sammlung Tychsen und der Universitätsbibliothek Rostock.* Erlangen: Harald Fischer Verlag, 2002. CD-ROM.

Talmage, Frank, ed. *Sefer ha-nizzahon of Yom Tov Lipman Muelhausen.* Altdorf-Nuremberg:
N.p., 1644. Photo offset ed. Jerusalem: Merkaz Dinur, 1984.

Ta-Shma, Israel Meir. *Halakha, minhag, u-metzi'ut be-Ashkenaz, 1000–1350.* Jerusalem:
Magnes Press, 1996.

———. "Issur shtiyat mayim ba-tequfah u-meqoro." *Mehqerei Yerushalayim be-Folklor Ye-hudi* 17 (1995): 21–32.

———. "The 'Open' Book in Medieval Hebrew Literature: The Problem of Authorized Editions." *Bulletin of the John Rylands University Library of Manchester* 75 (1993):
5–16.

Teshuvot ha-geonim. Ed. Jacob Mussafia. Lyck, Poland: Siebert, 1864. Photo-offset ed. Jerusalem: N.p., 1967.

Teshuvot ha-geonim sha'are teshuva. Ed. Ze'ev Leiter. Pittsburgh: Makhon ha-Rambam,
1946.

Thiele, Edwin. *The Mysterious Numbers of the Hebrew Kings: A Reconstruction of the Chronology of the Kingdoms of Israel and Judah.* Grand Rapids, Wis.: W. B. Eerdmans, 1965.

Thomas, Jack. *Le temps des foires: Foires et marchés dans le Midi toulousain de la fin de l'Ancien Régime.* Toulouse: Presses universitaires du Mirail, 1993.

Thomas, Marcel, Avril François, and Wilhelm Schlag, eds. *The Hunting Book of Gaston Phébus: Manuscrit Français 616, Paris, Bibliothèque Nationale.* London: Harvey Miller,
1998.

Thorndike, Lynn. "Computus." *Speculum* 29 (1954): 223–238.

———. *The Sphere of Sacrobosco and Its Commentators.* Chicago: University of Chicago Press, 1949.

Thurston, Herbert. "Easter Controversy." *Catholic Encyclopedia Online.* http://www.newadvent.org/cathen/05228a.htm (last accessed September 14, 2010).

Timm, Erika. "Die 'Fabel vom alten Löwen' in jiddistischer und komparatistischen Sicht."
Zeitschrift für deutsche Philologie 100 (1981): 109–169.

Timm, Erika, with Hermann Süß. *Yiddish Literature in a Franconian Genizah: A Contribution to the Printing and Social History of the Seventeenth and Eighteenth Centuries.* Jerusalem: Akademon Press, 1988.

Tishby, Isaiah. "The Controversy over the Zohar in Sixteenth-Century Italy." (Hebrew).
Peraqim (1967–1968): 131–182.

Toch, Michael. "Geld und Kredit in einer spätmittelalterlichen Landschaft." *Deutsches Archiv für Erforschung des Mittelalters* 38 (1982): 499–550.

Trachtenberg, Joshua. *Jewish Magic and Superstition: A Study in Folk Religion.* New York:
Atheneum, 1977.

Turniansky, Chava. "The Events in Frankfurt am Main (1612–1616) in "Megillas Vints" and in an Unknown Yiddish 'Historical' Song." Pp. 121–137 in *Schöpferische Momente des*

europäischen Judentums in der frühen Neuzeit, ed. Michael Graetz. Heidelberg: Universitätsverlag C. Winter, 2000.

Tychsen, Oluf Gerhard. *Beurteilung der Jahrzahlen in den hebräisch-biblischen Handschriften.* Rostock, Ger.: In der Koppenschen Buchhandlung, 1786.

———. *Bützowische Nebenstunden verschiedenen zur morgenländischen Gelehrsamkeit gehörigen Sachen gewidmet.* Vol. 6. Bützow, Ger.: N.p., 1769.

Tyrnau, Isaac (attributed). *Minhagim.* Fürth: N.p., 1742.

Ulmer, Rivka. *Turmoil, Trauma, and Triumph: The Fettmilch Uprising in Frankfurt am Main (1612–1616) According to Megillas Vintz.* Frankfurt am Main: Peter Lang, 2001.

Venture, Mardochée [M. V.]. *Calendrier hebraïque, qui contient tous les Roshodes, samedis, solemnités et jeunes de l'année: Avec les nouvelles lunes & Tecufot, suivant Rab Semuel pour 100. années consécutives, depuis l'année de la création du monde 5525. jusqu'à l'année 5624. . . . Amsterdam: N.p., 1765.*

Vilna-Horodna Calendar, 1825/26 and 1826/27. *Kalendarz starozakonny na rok 5587. Dozwala sie Drukować. Wilno, 17 Maia 1826.* N.p.

Voigt, Johann Henrich. *Calendarische An und Vorschläge von Vergleich und Vereinigung des Alten und Neuen Styli in einen Leopoldischen Reichskalender.* Stade, Ger.: Ernesti Gohls, 1672.

Volks-Kalender für Israeliten and *Jahrbuch des Nützlichen und Unterhaltenden für Israeliten* (later *Jahrbuch für Israeliten*). Editors: 1853–1859, K. Klein; 1864–1865, J. K. Buchner. Imprint varies: 1842–1847, Brieg E. Wollman; 1853, Stuttgart: Dittmarsch und Comp.; 1859, Mainz: Le Rour'sche Hofbuchhandlung; 1863–1865, Leipzig: In Commission bei C. L. Fritzsche.

von der Osten, Gert, and Horst Vey. *Painting and Sculpture in Germany and the Netherlands, 1500 to 1600.* Baltimore: Penguin Books, 1969.

Vries, Levi Abraham de. ספר מגלה תקופות *Das ist Entdeckung derer Tekuphoth, oder des schädlichen Bluts / Welches über die Juden vier mahl des Jahrs komt / laut ihrer eigenen* לוחות *oder Kalender / Aus Liebe zure Wahrheit entworffen von Levi Abraham de Vries, Gewesenen Rabbi und Beschneider der Jüdischen Kinder in Amsterdam, nun aber Bekenner seines Heylandes Jesu Christi.* Flensburg, Den.: Christoph Vogeln, 1733.

Wacholder, Ben Zion. "Biblical Chronology in the Hellenistic World Chronicles." *Harvard Theological Review* 61 (1968): 451–481.

———. "Chronomessianism: The Timing of Messianic Movements and the Calendar of Sabbatical Cycles." *Hebrew Union College Annual* 46 (1975): 201–218.

Wachtel, David. "The Ritual and Liturgical Commemoration of Two Medieval Persecutions." Master's thesis, Columbia University, 1995.

Wagenseil, Johann Christoph. *Belehrung der Juedisch-Teutschen Red-und Schreibart.* Königsberg: P. F. Rhode, 1699.

Wallis, Faith, trans. *Bede: The Reckoning of Time.* Liverpool, Eng.: Liverpool University Press, 1999.

Weinberg, Joanna. "Invention and Convention: Jewish and Christian Critique of the Jewish Fixed Calendar." *Jewish History* 14 (2000): 317–330.

Weinberg, Magnus. "Der Sulzbacher Wandkalender für das Schöpfungsjahr 5483 (1722/23)." *Jahrbuch der Jüdisch-Literarischen Gesellschaft* 17 (1926): 89–94.

Wieck, Roger S., ed. *Time Sanctified: The Book of Hours in Medieval Art and Life.* New York: George Braziller, 2001.

Wiesemann, Falk, with contributions from Fritz Armbruster, Hans Peter Baum, and Leonhard Scherg. *Genizah: Hidden Legacies of the German Village Jews.* Vienna: Bertelsmann, 1992.

Wischnitzer, Rachel. "The Moneychanger with the Balance: A Topic of Jewish Iconography." *Eretz Israel* 6 (1960): *23–*5.

Wiznitzer, Arnold. *Jews in Colonial Brazil.* New York: Columbia University Press, 1960.

Woerden, Isabel Speyart van. "The Iconography of the Sacrifice of Abraham." *Vigiliae Christianae* 15 (1961): 214–255.

Woolf, Daniel. *The Social Circulation of the Past: English Historical Culture, 1500–1730.* Oxford, Eng.: Oxford University Press, 2003.

Yahalom, Joseph. *Mahzor Eretz-Yisra'el: Codex ha-genizah.* Jerusalem: Magnes, 1997.

Yassif, Eli, ed. *Sefer ha-zikhronot, hu divre ha-yamim le-Yerahme'el.* Jerusalem: Tel Aviv University, 2001.

Yerushalmi, Yosef Hayim. *Zakhor: Jewish History and Jewish Memory.* Seattle: University of Washington Press, (1982), 1996.

Yosef ben Shem Tov ben Yehoshua Hai. *Sefer she'erit Yosef.* With commentary by Daniel ben Perahya ha-kohen. Salonika, Greece: N.p., 1568.

Yuval, Israel Jacob. *Hakhamim be-doram. Scholars in Their Time: Spiritual Leadership of German Jews in the Late Middle Ages.* (Hebrew). Jerusalem: Magnes, 1988.

———. *Two Nations in Your Womb: Perceptions of Jews and Christians in Late Antiquity and the Middle Ages.* Trans. J. Chipman. Berkeley: University of California Press, 2006.

Zacuto, Abraham. *Sefer Yuhasin ha-shalem.* 1st ed., Herschel Filipowski, ed., n.p.; 3d ed. Jerusalem: N.p., 1963.

Zalkin, Mordechai. "Scientific Literature and Cultural Transformation in Nineteenth-Century East European Jewish Society." *Aleph* 5 (2005): 249–271.

Zeltner, Gustav Georg, with Carl Friedrich Lochner. *Genaue Untersuchung dess seltsamen Jüdischen Wahns von dem Tekupha-Blut, und noch seltsamern Vorgebens, dass daraus ein sonderbar kräfftiger Beweiss für die Christliche Religion zu nehmen: Welche in ein kurtzes Send-Schreiben an Tit. Herrn M. Carl Friedrich Lochner, . . . Pfarrer dess Marckts Fürth verfasset, und damit sich zugleich Seiner, al seines Hochwerthen Freundes, fernern angenehmen Zuneigung und Liebe empfohlen hat D. Gustav Georg Zeltner, Pfarrer zu Poppenreuth.* Frankfurt: Johann Friederich Rüdiger, 1734.

Zerubavel, Eviatar. "Easter and Passover: On Calendars and Group Identity." *American Sociological Review* 47, no. 2 (1982): 284–289.

———. "The French Republican Calendar: A Case Study in the Sociology of Time." *American Sociological Review* 42 (1977): 868–877.

———. *Hidden Rhythms: Schedules and Calendars in Social Life.* Berkeley: University of California Press, 1985.

———. *The Seven Day Circle: The History and Meaning of the Week.* New York: Free Press, 1985.

Ziggelaar, August. "The Papal Bull of 1582 Promulgating a Reform of the Calendar." Pp. 201–239 in G. V. Coyne, M. A. Hoskin, and O. Pederson, eds., *Gregorian Reform of the Calendar: Proceedings of the Vatican Conference to Commemorate Its 400th Anniversary, 1582–1982.* Vatican City: Pontifica Academia Scientiarum, 1983.

Zika, Charles. "Hosts, Processions, and Pilgrimages: Controlling the Sacred in Fifteenth-Century Germany." *Past and Present* 118 (1988): 25–64.

Zimmels, H. J. *Ashkenazim and Sephardim*. Farnborough, Eng.: Gregg International, 1969.

Zimmer, Eric. *Fiery Embers of the Scholars: The Rabbinate in Germany in the Sixteenth and Seventeenth Centuries*. (Hebrew). Beersheba, Israel: Ben Gurion University, 1999.

———. "Jewish and Christian Hebraist Collaboration in Sixteenth Century Germany." *Jewish Quarterly Review* n.s. 71 (1980): 69–88.

———. *Rabi Hayim b. R. Betzal'el me-Fridberg: Ahi ha-Maharal mi-Prag*. Jerusalem: Mosad ha-Rav Kook, 1987.

———. "R. David b. Isaac of Fulda: The Trials and Tribulations of a Sixteenth Century German Rabbi." *Jewish Social Studies* 45 (1983): 217–232.

Ziskind, Jonathan. *John Selden on Jewish Marriage Law: The Uxor Hebraica*. Leiden: Brill, 1991.

Zuckerman, Arthur J. "The Nasi of Frankland in the Ninth Century and the *Colaphus Judaeorum* in Toulouse." *Proceedings of the American Academy for Jewish Research* 33 (1965): 51–82.

Zunz, Leopold. *Die Ritus des synagogalen Gottesdienstes*. Berlin: J. Springer, 1859.

———. *Sterbetage*. Berlin: M. Poppelauer, 1864.

———. "'Verfassen und übersetzen' hebräisch ausgedrückt." Pp. 50–67 in *Gesammelte Schriften*, vol. 3. Berlin: L. Gershel, 1876.

INDEX

Aachen, 152

Adam and Eve: illustration in sifre evronot, 89, 92; polemical subtext of, 93, 94; reception of calendrical knowledge, 92, 93, 120

Agobard of Lyons, Bishop, 149

Abudarham, David, 26

al-Bīrūnī, Abu Rayhan, 164

al-Khwarizmi, 13

Allerheiligenmarkt. See All Saints Day

All Saints' Day (*Allerheiligenmarkt, kol ha-qe-doshim*), 130, 137, 141, 149

Almanach des Centenaires, 35

Almanacs, 29, 32, 167; printing of, 33, 34, 41–43, 59, 139; political use of, 41, 198; as additions to calendars, 209–211

Altona, 66, 137–138

al-Qirqisani, Jacob, 14

Amsterdam, 66, 71, 138, 155, 186, 205

Anglican calendar, 42

Annunciation, 94, 127–129, 176

Apocrypha, calendar and, 11, 86, 89, 93

Aron, Abraham, 157

Astrology, 13, 21, 25, 26

Astronomy, 10–11, 13–14, 106; Greeks and, 11, 16; Jewish interest in, 14–17, 25–26; works of, 13–27;

Avodah zarah (tractate of BT), 121

August, Sigismund, 38

Baraita de Shmuel, 13, 89

bar Hiyya, Abraham. *See* Savasorda, Abraham bar Hiyya

bar Samson, R. Jacob, 25, 26, 165–166, 170

Basel, University of, 49

Bede, 9–11, 30–31, 101, 192

Belin Ashkenazi, Eliezer ben Jacob, 55–57

Berav, Jacob, 52

Berlin, 66, 134–135, 181, 185–186

Beurteilung. See Tychsen, Oluf Gerhard

Bible, and calendar, 11, 21, 34, 81, 87, 89, 93–95, 117, 201, 208

Bloodletting, 27, 33–34, 68

Bolechow, Ber of, 117

Bonnevilli, Baldassare, 65

Book of Martyrs (Foxe's), 144

Books of Hours, 2, 30, 32, 81, 94, 108

Braunschweig, 154, 156

Broadsides, 33–34

Budweis, 155

Business of Jews, 1, 116, 131, 211; at markets and fairs, 142, 150, 152, 157-159

Calendar (artifact): American Jewish, 69–71; glyphic, 30; Italian, 24–25, 58; layout of, 85, 141–142; paper quality of, 34, 68; perpetual, 10, 16, 30, 32, 59, 192; pocket, 35, 65–68, 69, 136, 199, 211; production and preparation of, 29–36; print culture and, 29–36, 49–68; role of printers, 60–61, 64–68; sale of, 32–33, 36, 43, 57–58, 134, 139; special interest, 35; *Schreibkalender* (see *Schreibkalender*); Soviet, 40; symbols on, 30, 34, 71, 87, 89, 98–99, 101–105, 108; wall, 60–61, 65–68, 124, 128, 136, 154, 199, 203, 206

Calendar (concept): Christian calendar in Jewish, 116, 119, 123–132, 140; Christian holy days, 32, 34, 116, 122, 126, 128, 136, 142–143; confessionalization and, 28–29; cultural influence on, 5–6; dissatisfaction with Christian, 11; dissemination of, 59–68; English, 43; mnemonics for, 9–10, 23, 30, 55, 77, 108; Muslim, 21–22, 26, 38, 196; Orthodox, 38, 131; Ottoman, 58; national identity and, 29, 41–46; Paul and, 117; political conflict and, 28; Reformation and, 2, 29; responsa/queries regarding, 115, 163, 164–165; *semikha* and, 47–48

Calendrier des bergers, 32

Censorship: of Jewish calendars, 36, 132, 134, 136–139, 207; of sifre evronot, 124, 130

Charlemagne, 10

Christ. *See* Jesus

Christian: accusations against Jews, 144–146; Hebraists, 48–50, 130, 138, 204; Jewish blasphemy regarding, 122–123; paschal lamb and, 117–118; ritual acts against Jews, 146–148

Chronology, 9, 11, 52, 58; *anno domini* (Christian Era), 22, 38, 89, 122; *anno mundi* (*Era from Creation*) 58, 94, 189–191; Era of Contracts (Seleucid, *shtarot*), 58, 191, 193, 197; Era from

אלו הן שמות רבה... לידתן/ לידה האב... לבני אדם... שמות...

...רבעים ותתנון הבדילה... ישב... לבדא... הוא א"...

...רבעים ותתנון... אם תובעת הוא ג' ... ... לזיות ... תלוק לב רבעים לחלק...

כ"ש ... וכן ... פרנם ... היו ... הדברים ... ... וכן ... שם ... ולחלק...

כל ... ... ולאמר לך יתנון ... ... וכן ... ... הדבור ... ... חלק...

הוא יתנון ורל הנא שם ... ... בכרבים ... ...

...יושו ...

וזאת תובעת ... וזאת ... ... תלוקין בדא ... תובעין ... ...

...מזונות מתנות ... כ"... ... ...

...ותלקין ... לקחת ... ...

...הכבד ... וחלק כל ... ... יב ... ...

וכורכד ... ... נשן או אודהלנד ...

וזאת תובעת תאני שאודהל ... ... היתנון ... ... לעדין

...בכל שני ... ... כד ... ... שאודהל ...

...שואו ... ... שם תובעת היתנון וכה ... ...

וכן אמרת ...

סליק

חלק היתנון והמונות וגזלות

אחרי זאת חלק שירי נשברים

אלו הן הכלות השוטעים צ{...} כופכיכם ולאלגעלות

לבנה
סרטן
♋
גבריאל

כוכב
תאומיםבתולה
♊ ♍
מיכאל

צדק
קשתודגים
↗ ♓
צדקיאל

שבתי
דלי גדי
♒ ♑
קפציאל

חמה נוגה
אריה מאזני שור
♌ ♎ ♉
רפאל

מאדים
טלה עקרב
♈ ♏
סמאל